Philip Alexander Bruce, William Glover Stanard

The Virginia Magazine of History and Biography

Philip Alexander Bruce, William Glover Stanard

The Virginia Magazine of History and Biography

ISBN/EAN: 9783337388614

Printed in Europe, USA, Canada, Australia, Japan

Cover: Foto ©ninafisch / pixelio.de

More available books at **www.hansebooks.com**

THE

VIRGINIA MAGAZINE

OF

HISTORY AND BIOGRAPHY

PUBLISHED QUARTERLY BY

THE VIRGINIA HISTORICAL SOCIETY

FOR THE

YEAR ENDING DECEMBER 31, 1920

VOL. XXVIII

RICHMOND, VA.
HOUSE OF THE SOCIETY
707 E. FRANKLIN ST.

Reprinted with the permission of the original publisher
KRAUS REPRINT CORPORATION
New York
1968

Reprinted in U.S.A.

TABLE OF CONTENTS

William Gordon McCabe

THE BELOVED AND HONORED
PRESIDENT OF

THE VIRGINIA HISTORICAL SOCIETY

DIED

JUNE 1, 1920

Mr. Armistead C. Gordon, a member of our Board, will, at the request of his colleagues, prepare an "In Memoriam," for publication in a future number of the Magazine.

THE

VIRGINIA MAGAZINE

OF

HISTORY AND BIOGRAPHY

VOL. XXXVIII JANUARY, 1920 No. 1

MINUTES OF THE COUNCIL AND GENERAL COURT, 1622-1629.

From the Originals in the Library of Congress.

(Continued.)

Oathes taken before S'r George Yeardley, Knight Etc. & Mr. Wiliam Clayborne, Secret. on the 16th day of March 1626.

John Wayne sworne & examined sayth that twoe weekes before their arrivall in this river in the ship called The Plantation ther was a falling out between Thomas Hitall & Thomas Lawley, wheruppon Robt. Cooke interposed himselfe & towld the s'd Lawley he would not suffer him to abuse any of his mates, upon w'ch the fell to words & the s'd Cooke tooke the s'd Lawley by the coller & thrust him from him, & settled him upon a chest that was nere to him & soe this deponent forthw'th p'ted them & saith that there was noe other blowes betweene them, nor did the s'd Cooke set his fiste or his knee upon the s'd Lawley's brest or offered him any further violence whatsoever, & further this deponent saith that he never saw the s'd Lawley at any tyme to spitt blowd nor ever heard him complayne of any hurt that he had receaved by means of the s'd Cooke.

Christopher Cutler sworne & examined sayth & affirmeth in all poynts as John Wayne aboves'd.

Edward Gaven, aged 38 years, sworne & examined sayth that about a monethe agoe in his going up w'th Thomas Lawley to his plantacon stayed for the tyde over nyght at Capt. Martyns. The tyde being come he called for his people to come abourd & spying the s'd Thomas Lawley to be behind he demanded of him why he would not go as fast as the rest, the s'd Lawley answered while he was aboard the shipp called the Plantacon ther was one gave him a blowe w'th his elbowe one his brest w'ch hath made me ever since then such a payne that it greaves me to goe & I can scarce fetch my breath, soe they went into the boate & the next day after arrived at the Shirley hundred & the where the s'd Lawley fell very sicke & being not able of himself to come out his bed this deponent helping him, the sayd Lawley sayd these words Oh Lord Master the blowe that Hobin gave me will surely be my deth, & then when one q'rter of an hower after he departed this life, this deponent sayth further that the sayd Lawleys brest after he was dead, seemed blacker than any other p'te of his body, this deponent sayth alsoe that he never saw the s'd Lawley at any tyme to spit blowd neither did ever hear him the s'd Lawley complain of spiting blowd.

John Fitz Humphreys aged 23 years sworne & examined sayth that about a fortnight before they made the land in the ship The Plantacon one Robt. Cooke and Thomas Lawley squabled aboard the shipp & were ready to fall by the eares wheruppon divers caled to this deponent & willed him to come & p't them,but before he came they were p'ted & stod wrangling & squabling together & suddenly after being in goeing to bed the s'd Lawley complayned to this deponent that his brest was very sore & sayd that Robert Cooke tripping up his heeles fell upon him w'th his kne upon his brest & the next morning the s'd Lawley shewed this deponent his brest wch he sayth was very black at that tyme & sayth that that day the s'd Lawley did spitt blowd & divers tymes after before he dyed in this deponts syght. This depont sayth that he willed the s'd Lawley the next day after he complayned to him to tell their Master of yt but Lawley answered he would not troble the M'r, he willed him to tell the Chirurgeon of yt that he might have some remedy for it; but he answered, I have had already something of the Chirurgeon for my ague, & calls to me for a note under my hand for yt, & I am loth to put my M'r to any more charges, & I will take noe more of his medicines. This deponent fourther sayth that the s'd Lawley being very sick at Sherly hundred often said both to him & others that the blow w'ch he had abourd the ship would kill him.

A Court at James Citty the 26th of March 1627, being p'sent

S'r George Yeardley, Knt., Govern'or Etc.

Mr. Doctor Pott
Capt. Smyth
Mr. Claybourne

At this Court Capt. Wilcoxes (1) made a request to have 500 acres of land granted unto him on the Eastern shoare uppon the old plantation creeke abutting on the Northeast uppon the land of John Blower, unto w'ch the Court hath condescended in favor to the said Capt. Wilcoxe & that he may not be unfurnished of ground to plant his servants uppon, w'ch he hath now brought over in the good shipp called the Plantation, provided that the said Capt. Wilcoxe doe as soon as may he make proofe that the said five hundred acres shall be due him by the transportation of the said servants or some of them or by any other way or means.

(1) Captain John Wilcox came to Va. in 1620 and was a Burgess in 1623. His will stating that he was formerly of Plymouth, England, was proved June, 1628. See this Magazine 11, 77. 78.

Quarter Court

A Court at James Citty the 3th of Aprill 1627, being present:

S'r George Yeardley, Knt., Governor Etc.

Capt. West
Doctor Pott
Capt. Smyth
Capt. Mathews
Mr. Secretary
Capt. Tucker
Mr. ffarrar

It is ordered that Mr. Jonas Stockden, Minister & Mr. Francis Chamberlaine doe w'thin fifteene dayes after ye date herof give a securitie unto ye Governor for the paiment of fiftene hundred sixtie and five pounds of principall merchantable Tobacco in leafe stript for the use of S'r Francis Wyatt, Knt., to be paid at or before the 20th day of November next ensuing at the Stores at James Citty uppon the forfeiture of three thousand one hundred and thirty waight of the principall Tobacco

At this Court was delivered in the last will & Testament of Thomas Dunthorne, deceased, and proved to be the true will of the s'd Tho Dunthorne by ye oath of Jonas Stockden, minister, and that the s'd Thomas Dunthorne was at the making thereof in perfect sense and memorye

At this Court Mr. Harmer delivered uppon his oath unto Will'm Hambry an account of all the goodes and estate of the Lady Dale (2) both of cattle, Tobacco, corne, and of whatsoever hath remained in his Custody since the time that the said Mr. Harmer received the same from Mr. Henry Watkins.

---

(2) Sir Thomas Dale, in his will proved Jan. 15, 1620, left his whole estate to his wife, Dame Elizabeth Dale. Her will was dated July 6, 1640, and proved Dec. 2, 1640. Her debts were to be paid out of her estate in the hands of the East India Company and her estate in Virginia. She gave her niece, Mrs Dorothy Throckmorton 500 acres in Virginia, with the appurtenances. To Edward Hamby, son of Mr. Richard Hamby, all her land in Charles Hundred in Virginia, with the appurtenances. All the remainder of her estate in

At this Court Mr. George Keth, minister, did promise on his going down to Kecaughtan (uppon an assurance made unto him from Thomas Godby for 200lb of Tobacco to be paid the last of October next ensueing) to seale and deliver unto the said Thomas Godby, one bill of sale of one hundred acres of land to him and ye said Thomas Godby and his heires and assignes forever, being the divident of the said George Keth & lying & abutting next unto ye Gleab land at Elizabeth Citty.

It is ordered that Left. Giles Allington shal have a com'ission of Administration uppon the whole estate of Caleb Page, deceased, the 2th of Aprill last past and that the said Giles Allington doe put in securitie to the Court to deliver of an Account and surrender the said estate when it shall be lawfully required. And Robert Adams of Martin's Hundred hath offered to be bound w'th the said Giles Allington for ye same.

Lt. Giles Allington sworne and examined sayeth that Caleb Page on Sunday last the day before his death said these wordes before divers yt were then p'sent: Neighbours bear witnes that I give unto my man Henry Hart two yeares of his time.

[125]

Whereas by an Act made at the Quarter Court in October there was a proclamation published to forbid any person of what qualitie soever to buy any com'odities aboard any shipp uppon the penaltie of 500 l. of Tobacco and the said com'odities or the value, of the same, it is at this Court thought good to mitigate the sayd fine being too extreme, and now further ordered that every one yt shall offend as aforesaid in buying of any com'odities aboard any shipp shall forfeit one hundred weight of Tobacco and the saide

Virginia or elsewhere, after some legacies, was to be divided into two parts. One part to go to the children of Sir William Throckmorton, knight and baronet, deceased, and William Sanborne, and the other part to her friends and executors, Mr. Richard Hamby and Mr. William Shrimpton. Lady Dale was Elizabeth, daughter of Sir Thomas Throckmorton, and married Sir Thos. Dale in 1611.

com'odities soe bought or the value of the same as often as they shall soe offend. It is ordered that Michael Wilcoxes for buying 12 l. of sugar aboard the Charitie doe forfeite one hundred weight of Tobacco and twelve pounds of Tobacco for the said sugar, and 30 l. of Tobacco for going aboard.

Whereas there remaineth one trunk of apparrell & linnen belonging unto Capt. Willia' Holmes, deceased, of which there is noe man to take charge, the Court doth thinke fitt for the good of his widdow, that Doctor Pott doe take the said trunke with the apparrell & linnen into his custody, and to make sale thereof to the best profitt, and to deliver up an account of the same unto any Attorney for ye said widow.

Wheras notw'thstanding an Order of Court made in October last past there be many that have neglected to prove the Wills & Testaments and bring in the Inventorys of persons deceased it is thought fitt and hereby ordered that Mr. Will'm Claybourne Secretary doe in more especiall manner take care and provide that the like negligence be here after prevented. And further that Mr. Claybourne shall have full power and authoritie to sum'n such as doe offend in this case to appeare at the Court at James Citty before ye Governor & Councill of State, there to answer unto ye same.

Whereas by some information received now of late fro' other Indians we understand there is a purpose in these Indians our Inimies to make a generall assault uppon all o'r plantations this Spring; it is ordered that notice be given by proclamation through the Colonie that according to a former proclamation published, all dwelling houses or plantations be strongly palizadoed about and that all men doe constantly stand uppon theire guard, keep sentinell uppon theire workmen by day, and keep good watch by night, shutting and making fast the gates of their forts, not suffering any single man to stragle abroad, wherby all danger may be prevented.

It is ordered that Will'm Kempe, yeoman, shall not any further molest or trouble Mr. George Keth concerning his suite of 500 l. weight of Tobacco, w'ch the said Will'm pretends to be wanting in the estate of the orphan Sara Spence the daughter of Ensigne Wm. Spence deceased, untill such time as any such Inventory may be found whereby anything may be proved that the said 500 l. weight of Tobacco is unpaid by the said George Keth.

At this Court there was leave granted that Mr. Secretary Claibourne should have a Com'ission to goe w'th a boate & a sufficient Company of men into the Bay, And to discover any rivers or Creekes w'thin the Bay up to the heads of the same and trade w'th the Indians for corne skins or any other Comodities whatsoever.

A Court at James Citty the 4th of Aprill 1627 being present

S'r George Yeardley, Knt., Governor Etc.

Capt. West
Doctor Pott
Capt. Smyth
Capt. Mathews
Mr. Secretary
Capt. Tucker
Mr. Farrer.

At this Court were read all the examinations and depositions formerly taken concerning the report of some bad behavior betweene Capt. Will'm Epes & Mrs. Alice Boice lately to have happened at Martins Brandon, all w'ch being duely weighed and debated on, the opinion of the Court is that it is noe way proved or manifest by those depositions that Capt. Epes and Mrs. Boise have offended the Law but that they are cleane and guiltlesse.

At this Court Mr. Howe delivered upp on his oath an account of the Estate of Luke Aden.

At this Court the Governor did testifie that presently after the arrivall of the tenants belonging to the Secretairy from

England hhimselfe did advise Mr. Porey to send the said tenants over the Bay & to plant there, w'ch accordingly he did and soe made choice of the 500 acres of land belonging to his place, afterwards when himselfe went over and seated the said tenants uppon the same.

It is therefore ordered that there be 500 acres of land laid out, at the place commonly called the Secretairy land on the Eastern Shoare and heretofore planted on by the tenants belonging to the Secretaryes place. And that if it happen any people to have seated themselves w'thin the bounds thereof, that they doe either compound w'th the Secretary, or else deliver upp the land into his possession. It is also hereby provided that if by this means the people shall forsake the place and the same be left unplanted that the Secretarye doe take some order to see the same again repeopled & planted.

(To be Continued)

LETTERS OF WILLIAM BYRD, FIRST.

(From the Originals in the Collection of the Virginia Historical Society)

Concluded

To Perry and Lane

Virginia June 3d 1691

Gent:

I recd most (if not all) of yours this year with what you w: I as morry were so considerable, since I could not have freight enough proportionall to answer itt, being I thinke very hardly used therein, you left itt wholly to P. P. who att first promised mee upward of 400 Hds in Porter & Allison. Some time after hee told mee, that I must not expect above 400. Accordingly I proceeded & bought Tobo but just as I had finished all, & was going to Towne, hee tells mee Harry Duke (1) had shewn him a letter & hee must have Some & Toppin more, therefore I must have but 350 Hds (besides bulke). After some words, I desired him to assure me of them, wch hee did, & I left notes att his house, as I went downe for twice that quantity, hee was not so kind all the while I was there to lett mee know ye contrary, when I could have hired a ship att £15:10 p tun, but last weeke (when the ships were goeing downe) hee gave mee an Accot that Allison had but 80 Hds & Porter 180 (2 whereof furres) besides bulke; by wch means. And these Masters (as well as those from Mr. North) cheating in their Ladeing by stowing away great quantitys in Bulke of their owne.

(1) Henry Duke, of James City County, who was appointed member of Council 1702, and died 1713.

I have ab^{t} 250 H^{ds} of New besides Some Old Tobacco left, I desire therefore that you positively order what freight I shall have (wch I expect may bee ab^{t} 500 H^{ds}) that I may not bee at ship uncertainty'e, and att every Ones disposeall: otherwise I desire you not to send mee above halfe the Goods wrote for, wch will bee then too much; I have sent you what skins & ffurres I had by mee (to help to clear Something) wch had been much more, had not the Indian trade been prohibited (all last winter). Now ye Assembly have laid itt open but wth so great an Imposition* on all commoditys of that sort, that I fear itt can never bee worth while onely those goods wee have by us must bee sold, I have sent for little but plains haveing sufficient of all ye rest by mee.

I desire you would Send me the furniture Sent for last year, & omitted I have Sent for a Considerable Cargo of English Goods, wch I desire if freight may bee had, & Tob^{o} like to doe anything; I suppose what Sent you this year may prove weighty & good, hope itt may answer Something.

If you have an Oppertunity I desire you to send 3 or 4 halfe tunes of Rheinsh wine from Rotterdam, for that I had two years Since from Mr Senserf proved So well, that I have been desired by Severall to procure Some as good.

How far our New Law about Townes may Affect trade I cannot yett guess, wee must expect ye confirmation of itt from England, & then I believe Some of the Ports may come in a little time to Something; Some time Since I rec^{d} yours by Emberly & should have been glad to have Seen my Acco^{t} wch I yett daily expect.

I returne you many thankes for your care of my Child^{n} & hope you'l indeavor to put out the Girls for their most advantage wth out any unnecessary charge; & for my Son I hope hee may bee so imployed, as (at least) not to loosse anything hath been bestowed on him. I cannot advise att

---

(2) Act of Assembly, April, 1991. See Hening's *Statutes at Large of Virginia*, III, 63.

this distance, but desire hee want nothing (in reason) for his necessary accomplishm[t].

I am Oblidged to you for your care ab[t] y[e] Aud[rs] place, & I hope you'l put itt out of dispute. My L[d] Effingham, M[r] Blaithwait & M[r] Povey haveing assured mee of their assistance therein, hope now you'l effect itt and not lett mee lye open to every one that will bid mony for itt.

Newham promised mee to take in four H[ds] of skins & ffurres, but after I had Sent them downe (hee being full) to Point Comfort, and I suppose they are on board the Wolfe, Capt. Geo. Purvis, Capt. Perry designes downe, hope hee'l take bills of Ladeing or a rec[t] for them, y[e] contents inclosed, there is allso Eight H[ds] on board Hogben, God Send all well to you: What farther offers shall write by the fleet therefore wth blessing to y[e] Child[n], due respects to all friends I take leave

Gen[t]
Yo[rs]
W. B.

Pray Send us a Considerable Quantity of Salt if possible & remember Paper for wee are in great want

---

To ——

Virg[a] June the 4th 1691

S[r]

This I hope will come Safe to hand by the Resolution wth 4 H[ds] Raw skins, 208 Hogs[hds] of Tob[o] in Caske, besides 51 in Bulke to bee divided Vizt. the ship to have two thirds & you 1-3 clear, to bee equally parted for quality in y[e] s[d] Proportions. The Bulke I could not expect much from, but however the 1-3 comeing fraight free, I thought might yield Something, better then lye here and rott, the Tob[o] in Caske I hope will prove well & weighty. I had not that quantity of skins & furs as usual, trade being Stopt all last winter, and now its open, a great imposition is laid on all Such Commodity's as are transported, wch I doubt will put a damp on ye trade. I thanke you for takeing mee So much fraight, but could have wished (though you Sent ye Charter pty's to mee) you had not Ordered away most of ye ffraight to others, Sikes takeing mee in but 70 od & Ware but 55, the former (they say) is a very rotten tool. I spared on your request so much of the fraight, that I have now 250 H^{ds} left on my hands, & could not give Satisfaction neither; therefore its mine as well as their desires that you would Secure every mans fraight certain (except Small quantitys wch may not be worth while) I hope you'l Secure mee for owne p'per use att Least 300 H^{ds} & if you can wth convenience you may adde another 100, I doubt not the complyance.

I have Sent for a Considerable Quantity of English Goods, allso Some apparell & Houshold Stuffe &c for my Selfe wch I hope (if goods gett well home) you'l comply wth & send wth ye furniture Omitted last year, by Some good ship.

Col. Xpher Wormeley (3) (who marryd Col^{o} Carters widow) designes to write to you, & hold a correspondence. I encouraged him, & promised to intimate the Same to you, I hope hee nor you will have occasion to complain thereof.

Inclosed is allso an Invoice from H. Gauler, & another friend of yours wch I desire you to Send by the first conveniency as directed.

I would allso desire you to Send mee to bee left att James City att Mr Gaulers 20 or 30 doz of Clarett or other fashionable wine thats very Good, 6 doz Canary, 6 doz of Cherry & 6 doz of Rhenish, wt^{h} one Q^{r}ter Caske of Brandy & 6 grs good Pipes:

I wish all things may come Safe & find you, your Lady & all friends in health; wee have (after a confused manner) in a hurry returned your token, you may charge mee those

(3) Christopher Wormeley, of Middlesex County, appointed member of Council 1683, and died 1701. The wife referred to was Elizabeth, daughter of Raleigh Travers, of Lancaster County, and widow of John Carter, Jr., of "Corotoman," in the same county. For note on Christopher Wormeley, see this Magazine, VII, 284, 285.

that have not pd their part & give mee an Acco^{t} thereof
My humble Service to all friends. I am

S^{r}

Yo^{r} Humble Servt

W. B.

Send mee a box of Smoaking Tobacco

To Mr. North

Virginia June the 8th, 1691

S^{r}

This Serves to cover the inclosed bill of Lading for 76 H^{ds} Tob^{o} of my owne, four of Mr Secretary's Coles & 2 of young Thom Cockes, I wish all Safe to you, my Service to all friends. I am

S^{r}

Yo^{r} Humble Servant

W. B.

To Mr North P Sikes
in ye Phoenix

To Philip Ludwell

Virg^{a} June ye 8th 1691

Hon^{d} S^{r}

I recd the favo^{r} of one from you Since you being in London, where I hope you injoy your health and all satisfaction. Wee have (I thanke God) been hitherto att peace, onely a great many little intrigues carryed on in our late assembly. An Acco^{t} of their proceedings (both touching the Colledge & other affairs) I doubt not but you'l receive att Large from others, there was an address design'd, that no person should bee capeable of holding any Office in this Government, unless hee were an inhabitant of the Same, whither it reflected on Mr Culpeper (4) or not I cannot tell, but it was

(4) "Mr. Culpeper" was Alexander Culpeper, Surveyor General of Virginia, who had been long resident in England.

quashed, & so its no great matter, theres now a resolve to settle the Bounds along ye main Blacke water, & So up to ye Appomatox Indian Towne & so to ye Monacan Towne, wch will cut of Some plantations allready Seated, & hinder the Surveyors Something, but I suppose those bounds will not continue Long, Mr James Blair, Com'^{ry}, our Minister comes home ab^{t} ye Colledge, & the other affairs are refer'd to Mr Jeffry's; please to give my humble service to all friends, & if Leasure will permit favo^{r} mee wth a line or two as occasion offers I am

Hon^{d} S^{r}

Yo^{r} faithfull Humble Servt

W. B.

To Col^{o} Ludwell und^{r} Covert E

To Mr. Methwold

Virg^{a} June ye 8th 1691

Hon^{d} S^{r}

I recd the favor of yours in my L^{ds} Pacquett, for wch I returne you hearty thankes & wish it were in my power to Serve you according to my desire: I have been from Home ere Since the beginning of Aprill but shall indeavo^{r} to provide all ye Stones & Seeds formerly omitted wth a fresh Supply of those formerly Sent, except the Sassafras wch my being abroad lost ye Season of Saveing the Seeds. If I could get a winter Passage I should hope they would doe much better; w^{ch} (God willing) s^{h}all indeavour: please to give my humble Service to yor Lady and all those I had ye hono^{r} to bee acquainted wth at Hale House, & please to accept ye Same from

Hon^{d} S^{r}

Yo^{r} most Oblidged Humble Servant

W B

To Mr Methwold p Comadore

To Lord Effingham

Virginia June ye 9th 1691

My L^{d}

I recd the hono^{r} of yor Exclcys of ye 26th of Fb^{r} & returne your L^{d}ship my hearty thanks, for your kind acceptance of my indeavours to Serve yor Exlncy for wch I have all the obligations imaginable. I have inclosed Sent yor Excellency p Ex^{ch} yor Salary till Lady day last as allso halfe the years House rent (the other p^{d} to ye Lt Govern^{r}) wth what else is come to my hands, yor L^{d}ships Acco^{t} is inclosed: by wch your Excellency may see what I have recd from ye Collecto^{rs} for ye rents I answer for 10' Countys. Col^{o} Cole Warwicke & Elizabeth City, Hee & Col^{o} Bacon for Isle of Wight, Col^{o} Bacon for Yorke, Hee & Col^{o} Page for N. Kent, & Col^{o} Page for James City, who have or will Acco^{t} to yor Excellency themselves as they say. Of £170 od mony charged on the Navy last year, they have promised to pay £103:06:10 but refused the rest, itt being for Clothing to ye Seamen &c. & the men (they Say) pd of ere the Acco^{t} came Home: Since wch the Dunbarton being found altogether unfit for Service, is laid up & some of her old Rigging Sold as much as amounts to £83:11:01 wch mony by Order of ye Lt Govern^{r} & Councell is paid to mee in Order to reimburse their Majesty's revenue here, I have not brought the s^{d} mony to Acco^{t} not haveing any certainty ye 1st p^{t} is pd, & expect farther Order ab^{t} ye Last; I shall not trouble yor Excellency wth the Matters of Government, nor proceedings of the Assembly Since your L^{d}ship will have all att Large. I beg your L^{d}ships pardon for this wide letter being Straitned in Time some of the Collecto^{rs} Acco^{ts} comeing in but yesterday, & too morrow being appointed for ye fleet to Sail.

I humbly beg the continuance of yor L^{d}ship's favour & returne my hearty thankes for yor Excellencys kindness in

Always business. I kiss your L^{d}ships Hands & wth the utmost respect take leave.

My L^{d}

Yo^{r} Exlncys most Oblidged & humbly
devoted Servt

W. B

To my Ld Effingham

To Mr. Povey

Virginia June ye 9th 1691

S^{r}

I recd the favo^{r} of yours of ye 25 Novemb^{r} & according to yor desire have Sent my former Acc^{t} drawne up after the first method, wth those warrants you returned mee, now (I hope) Sufficiently pfect, by the indorsements.

I have allso, by this Conveyance, Sent my last years Acco^{ts} to Mr Blathwait wherein I have continued the Same Method, & there being no Article in ye discharge but what hath ever been usuall, I hope that will take up Little of their L^{d}ships time to Passe itt. I have returned all the Warrants, they are all indorsed except my Ld Effinghams, Mr Blathwaits & your owne:

I desire to bee Satisfyed whither the Goven^{r} or Comander in chiefs Warrant to mee for payment of any mony's here out of their Ma^{tys} Revenue, may not bee Sufficient to justify mee (provided I bona fide pay the Same) Since by the Comission the Govern^{r} is impower'd to dispose of ye Revenue; & I thinke if hee passes a Warrant, I ought not to dispute itt, However I desire your advice therein.

I hope you will continue yor kindness in assisting to settle the matter about Mr Ayleway, that there may bee no farther dispute.

Inclosed is two bills of Ex^{ch}, One for £100 yor Salary, & the other for £20 wch I hope will bee pd accordingly. If wee have not a more considerable fleet next year then this there will bee much Tob^{o} left in the Country, & this Revenue will not bee able to Support the Government.

As oppertunity p'mits, I beg the favour of a Line or two on all Occasions, & that you would please to hint what was done in Mr Audito^r^ Bacons Acco^t^ wch I wrote to you about at Large of in my Last, I hope then to hear of the Passing of my Acco^ts^. I shall not trouble you farther att present, but wth humble Service take Leave.

S^r^

Yo^r^ Oblidged Humble Servant

WILLIAM B

To Mr Povey

To Mr. Blathwayt

Virginia June the 9th 1691

Hon^d^ S^r^

This serves to accompany Last years Acco^t^ wth the Warrants for payment of what I have discharged my selfe by, & presume there bee no great dispute in any of those Articles, being onely what is usuall

I re^d^ a letter from ye Navy Office wherein they promise to allow in pte of ye bill on them £103:06:10: but the remainder being £66:16:3 for Cloths for ye Seamen belonging to ye Deptford Ketch they refuse by reason the men were pd of ere the acco^t^ came to hand; When I recd itt I dispatched it by the first conveyance, wch was by the fleet last year. The Dunbarton hath had Severall Surveys on her, & is found unfitt for their May^tys^ Service, & therefore ordered to bee laid up, as you will find by the Orders of Councill. There was Some Old Rigging &c^a^ Sold, that formerly belonged to ye Dunbarton the mony was put into my Hands, & amounts to £83:11:01: wch will o're pay the Sum the Navy is indebted to their Majesty's Revenue here. And Since here was nothing intended but what was for y^r^ Ma^tys^ immediate Service, I hope the R^t^ Honble the Com^rs^ of ye Navy will allow the Same.

I have Setled the acco^t^ of Quitrents, & added what Compositions are come to hand, & Some Small fines, In the main the Q^{t}rents are advanced considerably, & hope will more & more, as a true Rent Roll can bee gitt in.

Inclosed is Ex^{ca} for your Salary the last year, wch I hope will be pd accordingly.

I shall not give you farther trouble, but beg the continuance of your favours, I kiss your hands & take leave.

Hon^{d} S^{r}

Yo^{r} Oblidged & Humbly devoted Servt

W B

To m^{r} Blathwait

To the Commissioners of the Navy

Virg^{a} June ye 9th 1691

R^{t} Honble

I recd the favo^{r} of yours of the 31th of Novr last, And am sorry yor hon^{rs} are pleased to dispute that part of my bill relateing to the Cloths Supplyed to Seamen belonging to their Majesty's Ketch the Deptford, Since it was wholy designed for their Majesty's Service, & when the Acco^{ts} came to my hands, I forthwith Sent them with ye first Conveyance; Since wch Their Majesty's ship the Dunbarton haveing been found (by Severall Surveys that have been made on board her) alltogether unfit for Service is ordered to bee Laid up, & Some old Rigging &c^{a} belonging to her being Sold, I have re^{d} bills for £83:11:01 Out of wch I hope you'l please to reimburse their Majestys Revenue here; And the overplus shall bee readily Accompted for what is done was by order of their Maj^{tys} Lt Govern^{r} & Councill

I am

R^{t} Honble

Yo^{r} Hono^{rs} most Humble

& Obedient Servt

W B Aud^{r}

To ye R^{t} Honble Com^{rs} of
their Majestys Navy

To Mr. Harpur

Virg^{a} June ye 9th 1691

S^{r}

I wrote to you last year by m^{r} Sheerwood & gave you what Acco^{t} I could of yor business, am Sorry it was no better; hee made mee propositions this year about Tobacco but haveing no advice from you, I dare not meddle in itt, for unless you could Secure fraight Tobacco would bee of no use, I wish you would imploy Somebody else in this affair who lives more convenient then I. m^{r} Sheerwood hath had £5 already of mee in that affair hee is well acquainted wth the matter & lives much more convenient.

I am sorry I have put you to so much charge to so little purpose haveing been out £7 & 1 Hogh^{d} Tobacco, wch I may bee ashamed to aske haveing Scarce better'd your Cause a farthing: However (if you thinke good) Send what you please in to mee, in wine, to drinke yours & all our friends good healths; If eather in this or anything else I can Serve you May Comand

Yo^{r} friend & Servt

W B

Service to all att ye Clubb
To m^{r} Harpur

To Perry and Lane

James City in Virg^{a} June ye 9th 1691

Gen^{t}

This Serves chiefly to accompany the bills of Ex^{ca} herewth inclosed amounting to   their are many very Small the Collect^{rs} not dareing to trust the Masters, & take their bills Some haveing Sufferd thereby allready, therefore its but reasonable that all owners & merch^{ts} that hire ships, should give them letters of Creditt for their Clearing & necessary charges, otherwise I know no man here hath reason to bee their Security, Since if the ship miscarrys they are like to Suffer, Neither Ought the Masters to have the allowance of the 10 p C^{t} unless hee can give his owne or acceptable bills of Ex^{ca} for his Ladeing, & I hope you'l indeavour itt: Below is an Acco^{t} of what bills charged on you, all wch I would have you charge to ye Audito^{rs} Acco^{t} except y^{e} £20 to m^{r} Povey, wch charge to my p'ticular, the fleet designed to Saile too morrow, & I fear my letters may bee late, therefore shall not inlarge, but wth due respects to all friends I remain

Gen^{t}

Yo^{r} Humble Servt

	£		
To m^{r} James Blair....................	200	..	..
To ye Lt Govern^{r}....................	341	10	..
To my Ld Effingham..................	670	00	7
To m^{r} Blaithwait....................	100	00	00
To m^{r} Povey.........................	100	00	00
To m^{r} Stephen ffarrar................	5	..	..
To ye Lt Govern^{r} more..............	14	..	..
	1430	10	7
To m^{r} Povey	20	..	..

If possible procure mee an ingenious Youth that writes well from ye Hospitall

W B

Remember mee a Box Smoaking Tobacco (5)

To Messrs Perry & Lane, a Duplicate one p Comadore & one p

---

To Perry and Lane

James City in Virginia June ye 10th 1691

Gen^{t}

This onely to be left wth m^{r} Secretary Coles (who if any more bills of Ex^{ca} for mee comes to his hand ere the fleet

(5) It seems curious that any one in Virginia should order smoking tobacco from England; but it was doubtless prepared there in a way to make it more agreeable than the unprepared leaf.

Sails) hath promised to inclose them herein to you. I wrote last night & Sent those I had, I wish all (designed) well to you. My Service to all friends. I am

Gen^t^

Yo^r^ Humble Servt

W B

To Messrs Perry & Lane

To Stephanus Van Cortlandt,(6) New York

Virg^a^ Aug^st^ ye 3^d^ 1691

Hon^d^ S^r^

The great Civilitys I recd from you dureing my Stay at N Yorke have incouraged mee to trouble you herewith wch I hope yor goodness will excuse, I would beg ye favo^r^ of yo^u^ (if yor convenience & a Safe conveyance will permit) to purchase for mee Some Wampum to ye Value of 50 or 60^t^ Lt^g^ ab^t^ 2-3 in black ye other in white, to large, even, & well Strung, & please to Send it to mee in James River, if no ships come So high as my habitation let them leave itt att James Towne, or wth our Lt Govern^r^: I will thankfully repay you for ye same by bills of Ex^ca^ for London, wch I will return to you, or deliver them to yor Order here, or pay our Lt Govr wch may bee most for yor Convenience, wch I hope you'l not Question Our Govern^r^ hath Spoke to mee to inquire after two Indians wch came from you a man and a woman wch I have, & understand they were in the farthest part of the Tuskerora Country, ab^t^ 300 miles fro' hence I shall Send that way Some time this moneth, & have ingaged my traders (if possible wth any reasonable charge to

---

(6) Stephanus Van Cortlandt (1643–1700) was one of the most eminent men of the Colony of New York. He was probably Mayor of New York during Byrd's visit, as well as a momber of the Governor's Council. The Livingston referred to was, no doubt, Robert Livingston (1654–1725), also a very prominent man. The Schuyler of Albany was Peter Schuyler (1657–1724), first mayor of that city.

Most of the New Yorkers named did a large Indian trade, and could therefore procure wampum. Byrd, evidently, deemed this the best currency for use by his traders who were going to the Cherokee country.

redeem), wch they have promised to doe, & doe not question itt, unles they are gone to a Nation. ab^{t} 100 miles farther, to w^{ch} (its S^{d}) they pretend to belong, Black wampum would oblidge Indians more than anything, wch wee want. However hope to retrieve them, though twill bee Something dearer English Goods being plenty amongst those Indians, S^{r} I beg you^{r} pardon for this trouble & if I can any way Serve you here please freely to command

Hon^{d} S^{r}

Yo^{r} most Humble Servt

W B

My Service to m^{r} Schuylers both at Yorke & Albany Allso to m^{r} Livingston & all fr'ds. If Gravenradt comes for our parts it will bee a most ready Conveyance. If I could procure a Pipe of good Madera (for my Selfe) any under £15 St^{g} itt would bee wellcome & if yor convenience p'mits please to Send mee one, & I will pay you by Ex^{ca} as above

Please to returne mee a line or two by the Messenger

W B

To Stephanas Van Cortland, Esqr N Yorke

To ——, New York

Virg^{a} Augst ye 3^{d} 1691

S^{r}

Yo^{rs} to m^{r} Secretary Cole by John Perry wth the Indian came Safe, And according to yor demand I am Ordered by the Lt Govr & Councell to returne you the S^{d} Sum by bills of Ex^{ca} wch are inclosed, & if the like occasion should happen that I could Serve you here I should very readily doe itt, & shall bee willing on all occasions to shew my Selfe

S^{r}

Yo^{r} ready friend to Serve you

W B

I returne you & your wife (to whom my Love & respects) thankes for ye great civility's I rec^{d} at yor house in N Yorke

W B

To the Governor of Virginia?

May it please yor Exlncy

Last night Yarborough came to my house & gave mee an acco^{t} that pursuant to the Orders they had re'd, they went toward the Toteroes but comeing to ye Nottoway river they found the waaters so high they could not passe, wherefore they Sent Pansioela to the Totero's to acquaint that others were there wth the Boy, & On friday night (the Kings Son of ye Toteros) One Saponee: wth Nomterccola ye great man of ye great man of ye came to them, & recd the Boy with great Satisfaction, they pretend they would have come in & pd their tribute at Towne, but that they were uncertain of ye time, but promise to bring it in next Gen^{ll} Court; Nantuccola seems to Speake Suspiciously of them, y^{t} if they had not speedily recd their boy, Some mischief would have follow'd, but affirmes that neither Saponees nor Toleros, had lately been near the English, they haveing been a considerable time all at home till about tuesday last, when most of the Toteras went (as they Said) a hunting on the South Side Maherin River, Neither Saponees nor Torteras have of late years planted any Corne, till this year, & now they have a considerable quantity of rare ripe corne growing. So that on the whole matter what to guesse I know not unlesse the Senecas have been sculking about ye English plantations to looke for ye Appomatocks, If so I suppose they are gone of on Sight of our Rangers, shall not trouble yor Exlncy farther, but humbly take leave & remain

My L^{d}

Yo^{r} Exlnay's humble & Obedient Servt

W B

(Concluded)

VIRGINIA GLEANINGS IN ENGLAND.

(Contributed by Reginald M. Glencross, 176 Worple Road, Wimbledon, S. W. 19, London, England.

(Continued.)

SAMUELL SWONE, of Brasted, co. Kent, gent.

Dated 1 Jan. 1603. Codicil 29 June 1604.
Proved 15 Jan, 1604-5.

To the poor of Brasted, 20s.

To my wife, MARTHA, all my goods and chattels for the bringing up of, MARTIN, SAMUELL, WILLIAM, ELIZABETH, ANNE, MARTHA & MARIE, my children.

And touching the disposition of all that part of my lands and woods in the parish of Sondrish, co. Kent, which I late purchased of my nephew, WILLIAM SMITH, called Shutwell Bothome and 3 acres of land, called Longe croft, which I purchased of WILLIAM MYDLETON, lying in Brasted, and one acre of meadow, which I purchased of HENRY CROW, also in Brasted, I bequeath to my kinsmen and friends, WILLIAM CROW, gent., THOMAS MARSHAM, cittizen and merchant tailor of London and EDWARD DUCKET, cittizen and mercer of London, they to sell the same, and the money arising by such sale to be paid to my daughters, ELIZABETH, ANNE, MARTHA & MARIE.

Sole Executrix:—my wife MARTHA.

GILES CROWE; ROBERT MELLERSH; BRYAN WILTON: Witnesses.

Codicil dated 29 June 1604.

Whereas THOMAS OVERY mortgaged unto me one acre of meadow in Brasted which is now forfeited unto me, never-theless I bequeath the same unto him again, upon condition he pay such debt as is owing to my Executrix.

EDWARD DUCKETS; ROBERT MELLERSH; THOMAS MARSHAM: Witnesses.
Proved 15 Jan. 1604-5 by the Sole Executrix named. **Hayes 5**

RICHARD SWANN, of Charing in co. Kent, gent.

Dated 5 May 1609. Proed 17 June 1609.

To the poor of Charing, 10s. and Lydd, 10s.
To my brother, JOHN SWANN, gent., an annuity of £20. to be paid out of my part viz., the moyety of those lands lying in Lydd which I hold together with one Sir FRANCIS SWANN, Knight, of the parish of Denton, in said co., also the yerely rent which is due unto me by Sir FRANCIS, viz., £3. 6. 8. being the moiety of a legacy unto me by the Will of FRANCIS SWANN, my father, which ever since the death of WILLIAM SWANN my brother remayneth yet unpaid. To my brother, CHRISTOPHER DEERING, of Charing, gent. 40s. and to my sister his wife, £5. To my cosin, JOHN DEERING, sonne of my said brother, all the goods and chattels in his hands jointly used between him and me. To my cosen, THOMAS DEERING, one other sonne of my brother, £10. To my cosen, FRANCIS DEERING, one other of my brother's sonnes, £10. To my cosens, JANE & MARTHA DEERING, the daughters of my brother £5 each. To my cosen, CATHERINE HUDSON, the wife of my cosen, GEORGE HUDSON 20s. To the children of my cosen BOULE, late of Warhorne, in said co., deceased £5. To my cosen, FRANCIS BRINGBORNE, 26s. 8d. and to my cosen JOHN BRINGBORNE, 10s. To my cosen BETTES, his wife, 10s. To my cosen, MANNERING, his wife, 10s. To Mr. FRANCIS STONARD, 10s. To STEPHEN PEMBLE, late of Egerton, 20s. To the poor silenced ministers in London £10. To ROBERT VIRGINE, 2s. To ROBERT PORTER, 2s. To HENRY OLIVER, 2s. To THOMAS OLIVER, 2s. To HENRY PROSSER, 2s. To COATS, 12d. To THOMAS

RAYNES, 12d. To PRISCILLA OLIVER, 2s. 6d. To PHINE BATCHELER, 2s. 6d.
Residuary Legatee and Sole Executor:—my brother, ANDREW SWAN. Overseer:—my brother, CHRISTOPHER DEERING.
JOHN HUDSON; THOMAS OLIVER, senior; JOHN BUSSON: Witnesses.
Proved 17 June 1609 by the Sole Executor named. **Dorset 55.**

WILLIAM SWAN, of Southfleete, in co. Kent, Knight.

Dated 10 Feb. 1618. Proved 15 March 1618-19.

To be buried in my chappell in the churche of Southfleete amongst myne ancestors. To the poore of Southfleete, an annuity of 20s. to be paid out of one tenement and land therto belonging, lying in a village neere Stonwood, in the parish of Stone, in said co., in the tenure of one PRICE. To the poore of the parish of Swanscombe, £5. To my daughter, MERIELL SWAN, £1,000. To my second sonne, GEORGE SWAN, £1,000. And whereas I have made him joynt purchaser with his elder brother, THOMAS SWAN, of a farm, called Boteshams, and the land belonging in Southfleete, my will is that at his age of 21 he is to surrender his estate therein to his brother THOMAS, on payment of £500. To my third sonne, WILLIAM SWAN, £1,000. To my sonne, THOMAS SWAN, all my plate and household stuffe whatsoever. Residuary Legatee and Sole Executrix:—my wife, Dame MERIELL.
Overseers:—The Revd. father in God JOHN, now Lord Bishop of Rochester, Sir GEORGE WRIGHT, Knt. and Sir HUMFREY MAYE, Knt., Chancellor of the Dutchey of Lancaster.
All my lands tenements and hereditaments, to my eldest son, THOMAS SWANN, and his heirs males. For default of such issue, to my sonne GEORGE aand his heirs males. For default of such issue, to my 'sonne WILLIAM

SWANN, and his heirs males. For default of such issue to the heirs males of JOHN SWANN, of Higham, co. Kent. gent. To my kinsman, THOMAS BIRKETT, that now serveth me £10.
WILLIAM BLAND; JOHN BACKHOWSE; JOHN HUNT; CHARLES GRYMES: Witnesses.
Proved 15 March 1618-19 by the Sole Executrix named. Parker 29.

CHARLES SWANN, of Southfleete, co. Kent, gentleman, lying sick in the house of one Mr. William Platers in Ditchlingham, co. Suffolk, gent., and fearing death he desired to see and speak with his brother in law, Paule Hill.

[No date] ["a little before his death"] Proved 11 Aug. 1618.

He declared as follows:

To my sister Hilles children, all my estate whatsoever, to be equally divided among them.
Executor:- my brother in lawe, Paule Hill.

"My brother Sir William Swann, is not to have twoepence of my estate."

Richard Baispoole; William Smythe; and others: Witnesses.

Proved 11 August 1618 by the Sole Executor named.
81 Meade.

[Samuel Swan or Swonne, whose will appears just above, does not appear in the pedigree of Swan of Denton, in *Berry's Kent*. He was probably of the Southfleet branch, and his Christian name would indicate a possible ancestry of the Virginia and North Carolina family. William Swann, the emigrant to Virginia, was born in 1585, so might have been the son of that name mentioned in Samuel Swan's will. Richard Swan, whose will has the second place, was a son of Francis Swan, of Wye, Kent. Richard Swan was a half-uncle of Sir Francis Swan of Denton.

Sir William Swan (will proved 1619) was the father of Sir Thomas Swan, whose will was printed in this Magazine XXVII, 154, and Charles Swan was a nephew of Sir William.

Several Swan wills and a note were printed in this Magazine, XXVII, 153-156.

We are indebted to Captain T. A. Ashe, of Raleigh, N. C. for the following copy of a family record prepared by Samuel Swann (son of Col. Thomas Swann of Virginia) who removed to North Carolina.

"The following is a copy of a paper compiled by Samuel Swann who died in 1707, (in Perquimans Co.—Albemarle, N. C.)

"My Grandmother, Judith Swann, was born on the 5th day of February 1589, being Wednesday and died on the 16th, day of March 1636 in the 47th year of her age and was buried at Swann's Point.

My Grandfather William Swann married again the 1st day of May 1637, and died the last of February following in the 52nd year of his age and was buried at Swann's Point.

My father, Col. Thomas Swann was born in May 1616,—was married to his first wife Margaret Debton the 13th of January 1639, by whom he had two sons and one daughter, to wit: Susannah Swann who was born the 26 October, 1640—and died the 25th of November 1660, without issue—having been married to Maj. William Marriot eight months and 22 days—and was buried at Swann's Point. William Swann—who was born 30th October 1644 and died young in London, England and was buried there. And Thomas Swann who was born the 23rd of March 1645 and died without issue at St. Edmunds Bury in Suffolk England the 19th of February 1666, and was there interred.

My said father's first wife died the 5th of April 1646 and was was buried at Swann's Point.

My father was married to his second wife, my dear mother, Sarah Cod, the 13th of January 1649, by whom he had issue, likewise, two sons and one daughter— Sarah; who was born the 15th of October 1651 and died the 9th of August 1652, and was buried at Swann's Point. Samuel who was born the 11th May 1653, and Sampson who was born the 28th May 1654, and died the 1st of November 1668, and was interred at Swann's Point.

My said mother departed this life to a better, the 13th of January 1654, having been married that day, just five years and was buried at Swann's Point.

My father was married to his third wife, Sarah Chandler, the 30th of July 1655, by whom he had two sons and two daughters, viz, Judith, who was born the 22nd April 1656 and died the 30th March 1668 and was buried at Swann's Point. Anne, who was born the 9th, of July 1657 and died the 21st of August 1659 and was buried at Swann's Point. A son—not baptized, who was born the 11th of December 1658 and died the 20th of the same month—and another son born 1st November 1662 and died at the birth.

My said father's third wife died 10th November 1662—and was buried at Swann's Point.

My father was married to his fourth wife, Ann Brown, widow and relict of Henry Brown, one of the Council of State, the 23rd day of * * * * *—who died the 12th of August 1668, without issue and was buried at the Four Mile Tree.

My father married his fifth wife. Mary Mansfield the 20th of December 1668, by whom he had issue one son and three daughters—Mary who was born the 5th of October 1669, who married Mr. .Richard Bland, Thomas and Frances, at one birth, who were born the 14th December 1670.

Frances died 14th April 1676 and was buried at Swann's Point.

Thomas married Eliza Thompson, daughter of William Thompson.

Sarah who was born the 8th of and was first married to Mr. Henry Randolph and after his death to Mr. Giles Webb.

My honored and dear father, Col. Thomas Swann departed this life for a better the 16th of September 1680, being 64 years and was buried at Swann's Point at my Grandfather's feet.''

Extracts from a paper drawn up by Hon. Samuel Swann, Collector of His Majesty's Customs at Roanoke.''

My dearly and most entirely beloved wife Sarah, daughter of William Drummond Esq., was born the 2nd day of March 1654, being Friday, about 2 of the clock in the morning, and was married to me the 24th March 1673 being Tuesday,—by whom I had seven sons and two daughters.

My dear and most entirely beloved wife Sarah Swann departed this life to a better on Saturday the 18th of April 1696 about 8 o'clock in the morning in North Carolina, and was buried at Swann's Point in Surry County at her own mother's feet on Friday the 28th of the same month, being 41 years one month and 16 days old, having been married to me 22 years and as much more as from the 24th of March to the 18 of April aforesaid.

My dear and entirely beloved wife Elizabeth daughter of Alexander Lillington of North Carolina, was born the 17th of June 1679, married to me the 19th of May 1698, being Thursday, the widow of John Tandall, by whom I had issue as follows—viz:

1 Elizabeth who was born the 26th of June 1699, being Monday, about 12 o'clock at noon; baptized the 9th October following, being Monday. 2 Sarah who was born the 29th of December 1701, being Monday about a quarter of an hour before sunset—was baptized the 2nd of February, following, being Monday. Samuel who was born the 31st of October 1704 being Tuesday at 1 o'clock in the afternoon. The Moon being full at 12 o'clock, was baptized on Thursday the 23rd of August 1705. 4 John Swann, who was born the 25th of April 1707 being Friday about half an hour before Sundown and was baptized by William Gordon.

Addendum of Col. Edward Moseley.

Some of his children by his first wife were "buried at my plantation at Lawns Creek"—so there he probably resided before coming to Albemarle, only William, Thomas and Henry, issue of his first marriage, seem to have survived—to attain manhood. One of that branch was John Swann, Member of Congress. The District Attorney in New York (1919) descends from Sarah, No. 2 who married a Jones—one of her sons returning to the name of Swann, about 1790.

The Honorable Samuel Swann Esq., Collector of His Majesty's Customs in Roanoke departed this life the 14th of September 1707 just at daybreak at his dwelling plantation in Perquimans and lies interred there, at whose death and funeral, I the subscriber was present.

EDWARD MOSELEY.

WILLIAM TURBERVILE of Winifrith Newborough, county Dorset, gent. Will 30 April 1630; proved 15 February 1630/1. To repairing Winifrith Church 20s., and to the poor 20s. To grandchild Elizabeth Clavell daughter of Edward Clavell gent, a lease of lands in common fields of Winifrith. To Marie, Richard, Grace, Edward, and Fraunces 5 other children of said Edward £20 apiece at 21. To William and John Smeddmore my grandchildren £5 each when 21. To my grandchild John Turbervile £100 which his father in law Mr. William Harbin borrowed of me. To be employed by my brother George Turbervile in advancing John. My wife to give bonds to my grandchild and heir John Turbervile, or if he die to his brother Thomas. Residuary Legatee and Executrix: Wife Elizabeth for life. Overseers: Brother George Turbervile and Robert Stricklande. Witnesses: George Turbervile, Thomas Hayte, Willm Edwards, Robert Strickland.

St. John, 20.

JOHN TURBERVILE of Wolbridge, county Dorset, Esquire. Will 5 December 1633; proved 30 April 1634. My body to Ile of Beere church where my dear Lady and wife, my father and other of my ancestors lie. To poor of Beere aforesaid £10 as stock. To repaire of Beere church 40s. To church of Stoake 40s. To poor of Stoake 10s. To churches of Woll and Winfrith 40s. apeece. To poor of Woll and Winfrith 20s. To my serving men (except Thomas Trew) £5 apeece. To Thomas Trew £6. 13s. 4d. To Mary Trew his wife £5. To every of my covenant servants 20s. apeece. To my brother George Turbervile two closes in East Burton, county aforesaid, for 20 years paying to my heir 4s. yearly. To my cosen Mathew Turbervile £10. To Grace and Mary his daughters £10 apeece. To the sons of my nephew William Turbervile deceased viz: John and Thomas Turbervile £5 apiece to be paid to my sister Elizabeth Turbervile their grandmother to their use. To my cosin Mrs. Elizabeth Rainger £50 to the use of her and her three sons George, Richard, and Samuel Reinger equally. To my cosin Margaret Streete and to her children by Poore and Streete £40. To my cousin Edward Clavells wife Bridgett and her children £30. To Elner and Mary daughters of my nephew Thomas Turbervile gent deceased £40, And to his sons Thomas and George Turbervile £40. To Margery Reade widow £5. To Mary Watkins £5. To Widow Steventon als Burgan £3. To my cosin Margery Loope as a token 40s. To Thomas Christophers the Keeper and his wife 40s. apiece. To my son in law Mr. Thomas Thornhurst £10. To my cosin Dorothy Turbervile widow, relict of my nephew Thomas Turbervile £10 token of my love. To the poor at my funeral £6. To said Dorothy Turbervile, widow, my farm of Wolbridge and my lands in East Burton to have and to hold until her son and my heir John Turbervile shall be 22 years, paying therefore £13. 6s. 8d. yearly. My two closes at West Burton, Winfrith, county Dorset to my nephew Mathew Turbervile gent untill such time as my heir John Turbervile shall be of 22 years paying during said term 10s. yearly. Concerning my plate, household stuff etc. at Wolbridge, Beere, West Burton or elsewhere I bequeath the same to my heir John Turbervile, said John Turbervile and his mother Dorothy executors. John Fussell of Blandford, county Dorset gent and my well beloved brother George Turbervile gentlemen, Overseers. For their love 40s. apiece.

Witnesses: John Gallton, Clarke, Mathew Turberville, Thos. Trew. Probate was also granted 15 September 1638 to John Turbervile.

Seager, 27.

[The first of the Turberville family in Virginia, was John Turberville, who, as is shown by a deed made by him in 1726, bought land in Lancaster County from Henry Fleet on Nov. 9, 1680. He was J. P. for Northumberland in 1692 and for Lancaster 1699 or, and a member of the House of Burgesses for the last named county in 1703 and 1704. He appears to have made no will but the inventory of his personal estate was recorded in Lancaster Oct. 9, 1728. Various deeds show that he had an only son and heir, George Turberville, of Westmoreland county. The Virginia Turbervilles, as shown on various book plates and tombs, bore the same arms as Turberville of Dorset: Ermin a lion rampant gules crowned or. Crest: A castle argent, portcullis or.]

WILLIAM WALTHALL, citizen and Alderman of London.

[P. A. B. St. Peter's Cornhill.]

Dated 16 July 1608. Adm. 3 Sept. 1608.

To be buried in the parish churche of St. Peter, in Cornhill in the vault where my late wife Ciceley was buried, being in the chauncell and in the upper end of the South Ile.

To the poore of the parish, £20.

All my goods and chattels to be valued and devided into three parts. But forasmuch that before the marriage with my wife Dame Margaret Goddart there was an agreement made as will appear by her deed made to my brother Thomas Walthall and my sonne in law, Arthur Robinson that she will accept £8,000 in lieu of her full thirdes. Also she hath agreed, and I have entered into covenant to Sir Thomas Bennett and Sir William Romney to pay £1,900 to her 4 children, Giles Garton, Simon Garton, Elizabeth Dent & Alice Greene that so much of the said £1,900 as shall happen to be unpaid shal be defaulted out of the said £8,000. Provided also that she pay out of the same all that I have disbursed for her sonne Giles Garton for the procuring his pardon to save his life and living from the danger of the Lawe, "for the surplus and charges of Billinghurst land more then the rentes, with the money to John Quarles which amounts to £750." not doubting but my wife will give allowance thereof to my executors as she promised me before her sonne in law, Mr. Francis Dent in the litle parloure in my house in Fenchurch streete, 20 March 1607.

One third part, unto my three children, Thomas, Luke & Elizabeth, equally amongst them. And the other third part, I reserve to myself towards the performance of my legacies.

To St. Thomas Hospitall in Sowthwarke, whereof I am a governor, £40. To the Hospitall of St. Bartholmewes, and the poor house of Bridewell £20 each.

To the poor of Bedlam, 6£. 13s. 4d. To the two Compters in the Poultrey and in Wood streete and to Ludgate. £100 between them.

To the prisoners at Newgate, the Marshallsea, Kynges benche, and the White Lyon in Sowthwarke, £30 between them. To all householders in the ward of Bishopsgate 2s each so far as £20 will perform. (Numerous bequests to various other charitable institutions etc, etc.) To William Batte, my godsonne, £10. To Mr. Batt's two daughters, that were godchildren to my wife and daughter Margaret, £3. 6. 8. each. To Anne Payne, my goddaughter, £10. To Elizabeth Bainbrig, my goddaughter, £6. 13. 4. All my other godchildren 10s. each. To "that olde woman my cosen Flower", £6. 13. 4. To the children of Robert Bristowe, 40s. each. To my brother Paynes, three daughters, Margaret, Mary & Johane, fyve markes each. To my brother Banbriggs children, 40s. each. "To two kinsmen I have abowte Dover in Kent of my mother's side, to witt,

Roert & Stephen Vincent," £10 each. To my sister, Johane Dutton, 100 markes. To Margaret Fisher, and her husband, £200. £100 of which her husband oweth me by his bond and Richard Walthall's. To their eldest daughter who hath married one Burne of Darbie, £30. To Johane Stables, my sister Dutton's daughter, £50 and £25 each to the children she had by her husband Higgins. To Anne Hubberde, mayde when my children were young, £6. 13. 4. To Ciceley, our mayde that dwells at Darbye, 40s. To Nanne and Alice that were maydes and married Feltmakers, 40s. each. To Jane Elsworthe, a poor woman, 40s. To Emme, mayde, now with me, £30. To Richard Walthall, my brother Anthony Walthall his sonne, £200. To his sonne William Walthall, my godsonne, £50. To my brother Thomas Walthall, his children, viz., John & Thomas Walthall, £100 each. To my sister Anne Walthall, my brother's wife, £20. To Godfrey Reyner, £5. To my brother Sylvester,. £10. To Mrs. Crockstone & Mrs Lewse £5. To olde John Howland, £5. To Dr. Ashpoole, a ring of golde, of 40s. To Shelley and his wife that keepeth my house at Hackney, £4. To Mr. Johnson, the preacher at Hackney, 40s. To my three children, Thomas, Luke and my daughter Elizabeth Robinson, all my plate and household stuffe, equally divided. To the Worshipful Company of Mercers, £500. To my sonne Thomas Walthall, the house and land that I lately bought of John Bowyer, gent., that lyeth in Hackney. To Lambert Osbaston, on the Bridge, £5. To his wife and Mrs. Eaton her sister, each of them rings of golde 40s. value, "and to Mrs. Thomas." To Mrs, Varder, nowe the Matron of St. Thomas Hospital in Sowthwarke, £3. 6. 8. To Mrs. Dixon in St. Peter's Parish, £3. 6. 8.

To my friends rings of gold, (the womens rings to be of 40s. value and the mens 50s.) vizt. Sir Thomas Bennet and his Ladye, Sir William Rumney and his Ladye, Sir Stephen Soames and his Ladye, Sir William Craven and his Ladye, Mr. Robert Sandye and his wife, Mr. Vernon, my brother and sister Stampforde, my sister Dutton, my cosen Richard Walthall and his wife, my sonne Dent and his wife my sonne Cowley and his wife, my sonne Poole, my brother Bambrig and his wife, Thomas Fisher and his wife, my sonne Moore, Giles Garbin, Simon Garbin, George Green and his wife, Godfrey Reyner and his wife, my two deputies and their wives, in Farrington without, Mr. Cawdwell and Mr. Hudson, my cousin Richard Walthall of the Manptwiche, Mr. Humphrey Walcott and his wife, Edmund Sleighes and Gervis Sleighes of Derbye, William Batts, on the Bridge, Richard Chambers and his mother Dorothy Chambers, Mrs. Awdley of Hackney, Mr. Humphrey Bashe and his wife, Sir John Manners of Haddon in Darbieshire, and Mr. Alderman Lemman.

Whereas my late brother Anthony Walthall deceased, "fell into decay and brake", about 1581, at which time his creditors "sewed out the statute of banckrupts," and by virtue thereof did seise certeyne household stuffe in his dwelling house in St. Margaretts parish in Lothbury, to the value of £100, which the said creditors left in trust with me, but owing to long keeping the same is perished and spoiled with "moathes, rattes and vermyn and ruste and wormes," Therefore I leave £200 in trust with the Mercers Company in London, in place of the said household stuff. "What is not perished" is in the hands of Sir Thomas Middleton, Knt. who marryed the widow of John Olmested. Md. Mr. William Walthall dyed 3 Sept. 1608 and this will was found lying upon a table in his compting house, being present at the fynding of the same, Ladye Margaret Goddart his wife, Mr. Thomas Walthall his brother, Mr. Arthure Robinson his sonne in lawe and his wife, his two sonnes Thomas Walthall & Luke Walthall and his cosen Mr. Richard Walthall.

3 Sept. 1608. Administration granted to Elizabeth Robinson als Walthall, daughter of said deceased, no Executor being named.

85 Windebanke.

LUKE WALTHALL citizen and Mercer of London.*
Dated 30 May 1617. Adm. 16 Dec. 1617

To the poor of the parish of Westham, co. Essex, £4. and to the poor of the parish of St. Peters in Cornhill, London, £4·

Residuary Legatee and sole Executor: my eldest sonne, William Walthall.

Overseers: Charles Pressey, Esq., Humfrey Browne of London, merchant Edward Panton, gentleman and Thomas Hobson, merchant.

Robert Jenyngs, vicar of Westham, Raphe Turner & John Thomas, Scrivener, Witnesses..

16 Dec. 1617. Administration granted to Mary Walthall relict of said deceased, to administer, during the minority of William Walthall, the son and sole executor named.

120 Weldon.

THOMAS WALTHALL, thelder, citizen and mercer of London.

[P. A. B. of St. Peters Cornhill·]

Dated 14 May 1611. Proved 11 May 1613.
[at top of Will]
Dated 23 April 1613. [at end of Will]

To be buried in the parish church of St. Peter's on Cornhill in London, near unto the place where my brother Alderman Walthall, was buried.

My executors to provide for 50 poore men, mourning gownes of black, six of them to be of the chief porters of the Mercers Company, and they to carry my corpse to the ground.

To the poore of St. Peter's, on Cornhill, 5 marks. To James Buffeilde, a poor water bearer, 20s. To the "Wandringe and Roagish poore", 5 markes to be distributed amongst them by two pence each. To Christs Hospitall, £5. My goods and chattels and things whatsoever, to be divided into three parts. One third to my wife, another third to my two sonnes and another third to perform my legacies etc. I owe certain legacies given by my late brother William Walthall, deceased which are not yet due, but as they become so, my executors are to see them paid. The house wherein I dwell, "being a lease belonging unto the worshipful Company of Mercers", my Wife to enjoy the same, and after her decease my two sonnes John & Thomas Walthall. To some learned man to preach at my funeral, 20s. To my godsonne Humfrey Walcott, the younger, a guilte cupp, of 5 markes value. To my sonne, John Walthall, my seale ring, with my Armes ingraven on it. To my second sonne Thomas Walthall, another golde ring, with my usual mark ingraven in the same. To Mr. Godfrey Reynor, a golde ringe, prayeing him to be helpful unto my sonne John in getting in my small estate which is abroad. To my friend Mr. Thomas Chapman, scrivenor, a cupp of guilte of 5 markes value. To my friend Mr. John Vernor, a ring of golde, of 40s. value. To John Walcott, the sonne of Mr. Humfrey Walcott, of London, grocer being now Student in Trinity Colledge, Cambridge, 40s. To my sonnes Tutor, Mr. Cearle, 40s. To my sonne John the tenement, at the old Jurie ende, now in the occupation of Francis Childe, a Chandler.

Executors: My wife Anne Walthall and my sonne John Walthall.

Overseers: Mr. Humfrey Walcott, thelder, grocer, and my brother in lawe Mr. Humfrey Robinson, grocer and my friend Mr. Thomas Dalbye.

Proved 11 May 1613 by the Executors named.

[No Witnesses.]

47 Capell.

[William Walthall, merchant, lived in Henrico County, Va., as early as 1656. He probably came from London. In his will, dated Aug 2. 1669, Raphael Throckmorton, of London, bequeathed £10 to "my dear wives brother Mr. William Walthall, now living in Virginia". If the marriage of Raphael Throckmorton could be found in some London register, William Walthall of Virginia, might be connected with the testators above.]

HENRY WOODHOUSE of Waxtonsham alias Waxham, in co. Norfolk, Knight.

Dated 18 Sept. 1624. Admon 4 Feb, 1624-5.

Whereas by Indenture made between me, of the one part and Nicholas Bacon, of Redgrave, in co. Suff, Esqr. now Knight Baronet, of the other, bearing date 2 June 17 Eliz. It was covenanted by me to convey the mannor of Waxham alias Waxtonsham, with all the lands and tenements belonging, to William Woodhouse, my eldest sonne, nowe knight, and to his heirs males. And whereas I afterwards did by fine and recovery convey the said mannor and lands to the intent of the said Indenture as by the records of the Court of Common Pleas it doth more plainly appear. Now I. being indebted to John Dee, citizen and goldsmith, of London for £400 and to William Engham of London, gent. for £100, I appoint unto them for the payment of the same, the profits of one close called the hundred acre close, concontaining by estimation 103 acres and one other close, called the midle Deanes, containing 50 acres, and another piece of ground called Lower Deanes, containing fower score acres, now in the tenure of Richard Cubit &John Lesingham, for 5 years. Residuary Legatee and Sole Executrix: my now wife, Dame Cicely.

James Sherringham, Samuel Walpoole, scriv. Witnesses.

4 Feb. 1624-25. Administration granted unto Thomas Elwin, one of the creditors of deceased, the Executrix, Dame Cecile Woodhouse, renouncing.

15 Clarke.

[Sir Henry Woodhouse, whose will is given above, was the father of Sir William Woodhouse, and of Captain Henry Woodhouse, Governor of Bermuda. Henry, son of the latter settled in Virginia. It is probable that the Sir William Woodhouse, who died 1639, and whose will has been printed XXVI, 40, was not father of Capt. Henry, as there stated, but his brother.

See this Magazine XXVI, 38-40, and references there given.]

VIRGINIA IN 1681-82

Instructions to Lord Culpeper.

Continued.

57 To encourage Trade and the African Compy.

You are to give all due encouragement and invitation to merchants and others who shall bring trade unto our said colonie or any way contribute to the advantage thereof, and in particular to the Royal African Company of England.

58 To Suffer none to trade in Africa within the Charter of the Company without leave.

And you are to take care that there be no trading from Virginia or any of the Territory depending thereon to any place or part in Africa within the Charter of the Royal African Comapny. And you are not to suffer any ships to bee sent thither without their leave or authority.

59 To endeavour that their payments be duly made.

And as wee are willing to recommend unto the said Company that the said Colonie may have a constant and sufficient supply of Merchantable Negroes at moderate rates in money or commodities, you are to take special care that payment be duly made and within a competent time, according to their agreement. It being against reason to expect that any should send good wares to a known bad market.

60 To observe the Treaty of Madrid 1670,

Our Will and Pleasure is, and wee do hereby strictly commend and enjoyn you carefully to observe all the articles contained in the late Treaty for the composing

between England and Spain.

of differences and the establishing of Peace in America concluded at Madrid the 8-18 day of July, 1670, between Us and the Crown of Spain, an authentick copie whereof you shall herewith receive.

61
To give an account of all Injuries done by the Spaniards there, and not to Suffer any other reparation than is directed by Treaty.

And in case any private injury or damage shall be offered or done to any of our subjects in those parts by any of the subjects of the King of Spain, you shall take care to give Us an account with all convenient speed by one of our principal Secretary's of State or to the Lords of Our Privy Council appointed a Committee for Trade and Foreign Plantation. And not to permit or encourage reparations thereof to be sought in any other way than what is directed and agreed in the said Articles of Madrid.

62
To give an acc't of the strength of the neighbours.

And Our Will and Pleasure is that you doe from time to time give unto Us and the Lords of the Commitee for Trade and Plantation an account of what strength your bordering neighbours have (bee they Indians or others) by Sea and Land, and what correspondency you doe keep with them.

63
A Law for ascertaining what Estate Jurors ought to have to bee prepared and sent over for approbation.

And whereas, wee think it fit for ye better administration of Justice that a Law bee passed in the Assembly wherein shall be set the value of Men's Estates, either in goods or Lands under which they shall not bee capable of serving as Jurors, Our pleasure is that at the first opportunity of transmitting any Laws hither for Our approbation according to Our Instructions before expressed you preprae and send one to that purpose.

64

To admit no appeals to the Assembly. Appeals above £100 to be submitted to the King and Council, Security being given by the Appell^{t} to the answer costs, and to pass a Law for the limitation of Appeals to the Government & Council.

You are not for the future to admit or allow of any appeals whatsoever to bee made from the Governor and Council unto the Assembly. But whereas wee judge it absolutely necessary that all Our Subjects may have liberty to apeal to Our Royal Person in cases that may deserve the same. Our Will and Pleasure is that if either party shall not rest satisfied with the Judgment or Sentence of the Governor and Council, they may then appeal unto Us in Our Privy Council, provided the matter in difference exceed the real value and Summ of One Hundred pound sterling, and that Security bee alsoe given by the Appellant to answer such charges as shall be awarded in case the Sentence of the Governor and Council in Virginia bee confirmed. And provided alsoe that Execution bee not suspended by reason of any such appeal unto Us. And whereas, it may not bee let that appeals bee too frequently and for too small a value brought unto Our Governor and Council; you shall therefore with the advice of the Council propose a Law to be passed wherein the method and limitation of Appeals unto the Governor and Council may be setled and restrained in such manner as shall be found most convenient and easy to Our subjects in Virginia.

65

To endeavour to pass a Law against the inhumanity of Masters & Overseers and

You shall endeavour to get a Law passed for the restraining of any inhuman severity which by ill masters or overseers may be used towards their Christian Servants or Slaves. And you are alsoe with the assistance of the Council and Assembly, to find out the best means to facilitate and ento encourage the conversion of the Negroes to Christianity with regard to the property of the Inhabitants and Safety of the Island.

courage the conversion of Negroes to the Christian Religion, wherein you are to leave a due caution and regard to ye property of the Inhabitants and safety of the Colonies.

66
To recommend to the Assembly to raising a publick stock and building of workhouses for the poor.

You are to recommend to the Council and Assembly the raising of stocks and building of Publick Workhouses in convenient places for the imploying poor and indigent people.

67
To take a survey of Landing places and Harbours, and to erect fortifications at the publick charge.

And you shall cause a survey to be taken of all the considerable Landing places and Harbours in the said Colonie, and with the advice of the said Council erect in any of them such Fortifications as shall be necessary for the Security and advantage of Our Said Colonie which shall be done at the Public Charge of the Country; not doubting of the chearful concurrence of the Inhabitants thereunto from the common security and benefit they will receive thereby.

68
To dispose the planters to build Towns upon every

You shall likewise endeavour all you can to dispose the Planters to build Towns upon every River, and especially one at least on every great River, as tending very much to their security and profit. And in order

River and to permit noe ships to unload but at such Towns. Building of James Town to be encouraged.

thereunto you are to take care that after sufficient notice to provide warehouses and other conveniences, noe ships whatsoever be permited to load or unload, but at the said places where the towns are settled. And whereas, wee are given to understand that Jamestown is not only ye most antient but the most convenient place for ye Metropolis of Our said Colonie, you are to direct all possible means to be used for the speedy Rebuilding of the same. As also to take care that the Chief Post ye usual place of your residence the Courts of Justice and other Public Offices attending the Government be setled and continued in that place. For the better accomplishing of which Our designs you shall in Our Name, let Our Counsellors and chief Inhabitants in that Our Colonie know that wee shall take it very well at their hands if they shall alsoe contribute thereunto, by building, every one of them, one or more houses, as occasion shall offer, and of the success thereof you shall from time to time give us an account by one of Our principal Secretaries of State and by Our Committee for Trade and Foreign Plantations.

69 All Servants are to serve the time prescribed by Law; Each to have 50 acres after the said term.

Our Will and Pleasure is that all servants that shall come to be transported to Our said Colonie of Virginia shall serve their respective Masters for the term prescribed by the Laws of that Our Colonie. And the said Servants shall at the end of the said term have 50 acres of Land set out and assigned to every of them respectively to have and to hold to them and every of them their Heirs and Assigns for ever under the Rent and Dutys usually paid and reserved.

70
To repeal the Acts in 1676 as also an Act concerning appeals how to be brought and all Acts allowing appeals to the Assembly, but appeals to the general Courts to be as formerly.

And whereas Wee are very much dissatisfied at several Laws passed at a Grand Assembly begun at Green Spring on the 20th of February, 1676, during the Government of Sir William Berkley, which are not only disagreeable to the Powers residing in the Government there but derogatory to Our gracious Proclamation bearing date the 20th of October in the 28th year of Our Reign and prejudicial to the good of Our said Colonie. You are therefore to signify Our Royal Pleasure at such time after your Arrival as you shall find most convenient for Our service. That such of the said Laws as are not yet repeal'd, viz, An Act limiting times of receipt and payment of Public Tobaccos, an Act regulating Ordinarys and the Prices of Liquors; An Act disposing Americaments upon Past Actions; An Act for Laying of Parish Levys; as alsoe one Act passed at a Grand Assembly begun at Middle Plantation on the 10th of October, 1677, viz.: An Act for signing Executions and Judgments in the Assembly; as likewise an Act made at a Grand Assembly held at James Citty the 3rd of March, 1662, entitled Appeals, how to be made and all others to the same effect allowing appeals to the Assembly, bee all forthwith repealed and declared void. Provided always that all appeals from the County Courts and other inferior Courts shall be made by the General Court in such manner as formerly until Our further Pleasure bee known therein.

71
To give an

You are likewise from time to time to give us by one of Our principal Secretarys

account of the wants of the Colonie.

of State and Our Committee for Trade and Foreign Plantations an account of the wants and defects of ye said Colonie and Territorys under your Government. What the chief products of them are, What new Improvements the industry or invention of the Planters hath afforded? What probable advantage may be gained by Trade? and which way you conceive wee may contribute towards them.

72
To encourage the manuring of Vines, Silk, Hemp, Flax, Pitch & Potashes, and to provide for the Same by Law.

And you shall particularly endeavour to advance the Plantation and production of Vines, Silks, Hemp, Flax, Pitch and Potashes, for which wee are well assured that Climate and Soile is very proper, and for the Encouraging thereof Wee are desirous that new and greater rewards be given in proportion to ye great benefit that Our Colonie would in a short time reap thereby. And that provision be accordingly made for it in the first Laws you shall transmit unto Us for Our approbation.

73
To consider of a restraint for the planting of Tobacco.

And whereas Wee have been formerly moved to put some restraint on the planting of Tobacco in that Our Colonie We recommend the consideration of this matter to you and Our Council there, wherein you may likewise consult the Assembly if you see fit. To the end that upon due deliberation of what is best for that Our Colonie and upon notice thereof given to Us by one of Our principal Secretarys of State and to Our Committee of Trade and Plantation, Wee may order and establish such good rules as may be for the Publick benefit of Our Subjects there.

74 In case any Patent Office bee vacant to provide one to officiate till the King's pleasure be known, taking security for the mean profits.

And whereas Wee have thought fit to dispose of certain Offices and Places in Our said Colonie of Virginia by Letters Patent under Our Great Seals of England, Our Will and Pleasure is that you take care that the said several Offices and Places be freely and without any molestation enjoyed and held by the respective persons to whom granted or their sufficient Deputys. And in case any of the said Patentees or their Deputys shall misbehave themselves in the discharge of any of the said Offices, Our Will and Pleasure is that you only suspend them from ye execution of their said Places till you shall have represented the whole matter and receive Our Pleasure and determination thereupon, taking care that those who shall in the meantime be appointed by you to execute any of the said offices give security to be accountable for the clear profits of the same to the respective Patentees.

75 To the Governor £2000 and for life and £150 p annum till the Colonie provide a house to Officers civil and military as formerly and to transmit the accounts.

And whereas, by the advice of Our Council, we have thought fit to establish and allow a comfortable subsistance and salary for you, Our Governor and Our other chief Officers in that Our Colonie, you shall according to Our said Establishment receive and take to your own use as Governor out of the first moneys raised or to be raised there the yearly summe of Two Thousand Pounds, from the death or other avoidance of Sir William Birkley, Our late Governor there, payable per diem during your natural life. As alsoe the summe of One Hundred and fifty pounds yearly until Our said Colonie shall have provided a house and plantation for you and Our Governor for the time being, which Wee expect and command to see done with all speed. And you shall alsoe pay out of the Next Revenues of Our said Colonie to the Councillors and other Judges and Officers, as well Civil as Military, and to the Marsnal Clerks of the Assembly, Gunners and Matrosses the several Salaries and Allowances formerly paid, or such other reasonable ones as you with the advice of Our Council there shall think requisite, A true account whereof you shall from time to time transmit unto Our Lord High Treasurer or the Commissioners of Our Treasury for the time being, and to the Lords of Our Privy Council appointed a Committee for Trade and Foreign Plantations.

76 To use all means for preventing abuses in the payment of Tobacco duties, and to take care that ye several officers be diligent etc.

Whereas upon considering the entries in Our Custom house here in England with the payment of the two shillings per Hogshead on Tobacco and other duties and imposition due to Us in Virginia. We are certainly informed of great frauds and abuses both in the payment thereof by Masters of Ships and others and in the collection by Our Officers, you are to use all legal means for the prevention thereof and for the Improvement of Our said Revenues. And whereas sush abuses cannot be committed without the apparent negligence of the collectors or their connivance with the said Masters of Ships and other persons, you are strictly to charge and command them and every of them in Our Name to be more diligent and carefull for the future, under penalty of forfeiture of their respective places by your putting others in their stead on the first offence and of Our Highest Displeasure. And you are from time to time to give Us a particular account of your proceedings herein and of the Dutys and Impositions collected and disposed of pursuant to former directions signified in that behalfe.

77
Power to enhance the price of Foreign Coyn by proclamation in all payments except upon the act for 2s per hogshead wch are to be in sterling money.

And whereas it hath been represented unto Us that it is necessary for the good of Our said Colonie to raise the price of Foreigne Coyne, Our Will and Pleasure is that you proceed therein in such manner as with the advice and consent of the Council you shall in your discretion find convenient soe as the enhancement of the price bee made and signified by Proclamation, excepting always what shall be given in payment upon the Act of 2sh per hogshead on Tobacco exported and for other Dutys payable to Us and to the Government which are all to be satisfied in Sterling Money according to the same value as formerly and not otherwise.

78
All Levy's Fines and Forfeitures to be to the King.

And whereas in Laws for levying of money and raising a Public revenue and in Penal Laws there have been hitherto clauses whereby the Levies, Fines and Forfeitures are appropriated unto the Publick without any mention made of Us or unto Us for the Publick use which are derogatory to Our Right of Sovereignty; you shall take care that the same be altered and made agreeable to the stile of such Laws within Our Kingdom of England.

79
Writs to issued in

And for a further mark of Our Supreme and Immediate Authority, Wee do hereby signify unto you Our Express commands the King's name. That all Writs bee issued in Our Royal name throughout Our said Colonie and Dominion notwithstanding any former usage to the contrary.

80 That an order of the 22nd Dec. 1681 disapproving the declaration of the Assembly under the Government of Colo. Jefferies be entered in the Council Book, and to propose a bill to declare His Maj[ties] rights to command the records.

And whereas Wee were pleased by Our Instructions dated in December, 1679, to direct you to signify Our high resentment of a seditious Declaration made by the Assembly of Virginia during the Government of Coll. Jefferies whereby they set forth that Our Commissioners having called for and forced from the Clerk of the Assembly all the original Journals of the Assembly, which power they supposed wee would not grant them, for that they find not the same to have been practiced by any of the Kings of England, and did therefore take the same to be a violation of their privilege desirnig with all satisfaction to be given them that noe such violation of their privilege should be offered for the future. W[ch] significance of our resentment you have hitherto suspended by the advice and Petition of the whole Council there. To the end therefore that such unwarrantable proceedings of that Assembly may not be taken for a president hereafter and seem to have Our Allowance, Wee have therefore thought fit by an Order in Our Privy Council dated 21st of December 1681, to signify Our Pleasure herein and to declare that although wee are pleased to pardon the persons who have offended herein, Wee do nevertheless wholly disapprove the said Declaration and have directed that not only all Records to that effect may be taken off the File and razed out of the Books in Virginia which said Order Our Royal Will and pleasure is that you cause to be entered in the Registry of Our said Council there, and that you likewise propose a Bill to the next Assembly for condemning the said proceedings and declaring the right of Us and Our Officers to call for all the Publick Records and Journals whenever it shall be thought necessary for Our Royal Service.

81
To take order in all things for the good of the Colony till further directions soe as not to declare warr without command.

And if anything shall happen that may be of advantage and security to the said Colonie and other the Territorys depending thereon, which is not herein or by Our Commission provided for, Our Will and Pleasure is and Wee do hereby allow unto you with the advice and consent of the Council to take order for the present therein: Giving Us by one of Our principal Secretarys of State and to the Lords of Our Privy Council appointed a Committee for Trade and Foreign Plantation speedy notice thereof, that soe you may receive Our ratification if Wee shall approve the same. Provided always and Our Will and Pleasure is that you do not by color of any power or authority hereby given you commence or declare warr without Our Knowledge and command therein except it bee against Indians, of which you shall give Us a particular account with all speed.

82
To give an acc[t] of proceedings.

Lastly, you shall upon all occasions give unto Us by One of Our principal Secretarys of State and y[e] Lords of Our Privy Council appointed a Committee for Trade and Foreign Plantation a particular acco. of all vour proceedings and of the condition of affairs within your government:

The Instructions dated the 6th Decr 1679 made void.

Our Will and Pleasure being that Our former Instruction given you the Sixth day of December, 1679, doe from the date hereof become void and of none effect.

A True Copy Teste

J. W. GREENWOOD.

AN INTERESTING COLONIAL DOCUMENT

A while ago, on unearthing some papers of Colonel Robert Burton of Granville County, N. C., I ran across an old paper, mutilated and in part indecipherable, entitled "A General Meeting of the Freeholders of the County of Mecklenburg on the 29th day of July, 1774." So far as I can learn, this paper has not hitherto found its way into print. Accordingly I am submitting it for publication of the Virginia Magazine of History and Biography.

Bancroft attributes the credit for inaugurating the system of intercolonial committees of correspondence to that "young statesman of brilliant genius," Dabney Carr. From the investigation of Dr. Eckenrode, it would seem that the "first intercolonial intelligence bureau" owed its inception to "the fertile brain of Richard Henry Lee."*

After Dunmore, the governor of Virginia, dissolved the Assembly on May 25, 1774, the Burgesses "retired from the official state house to the Williamsburg tavern, where in that so-called Apollo room, dedicated to colonial mirth and revel," they decided to propose a general congress of the colonies. In particular the meeting issued a call for the election of delegates from the counties to a convention of the colony; and this convention was set to meet at Williamsburg on August 1, 1774.

The object of the meeting at Williamsburg was to consider further the state of public affairs and, more particularly, to appoint deputies to the general congress, which was to be convened at Philadelphia on the 5th of September following.

The first of these committees, it appears, were formed in the Virginia towns in May and June, 1774.†

*H. J. Eckenrode: The Revolution in Virginia. 33.

†Magazine of History (1906) 3,153.

"Dunmore (afterward Shenandoah) County also elected a committee on June 16, 1774, and Fairfax on June 18, at a meeting over which George Washington presided."**

Other counties followed, but a number of them did not elect committees; and some, notably Mecklenburg, did not even choose representatives in time. But, as the paper printed below evidences, the Mecklenburg meeting nevertheless expressed in formal declaration their sentiments upon the grave matters then at issue.

Before printing the papers, a word upon Robert Burton may be in order. He was born in Mecklenburg County, Virginia, in 1747; and settled in Granville County, North Carolina, about 1775. He was married to Agatha, only daughter of Judge John Williams and Agnes Bullock, the widow of Lord Keiling, on October 12, 1775.‡ Through this connection, he became interested in the Transylvania Land Company and made a hazardous trip to Boonesborough and return (1775-6), to visit the rich Kentucky lands recently purchased fro mthe Cherokee tribe of Indians through the agency of Colonel Richard Henderson, president of the Transylvania Land Company. In 1785, he was elected a delegate to the Continental Congress; but did not report at Philadelphia until May 22, 1787. In recognition of the fact that John Paul Jones derived his appointment in the American navy from North Carolina, Burton in 1789 presented to the State of North Carolina a replica of Houdon's bust of Jones. In 1801, Robert Burton was one of the Commissioners from N. C. to settle the long-disputed boundary between North Carolina, South Carolina, and Georgia. He died in 1825.

Below follows an exact transcript of the document found among the papers of Colonel Robert Burton. I am herewith presenting the original to the Virginia Historical Society.

ARCHIBALD HENDERSON.

University of North Carolina,
Chapel Hill, N. C.
September 22, 1919.

**Eckenrode, ibid, 34. ‡Marriage find at Oxford, N. C.

A GENERAL MEETING OF THE FREEHOLDERS OF THE COUNTY OF MECKLENBURG ON THE 29th DAY OF JULY, 1774.

ROBERT MUNFORD, MODERATOR.

Whereas by the Delay of the Writ of Election for this County, we are prevented from choosing Representatives, in time, in whom we may confide, to express our sentiments, upon the important matters Recommended to the members of the late house of Burgesses by some of the Northern Colonies, the Consideration of which is Refer'd to the first day of August next.

Nevertheless we deem it expedient to Transmit our Opinions to the said meeting, lest we should be supposed Inattentive to the common cause of America at this Alarming Crisis.

We therefore unanimously declare—

That we entertain the most Cordial Affection to his Majesty's Person and that nothing, on our parts, shall ever impede our duty to our King, or conduce to violate the sacred Bonds of Amity and Allegiance condition'd between us.—

That as our King and Father we look up to him with Reverential awe and Filial Piety, not imputing to him the evils we feel but Imploring the Assistance of his Royal Person on our behalf.—

That in Return for our Loyalty and firm Allegiance, we are Intitled to his Majesties Protection, whenever our Civil Rights, as British Subjects, are Invaded. —

That the congeniality of our constitutional principles, with those of Great Britain, long [un?] interrupted usage, the Faith of Kings, natural Justice and [mutilated] Right, have confirm'd to us our civil liberties [words indecipherable].

That the King at the head of his American Assemblies, constitutes a supreme Legislature in the Respective Colonies.—

That to admit a supreme Legislative power in the British parliament over the Colonies is giving the Crown a double Influence, and enlarging the limited Rights of the Prerogative, in a manner dangerous to American Liberty.

That the Right of Taxation is an Appendage to Freedom, and that no Power on Earth can justly deprive us (of) our property, without our consent.—

That the right of granting aids to our sovereign, for the Exigencies of Government, or the support of the Crown, in measure and manner best suited to our state and Circumstances, is constitutionally vested in the people of this Country.—

That we will contend for this inestimable privilege, at the Hazard of our Lives and Fortunes, it being our best security against the Alienation of the Royal Favor, a Privilege that may disarm Tyranny itself and draw the smiles of sovereignty upon us.—

We will therefore most cheerfully concur in every Justifiable Measure to Procure a Repeal of all such acts of the British parliament, as either Express or imply the parliament's Right to Tax America.—

We sympathise with our Distressed fellow subjects in the Town of Boston, who by the late Act of the British parliament, are cutt off from the common benefits of Humanity; we wish to administer to their Relief, and will readily adopt every measure productive of this end, that may be consistent with our duty to our King, and warranted by those moral Obligations, that should ever subsist among Mankind. Virtue forbids, 'tho Policy may licence, a violation of that Faith we Owe to our King and to his People.

End.

VIRGINIA STATE TROOPS IN THE REVOLUTION.

(From State Auditor's Papers, Now in State Library.)

(CONTINUED)

			£	s	d
	12	Ditto paid John Sankard for Nathan Bagnel for a Quantity of Duck furnished the Army	11	10	
		Ditto paid John Tazewll for Lead sold the Country	3	9	2
		Ditto paid Thomas Miller for use Richard James for Arms purchased for the use of the Public	99	6	4
		Ditto paid William White for a Gun furnished the Army	3	9	2
1776 February		To Cash paid John Skinner for Wood furnish'd the Army	8	15	
		Ditto paid Ditto for Sarah Dixon for Wood supplied the Army	3	12	6
		Ditto paid Ditto for John Fields for Ditto	7	5	
		Ditto paid Ditto for John Armistead for Beef furnis'h the Army	3	10	10
		Ditto paid Thomas Warren for a Gun furnish'd the Public	3		
		Ditto paid Isham Allen for Provisions & Fodder to the Army	2	3	9
		Ditto paid Thomas Wilks for a Gun sold for public use	4		
		Ditto paid James Anderson Balance of his account settled for Smiths work done for the use of the Public	119	2	10½

Day	Item	£	s	d
	Ditto paid George Lyne for Forrage etc., furnished the Army	13	5	
13	Ditto paid Joseph Scott for his pay as an Adjutant in theArmy	17	17	
	Ditto paid Thomas Prosser for Drum & Colours to the Henrico Militia	5		
	Ditto paid Ditto for a Gun furnished the Public Service	2	10	
	Ditto paid Jeremiah Underwood for Provisions furnished the Army	11	8	
	Ditto paid William Dalton for a		1	
	Gun furnish'd for the use of the Public	4	2	6
	Ditto paid Ditto for Willoughby Old for provisions furnish'd ditto	7	10	
	Ditto paid William Ellison for a Gun sold for the use of the public	2	5	
	Ditto paid Edward Wilkinson for John Davis for a Gun for the public	4		
	Ditto paid John Morris for Fodder furnished the Army	45	11	4
14	Ditto paid William Pearson for Leather furnish'd the Public	8	5	9
	Ditto paid Samuel Boush for Rob Waller for Corn furnish'd the Army	14		9
	Ditto paid John Page for use of Samuel Deney balance due him for srrvice in mounting cannon for Public use	25	5	
	Ditto paid William Sclater for Arms furnish'd the Public service	13	10	
	Ditto paid Thomas Keith for Wagonage to the Army	62	10	

		Ditto paid Robert Anderson for work done on a Rowe Galley	4		
		Ditto paid Henry Davis for John Talbot for Sundry Arms sold the Public	150		
		Ditto paid David Minge for necessaries furnish'd the Militia at S. Point	77	13	8
1776 Februa'	14	To Cash paid Burges Ball balance by his Recruiting Money	20	1	
		Ditto paid Ditto for Arms furnished the public service	8	7	6
		Ditto paid James Dilland for Board & Necessaties to a sick soldier	10		
	15	Ditto paid Alexander Purdie for sundries supplied to the Army	4	1	
		Ditto paid Thomas Walker for Brushes & Peckers furn'd the Army	6	16	
		Ditto paid John Dandridge for a Gun furnished the public service	3	10	
		Ditto paid Sarah Spotswood for Nursing sick soldier	2	10	
		Ditto paid Jacob Faulcon for 2 Barrells Corn to the Army	1		
		Ditto paid Benjamin Fox for Fodder furnish'd the Army	17	6	
		Ditto paid Daniel Taylor for Fodder furnish'd the Army	8		
		Ditto paid Captain William Goosley for pay of his Company & Provisions furnish'd the Troops stationed at York	231	3	4
	16	Ditto paid William Barrett for Ferriages the Troops	9	3	6
		Ditto paid John Cosby for Provisions to a Guard of M. Men on Duty	24	13	

	Ditto paid Joil Sterdivant for pay of a Guard of Militia on Duty....	36	19	3	
	Ditto paid James Barbour for Drom furnish'd the Culpepper Battallion	25	5		
	Ditto paid P. R. Francis Lee for the Recruiting service furnish'd his Company	26	13	4	½
	Ditto paid C. Tompkins for Provisions furnish'd his Company..	50			
	Ditto paid Merit Westwood for Wood furnish'd the Troops at Hampton	35	5		
	Ditto paid for John Cowling for Ditto	12			
	Ditto paid Ditto for John Maloy (say Francis) Ditto	27			
	Ditto paid David Jamison for Medicines, etc., furnish'd the Troops at York	8	9		
	Ditto paid William Lively for a Gun sold the Public	2	10		
	Ditto paid William Smith for 38. Gun furnish'd his Company M. Men	101	15		
17	Ditto paid William Aylett for Corn furnish'd the Army	52	6		
	Ditto paid Ditto for George Reid Guns furnish'd the Army	19	17	6	
	Ditto paid SamEel Boush for John Jones for a gun to the Public......	4			
	DittT paid Ditto for Thomas Bressie pay of a guard at the Great Bridge	42			
1776	ToCash paid Samuel Boush for Samuel Butt for a Mare lost in the service	13			

	Ditto paid Hreny Laughton for Dixon & Hunter Blank returns to the Army	4	5	7½
	Ditto paid Simon Triplett for Waggonage to the Public Service	26		
	Ditto paid Ditto for Joseph Farmer for Ditto	11		
	Ditto paid Ditto for Johnathan Davis Ditto	16		
	Ditto paid Ditto for Samuel Evans Ditto	5	13	6
	Ditto paid Augustine Moore for Ditto	15	10	
	Ditto paid Solomon Shepherd for Cap'n Charles Connor for pay of his Company of Minute Men in Princess Anne District	197	11	6
	Ditto paid Ditto for Cap'n Murdough pay of his Company of Minute Men	62	17	6
	Ditto paid Ditto for Cap'n Washington for conveying Prisoners to Wms'burg	46		
	Ditto paid Ditto for Lewis Almond for Ferriages to the Troops		11	
	Ditto paid William Stone for Waggon hire to the Public	9	10	
	Ditto paid Chisley Jones for a Gun furnished the Public	2		
	Ditto paid Solomon Shepherd his Expenses in attending the Committee on Public Account	7	10	
	Ditto paid William Smith for pay of his Company on Duty	24	19	8
19	Ditto paid Thomas Walker for Cap'n John Washington for pay of his Company of M. Men Princess Anne District	120	15	

		Ditto paid Joseph Jones for Robt. Johnson for Sundry Medicines to to the Army	15	14	
		Ditto paid John Langley for Wood furnished the Army	x8	19	
		Ditto paid Ditto for Jo. Langley for Ditto	10	15	
		Ditto paid Ditto for Thomas Hampton for Fodder furnished the Army	1	1	12
		Ditto paid James Hill for John Draper for 2 Guns to the Public	8		
		Ditto paid Anthony Noble for furnishing Muskets for Public use	200		
	20	Ditto paid Doctor Alexander Skinner for Expenses of the Public Hospital	24	5	1
		Ditto paid Ditto for Sundry Medicines furnished the Army	195	5	7
		Ditto paid Robert Prentes for Gun furnished the Public Service	9		
		Ditto paid Ditto for Sundries furnished for the use of the Army	7	10	3
		Ditto paid Jacob Bruce for boarding sick soldiers	3	5	
		Ditto paid Ditto for Iron Work done for the Army by Robt. Bond	31	15	5
		Ditto paid Charles Barham for pay of a guard stationed at James River	23	17	4
1776 February	19	To Cash paid John Draper for conveying Lieut Batutt a Prisoner to Richmond	1	10	
		Ditto paid Thomas Peyton for his Company of Minute Men	198	5	1
		Ditto paid Richard Matthews for Jos. Lowell for dieting a Company of Volunteers	1	7	6

	Ditto paid William Westwood for wood furnished the Army..	9	5	
	Ditto paid William Minifee for Waggonage to the Public............	26	3	3
	Ditto paid Leonard Henley for a Gun furnished to the Army.....	3		
	Ditto paid Charles Jones for a Gun Ditto..................................	3	10	
	Ditto paid Henry Delaney for Public Express Hire..........................	5		
	Ditto paid George Brook for Thomas Hughes for a Gun sold the Public....................................	5	10	
	Ditto paid Ditto for William Pleese for Horse Hire..................	2	5	6
	Ditto paid John Hunter for painting public guns, etc.....................	2	15	6
	Ditto paid William Ratcliff for Fodder furnished the Army........	12	6	
12	Ditto paid John McLacklin for Express Hire................................	11	18	8
	Ditto paid Benjamin Tomilson as an Express from Luenburg...	2		
	Ditto paid Robert Gibbons for repairing Public Arms..............	7	1	1½
	Ditto paid Appolles Cooper Balance of Captain Wests Recruiting Money....................................	2		
22	Ditto paid Cap'n Gibson for Forage & Subsisence for his Company	57	17	6
	Ditto paid Jacob Cures for repairing sundry arms for the Public..	40	17	6

(To be continued)

NOTES AND QUERIES

ORIGIN OF THE STONE FAMILIES OF VIRGINIA.

E. A. STONE, D. D. (Deceased).

Among the early settlers of Virginia there were several of the name of Stone. The majority of those who came during the first one hundred and fifty years is given here, with some others. In point of time and prominence, there was first (1) Captain William Stone, who settled in Accomacke Co., in 1629 or earlier. He brought with him four brothers, Andrew, John, Matthew and Richard. None of these left any children, Later, about 1648, William Stone moved to Maryland and was appointed Governor. Two of the sons of William Stone, viz: Thomas Stone and John Stone left children. The descendants of these are traced through Charles Co., Maryland. Another (2) William Stone immigrated to Va. in 1662-3, and received from Sir Wm. Berkeley a grant of 750 acres in New Kent Co. for transporting 15 persons into the colony. His wife was Mary—their descendants are quite numerous. They left four children. There was a (3)James Stone, merchant of London, who with others received 8000 acres in Charles City county, granted by Sir John Harvey, and another grant from Sir Wm. Berkeley of 564 acres in York county. The first grant was made in 1636, and the second in 1647. That he removed to Virginia is uncertain. In York Co. there is on record a will of another (4)William Stone, dated Nov. 25, 1729, and probated the following February. His wife's name was Sarah. He names four children, and from the records it appears they, in part at least, moved into Lunenburgh Co. Their descendants are quite numerous. There was a (5) Theophilus Stone also in York Co. in 1646, but there is very little known of his history later.

In "old" Rappahannock another group of Stones are found. Oct. 20, 1672, (6)William Stone bought of Giles Cale 200 acres of land. This is the earliest record of him in this country. Later he purchased various other tracts of land, until he owned over one thousand acres. His will is dated 1704. He left a wife Sarah and five living children—one daughter had died earlier. He died about 1710-11 as appears from the court records. The widow lived about twety years after William Stone's death.

There was living in the same county (7)Col. John Stone, who was prominent in its affairs from 1672 until about 1691-2. He married Sarah Walker, widow of John Walker, and when he died left only one child, a daughter.

The records show that there was living in the same county a(8)Francis Stone, wife Elizabeth, who also were prominent from 1685 onward. Francis Stone received a grant of land in 1711 from Lady Fairfax, in Stafford county. Other grants were made later by the same to Francis Stone. There is one mention made of (9)David Stone associated with Francis Stone in 1685, but no other record has so far been found of him. It would seem that there four Stones, William, John, Francis and David were possibly related, most probably brothers. There were grants of land as late as 1727, and again in 1739 made to Francis Stone, one in Stafford Co., the other in Prince William Co. It is possible that this later Francis Stone was a son of Francis Stone who received the grants made earlier.

There was a (10) Humphrey Stone who received in New Norfolk Co. a grant of 200 acres from Sir John Harvey in 1637; there is little else known of him.

There was to a (11)John Stone a grant of land made in Henrico Co. in 1718 and another in King and Queen Co. in 1725.

(12)Thomas Stone, of Brunswick Co., "imported himself in the year 1740". He was prominent in the affairs and a vestry man in St. Andrews Parish. His will is dated April 16, 1795, and proven ten days later. His son (13)Richard Stone received in 1746 a grant of 400 acres from William Gooch.

There is a record of the marriage of (14) John Stone and Nancy O'Bissell dated Nov. 10, 1687, in Middlesex Parish.

(15)Eusebius Stone, of Caroline County, received from William Gooch, 400 acres in Orange County in 1735.

(16)Jeremiah Stone was transported into James City county Aug. 11, 1637.

There was a (17)John Stone came to Virginia as early as 1621 and of George Sandys 100 acres in Archers Hope. No other record at hand.

There was a (18) Thomas Stone in Westmoreland Co., Va., made a will in 1718, in which he annuls all previous wills. This will was probated in a short time. In it no mention or reference is made to a wife or children, no heirs designated. There was however another (19) Thomas Stone whose wife was Jemima Sturman, whose name appears in records from and after 1724. This Thomas Stone separated from his wife, and their son (20)Joseph Stone was given to the guardianship of his uncle, William Sturman. The probability is that this second Thomas Stone was the son of the Thomas whose will was made in 1718, and a comparison of the records makes it probable that he came to America in 1676, with his brother William, who settled in St. Mary's Co., Md., while Thomas came over in Westmoreland Co., Va. Everything in the records show that the two family lines were related. There was about 1740 to 1750 several of Gov. William Stone's descendants who left Charles Co., Md., and emigrated to Stafford Co., Va.; most of them settling in that portion of the county which later became Prince William Co. They were

(21)Barton Stone, (22)Samuel Stone, Thomas Stone, (23)William Stone and (24)Benjamin Stone, all related closely and all descendants of the Provincial Governor. Some of the descendants still live in that region. Other (24)Stone families found their origin in the counties farther north, some of them, if not all, being of German descent, whose names were Anglicized after coming to America. There are probably others, but this list shows the complications which necessarily arise in tracing out the various families and their descendants

---

Willison Bible Records.

This volume of the Bible with the other of the New Testament belonged originally to Sir William Callander of Bancloigh & Dorator, in the Shire of Sterling, North Britain, and is Presented as a memorial of the ancient Family of Callander from John Willison in Port Glasgow, to his son James Willison of Dorator, at Cabin Point, James River in the Province of Virginia North America an Dom 1704. The ible was printed at London, by Christopher Barker, 1585.

Beginning of family record.

(1st) James Willison son of the above John Willison and Margaret Dunbar was born in Port Glasgow, North Britain, February 15th, 1751, N. S., and was married to Mary I'Anson, daughter of John I'Anson, M. D., and Lucy Cocke. Their issue as follows viz.:

(1st) John Willison Born in Prince George County Virginia, October 22d, 1778, baptized 4th January 1779 by theRev. Mr. Benjamin Blagrove. Godfathers Archibald Dunlop, Thomas I'Anson, Godmothers Mary Mackie and Margaret Ross.

(2) Archibald Dunlop Willison, Born in Prince George, Dec 12th 1779 Baptized March 12th 1780 By the Revd William Harrison,Thomas Peter, and James Tait Godfathers; Mrs. Thomas Peter and Mrs. Tait Godmothers.

(3rd) Lucy Willison Born September 5th 1782, in Surry County at Cabin Point, and baptized Nov. 1st 1782 by the Revd. Mr. Thomas Hopkinson, John Stewart and Robert Peter, Godfathers; Mrs. Fletcher & Miss Nancy Cocke, Godmothers.

Archibald Dunlop Willison departed this life August 20th 1784 and lyes buried at the Family burying ground at Colin Cocks.

(4th) Margret Dunbar Willison was born at Cabin Point, in Surry County September 23rd 1784. Baptized by the Revd. Mr. John Burgess. Archibald Campbell, M. D. & Colin Cocke Godfathers, Miss Polly Allen and Miss Peggy Belsches Godmothers.

(5th) Mary I'Anson Willison was born at Dorator near Cabin Point in Surry County September —th 1787, and baptized by the Revd. Mr.

John H. Burgess at Little Town. Mr. Archibald Campbell and Mr. Chs. Thomas I'Anson Godfathers, Mrs. Mary I'Anson Godmother.

James Willison Died at Dorator on Monday 25th June 1787 and was buried at the family burying ground over the Creek.

Mary Willison wife of James Willison departed this life on —th September 1787, and was buried at the family Burying ground at Colin Cocke's over the Creek on —th 1787.

Lucy Willison departed this life February 23d 1794 and lies buried at the Family burying ground at Colin Cockes.

Mary I'Anson Willison departed this life on Saturday February 6th 1796 and buried at the family burying ground over the Creek.

Margret Dunbar Willison was married to Colin Campbell of Surry County the 7th October 1801 and died on Saturday evening the 24th April 1802 and buried at the burial ground.

John Willison son of the above James Willison, was married by the Revd. Mr. Chapin to Miss Mary Burbidge Dandridge of New Kent County on Monday 26th August 1805. (Daughter of Bartholomew Dandridge). Issue:

(1st) Frances LucyWillison born in Charles City County at Mr. George Minges (Rowe) June 14th 1806 baptized by Revd. Mr. James Madison Godfathers George Minge, Braxton Harrison, Godmothers Martha Halyburton and Miss Susanna Armestead.

(2) Martha Dandridge Willison Born in Charles City County at Mr. George Minges (Rowe) November 18th 1808.

(3) John Willison born in Charles City County at Mr. George Minges (Rowe) November 17th 1810.

(4th) James Dandridge Willison was born in Charles City County at Mr. George Minges (Rowe) February 22, 1813.

Martha Dandridge Willison departed this life on Wednesday night 3 o'clock the 25th October 1814 and buried in Mr. George Minges Family burial ground in Charles City (Rowe) on Friday the 28th Instant by the Rev. Mr. Bowrey.

(5th) Mary Elizabeth Willison born Charles City Co. at Mr. George Minges (Rowe) June 1st 1815.

(6) Martha Dandridge Willison born in Surry County August the 9th 1817.

John Willison departed this life on Tuesday night 12 o'clock the 29 of December 1817, and was buried at the (Rowe) in Charles City County.

Martha Dandridge Willison departed this life on Monday night 10 o'clock 28th August 1820 and was buried at the (Rowe) Charles City County.

John Willison departed this life at Manchester, Mississippi, Dec. 1837 and was buried in the burying ground of that town with Masonic honors.

Mary B. Willison departed this life in Petersburg on Friday night November 16th 1839 and was buried at Blandford Church burying ground.

James Dandridge Willison was married by the Rev. Mr. Burtolk on

Thursday June 1839 to Miss Cathrine H. McIntosh daughter of Gen. Wm. McIntosh, Fort Gibson, Ind. Ter. Issue:

(1st) Kiamesha Dandridge Willison was born June 14th 1840 near Fort Gibson, I. T.

(2nd) William Dandridge Willison was born June 16th, 1842, near Fort Gibson, Ind. Ter.

William Dandridge Willison departed this life 1843.

(3rd) Mary Burbidge Willison was born Nov. 25th, 1844, near Fort Gibson, I. T.

(4th) Sallie McIntosh Willison was born Nov. 16th, 1846, Fort Gibson, I. T.

(5th) Rubie Dandridge Willison was born Feb. 5th, 1848, Fort Gibson, I. T.

(6th) Sue Dandridge Willison was born Dec. 13th, 1850 near Jefferson, Texas.

Sue Dandridge Willison, died 1851 and was buried in the family cemetery.

(7th) James Dandridge Willison was born Dec. 31st, 1852, near Jefferson, Texas.

Kiamesha Dandridge Willison was married to Thomas Harding Scott, Jefferson, Texas.

(8th) Lucy Bowers Willison was born April 1861, Jefferson, Texas.

Rubie Dandridge Willison was married Feb. 5th, 1856, to Walter R. West Red River Co., Texas.

James Dandridge Willison departed this life near Jefferson, Texas, in the 58th year of his age on the 14th of May 1870 and was buried at the family burying ground.

Sallie McIntosh Willison was married Aug. 1871 to Wm. L. Hailey by Rev. E. G. Benners, Jefferson, Texas.

Mary Burbidge Willison was married in 1872 to Geo. Shannon near Muscogee, I. T.

Lucy Bowers Willison was married 1882 to Henry C. Fisher at Fisher Town, Creek Nation, I. T.

James D. Willison was married to Miss Mary Mackey, Jan. 9th, 1879 by the Rev. H. F. Buckner at Texana, Cherokee Nation, I. T. Issue:

(1st) Howard Dandridge Willison was born Oct. 19th, 1879 near Eufaula, I. T.

(2nd) Irine Bowers Willison was born June 27th, 1881, near Eufaula, I. T.

(3rd) James Mackey Willison was born April 27th, 1885, at Gibson Sta., I. T.

(4th) May Cathrine Willison was born April 27th, 1885, at Gibson Sta., I. T.

May Cathrine Willison died Sept. 2nd, 1887 and was buried at family burying ground near Gibson Sta., I. T.

(5th) Hellen Willison was born Aug. 18th, 1891, Gibson Sta., I. T.

The Gibson Family.

For some time past I have been interested in the Gibson family and have come into possession of some little information which may be of service to your magazine and the public interested in this family, by elucidating and untangling at least a few of the Jonathan Gibsons which have been a source of complication to you and other Virginia genealogists; and whereas I cannot untangle the entire family of Gibsons, having myself come in two ways from them, I can add a few additions and corrections which are authentic, being based on personal family knowledge, one old will and some recent letters which were written me within the past year by a most remarkable old lady, Mrs. Lucy E. (Gibson) Buckner of Culpeper, Va. My great grandfather, Wm. Berry, Taylor was son of Lieutenant Jonathan Taylor and Ann Berry. Jonathan was 3rd son of Col. Geo. Taylor and Rachel Gibson—the daughter of Jonathan[1] Gibson, probably the Jonathan styled Sr. of St. Marks Parish, Orange Co., who died 1745 from accidental poisoning. He is also probably the one who was brother of Bishop Edmund Gibson of London, as the Bishop was born 1669, died 1748, contemporaneous. Jonathan's marriage seems still unsolved. Now this Wm. Berry Taylor married, 26 of November, 1795, Susan Harrison Grayson Gibson, and in December, 1796, he moved to Kentucky and settled on a thousand acre tract which he bought of his uncle, Col. Francis Taylor—this having been a Revolutionary land grant signed by Patrick Henry. Here he built a large brick house, and this homestead has remained in the family in an unbroken line of possession until one year ago. I have recently written an account of it for the "Kentucky Magazine of History," as there have been two very distinguished descendants in the Navy, Rear Admiral Robert Mallory Berry, who in 1881 commanded the Jeannette Relief Expedition to the Arctic in search of DeLong's Party; and Rear Admiral Hugh Rodman, prominent as Commander of our Dreadnaughts in the late war; and desides these, many well known and representative Kentuckians. The homes of my grandmother, Sarah Frances (Taylor) Berry, and that of her sister, Mrs. Robert Mallory, have also remained in the family until this past year, so the Bibles and information have been kept intact. I tell you this to assure you that what information I give can be relied upon. Now the wife of Wm. B. Taylor was, as I have said, Susan Harrison Grayson Gibson, she generally signing her name with both Harrison and Grayson in it. But her father in his will calls her Susanna Grayson, I am inclined to think that she personally added the Harrison after her mother who was Susanna Harrison, the wife of Jonathan[3] Gibson of Fauquier Co., Va., who died 1791, (see will of Thomas Harrison, Jr., *Va. Mag. of Hist.*, Vol. 23, p. 332, which names daughter Susanna Gibson and son-in-law Jonathan[3] Gibson). The very old members of my family knew many of this particular branch of Gibsons, as my great grandfather Wm. Taylor was a very rich and generous man, being the largest land owner in this section, and after his wife's eldest brother, Col. Thomas Gibson (see Hayden's account of him), had been, by his father Jonathan Gibson, given all of the estate except slaves, and had as promptly as possible by his dashing and extravagant ways spent it all, his sons and daughters were gradually brought out to Kentucky to be looked after by their uncle-in-law, Wm. B. Taylor. Fortunately they were much beloved and there was always great intimacy.

William^{7} Gibson, the eldest of Thomas and his wife Charlotte Beale, lived at first at his aunt's, Mrs. Taylor's, and married their daughter, Susan Taylor. I will give more of this branch later. I am not asking you to publish this as an article, but hoping that what I can furnish may be added to other information as you gather it, and that some thing worth while be cleared on the Gibson family and appear in your Magazine, as there are many interested.

The Jonathan Catlett Gibsons in Dr. Slaughter's Culpeper Records, are all explained by Mrs. Buckner's Letters. I will send abstracts from them along with this. Her information in regard to the relationship to Bishop Edmund Gibson corresponds perfectly with all that our branch of the family in Kentucky have been hearing for generations.

I will insert the will of Jonathan^{3} of Fauquier, showing the marriages as I knew them to have existed. Mrs. Buckner is a great grand child of this Jonathan, her grandfather having been Col. Jonathan^{4} Catlett Gibson. of the Rev. married a Miss Mallory, and her father Col. Jonathan Catlett^{5} Gibson of 1812, who married first Martha Dandridge Ball and married second, Mary Williams Shackleford. Mrs. Buckner^{6} of this last marriage.

I will also insert the Bible of Wm. Berry Taylor and Susan Harrison Grayson Gibson. Some day this may be of service.

WILL OF JONATHAN GIBSON, OF FAUQUIER CO., VA., MADE 22 JULY, 1788, PROVED 26 SEPT., 1791.

1. Son Thomas married 1782 Charlotte Beale; (Fauquier Co. Rec.) son Wm. Gibson married first Susan Taylor of Kentucky and second Susan Gibson of Virginia.

2. Son John married Ann Eustace, 1783, is given in Fauquier Rec. I believe this is intended for this John.

3. Daughter Ann Grayson, married Aug. 14, 1787, first wife of Col. Jos. Blackwell, born 1755, died 15 Sept. 1823; his second wife was Mary Waddy Brent (Hayden Genealogies) *p. 268.

4. Son Jonathan^{4} Catlett married a Miss Mallory according to Mrs. Lucy E. Buckner of Culpeper.

5. Daughter Susanna Grayson, married 26 Nov. 1795, Wm. Berry Taylor, settled in Kentucky, my great grandmother.

6. Daughter Mary married 7 Dec. 1797, William Mallory; Sons Robt. M. C. and son Gibson, daughter Hannah married Edwin Gibson, her first cousin.

7. Grand daughter Margaret Catlett Gibson:
Grand daughter, child of daughter Ann Grayson Blackwell.
Niece Margaret Adie:
Witnessed by John Mauzy and Mathew Harrison; Exr. Benjamin Harrison, a brother-in-law, Joseph Blackwell, son-in-law going on his bond. *On p. 326, vol. 23 Va. Mag. it states "Col. Jos. Blackwell, married first 14 Aug. 1787, Ann Grayson Gibson, daughter of Col. John Gibson of Fauquier Co., and Mary Waddy (Brent) Gibson. I can not understand this statement, and believe it is incorrect, the will above cited disproving it. Hayden names children Susan Gibson Blackwell and Wm. Taylor Blackwell, born 1793, and Ann Grayson Blackwell.

Fitzhugh Catlett left some information taken from old Catlett Bibles. One states that

John Catlett 3rd married for his first wife Miss Taliaferro and had a son John[4], married Alice[2] Gibson.

John Catlett 3rd married for his second wife Mary Grayson, 20 Oct. 1726; their daughter Mary Catlett married Jonathan[2] Gibson, Jr., who with his sister Alice[2] were children of Jonathan[1] Sr., Burgess and Justice for Caroline, 1736-38-40. Was of Orange and of the Vestry of St. Marks. He also states that "their son was Col. Catlett Gibson, married Martha Dandridge Ball". This is a mistake as Mrs. Buckner writes that her father's first wife was this M. D. Ball, and that his father was Jonathan Catlett[4] Gibson who married Miss Mallory.

My conclusions are that the first Jonathan[1] Gibson died 1745 and left a son, Jonathan[2], Jr., of Caroline and King George. He is the one who married Mary Catlett and that their son was Jonathan[3] Gibson who died Fauquier Co., 1791. He names children with Catlett and Grayson in their names—his mother having been a Catlett and her mother a Grayson. I will send you copies of these letters of Mrs. Lucy Ellen (Gibson) Buckner. Her grandfather, Col. Jonathan Catlett[4] Gibson, of Rev. and her father Col. Jonathan Catlett[5] Gibson of 1812.

Fitzhugh Catlett also stated that Margaret Catlett, daughter of John Catlett 2nd, who died 1724, had married John Gibson of Orange, but that the Jonathan was called John. I believe it was intended for John as stated in Bible, and not Jonathan at all, because Rachel Gibson (who married Col. George Taylor) was born 4 May, 1717, and Margaret Catlett was left an estate in 1724 if she never married. She forfeited it to marry. I believe that she married the brother of Rachel[2] instead of her having been the mother of Rachel. That leaves us still with no definite marriage for the 1st Jonathan[1] Gibson in this country, the father of Rachel. I am also inclined to think that Rachel[2] had a sister Alice[2] who married John Catlett 4th and a brother John[2] married Margaret Catlett: besides a brother Jonathan[2], Jr., who married Mary Catlett, a niece of Margaret Catlett above mentioned.

In these theories I may be wrong, but up to the present I have found nothing that disproves them. And I am in hopes that it may be of service and yield fruit and can be substantiated.

BIBLE OF WM. BERRY TAYLOR AND SUSAN HARRISON GRAYSON (GIBSON) TAYLOR, of Oldham Co., Ky.

William B. Taylor, born 26 Feb., 1768; died 2 Feb., 1836; married 26 Nov., 1795, Susanna Harrison Gibson, born 26 Nov., 1775; died 23 Feb., 1838.

Ann Berry Gibson Taylor, born 10 May, 1798, married Thomas Throckmorton Barbour.

Mary Berry Taylor, born Feb., 1800, married William Todd Barbour. (Sons of Thomas Barbour and Mary Taylor of Va.)

Elizabeth Coates Taylor, born 28 Jan., 1802, married Dr. William Willett.

Francis Madison Taylor, born 10 June, 1804; died at 19 years.

William Berry Taylor, died young.

John Gibson Taylor, born 25 July, 1810, married Oretta Barnes.

Susan Harrison Gibson Taylor, born 7 Nov., 1812; married her 1st cousin William Gibson, son of Col. Thomas and Charlotte Beale.

Sarah Frances Taylor, born 5 April, 1815; married Edmond Taylor Berry, daughter Alice E. Berry married S. F. J. Trabue.

Mathilda Catherine Taylor, born 30 April, 1820, married Hon. Robert Mallory M. C., her 1st cousin, son of Mary Gibson.

William Willett Taylor, born 4 March, 1823, married Alice Sandford.

Some of the Gibsons have heen quite prominent in Virginia and their descendants there and in other localities, and I have been sorry that there has been no little investigated about them. After my experience with Mrs. Buckner, I felt encouraged to look further for more information.

With the hope that this may prove useful, I am

Very truly,

(Miss) Alice E. Trabue.

P. S.

The Colonial Services ascribed to Jonathan[1] Gibson, Sr., died 1745, of Orange, may have been held in part by the 2nd Jonathan[2]; they both held lands in Orange anu probably other counties, also Caroline, King George, Essex, etc., until they are hard to unravel.

My dear Miss Trabue:

I received your letter, it was interesting to me and I read it with pleasure. I wish I could aid you in researches, but am afraid I cannot do so. I am only a member of the Gibson family and by no means a genealogist or predisposed to be an expert in that science.

I will, however, give you some particulars of my immediate family which may interest you.

My father was Col. Jonathan Catlett Gibson, he enlisted in Orange Co. in a company and fought in the war of 1812, and with his regiment, saw the Capitol burned and helped to drive the British from Washington. At the close of the war, he studied law in the office of his brother John Gibson, in the little city of Dumfries in Prince William Co., Va. This indicates that the two names were considered in England separate and distinct and the same iteration occurs in many families in the United States. It pleases me to know that the name of Jonathan descended from the Bishop's Brother, who certainly showed a friendly interest in our family. If my brother, Col. Jonathan Catlett Gibson (a Civil War veteran), claimed to have seen the letters (there were three of them) he certainly did as it was no secret in the family. Unfortunatey they were burned in my fathers office in the Civil War. They would have been of no worldly value as the Bishop had married, but we would have prized them as heirlooms. Many valuable presents were sent to our family by the Bishop's descendants. I handled his prayer book he used in his last days. My brother had it.

In every generation, since I could remember, there have been Jonathans as I told you my father was Jonathan Catlett Gibson, my brother was Jonathan Catlett Gibson and his grandson of the same name is now Lieutenant in our Army in France.

I have always known we were connected with the families of Taylors, Harrisons, Pendletons, Eustaces, Catletts and others, but as I have led the life of a busy housekeeper on a farm, I have provided no data to record their marriages; if I had they would have been destroyed during the Civil War. The Gibson family is one of the largest in this country. I would not be surprised if I were to go to the Island of Madagascar to find a descendant of the Gibson family there. The immediate descendants of the Gibson family as they came from England were large and wealthy planters. To that class General Washington and his wife belonged. The next generation were comfortable farmers and good livers; to that class my father belonged, he was also a successful lawyer. His first wife was Martha Dandridge Ball, a near relative of the Washingtons. She died and left two daughters, Frances Ann and Martha Dandridge, named for Washington's wife.

My father then married Mary Williams Shackleford, who had twelve children. I am the second child of the last wife, now very old (91); the rest are all dead.

I have written you a gossiping letter. Hoping that if not satisfactory, it will be agreeable.

I am yours truly,
Lucy E. Buckner."

I will copy the others only in parts as there are many side remarks not bearing on the genealogical side and of no value in research. This was about August, 1918.

2ND LETTER.

Sept. 27, 1918.

Dear Miss Trabue:

Although I have not replied to your last letter, I have not lost sight of the subject of our correspondence.

My uncle John Gibson (better known as Col. Jack Gibson) settled first in "Dumfries", a small city in Prince William County, much frequented by the elite of the county, but settled principally by merchants. .... My uncle Jack Gibson married a daughter of one of these Frenchmen, a Miss Muschette. ....
The city was gradually deserted. My uncle retired to a farm in Prince William Co., where he practiced law and kept an open house in accordance with old English ideas. He did not have any childred but raised several nephews, all of whom were killed in the civil war.

Our Virginia Bishop has made our acquaintance and claimed us as relations (Bishop Robert Gibson). I regret that we have no Coat of Arms. It was destroyed when the correspondence was burned and we do not remember it. If I hear anything more of interest on the subject, I will communicate to you. I am flattered that you should think my letters of any consideration.

Your truly,
Lucy E. Buckner.

3RD LETTER.

October 10, 1918.

My Dear Miss Trabue:

I received your last letter two days ago, with the beautiful and very acceptable present of the Coat of Arms of the Gibson family. It is particularly interesting now that the English Colonies have all rallied to the support of the Mother Country.

We are proud of being descended from a family that produced Bishop Edmund Gibson, and such a superb literature. Thank you again for your ingenious copy; you must be an artist. And now to business. My grandfather married a Miss Mallory he had five sons: John, Jonathan, Thomas, Edwin and William. You know how Col. Jack and Jonathan, my father married. Thomas and William both married sisters, Miss Grays. Edwin married his first cousin, Hannah Mallory, a good deal of this kind of thing was done in Eastern Virginia at that time.

My memory does not extend any further back than my grandfather's immediate family. Grandfather Gibson had four daughters. Frances and Nancy, Betsy married a Terrell. The two latter married planters, the two first did not marry at all. They were thoroughbred ladies, all, and would have appeared well in any society. They lived to a good old age, except Susan............. Wishing that I could really have helped you, I am truly your friend,

Lucy E. Buckner.

4TH LETTER.

Oct. 26, 1918.

My dear cousin:

I am very proud indeed to claim you as a kinswoman. I have no doubt you are correct in you researches, but my memory does not extend further back than my paternal Grandfather Jonathan Gibson.

My father was Col. Jonathan Catlett Gibson, who fought in the War of 1812, and my mother drew a pension. She was his second wife, twenty years younger than he was. She was Mary Milliams Shackleford of French extraction. You know his first wife was Martha Dandridge Ball, cousin of George Washington and named for his wife.

To resume my remarks about the Gibson family, my uncle John was the head of the family as the oldest son. He had a large landed estate in Prince William Co. His residence was not a castle by any means but an old Colonial of four stories with smaller houses on each side. One side with chambers for men of the family and office for Library. On the other side kitchen and other domestic buildings. A kitchen garden and a garden where every variety of flowers were cultivated. Much of my young days were spent there. As I am a failure as a genealogist, I have become a gossip. My uncle was a very handsome man, immacuate in his dress and deportment, and I often thought he looked like a French Noble just stepped down from the canvass.

I can account for that now since he must have had some French blood. A type of men sometimes survives many generations. I forgot to say that the name of the place is "Fleetwood", being historic from the fact of its being the winter quarters of a large part of the Federal army three miles from the town of Brandy where a battle was fought. Three miles from Cedar mountain where another important battle was fought. You know Virginia was the battle ground. My uncle entertained visitors not only sometimes but all the time, the best people as well as the poorest. I dont suppose any noble in England ever enjoyed more comfort or kept a better table, all the products of the cities. He had a large number of slaves and his wife never did a "hands turn" of work in her life.

(Here is a description of the negro quarters.)

I did not hear there any dissatisfaction with slavery. My uncle loved the mother country and wrote to England for a souvenir of the Bishop. They sent him from the palace of the Bishop a box containing a full dinner service of rare old china and cut-glass. It came across the Atlantic with one slight accident, a plate was broken and he sent it back to England and had it riveted with silver. I have been told that "Fleetwood" was almost destroyed during the Civil War. My aunt had all of her silver and everything of value stolen.

My Father and my uncle John were two of Nature's noblemen, but they were different. My Father, though he fought against Great Britain, was a more typical Englishman in his appearance, habits and tastes. He loved sports, kept stables of race horses and valued them. Of course he did not make any thing for it is said of the Gibsons that they die poor, but they are honorable, truthful and unselfish.

As for my brothers, my eldest brother was killed on the way to Gettysburg. Col. Jonathan Catlett Gibson was an officer in the Confederate Army, wounded badly three times, a widely known and successful Lawyer. Hon. Eustace Gibson so badly wounded he was retired from the Army and served four times in Congress from West Virginia, died finally of his wounds, was considered more than an average lawyer and orator. Edwin Gibson fought through four years with Mosby without a scratch, and died from an accident. All of the family have died and I alone am left. Being next the oldest child, of course I am very old, 91. I am living with my grand-daughter and her husband, Mr. Raleigh T. Green, Editor of Culpeper Exponent, Culpeper, Va.

Very truly your friend and relative,

Lucy E. Buckner.

RUCKER—VAWTER—MEDLEY—SHELTON—MAY—BURTON.

In *Va. Mag.*, Vol. XIX, No. 2, April, 1911, p. 198, is query by Mrs. B. H. R., of Rolla, Mo. I can answer a part of her query.

In Will Book 1, at p. 248, Orange C. H., is will of John Rucker, date "XI" Jan'y 1742, proven, 28, Jan'y 1742; names his wife Susannah and his 12 children and among them "Peter". Appts. wife Susannah, son Peter Rucker and friend George Taylor Exors.

In same Will Book at p. 299, is will of Peter Rucker, date, 18th. Jan'y, 1742-3, proven 23 Feb. 1743; lends to wife Elizabeth Rucker, all estate, real and personal during life, and after her death gives certain personal property to daughter Margaret Tinsley and son-in-law Isaac Tinsley; son Ephraim Rucker and to daughter Ann Cook and son-in-law Shem Cook, and balance to be sold and divided among his children by name as follows: Thomas Rucker, Elizabeth Pearce, Wm. Rucker, Mary Offott, James Rucker, Ephraim Rucker and Ann Cook. Appts. James Rucker and Ephraim Rucker Exors.

On Oct. 6, 1917, I found in Will Book A. in Culpeper C. H., at p. 65, the will of John Vawter, from which I made the following notes:

Date, 23, May, 1748. "I John Vawter of Essex County", Proven in Culpeper County, 16 Nov., 1752. All personal estate, as well in Orange County as in Essex County be not apportioned but sold at auction and pay just debts and remainder be divided as follows—One third part to loving wife Margaret Vawter, the rest to be equally divided among my children namely, Winifred, Bartholomew, Richard, Margaret, Angus and David Vawter.

2ndly. What land I have I give as follows—the land I purchased of young Hawkins I lend to my wife for life—150 acres, and after her death to my son Bartholomew Vawter, paying to my son Angus Vawter twenty pounds, the son David Vawter fifty pounds. 3rdly. To daughter Winifred Vawter, 130 acres which was given me by my father-in-law Daniel Noel.

4th. "To my daughter Margaret Rucker 150 acres at the Great Mountains, that which lays most convenient to her."

5th. The remainder of the tract being 500 acres, be equally divided by an east and west line in two parts; and I give to my son Richard Vawter his choice, and the other to my son Angus Vawter.

6th. To my son David Vawter three hundred and eighty acres adjoining the old Ct House (?) tract in Orange County to him and his heirs forever.

Appoints wife Margaret and son Bartholomew Executors.

Witnesses—Edward Vawter, Eliza. Vawter, Samuel Vawter.

In same Will Book A, at p. 138, is will of Margaret Vawter, of Culpeper Co. of date, 18 Sept. 1756, and proven, 21 Oct. 1756.

Gives to son David Vawter certain personal property and he to pay his sister Winifred McBen fifty shillings. To son Angus Vawter, a negro.

"Unto Ephraim Rucker and Margaret his wife," a negro.

"Remainder to my sons Richard Vawter, and Angus Vawter and my daughter Winifred McBen." Appoints Ephraim Rucker Executor.

According to Mrs. Grace Vawter Bicknell in her first book—"The Vawter Family." who says at p. 4. "(1691). 2. John, son of John[1], married a Beverly (probably). Children: Bartholomew, Angus, Richard, Beverly, David, Margaret, Winifred."

Mrs. Bicknell doubtless never saw the above wills, and I have found nothing to indicate that there was a son, Beverly Vawter. At pp. 24, 25, &c., Mrs Bicknell quotes from the MS. of Col. John Vawter, born Jan. 8, 1782, who gives a remarkably accurate and concise history of the early Vawters in America, and he gives the same children as named in the wills above.

Col. John[5] Vawter gives his pedigree as follows: son of Jesse[4], David[3], John[2], John[1], who came from England to Virginia with his brothers, Bartholomew and Angus, prior to 1700.

Another will I found in Culpeper, gave much genealogical data I was very glad to find and may help Mrs. B. H. R. It is in same Will Book A, at p. 203, and is that of the old bachelor, Robert Medley, of Culpeper Co., "being sick and weak" &c.: of date 9 Aug. 1759, proven 20 Sept. 1759, and my notes from same are as follows:

"I give my beloved Cousin" (..? ..nephew) "Ambrose Medley son to Jacob Medley my Manor Plantation with 200 acres of land and in case he should die without issue that then the said land and Plantation shall fall to Reuben Medley, son to said Jacob Medley, and that if the said Reuben Medley should die without issue, the said land and Plantation shall fall to my beloved brother Jacob Medley. I give to my brother-in law Reuben Shelton 200 acres joining my Plantation during his life and after death to fall to his eldest son Thomas Shelton."

"I give to my Honored Mother Ellinor Medley 5 pounds cash if she be living and if dead to fall to Thomas Hundley for the education of his children."

"To beloved brother James Medley my riding mare."

"To beloved brother Isaac Medley 15 pounds cash."

"To my brother-in-law May Burton 15 pounds and after his death to fall to his son May Burton, Jun."

"To beloved brother John Medley 10 pounds and after his death his son John, Jr."

"To my Cousin" (niece) "Susanna Medley 15 pounds and after her death to her sister Elizabeth and in case Elizabeth died without issue to her sister Ellinor Medley."

To my brother Jacob Medley 10 pounds. "Remainder of estate "to be sold and divided among all my friends above mentioned." Appoints bros. John and Jacob Medley Exors. and they qualified.

QUERY.

David Vawter, born in Essex Co.,Va., in 1790, married Mary Rucker, who survived him, and she married 2nd, a Mr.---------- Rentfrow and died in Kentucky.

David Vawter lived in Orange Co. from about 1760 until his death.

Old Orange Co. Order Book shows: "March ------ 1785, Wm. Vawter granted administration on estate of David Vawter, deceased."

David Vawter and wife, Mary Rucker, had following children: Jesse, born Dec. 1, 1755; William, born ------------, 175- (?); Philemon, Winifred, Margaret and Mary.

William Vawter was a soldier in the Rev. War, and married Mary Rucker, as shown by the original marriage bond in Orange C. H. of date, 19th June, 1784. They removed at an early day to Versailles, Woodford Co., Ky., and where they were still living in 1810, as shown by U. S. Census of that year, and had 9 whites in family and 14 slaves. Later he moved to Boone Co., Ky., where he died Nov. 27, 1823.

The names of the parents, with all genealogical data, desired of these two Mary Ruckers.

The foregoing wills of John and Margaret Vawter and Robert Medley, as also the wills of James Collins, James Clark and others, in Culpeper Co., examined by me and found to contain most valuable genealogical data, are not shown in Green's Notes on Culpeper County.

Colonel George Wilson

Four years ago, you published an article about Lieut. Col. George Wilson, with affidavits of his disappearance in February 1777, and added a paragraph that this might be the same man as Lieut. Col. George Wilson of the 8th Penna. Regiment, killed at Quibblestown, N. J., in February, 1777. It was the same man. First, because there was no other Lieut. Col. George Wilson killed in the Revolution. Second, because the first affidavit was made by a Fayette County, Pa., man, and Fayette Co., which had in 1777 been Bedford Co., was the home of Lieut. Col. George Wilson of the 8th Pa.

According to the Histories of Western Pa., of Westmoreland Co., Pa., and Bedford and Fayette and Cumberland Counties, and to the Pa. Archives and to contemporary official documents published in the Pa. Archives, George Wilson was born in Augusta Co., Va. He fought as an officer in the French and Indian War, 1755–1762, lived in Cumberland County, Pa., was a Pennsylvania Justice of the Peace, and Lieut. Col. of the 8th Pa., being killed at Quibblestown, N. J., February, 1777, and is said to be there buried, the place being now called New Market. He called his place in Bedford Co., Pa., Springhill, after his old home place in Augusta Co., Va., The township there was than called Springhill township, and still exists as such in Fayette Co., which was set off from Bedford in 1783. This use of the name Springhill is enough to identify the man, without any other evidence.

In 1783, we find an application made for a Revolutionary Pension by Mrs. Samuel Williams, Sabina Williams, stating that she was the widow of Lieut. Col. George Wilson, and living in Fayette Co., Pa., and that in 1781 she had married Samuel Williams.

I am desirous to know the maiden name of Sabina Wilson, where she was born, where she married George Wilson, and what children they had.

I also would like to know if he was the son of Col. John Wilson of Augusta Co., Va., born 1702, and died 1773.

I would appreciate it if any of your readers will enlighten me.

Thanking you,

Faithfully,

George E. Fleming.

Box 419, City Hall Station, New York City.

LIST OF TITHABLES IN VA. TAKEN 1773.

Accomack	3660
Albemarle	3338
Amelia	5308
Amherst	2452
Augusta	2792
Bedford	2300
Botetourt	2014
Brunswick	4054
Buckingham	1817
Berkeley	
Caroline	4596
Charles City	1959
Charlotte	1930
Chesterfield	3251
Culpeper	4134
Cumberland	3661
Dinwiddie	2985
Dunmore	
Elizabeth City	1212
Essex	2850
Fairfax	2508
Fauquier	3115
Frederick	5406
Fincastle	
Gloucester	4238
Goochland	2238
Halifax	2047
Hampshire	939
Hanover	4413
Henrico	2329
James City	1872
Isle of Wight	2182
King George	1968
King & Queen	2928
King William	2765
Lancaster	1990
Loudoun	3126
Louisa	2283
Lunenburg	1720
Middlesex	1407
Mecklenburg	2611
Nansemond	2934

New Kent	2181
Norfolk	4286
Northampton	2000
Northumberland	2922
Orange	2071
Pittsylvania	2198
Prince Edward	1885
Prince George	2490
Princess Ann	2416
Prince William	2222
Richmond	2443
Southampton	2859
Spottsylvania	2518
Stafford	2675
Surry	1952
Sussex	2787
Warwick	816
Westmoreland	2701
York	2524
	76061
	79217
	155278
Tithables in Dinwiddle	1767—2864
Lunenburg	1769—1585
Amelia	4903

From Amelia County Order Book .... 1766—69
Noted in back of book.

WILLIAM LOVELACE, SERGEANT AT LAW
(Great Grandfather of Ann (Lovelace) Gorsuch)

GENEALOGY.

GORSUCH—LOVELACE: A CORRECTION.

Through a printer's error that was interpolated in the concluding instalment of the Gorsuch genealogy in the July-October 1919 number of The Virginia Magazine (Vol. xxvii; pp. 388-390) two pages of reading matter from uncorrected type forms which had already appeared in its proper place and in corrected form in the April 1919 number (Vol. xxvii; pp. 200-202). Confusion will therefore be avoided if under the sketch of Lovelace Gorsuch^4 of Dorchester County, the interested reader will run a pencil through the text beginning on page 388, line 29, with the words "Elisha^5 Gorsuch," etc, and extending to page 390, line 29, ending with the words "Both living 1844".

THE LOVELACE FAMILY AND ITS CONNECTIONS.

By J. Hall Pleasants, Baltimore, Md.

(Continued.)

V. Sergeant William Lovelace^5 (John^1, Richard^2, William^3, William^4). Born about 1525-1530. He succeeded his father as proprietor of Lovelace Place. He was admitted to Gray's Inn in 1549, and called to the bar in 1551. Elected a member of Parliament for Canterbury in 1558, he was returned on three subsequent occasions (*Hasted's* Kent; 2 *ed.;* ix; 54) He was doubtless attached to the doctrine of the Reformation as he was appointed July 19th, 1559, with William, Earl of Pembroke, John Jewell the celebrated Bishop of Salisbury, and Henry Parry, on an important commission for the Establishment of Religion. He was raised to the rank of Serjeant-at-Law in 1567, and attained great eminence in his profession. He served as one of the Justices of Assize for Oxfordshire, 27 February, 1571. He died March 23rd, 1577, the St. Alphage register under date of April 1st, 1577, containing the entry: "Sereiant Lovelas died the xxiijti day of Marche last past in London and was buryed in the body of Christe Churche" [i. e. Canterbury Cathedral]. In the nave of the Cathedral a raised tombe bearing his "portrait in long robes" with that of his first wife, Anne Lewes, existed until this portion of the

Cathedral was newly paved early in the nineteenth century (*Hasted's Kent; 2 ed.;* ix; 387). There must have been something remarkable about his death for May 3rd, 1577, Henry Binneman paid "vy d. and a copie" to the Stationers' Company, London, for the right to print "The Briefe Course of the Accidents of the Death of Mr. Serjeant Lovelace."

Sergeant Lovelace[5] married twice and left issue by both wives. His first wife was Anne, daughter of Robert Lewes*, Alderman, and Mayor of Canterbury in 1536 (*Hasted's Kent; 2 ed.;* xii; 606). She was buried February 25th, 1569, in the Cathedral. She left no will. He married secondly, about 1570, Mary, daughter of Sir Thomas White and the widow of Thomas Carrell. The will of "Mary Lovelace of Southwarneborne, Hants and St. Martin's, Ludgate, London, widow of William Lovelace Serjeant at the law", dated January 25th, 1577-8, proved April 29th, 1578, requests that she be buried at South Warnborough, Hants. She names her previous husband Thomas Carrell, her daughters Frances Carrell and Mabel Lovelace, both under twenty-one, several White brothers and sisters, and her step-children William, Thomas and Mary Lovelace (*Prerogative Court. of Canterbury,* 1578; Langley 17). The portrait of Sergeant Lovelace reproduced here is from a contemporary painting in the Dulwich Gallery, London, dated "AN°DNI, 1576", and displays the Lovelace arms with the motto "Virtute duce" (Gallery No. 372). It is painted on a panel (26 x 22 inches) and shows the Sergeant in his red robes.†

His will and the lengthy *inquisition post mortem* upon his landed estate, show that he left a very large number of properties in various parts of Kent, including among others Lovelace Place in Bethersden, "one house and the site of the Grey Friars in the City of Canterbury", and the old "Hospital of St. Laurence near the walls of Canterbury". (For *inquisition* see *Archaeologia Cantiana;* x; 201-2). The purchase of this last property involved him and his heirs in a long law suit with Roger Manwood, Chief Baron of the Exchequer.

*It was probably this same Robert Lewes, described as of Lenham, co. Kent, whose estate was administered upon October 24, 1567, by his widow Margaret Lewes, with a note that he died in Ireland (*Prerogative Court of Canterbury Administrations—The Genealogist;* i; 81.

†Excellent copies in oil of the same size as the originals, have recently been made of the three portraits now in the Dulwich Gallery, London, of Serjeant William Lovelace[5], his son Sir William Lovelace[6], the elder, and his grandson Sir William Lovelace[7], the younger. These were copied by Mrs. Strother-Stewart of Newcastle-upon-Tyne, an English artist, for Mr. Walter de Curzon Poultney of Baltimore, a descendant of the Lovelaces, and are now in his collection. The illustrations reproduced in the Magazine are from photographs of the *originals* at Dulwich.

"Grey Friars" was used as his Canterbury residence by his son, Sir William Lovelace[6]. The will of Sergeant William Lovelace[5], dated July 20th, 1576, with a codicil March 21st, 1577, and probated in the Prerogative Court of Canterbury (1577; Daughtry 15), May 9th, 1577, is a lengthy document, an abstract of which follows:

> I William Lovelace, esquier, serviant at lawe, do make my last will and testament this 20th day of Julie, 1576, in manner and forme following: I bequethe my soule to Almightie God, my Maker and Redemer, trusting by the merits of the passion of Jesus Christe to be partaker of the heavenlie Joyes; and my body to the earth, to be buried in the bodie of the cathedrall churche of Canterburye, betweene the twoo pillers near where my first weiff Anne, the daughter of Robert Lewes, sometyme mayor of Cantreburie, lyeth buried yff my bodie may be convientlie so farre carried. I will to be bestowed amongest the poore of the cittie on the day of my buriall, £6 13s 4d.; to the hospital of St. Johnes I give 20s., and to the hospital of Harboldowne, 13s 4d. To everie one of my servants that hath yearlie wages, a yeares wages, and to remaine in my house by the space of one monethe till they can be provided of service; and such of my householde servants and clerkes as have not wages, to be considered by the discrecion of my executours. Everie of my servants shall have a black coate at my deathe; and I will that some convenient tombe shall be made over me. I give to my daughter Marye that I had by my first wieff, £200, and the like sum to my daughter Mable that I had by my second wieff Marie, the daughter of Sir Thomas White, to be ymployed to their fynding after my death; and if either of them dye before they shalbe maried or not of thage of one and twentie years, the overlyver to have the porcion of her so dying. To my loving frende Mr. William Bewell of Cornewall, one of my geldinges, to be chosen by my executours. Forasmuche as it is not almost possible that any can in particularities provide order for all things, therefore I leave to my Executours or moast of them sufficient auctoritie to use their discrecions in all things as occasion shall offer and shalbe to them thought best. I make my Executours William Lovelace, my eldest sonne, Vincent Engeham, esquier, Richarde Cooke, gent., John Crispe and William Morebredd, and I give [to each] a mourning gowne and a ringe of 40s. and my name therein to be written; and I make my loveing frendes Sir Richard Baker and Sir Thomas Scott, Knightes, overseers of the same, to either of whom I give the like rings. I give to my wife Marie the use of all such household stuff, jewells, plate and goodes as she will herself during her lief. To my daughter Marie, her own mother's billamentes of goulde and her rynges; and to my

daughter Mable her mother's jewels and rynges, if they live to be maried. All the rest of my goodes to my son William at 21 or, in the event of his death, to my son Thomas at 21. Tc my sister Margaret Austen [Cooke?] now being widdow, £5. This is my last will as touching all my landes and tenements: My wieff shall have oute of the same £60 yerlie for her dower. I give to my son Thomas in tail male my manor and parsonage of Newenham and my manor of Monkton Mylfield. My executours shall take the yssues and profits of the rest and accompte for the same to my sonne William at his age of 21, the fyndings of my children to Schole and chardges of their education being deducted. In default of heires male to my sonnes, I will all myne in heritance in Bethresdence, co. Kent, unto Thomas Lovelace of Kingesdowne, esquier, being my cosen jarman, and suche heires of his bodie. In witness whereof I have hereunto setto my hande and seale and written all withe my hande.

WILLLIAM LOVELACE.

Witnesses of the will: Thomas Howtaine, Leonarde Lovelace, Thomas Wyn.

A codicill added 21 Marche 19 Elizabeth [1577]. If my wieff will inhabite in any of my messuages, I do allow that unto her so to do, deducting half the yearlie value thereof in her annuity. I appoint for my executours Mr. Vincent Engeham, Mr. John Crispe, sone to the late lieutenante of Dover Castell, Mr. Anthony Sentleger, John Barker and William Lovelace, my eldest sonne; and Mr. Justice Sowthcote to be overseer onelie. Written all with my owne hande.

W. LOVELACE.

Witnesses of the codicill: Stephen White, Thomas Hovenden, Thomas Howtaine, John Turner.

Proved 9 May 1577 by Vincent Engleman and Anthony Sentleger, with power reserved, etc., for the other executors.

Issue of Sergeant William Lovelace^5 (John^1, Richard^2, William^3, William^4) and his 1st wife Anne Lewes:

i Margery Lovelace^6 (John^1, Richard^2, William^3, William^4, William^5). Buried July 6th, 1560.

ii Nicholas Lovelace^6 (John^1, Richard^2, William^3, William^4, William^5). Buried February 1st, 1560-1.

iii Richard Lovelace^6 (John^1, Richard^2, William^3, William^4, William^5). Baptized September 14th, 1560; buried September 11th, 1561, at St. Alphage.

iv William Lovelace^6 (John^1, Richard^2, William^3, William^4, William^5). Baptized September 30th, 1561; buried October 12th,

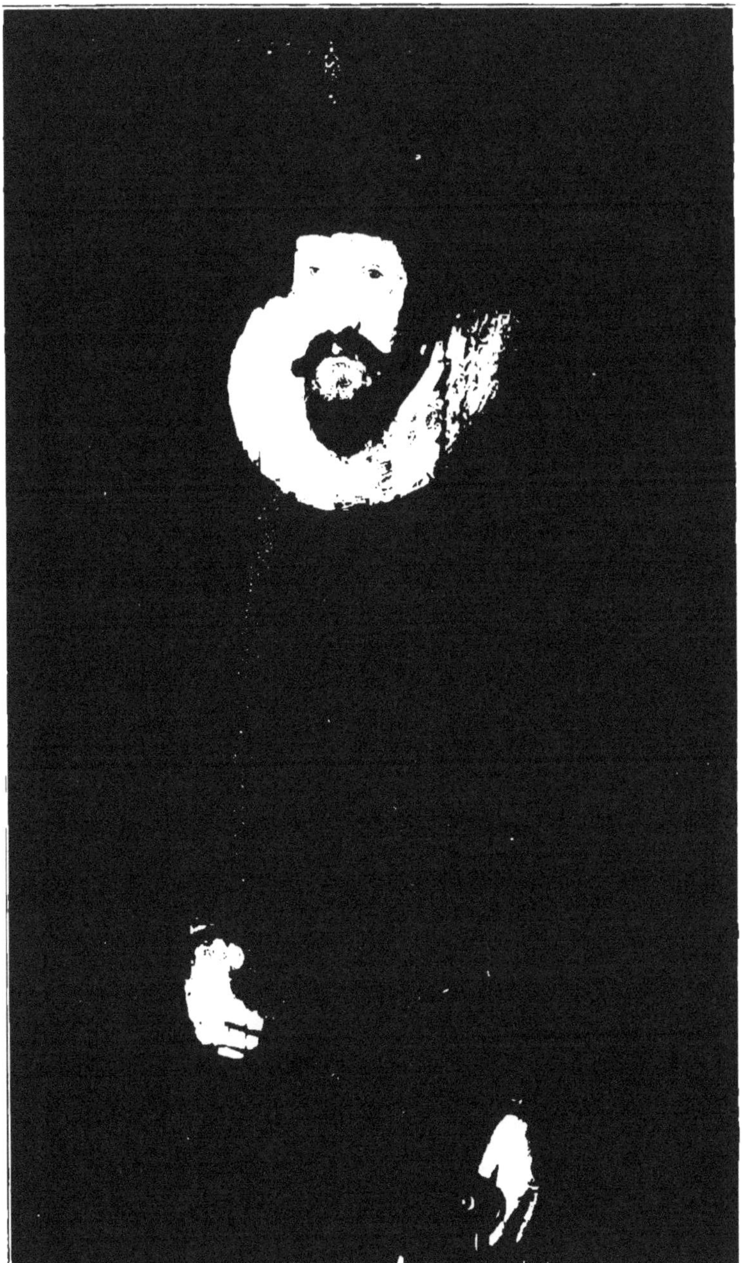

Sir William Lovelace
of Bethersden and Gray Friars
(Grandfather of Ann (Lovelace) Gorsuch)

1628; married Elizabeth Aucher. Knight and proprietor of Lovelace Place. See sketch post. VI.

v Thomas Lovelace^6 (John^1, Richard^2, William^3, William^4, William^5). Baptized April 25th, 1563. Died October 23rd, 1591; buried at Bethersden. This may be the pilgrim to Rome of this name, 1583. He inherited the parsonage of Newenham under his father's will. Died without issue.

vi Mary Lovelace^6 (John^1, Richard^2, William^3, William^4, William^5). Baptized October 8, 1564. The statement in *Hasted's Kent* that it was this Mary Lovelace who married her cousin Richard Lovelace of Kingsdown, Kent, is apparently incorrect (*Archaeologia Cantania* xx; 60-61). It is this Richard Lovelace of Kingsdown whose daughter Margaret married, August 24, 1619, Henry Coke, son of the Chief Justice, and became the ancestress of the earls of Leicester; some biographers have confused him with Richard Lovelace^9, the poet.

vii Anne Lovelace^6 (John^1, Richard^2, William^3, William^4, William^5). Baptized December 6th, 1567; died in infancy.

Issue of Sergeant William Lovelace^5 (John^1, Richard^2, William^3, William^4) and his 2nd wife Mary (White) Carrell:

viii Jane Lovelace^6 (John^1, Richard^2, William^3, William^4, William^5). Born about 1570: buried July 29th, 1572.

ix Mabel Lovelace^6 (John^1, Richard^2, William^3, William^4, Willam^5). Baptized August 19th, 1572; living 1577.

VI. Sir William Lovelace^6, knight (John^1, Richard^2, William^3, William^4, William^5). Baptized September 30th, 1561, at St Alphage, Canterbury. His principal residence was Lovelace Place, Bethersden, although his latter days were spent in Canterbury. While still a minor he was obliged to pay £800 to Chief Baron Manwood as a result of the law suit which he had inherited from his father in connection with the title to the "Hospital of St. Laurence", Manwood having postponed active proceedings until after the Sergeant's death, notwithstanding his profession at that time that "as the Sergeant was dead it was time their quarrels were forgotten". Not long afterwards young Lovelace's aunt, Margaret Cooke, pleaded with the Baron to settle the suit as her nephew "was but young, fatherless and almost without friends." Manwood replied "he might hang himself or sell his land" but clear the title he must. William Lovelace^6 appears in 1588, 1590, 1594, 1613 and 1627 in the Bethersden parish records (*Archaeoligia Cantiana;* x; 203-4). There seems no question that it was this William Lovelace who was admitted to Grey's Inn in 1580. He married, about 1580-1581, Elizabeth, daughter of Edward Aucher, Esq. of Bishopsbourne, Kent, of the distinguished family of that name. The Aucher family will be considered in a later paper.

William Lovelace[6] was knighted for the part which he took in suppressing the rebellion in Ireland, as is shown by the following: "July 30, 1599, Sir William Lovelace [was] knighted by the Earl of Essex, lord Lieutenant of Ireland at the rising of the camp after the fight in Ophaly" [Offaly] (*Shaw's Knights of England;* ii; 97). There is a letter from John Wightgift, Archbishop of Canterbury, to Sir Robert Cecil, Elizabeth's Secretary of State, dated January 8th, 1601-2, which reads: "Sir William Lovelace, Knight, my very good friend and neighbour of Canterbury, having wholly addicted himself to martial affairs, is very desirous to be employed that way in her Majesty's service. And therefore I request that you will have him in remembrance—From Lambeth the viiith of January, 1601." (*Calendar of the Manuscripts of the Marquis of Salisbury Hist. MSS. Comm.;* 1910;; p. 9). Whether he received this appointment or not is not known, but November 27th, 1604, license was given "to Sir Wm. Lovelace to serve in the wars under any Christian State or Prince in league with his Majesty during pleasure". (*Calendar State Papers—Domestic; 1603-1610;* 171). His military career has not been traced. He was a member of the Virginia Company and incorporator of the Third Virginia Charter, 1614 (*Brown's Genesis;* ii; 545, 939). In 1620 he was one of the magistrates of Kent who made the rate (*Archaeologia Cantiana;* x; 204) In 1624 he seems to have successfully contested Canterbury for Parliament in the court interest, for we have a certain Simon Penny, when examined, "desiring time to answer whether he had said that Sir William Lovelace had crossed himself before the French and Spanish Ambassadors, or intimated that he was a Papist, when urging some one to vote for Mr. Scott and Mr. Denne, rather than for Sir Wm. Lovelace, who is Captain of the City." (*Calendar of State Papers—Domestic; 1623-1625;* 155, 165). He was a correspondent of Sir Dudley Carlton in 1617, 1618 and 1619, as may be seen by reference to the *Calendar of State Papers.* He died in October, 1629 in his 69th year, having survived his wife, his son William and his only daughter Lady Mabel Collimore. His will shows that he was living at the time of his death in his "House of the Grey Friars". This picturesque old building, lying within the walls of the city of Canterbury, which he had inherited from his father, and portions of which are still standing, was built partly on some graceful old Gothic arches over the stream. The illustration of Grey Friars reproduced here is taken from an old print which the writer recently secured in Canterbury. Sir William Lovelace[6] was buried, as he requested in his will, "in the South Chappell of the parish church of Bethersden in the county of Kent near unto the South walls therein". Lady Lovelace was buried December 3rd, 1627, in Canterbury Cathedral. The portrait of Sir William Lovelace[6] shown here is from the

Gray Friars, Canterbury

painting of him in the Dulwich Gallery (Gallery no. 367—panel 42 x 32 inches).

The will of Sir William Lovelace[6] which disposes of his personal property makes no disposition of any of his lands. As his son Sir William Lovelace[7], the younger. who had died over two years before, by his will leaves sundry lands formerly owned by his grandfather Sergeant William Lovelace[5], there is every probability the elder Sir William Lovelace[6] had made over his lands to his son before the latter's death. The will of Sir William Lovelace[6] of Bethersden, dated 6 October, 1629, was proved 19 October, 1629, in the local Consistory Court at Canterbury, by Anne, the widow of his son Sir William Lovelace[7], the younger.

> I, Sir William Lovelace in my house of the Gray Friers within the Walles of the Citty of Canterbury, Knight, being sicke and weake of bodie—my bodie to be buried in the South Chappell of the Parish Church of Beathersden in the countie of Kent, neer unto the south wall therein—I bequeth unto James Collimore my best bever hatt, all my Books, my purple cloth cloke, my hose and doublet belonging if he will accept thereof—unto Thomas Yarley my servant all my other wearing apparell without exceptions or deductions and five pounds in ready money to be paid within one month—I earnestly desire my executrix whom I nominate to be my Ladie Anne Lovelace [i. e. his son William's widow] quietly to suffer him the said Thomas Yarley to enjoy Jordoines house during the life of the said Thomas—unto Nan Hewet my old gowne of kersey—unto Mary the wife of Edward Turfet of Cant: my cloth cote to make her a wastcote of—unto the foresaid James Collimore his Father's and Mother's pictures wch hang up in my chamber in the Gray Friars beseeching God to bless him and to make him his servant—unto Mabell Collimore six pounds wch I borrowed of Mr. Hawkins upon some part of my goods desiring my daughter Lovelace [i e. his son William's widow] to redeem the same because my crimson velvet bed is part thereof—unto Ned Ward my great fether' wch I use to muster withall desiring him to keep it for my sake—unto the poor of the Parish of Beatrisden twenty shillings. And as concerning all the rest of my goods, cattell, plate, utensills and money and money worth whatsoever I wholly give the same as it is conveied by Indenture unto [his grandchildren] Richard Lovelace, Thomas Lovelace and William Lovelace, except that my will and meening is that Elizabeth Lovelace shall have the moietie of all my goods, cattell and utensills aforesaid and money whatsoever when she shall attaine the

age of eighteen yeares because I know the said Indenture will be void in law for want of livery and seizure. In witness whereof I have hereunto set my hand and seal making my said daughter Executrix as aforesaid the sixt day of October above written anno Dni 1629, Edward Turfett, witness. Proved in the Consistory Court of Canterbury the 19th October, 1629 by Lady Anne Lovelace, widow, the Executrix.

Issue of Sir William Lovelace^6 (John^1, Richard^2, William^3, William^4, William^5) and his wife Elizabeth Aucher:

i Richard Lovelace^7. Baptized January 1st, 1582. Died in childhood. His burial is recorded in the register of Canterbury Cathedral: "October 24, 1602, Richard son ser. William Loveles". (*Harleian Soc. Reg.* ii; 112).

ii Sir William Lovelace^7. Baptized February 12th, 1583-4. Knight and proprietor of Lovelace Place. Died 12 August, 1627. Married about 1610 Anne Barne daughter of Sir William Barne, Knight. Ancestor of the direct Bethersden line. See sketch VII post.

iii Mabel Lovelace^7. Baptized December 26th, 1584, at St. Alphege, Canterbury. Buried July 12th, 1627, at Bethersden. Married Sir John Cullimore, mercer, 29 years of age, February 19, 1603, at St. Thomas The Apostle, London (*Harleian Soc. Reg.* vi; 9), who was buried July 30, 1620 in Canterbury Cathedral.

The above shows there was a son James, living in 1629. Their only daughter Mabel died unmarried at Dr. Harde's house, Canterbury, and was buried 1668 in the Cathedral (*Arch, Cant.* xx; 58).

(To be continued.)

THE GRYMES FAMILY.

(Continued.)

4. CHARLES^3 GRYMES, of "Moratticо", Richmond County, where he inherited lands under his father's will. He was at the Wm. & Mary Grammer School 1704 &c., and later at the College. He was Sheriff of Richmond County 1724 and 1725, a member of the House of Burgesses Feb. 1727-8, and died intestate, in 1743. The inventory of his estate was recorded in Richmond County in that year. He married Frances, daughter of Edmund Jenings, of "Ripon Hall," York County, Governor of Virginia, and had issue:

16. Frances^4, married Philip Ludwell, of Green-Spring, James City County. The Ludwell Family Bible contains the following:

"The daughter of Charles Grymes, of North Farnham Parish in the County of Richmond, in Virginia, Esquire, and Frances his wife, daughter of the Hon'ble Edmund Jenings of Rippon, in Yorkshire, in England, Esquire, who was born at Morattico, in the aforesaid County and Parish on ye 19th day of November, An. Dom. 1717. The marriage took place at Morattico aforesaid A. D. 1737"; 17. Lucy[4], born April 26, 1734. She is said by tradition to have been "The Lowland Beauty", who was one of the youthful Washington's loves. She married Henry Lee, of "Leesylvania" Prince William County, Dec. 1, 1753. She was the mother of General Henry ("Light Horse Harry") Lee, and the grandmother of Robert E. Lee.

9. PHILIP[4] GRYMES, of "Brandon", was born March 11, 1721, and died 1762. He was no doubt educated at William & Mary. He was a Burgess for Middlesex, at the session of Oct. 1748, appointed to the Council 1751, and was Receiver General 1749-1754. He married Dec. 8, 1742 Mary, daughter of Sir John Randolph, of Williamsburg (She died at Williamsburg, Jan. 10, 1768).

His will, dated Dec. 18, 1756, and proved in Middlesex Feb. 2, 1762, is as follows:

In the name of God Amen, I Philip Grymes of Brandon in the County of Middlesex being in good health and of sound mind & memory do make this my last Will and Testament in the following manner. My Soul I commend to Almighty God hoping for his most gracious Acceptance of it & Pardon for my Sins through the Merits and Intercession of Jesus Christ my Saviour & Redeemer. My Body I desire may be buried in the Church Yard near my dear Relatives with Christian Decency but as little ceremony as possible. I desire that Prayers only may be read, having observed, that Funeral Sermons are generally prostituted by fulsome Flattery and too often by untruths, not the least Regard being had to the Sacred Place and divine Presence in which they are delivered. I direct that there be no outward show of Mourning made Use of among my family, my wife only excepted, who may conform to the common Custom if she pleases, nor will I have any Tomb erected over me. As to my worldly affairs. First I will that all my Debts be duly and punctually paid.

Item. For the Support and Maintenance of my dear and well beloved Wife, I give unto her the Use and Occupation of my Mansion House and Plantation called Brandon with all the Outhouses Gardens, Orchard & Appurtenances, the Use of all my Servants and Slaves usually employed about the House & Gardens, and of all my Plate and Household Furniture of all Kinds and my Coach and Horses during her Widowhood. I give unto my said Wife all her wearing apparel, Watch, Rings, Jewels and all other Parapharnalia whatsoever. I also give unto my said Wife during her natural Life out of the Increase of my Estate a full third Part of the Provisions raised and Crops of all kinds made in the whole Estate, in Specie, she contributing one third of the charges & expenses in maintaining the Negroes and supplying the Plantation with all Things necessary for their support and Improvement and to the paiment of my Debts. And I do hereby declare that what I have hereby given unto my dearly beloved Wife is and shall be taken to be in Lieu Recompence & full satisfaction of and for all her Dower and Thirds in all or any of my Lands Tenements & Hereditaments and of whatsoever else she might claim or demand in and out of any of my Estate Real or Personal.

Item. I give and devise unto my eldest Daughter Lucy One Thousand Pounds and to my two younger Daughters Susanna and Mary Eight Hundred Pounds apiece when they shall respectively attain the age of Twenty One Years or marry, but if either or all of them should die before one of the Contingencies happen then the Legacy or Legacies of such Daughter or Daughters so dying shall fall into my Residuary Estate and be subject to the Disposition hereafter made.

Item. I give and devise unto my second son John Randolph Grymes and his Heirs forever all my Messuages Plantation Lands Tenements and Hereditaments with the Appurtenances lying and being in the County of King & Queen and all the Slaves, Stocks of all kinds and other Goods and chattels whatsoever belonging to the said lands at the time of my Death. I likewise give and devise unto my said son John Randolph Grymes and his Heirs for ever all my Lands Tenements and Hereditaments with the Mill and all Appurtenances lying and being near the upper End of Middlesex County together with all the Slaves, Stocks of all kinds and other Goods, and chattels whatsoever belonging to the said lands at the time of my death.

Item. I give and devise to my two sons Charles and Benjamin and their Heirs for ever all my Lands Tenements and Hereditaments with the appurtenances lying and being in the County of Culpeper with all the Slaves, Stocks of all kinds and other goods and chattels whatsoever belonging to the said Lands and Plantation at this Time of my death, which said Lands, slaves and other Premises shall be equally divided between my said Sons & held by them as Tenants in common until Division thereof be dully made, which I desire may be done as soon as convenient & each have his Part allotted him by my Trustees and Executors herein after named. But if it shall so happen that my son Philip depart this Life before he attains the age of Twenty one years then my Will & Desire is that my son John and his Heirs shall have all the Estate both real and personal herein devised to my said son Philip, my son Charles and his Heirs shall have all the Estate both real & personal in the County of King and

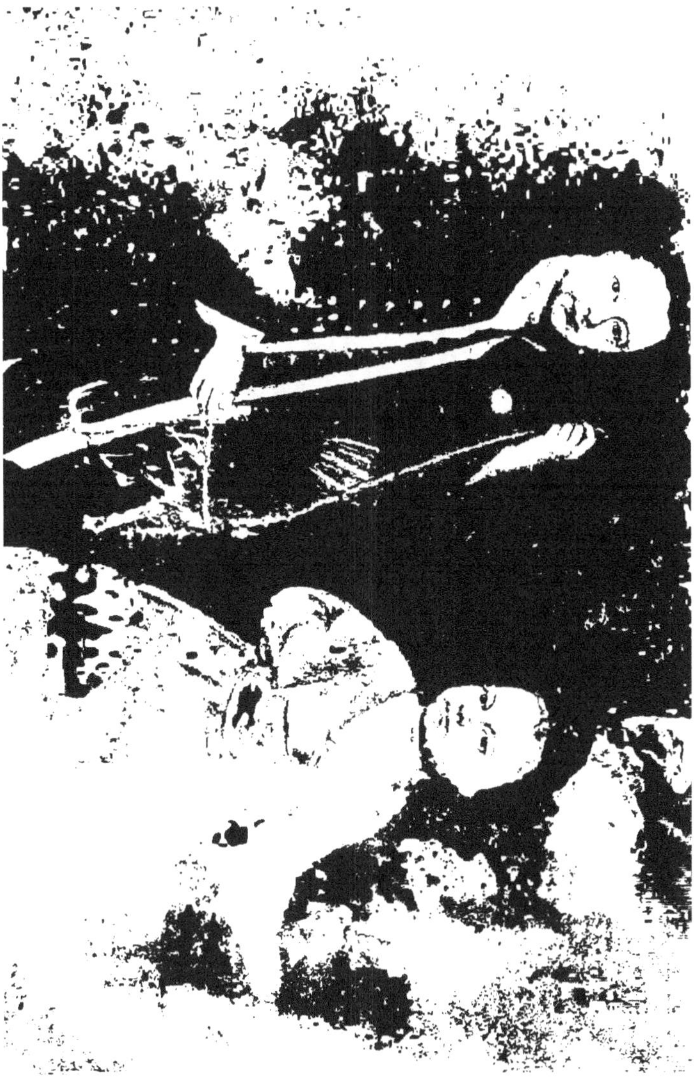

Queen herein devised to my said son John, and my son Benjamin and his Heirs shall have all the Estate both real and personal in the County of Middlesex herein also devised to my said son John, and if it shall happen that my son John depart this Life before he attains the Age of Twenty one years then and in that case my Will and Desire is that his Estate shall be divided between my said sons Charles and Benjamin and held by them in the same manner as if my son Philip had departed this Life before he had attained the age of Twenty one years, and if is shall happen that either of my said sons Charles or Benjamin shall depart this Life before he attains the Age of Twenty one years then my Will & Desire is that the Estate of him so dying shall be equally divided between the survivors and my son John and their Heirs, and whereas my Intention is to place and settle on those Lands in the County of Culpeper before my Death at least fifty working slaves. I do direct and appoint that if at the Time of my Death there shall not be fifty working slaves properly belonging to those plantations, that in such case, my Trustees and Executors or the survivors of them shall purchase so many young working Slaves, Men or Women or both as with these belongings to the said Lands at the time of my Death will fully compleat and make up the aforesaid number of fifty working slaves, and shall place and seat them upon those Lands for the Use of my said sons Charles and Benjamin & their Heirs for ever. The Charge and Expense of this Purchase to be defrayed and born out of my personal Estate & the Profits of my other Estate.

Item. My Will & Desire is that the Money arising from the sale of a Tract of Land in Spotsylvania County mortgaged to my deceased Father by Oswald Smith late of that County the legal Title of which becomes now vested in me as Heir at Law, having foreclosed the Equity of Redemption of the same, may be equally divided between Hannah and Susannah Potter who are entitled to the same in Equity. My Will further is, and I do hereby direct and appoint that all Goods and Merchandizes that I may have sent for to Great Britain at the time of my Death which shall happen to arrive afterwards, and all Goods and Merchandizes that shall be in the House at the time of my Death shall be made use of for the clothing my Wife, Children and Slaves and for furnishing my Plantation in the same manner as I might or should have used them if I had been living, and all the rest and Residue of my Estate both real and personal not herein disposed of I give and devise to my eldest son Philip Ludwell Grymes and his Heirs for ever. Lastly I declare my Will to be, that my four Sons as they shall repectively attain the Age of Twenty one years shall be possesed of the Lands Slaves and personal Estate devised to each of them, saving their Mothers Right of Dower if she shall be then living. But in the meantime my Will is that the several Estates real and personal hereby given to my said Sons and all my ready money and outstanding Debts shall after my Death be vested in the following Trustees, viz., My loving Wife my Brothers Peyton Randolph & Benjamin Grymes Esquires and my good Friend and Neighbor Major John Robinson the Survivor or Survivors of them in Trust. First for the satisfying and Paying All my just Debts and my Legacies out of my ready money and outstanding Debts and if the same shall not prove sufficient for that Purpose then to apply the Profits of my other Estate to discharge my Debts remaining unsatisfied. And afterwards in Trust for the Maintenance and Education of my children until my Daughters shall be married or entitled to their respective Legacies out of the said Profits. And as to the Overplus of Profits in Trust for raising and paying the Legacies before given to my Daughters. And when that is accomplished in Trust for the maintaining and educating each of my Sons out of the Profits of his own proper Estate during their Minority. And lastly in Trust, to account for & pay to each of my Sons as they respectively come to age all surplus Profits arising out of their respective Estates. And when any of my Sons attain the age of Twenty one years the Trust aforesaid shall cease and be determined as to his or their Estate or Estates: But in case the Sum of Money to be raised out of my Estate for the Payment of the Legacies be not then compleated the Sum wanting shall still be chargable upon them in proporation to the clear yearly value of the Estate delivered up, which shall be computed & finally adjusted by my Trustees aforementioned the Survivors or Survivor of them.

Item. I appoint my dear and well beloved Wife Guardian of my Daughters until they attain their full Age or marry; and I appoint all my aforementioned Trustees and the Survivors or Survivor of them Guardians of my Sons until they arrive at the Age of Twenty one years. And if any question Doubt or Controversy arise touching the Meaning and Exposition of this my Will during the Guardianship aforesaid, the same shall be fully determined by my said Trustees or the Major Part of them and what they shall judge or determine shall be binding upon all my said Children.

Item. I nominate and appoint my said well beloved Wife, my Brothers Peyton Randolph and Benjamin Grymes Esquires & my good Friend and Neighbor Major John Robinson Executors of this my last Will declaring that my Intention is not to release any Debt which either of them shall happen to owe me at the Time of my Death. Lastly I desire that my Estate shall not be appraised and that my Executors give no Security for the Discharge of the Trust reposed in them. And I do hereby revoke all former Wills made by me, declaring to be my true last Will and Testament. In Testimony whereof I have hereunto set my Hand and affixed my Seal this Eighteenth

Day of December in the Year of our Lord One Thousand Seven hundred & fifty six.

PHILIP GRYMES. (Seal)

Signed sealed published and Declared by the said Philip Grymes as and for his last Will and Testament, in the Presence of us who were present at the Signing & Sealing thereof.

Peter Randolph.
Chs. Carter jr.
John Skinker.
John Gilliam.

I Philip Grymes of Brandon in the County of Middlesex being in Health & sound disposing mind & Memory, do make this Codicil to this my last Will and Testament: Whereas since the making this my Will it has pleased God to bless me with another Daughter, whom we have named Betty, who is not provided for in the said Will, I do hereby give her the same Portion that I have alloted to each of her Sisters Susannah and Mary, to be paid in the same manner and out of the same Particular parts of my Estate as the other two abovementioned Daughters' portions are directed to be paid. In Witness whereof, I have hereunto set my hand and Seal this fifth Day of August, 1761.

PHILIP GRYMES (SEAL).

At a Court held for Middlesex County at the Court House in Urbanna, on Tuesday, the 2nd day of February, 1762.

The last Will and Testament of the Hon'ble Philip Grymes, Esq., dec'd, being presented by Benjamin Grymes and John Robinson, two of the Exrs. therein mentioned, was proved by the Oaths of Charles Carter, Jun'r, and John Skinker Gentn. two of the Witnesses thereto and ordered to be recorded. And the said Benjamin Grymes and John Robinson having taken the Oath of an Exor, Certificate is granted them for obtaining a probat in due form.

At a Court held for Middlesex County at the Court House in Urbanna, Tuesday, the 2nd day of March, 1762.

The Will of the Hon'ble Philip Grymes, Esq., dec'd, being brought into Court according to order, Peyton Randolph, Esq., and Mary Grymes, the other Ex'ors therein mentioned, took the Oath of an Ex'or, which is ordered to be Certified.

Test ROBERT ELLIOT, Clk.

Philip and Mary Grymes had issue:

18. Lucy, born August 24, 1743, died Sept. 18, 1834; married July 3, 1762, Thomas Nelson, of Yorktown, Governor of Virginia; Major General commanding Virginia Militia at the siege of Yorktown, and signer of the Declaration of Independence. She was buried at Fork

Church, Hanover County, where her tomb, giving dates of death and age, remains.

19. *Philip Ludwell.*[5]

20. John Randolph[5], born about 1746, died 1820. He entered Eton in 1760, and was probably later at one of the Universities or Inns of Court. He took the English side at the beginning of the Revolution, and joined Lord Dunmore in 1776 at the head of a troop. Dunmore was much elated at the accession of Mr. Grymes, and wrote Lord George Germaine that he was a great acquisition to the royal cause, and was "of the first family in Virginia, a gentleman of fortune, amiable character, strict honor, brave, active and able." John R. Grymes entered the Queen's Rangers under Simcoe, and served with credit as Major until 1778, when he went to England. When Napoleon was expected to invade England, Major Grymes was an officer in a force of American Royalists. Later he returned to Virginia and became a wealthy planter in Orange County. He married his cousin Susanna, daughter of John Randolph, formerly Attorney General of Virginia (also a refugee loyalist), and died without issue.

21. *Charles.*[5]

22. *Benjamin.*[5]

23. Susanna, born March 4, 1752; married March (another account says November) 28, 1772, Nathaniel Burwell, of "Carter's Grove," James City County, and later of "Carter Hall," Frederick (now Clarke) County.

24. Mary, born March 4, 1754; married, October, 1774, Robert Nelson, of Yorktown.

25. Peyton[5].

26. Elizabeth, married Dr. Matthew Pope, of Yorktown, a surgeon in the American Army during the Revolution.

(To be continued.)

OFFICERS AND MEMBERS

OF THE

Virginia Historical Society

JANUARY, 1920.

President.

W. GORDON MCCABE, Richmond, Va.

Vice-Presidents.

EDWARD V. VALENTINE, Richmond, Va.
LYON G. TYLER, Williamsburg, Va.
PHILIP A. BRUCE, University, Va.

Corresponding Seecretary and Librarian.

WILLIAM G. STANARD, Richmond, Va.

Recording Secretary.

D. C. RICHARDSON, Richmond, Va.

Treasurer.

ROBERT A. LANCASTER, JR., Richmond, Va.

Executive Committee.

C. V. MEREDITH, Richmond, Va.
J. STEWART BRYAN, Richmond, Va.
A. C. GORDON, Staunton, Va.
S. S. P. PATTESON, Richmond, Va.
S. H. YONGE, Norfolk, Va.
WM. H. PALMER, Richmond, Va.
DANIEL GRINNAN, Richmond, Va.
J. P. MCGUIRE, JR., Richmond, Va.
WM. A. ANDERSON, Lexington, Va.
EARL G. SWEM, New York, N. Y.
MORGAN P. ROBINSON, Richmond, Va.
and ex-officio, the President, Vice-Presidents, Secretaries and Treasurer.

LIST OF MEMBERS

HONORARY MEMBER

Keane, Prof. A. H., London, Eng.

CORRESPONDING MEMBERS

Bacon, H. F., Bury St. Edmund, Eng.
Banks, Chas. E., M. D.
Barber, E. A., Philadelphia, Pa.
Bryant, H. W., Portland, Maine.
Campeau, Hon., F. R. E., Ottawa, Can.
Champlin, J. D., Jr., New York, N.Y.
Craig, Isaac, Alleghany, Pa.
Hinke, Prof. W. J., Auburn, N. Y.
Hoes, Rev. R. R., Washington, D. C.
Judah, George F., Spanish Town, Jamaica.
Nicholson, Col. J. P., Philadelphia, Pa.
Richemond, Mons. Meschinet De, La Rochelle, France.
Ross, Hon. D. A., Quebec, Can.
Wright, W. H. K., Plymouth, Eng.

LIFE MEMBERS

Adams, Gilmer S., Louisville, Ky.
Adams, Wm. Newton, Bridgehampton, L. I.
Alexander, H. M., New York, N Y..
Ancell, Rev. B. L., New York, N. Y.
Andrews, A. B. L., Jr., Raleigh, N. C.
Bagnell, Mrs. Wm., St. Louis, Mo.
Barratt, Judge Norris S., Philadelphia, Pa.
Billings, C. K. G., New York, N. Y.
Blackwell, Henry, New York, N Y.
Blair, Mrs. Lewis H., Richmond, Va.
Blankinship, Dr. J. W., Berkley, Cal.
Bryan, Jonathan, Richmond, Va.
Bryan, Robert C., Richmond, Va.
Bryan, St. George, Richmond, Va.
Bryan, J. Stewart, Richmond, Va.
Bullitt, Dr. John C., Wayne, Pa.
Bushnell, David I., Jr., University, Va.
Cabell, J. Alston, Richmond, Va.
Cabell, Col. H. C., U. S. A., Portland, Oregon.
Childers, Col. Gracey, Clarksville, Tenn.
Cox, Mrs. Wm. Ruffin, Richmond, Va.
Clement, Capt. H. C., U. S. A., Governor's Island, N. Y.
Clements, Mrs. Helen I., St. Louis,Mo.
Cocke, Lucian H., Ronoake, Va.
Cook, Heustis P., Richmond, Va.
Deats, H. E., Flemington, N. J.
Dooley, James H., Richmond, Va.
Downman, R. H., New Orleans, La.
Earnest, Joseph B., Lexington, Ky.
Fothergill, Mrs. Robert, Richmond, Va.
Gary, J. A., Baltimore, Md.
Gibbs, Mrs. Virginia B., Newport, R. I.
Gratz, Simon, Philadelphia, Pa.
Hanna, Charles, A., Montclair, N. J.
Harrison, Fairfax, Belvoir, Fauquier Co., Va.
Harrison, Richard Fairfax, Fauquier Co., Va.
Hill, C. K., Harriman, Tenn.
Hobson, Mrs. Henry W., Jr., New York, N. Y.
Hotchkiss, Elmore D, Jr., Richmond, Va.
Hughes, R. M., Norfolk, Va.

Huntington, Archer M., Baychester, N. Y.
Hyde, James Hazen, Paris, France.
Jones, Judge Lewis H., Louisville, Ky.
Keith, Charles P., Philadelphia, Pa.
Kinsolving, Walter O., Austin, Tex.
Lee, Edmund J., M. D., Philadelphia, Pa.
Lee, W. H., St. Louis, Mo.
Mason, Wm. Peyton, Ft. Worth, Tex.
Miller, Dr. J. L., Thomas, W. Va.
Mitchell, Robert, Richmond, Va.
Moriarty, G. Andrews, Providence. R. I.
Morse, Willard S., Seaford, Del.
McCabe, Col. E. R. Warner, U. S. A.
McCabe, W. Gordon, Jr., Charleston, S. C.
McCormick, Cyrus Hall, Chicago, Ill.
Nolting, Miss Elizabeth Aiken, Richmond, Va.
Pillsbury, Mrs. Charles L., Minneapolis, Minn.
Raborg, T. M. T., New York, N. Y.
Richardson, D. C., Richmond, Va.
Robinson, Morgan P., Richmond, Va.
Rosser, Thomas L., Jr., Charlottsville, Va.
Rucker, Mrs. Booker Hall, Rolla, Mo.
Scott, Frederick W., Rchmond, Va.
Scott, Winfield, New York, N. Y.
Sharp, Willoughby, Jr., New York, N. Y.
Stires, Rev. Ernest, M. D. D., New York, N. Y.
Stubbs, Wm. C., New Orleans, La.
Swanson, Hon. Claude A., Chatham, Va.
Sweet, Mrs. Edith M., St. Albans, W. Va.
Talcott, Col. T. M. R., Richmond, Va.
Tedcastle, Mrs. Arthur W., Milton, Mass.
Waterman, W. H., New Bedford, Mass.
Watson, Mrs. Alexander McKenzie, Washington, D. C.
Webb, W. Seward, New York, N. Y.
Wickham, Henry T., Richmond, Va.
Williams, A. D., Richmond, Va.
Willson, Mrs. Howard T., Virden, Ill.
Williams, Thomas C., Richmond, Va.
Winslow, H. M., Harriman, Tenn.
Woodson, Captain R. S., U. S. A., St. Louis, Mo.

ANNUAL MEMBERS*

Abney, John R., New York, N. Y.
Adams, Walter, Framingham, Mass.
Addison, E. B., Richmond, Va.
Adkins, S. B., Richmond, Va.
Allen, Herbert F. M., Washington, D. C.
Ambler, Ben. Mason, Parkersburg, W. Va.
Ames, Mrs. Joseph S., Baltimore, Md.
Anderson, B. P., M. D., Colorado Springs, Col.
Anderson, Charles C., Richmond, Va.
Anderson, W. A., Lexington, Va.,
Andrews, Prof. C. M., Yale University, New Haven, Conn.
Antrim, Hugh, Richmond, Va.
Atkins, Mrs. G. W. E., New York, N. Y.
Atkinson, Thomas, Richmond, Va.
Atwood, Lewis R., Louisville, Ky.
Austin-Leigh, Richard A., London, Eng.
Axtell, Decatur, Richmond, Va.
Bacon, Mrs. Horace S., North Middletown, Ky.
Bagby, Mrs. Parke C., Richmond, Va.
Baker, C. C., Texas City, Texas.
Ballard, N. H., Brunswick, Ga.
Barbour, John S., Washington, D. C.
Barham, Dr. W. B., Newsoms, Va.
Barnum, Mrs. George, Winchester, Va.
Baskervill, P. H., Richmond, Va.
Bates, S. E., Richmond, Va.
Battle, George Gordon, New York, N. Y.
Bayne, Howard R., New York, N. Y.
Beer, George Louis, New York, N.Y.
Beirne, Capt. Francis F., Richmond, Va.
Bell, Landon C., Columbus, Ohio.
Bell, Robert O., Richmond, Va.
Belmont, August, New York, N. Y.
Berry, Mrs. C. D., Nashville, Tenn.
Best, Frank E., Chicago, Ill.
Beveridge, Hon. A. J., Indianapolis, Ind.

*This list includes subscribers to the Magazine.

Blackstock, Ira B., Springfield, Ill.
Blair, Miss Louisa Coleman, Richmond, Va.
Blow, George P., La Salle, Ill.
Boatwright, Mrs. Gertrude F. H., Roanoke, Va.
Boddie, John T., Chicago, Ill.
Boisseau, P. H., Danville, Va.
Bolling, Charles E., Richmond, Va.
Booker, Mrs. Hunter R., Hampton, Va.
Boreman, R. J. A., Parkersburg, W. Va.
Bosher, Mrs. Robert S., Richmond, Va.
Bowling, Benjamin L., Chicago, Ill.
Boykin, Miss Anna B., Richmond, Va.
Bradshaw, Mrs. Rosena, Paducah, Ky.
Brame, Miss Lucile, Knoxville, Tenn.
Branch, John K., Richmond, Va.
Brodhead, Mrs. Lucas, Versailes, Ky.
Brooke, George D., Cumberland, Md.
Brooke, Richard N., Washington, D. C.
Brooke, Major Richard, Weston, W. Va.
Brooke, Robert T., Birmingham, Ala.
Brooke, S. S., Roanoke, Va.
Brooke, Dr. T. V., Sutherlin, Va.
Brown, Prof. W. G., Columbia, Mo.
Brown, J. Tompson, Richmond, Va.
Brown, Wallace F., Richmond, Va.
Bruce, Hon. C. M., Washington, D. C.
Bruce, Philip Alexander, University, Va.
Bruce, Mrs. Mary Howard, Richmond, Va.
Bryan, George, Richmond, Va.
Bryan, Thomas P., Richmond, Va.
Budlong, Mrs. Milton J., New York, N. Y.
Bukey, Mrs. John Spencer, Vienna, Va.
Bullard, Mrs. B. F., Savannah, Ga.
Bullitt, Wm. Marshall, Louisville, Ky.
Burges, Richard F., El Paso, Texas.
Burwell, D. S. Norfolk, Va.
Byrd, Samuel M., Brook Haven, Miss.

Callahan, G. C., Philadelphia, Pa.
Callery, Mrs. J. D., Pittsburg, Pa.
Cameron, Col. Benehan, Stagville, N. C.
Cameron, Miss Mary H., Richmond, Va.
Campbell R. K., Washington, D. C.
Cannon, Mrs. G. Randolph, Richmond, Va.
Caperton, Mrs. James W., Richmond, Ky.
Capps, Rear Admiral, W. L., U. S. N., Washington, D. C.
Cargill, Mrs. T. A., Houston, Texas.
Carpenter, Pay Director J. S., U. S. N., Boston, Mass.
Carrington, Edward C., New York, N. Y.
Cartwright, Mrs. S. A. Brooke, Washington, D. C.
Cary, T. Archibald, Richmond, Va.
Catlett, Mrs. Richard H., Staunton, Va.
Chamberlayne, Churchill G., Richmond, Va.
Chandler, Dr. J. A. C., Williamsburg, Va.
Chandler, R. G., Chicago, Ill.
Chandler, Walter T., Chicago, Ill.
Chauncey, Mrs. Agnes C., Narberth, Pa.
Chilton, W. B., Washington, D. C.
Chowning, C. C., Urbanna, Va.
Christian, Judge Geo. L., Richmond, Va.
Christian, Walter. Richmond, Va.
Claiborne, Dr. J. H., New York, N. Y.
Claiborne, Mrs. Robert, New York, N. Y.
Claiborne, Rev. W. S., Sewanee, Tenn.
Clark, Mrs. Edward H., New York, N. Y.
Clark, W. Welch, Danville, Va..
Clark, Wm. Hancock, New York, N. Y.
Clark, Mrs. G. Harvey, Richmond, Va.
Clarke, P. N., Louisville, Ky.
Clement, Mrs. N. E., Chatham, Va.
Clyde, W. P., New York, N. Y.
Cobb, Wm. H., Elkins, W. Va.
Coffin, Charles P., Brookline, Mass.
Coke, Capt. John A., Richmond, Va.
Coleman, Aylett B., Roanoke, Va.
Coleman, Charles W., Washington, D. C.
Coles, Mrs. T. B., Brooklyn, N. Y.
Colston, Edward, Cincinnati, Ohio.
Connor, Judge H. G., Wilson, N. C.
Coolidge, Archibald C., Cambridge, Mass.

Corbin, Richard Beverley, New York, N. Y.
Corbin, Richard W., Newport, R. I.
Cotten, Bruce, Baltimore, Md.
Craig, Mrs. Lawrence R., Little Rock, Ark.
Cozzens, Federick B., Chicago, Ill.
Crenshaw, S. Dabney, Richmond, Va.
Cridlin, W. B., Richmond, Va.
Crockett, R. H., Franklin, Tenn.
Crump, Judge Beverley T., Richmond, Va.
Crump, James D., Richmond, Va.
Culleton, Leo., London, Eng.

Dabney, Dr. William M., Ruxton, Md.
Dabney, Prof. R. H., University, Va.
Daingerfield, Francis Lee, Alexandria, Va.
Dance, Mrs. Russell, Corinth, Miss.
Dandridge, Miss Mary E., Cincinnati, Ohio.
Darling, Mrs. Frank W., Hampton, Va.
Daughters, A. R., Washington, D. C.
Davis, Arthur K., Petersburg, Va.
Davis, Mrs. E. P., Columbia, S. C.
Davis, W. O., Gainesville, Texas.
Denham, Edward, New Bedford, Mass.
Denson, C. B., Raleigh, N. C.
Dickey, Judge Lyle A., Lihue, H. T.
Dillard, Dr. James H., Charlottesville, Va.
Doneghy, Mrs. John T., Macon, Mo.
Doremus, Mrs. C. A., New York, N. Y.
Downing, Prof. G. C., Washington, D. C.
Drewry Hon. P. H., Petersburg, Va.
Driven, Mrs. James L., Bardstown, Ky.
Duke, Judge R. T. W., Jr., Charlottesville, Va.
Dunn, John, M. D., Richmond, Va.
Dupont, Col. H. A., Winterthur, Del.
Duval, Mrs. Maria P., Charlestown, W. Va.
Dwight, Dr. E. W., Boston, Mass.

Eagon, Robert E., Dallas, Texas.
Easley, J. C., Richmond, Va.
East, John P., New York, N. Y.
Eaton, George G., Washington, D. C.
Eckenrode, Dr. H. J., Richmond, Va.
Eggleston, Dr. J. D., Hampden-Sidney, Va.
Ellis, Wade H., Washington, D. C.
Ellis, William A., Florence, Ala.
Embry, Judge Alvin T., Fredricksburg, Va.
Emple, Adam, New York, N. Y.
Eustace, Wm. Corcoran, Washington, D. C.
Evans, Miss Catherine, Richmond, Va.

Farrar, Edgar H., New Orleans, La.
Faulkner, C. J., Boydton, Va.
Feild, W. P., Little Rock, Ark.
Ferrell, Mrs. Chas. C. Anson, Texas.
Fife, Prof. R. H., Middletown, Conn.
Fitzhugh, Gen. Chas. L., Washington, D. C.
Fletcher, William Meade, Sperryville, Va.
Fountain, General S. W., U. S. A., Philadelphia, Pa.
Frances, Mrs. Charles E., Bedford, Ind.
Freeman, D. S., Richmond, Va.
French, Dr. Jno. Herndon, New York, N. Y.
Furlow, Floyd C., New York, N. Y.

Gaines, C. Carrington, Ploughkeepsie, N. Y.
Gaines, J. B., Leesburg, Fla.
Garland, Spotswood, Wilmington, Del.
Garner, J. W., Falls Church, Va.
Gilbert, Mrs. Wells, Oswego, Ore.
Gilbert, Mrs. R. M., New York, N. Y.
Gilbert, Prof. W. E., East Radford, Va.
Giles, T. Peyton, Richmond, Va.
Glover, Rolfe E., Richmond, Va.
Goddard, A. J., Freeport, Ill.
Good, D. Sayler, Roanoke, Va.
Goodwin, Rev. E. L., Richmond, Va.
Goodwyn, Tyler, Montgomery, Ala.
Goodwyn, Mrs. W. S., Emporia, Va.
Gordon, Armistead C., Staunton, Va.
Gray, Henry W., Jr., Hartford, Conn.
Gregory, George C., Rio Vista, Va.
Grinnan, Judge Daniel, Richmond, Va.
Grinnan, John C., Norfolk, Va.
Groome, H. C., Warrenton, Va.

Guthrie, Capt. John W., U. S. A.
Guy, H. I., Schenectady, N. Y.

Hairston, S. W., Roanoke, Va.
Hamilton, Mrs. Amelia C., New York, N. Y.
Hardy, Miss Stella Pickett, Batesville, Ark.
Harpel, Mrs. Almeda B., Des Moines, Iowa.
Harrington, Howard S., New York, N. Y.
Harris, Alfred T., Jr., Richmond, Va.
Harris, John T., Jr., Harrisonburg, Va.
Harrison, Mrs. Carter H., University, Va.
Harrison, Hon. Francis Burton, Manila, P. I.
Harrison, Geo. T., M. D., University, Va.
Harrison, Robert L., New York, N. Y.
Harrison, W. Gordon, Savanah, Ga.
Harrison, W. Preston, Los Angeles, Cal.
Hasbrook, Col. Charles E., Richmond, Va.
Hawes, S. H., Richmond, Va.
Heatwole, Prof. C. J., Athens, Ga.
Heath, James E., Norfolk, Va.
Hempston, W. D., Leesburg, Va.
Henning, Mrs. S. T., Shelbyville, Ky.
Herndon, J. W., Alexandria, Va.
Heyer, Mrs. Mary B., Wilmington, N. C.
Hibbett, A. J., Hattiesburg, Miss.
Higgins, Mrs. D. F., Joliet, Ill.
High, Mrs. J. M. Atlanta, Ga.
Hine, Col. Charles DeLano, U. S. A., Vienna, Va.
Hite, Rev. Lewis F., Cambridge, Mass.
Holladay, A. Randolph, Warminester, Va.
Holt, R. O., New York, N. Y.
Hord, Rev. A. H., Philadelphia, Pa.
Horsley, Dr. J. Shelton, Richmond, Va.
Houston, Mrs. E. M., Walton, Fla.
Houston, Miss Martha K., Columbus, Ga.
Howard, Mrs. Eleanor Washington, Washington, D. C.
Howard, Major McHenry, Baltimore, Md.
Howell, Arden, Richmond, Va.
Hughes, A. S., Denver, Col.
Hume, Mrs. Frank, Washington, D. C.
Hunt, Gaillard, Washington, D. C.
Hunter, James W., Norfolk, Va.
Hunton, Eppa, Jr., Richmond, Va.
Hutcheson, H. F., Boydton, Va.
Hutcheson, Mrs. J. C., Houston, Tex.
Hutchinson, Cary T., New York, N. Y

Jackson, H. W., Richmond, Va.
James, Mrs. J. O., Chatham, Va.
Jameson, Mrs. S. W., Roanoke, Va.
Jarman, Prof. J. L., Farmville, Va.
Jeffress, T. F., Drewry's Bluff, Va.
Jenkins, Luther H., Richmond, Va.
Jewett, W. K., Passadena, Cal.
Johnson, B. F., Wshington, D. C.
Johnston, Miss Mary, Warm Springs, Va.
Jones, Mrs. Bolling H., Alanta, Ga.
Jones, T. Catesby, New York, N. Y.
Jones, Mrs. Richard, New Orleans, La.
Jones, Meriwether, Richmond, Va.
Jones, W. Strother, Red Bank, N. J.
Joynes, Levin, Richmond, Va.
Junkin, Francis T. A., Chicago, Ill.

Kable, Mrs. W. G., Staunton, Va.
Keach, Mrs. O. A., Wichita, Kan.
Keim, Mrs. Betty L., Philadelphia, Pa.
Kemper, Charles E., Staunton, Va.
Kirby, Judge Samuel B., Louisville, Ky.
Kirk, Henry J., Bertrand, Va.
Klemm, Mrs. J. G., Jr., Haverford, Pa.
Lamb, Mrs. E, T., Norfolk, Va.
Lacy, Samuel W., Washington, D. C.
Lambert, Mrs. W. H., Germantown, Pa.
Lancaster, R. A., Jr., Richmond, Va.
Lawrence, Mrs. Graham, Shelbyville, Ky.
Leake, J. Jordan, Richmond, Va.
Lee, Blair, Silver Springs, Md.
Lee, R. E., Jr., Fairfax County, Va.
Leigh, Egbert G., Jr., Richmond, Va.
Lester, J. Calvin, Kansas City, Mo.
Lewis, Charles, Cincinnati, Ohio.
Lewis, Judge Lunsford L., Richmond, Va.

Lloyd, Mrs. Arthur S., New York, N. Y.
Lodge, Hon. H. C., Washington, D C.
Locke, Victor Murat, Antlers, Okla.
Long, Ernest M., Richmond, Va.
Long, E. McL., New York, N. Y.
Lorton, Heth, New York, N. Y.
Loyall, Captain B. P., Norfolk, Va.
Lukeman, H. Augustus, New York, N. Y.

Mallory, Col. J. S., U. S. A. Lexington, Va.
Markham, George D., St. Louis, Mo.
Mason, Mrs. Frank T., Atlanta, Ga.
Massie, Robert, Lynchburg, Va.
Mastin, Mrs. George R., Lexington, Ky.
Matthews, Albert, Boston, Mass.
Maury, C. W., Richmond, Va.
Mayo, E. C., Richmond, Va.
Mayo, P. H., Richmond, Va.
Mercer, Mrs. William P., Elm City, N. C.
Meredith, Charles V., Richmond, Va.
Meriwether, Mrs. Minor, Shreveport, La.
Merrill, Mrs. Lida W., Terre Haute, Ind.
Meyer, Mrs. August R., Kansas City, Mo.
Michie, Thomas J., Charlottesville, Va.
Mickley, Miss Minnie F., Allentown, Pa.
Miller, Rudolph P., New York, N. Y.
Minnigerode, Charles, Baltimore, Md.
Minor, Benj. S., Washington, D. C.
Mitchell, Kirkwood, Richmond, Va.
Moffett, Miss Edna V., Wellesley, Mass.
Moncure, James A., Richmond, Va.
Montague, Hill, Richmond, Va.
Morgan, Dr. Daniel H., Lanesville, N. Y.
Moore, Warner, Richmond, Va.
Moore, Mrs. W. C., Columbus, Ohio.
Morton, Richard Lee, Williamsburg, Va.
Morton, W. S., Charlotte C. H., Va.
Mosby, Mrs. J. B., Richmond, Va.
Munford, Mrs. Beverley B., Richmond, Va.
Munford, R. B., Jr., Richmond, Va.
Murrell, W. M., Lynchburg, Va.
Myers, Barton, Norfolk, Va.
McAllister, J. T., Hot Springs, Va.
McBryde, Dr. J. M., Blacksburg, Va.
McCabe, Capt. W. Gordon, Richmond, Va.
McConnell, Prof. J. P., Radford, Va.
McCormick, Robert H., Jr., Chicago, Ill.
McCorkle, Walter L., New York, N. Y.
McCormick, Harold F., Chicago, Ill.
McCutcheon, Mrs. B. B., Clifton, Forge, Va.
McFall, James, Philadelphia, Pa.
McGraw, John T., Grafton, W. Va.
McGaroarty, W. B., Falls Church, Va.
McGuire, Dr. Edward, Richmond. Va.
McGuire, Mrs. Frank H., Richmond, Va.
McGuire, John Peyton, Richmond, Va.
McGuire, Murray M., Richmond, Va.
McGuire, Dr. Stuart, Richmond, Va.
McKim, Rev. Randolph H., Washington, D. C.
McKinney, Mrs. Roy W., Paducah, Ky.
McIlwaine, Dr. H. R., Richmond, Va.
McIlwaine, W. B., Petersburg, Va.
McIntosh, Charles F., Norfolk, Va.
McNeil, Mrs. Walter S., Richmond, Va.

Neale, S. C., Washington, D. C.
Neilson, Miss Lou, Oxford, Miss.
Nichols, Rt. Rev. W. F., San Francisco, Cal.
Nicholls, Col. Maury, U. S. A., Norfolk, Va.
Nixon, Lewis, Metuchen, N. J.
Norvell, Mrs. Lipscomb, Beaumont, Texas.

O'Connell, Rt. Rev. D. J., Richmond, Va.
Osborne, W. L. H., Glide, Oregon.
Outerbridge, Mrs. A. J., Easton, Md.
Owen, Thomas M. Montgomery, Ala.

Page, Mrs. Mann, Elizabeth, N. J.
Page, S. Davis, Philadelphia, Pa.
Page, Rosewell, Beaver Dam, Va.

Page, Hon. Thomas Nelson, Washington, D. C.
Palmer, Col. William H., Richmond, Va.
Parker, Col. John, Browsholme Hall, Clethiroe, Lancashire, Eng.
Patteson, S. S. P., Richmond, Va.
Paxton, T. B., Jr., Chicago, Ill.
Payne, John B., Washington, D. C.
Payne, Marshall John, Staunton, Va.
Pegram, Henry, New York, N. Y.
Pegram, Lt.-Col. John C., U. S. A.
Penn, Mrs. James G., Danville, Va.
Pescud, Peter F., New Orleans, La.
Peterkin, Mrs. George W., Parkersburg, W. Va.
Pettigrew, Mrs. C. D., Pine Bluff, Ark.
Pettus, William J., M. D., U. S. Marine Hospital Service, Charleston, S. C.
Pinckney, C. C., Richmond, Va.
Pleasants, Edwin, Richmond, Va.
Pleasants, Dr. J. Hall, Baltimore, Md.
Poindexter, W. W., Lynchburg, Va.
Pollard, Henry R., Richmond, Va.
Prentiss, Judge R. R., Suffolk, Va.

Ramey, Mrs. Alice Lewis, Brownwood, Texas.
Randolph, Mrs. Robert Lee, Alexandria, La.
Reed, P. L., Richmond, Va.
Reid, Prof. Legh W., Haverford, Pa.
Richardson, Albert Levin, Baltimore, Md.
Richardson, Wm. D., Richmond, Va.
Ridgeley, Mrs. Jane, Chicago, Ill.
Rives, Mrs. W. C., Washngton, D. C.
RoBards, Col. John Lewis, Hannabal, Mo.
Roberson, Mrs. J. Fall, Cropwell, Ala.
Roberts, Mrs. James A., Marietta, Ohio.
Robertson, Frank S., Abingdon, Va.
Robertson, Thos. B., Hopewell, Va.
Robins, Dr. C. R., Richmond, Va.
Robinson, Alexander G., Louisville, Ky.
Robinson, Judge C. W., Newport, News, Va.
Robinson, P. M., Clarksburg, W. Va.
Robinson, Mrs. Poitiaux, Richmond, Va.
Rockwell, Mrs. Eckley, Washington, D. C.
Ryan, Thos. F., Oak Ridge, Va.

Sands, Alexander H., Richmond, Va.
Savage, N. R., Richmond, Va.
Scherr, Henry, Williamson, W. Va.
Schouler, Prof. James, Intervale, N. H.
Scott, Alexander V., Rosedale, Miss.
Scott, George Cole, Richmond, Va.
Scott, Thomas B., Richmond, Va.
Scott, W. W., Orange, Co., Va.
Shearer, W. B., New Orleans, La.
Shelton, Thos. W. Norfolk, Va.
Shelton, Mrs. T. J. Denver, Col.
Shepherd, Dr. Wm. A., Richmond, Va.
Shewmake, Oscar L., Surry, Va.
Shine, Dr. Francis Eppes, Bisbee, Ariz.
Shipley, Mrs. Walter, St. Louis, Mo.
Sim, John R., New York, N. Y.
Sitterding, Fritz, Richmond, Va.
Smith, Austin, Middletown, Ohio.
Smith, A. D., Fayetteville, W. Va.
Smith, Alda L., Belton, S. C.
Smith, Capt. Boyd, Richmond, Va.
Smith, Miss Edith W., Denver, Col.
Smith, H. M., Jr., Richmond, Va.
Smith, Willis B., Petersburg, Va.
Smith, Capt. R. C., U. S. N. New York, N. Y.
Southall, Rev. S. O., Dinwiddie, Va.
Spilman, Gen. B. W., Warrenton, Va.
Stanard, W. G., Richmond, Va.
Statham, Miss Mary B., Passadena, Cal.
Staton, Mrs. James G., Williamston, N. C.
Stechert & Co., New York, N. Y.
Steiger, E., New York, N. Y.
Stern, General Jo. Lane, Richmond, Va.
Stettinius, Mrs. E. R., New York, N. Y.
Stevens, B. F. and Brown, London, Eng.
Stewart, Miss Annie C., Brook Hill, Va.
Stewart, Miss E. Hope, Brook Hill, Va.

Stewart, Miss Norma, Brook Hill, Va.
Stewart, Miss Lucy W., Brook Hill, Va.
Stewart, Rev. J. Calvin, Richmond, Va.
Stewart, J. A., Louisville, Ky.
Stiles, Mrs. Barnett, Medina, Texas.
Stone, Miss Lucie, P., Hollins, Va.
Stoner, Mrs. R. G., Mt. Sterling, Ky.
Strother, Henry, Fort Smith, Ark.
Strother, James French, Welch, W. Va.
Strother, Hon. P. W., Pearisburg, Va.
Stuart, Hon. Henry C., Elk Garden, Va.
Swem, Earl G., New York, N. Y.

Taliaferro, Mrs. Richard P., Ware Neck, Va.
Tatum, Miss Edith, Greenville, Ala.
Taylor, Dr. Fielding L., New York, N. Y.
Taylor, Jacquelin P., Richmond, Va.
Taylor, John M., Richmond, Va.
Taylor, Prof. T. U., Austin, Texas.
Terhune, Mrs. E. T., New York, N. Y.
Terrell, R. A., Bermingham, Ala.
Thach, Mrs. Charles C., Auburn, Ala.
Thompson, J. Taylor, Farmville, Va.
Thompson, Mrs. Wells, Houston, Texas.
Thompson, Mrs. W. H., Lexington, Ky.
Thornton, R. G., Richmond, Va.
Throckmorton, C. Wickliffe, San Antonio, Texas.
Thruston, R. C., Ballard, Louisville, Ky.
Tidball, Prof. Thomas A., Sewanee, Tenn.
Tiffany, Mrs. Louis McLane, Baltimore, Md.
Torrence, Rev. W. Clayton, Herndon, Va.
Traber, Mrs. Herman, Muskogee, Oklahoma.
Trant, Mrs. Robert L., Washington, D. C.
Travers, S. W., Richmond, Va.
Traylor, M. G., Princeton, N. J.
Tuck, G. O., New York, N. Y.
Tucker, Alfred E., Wimbledon, London, Eng.
Tucker, H. St. George, Lexington, Va.
Tucker, Lawrence F., Norfolk, Va.
Tunstall, Robert B., Norfolk, Va.
Turner, D. L., New York, N. Y.
Tyler, D. Lyon G., Holdcraft, Va.

Valentine, E. V., Richmond, Va.
Valentine, G. G., Richmond, Va.
Valentine, M. S., Jr., Richmond Va.
Vincent, George A., Fairmount, W. Va.

Waddell, Judge Edmund J., Richmond, Va.
Waggener, B. P., Atchison, Kan.
Walker, G., A., Tarrytown, N. Y.
Walker, Mrs. J. A., Brownwood, Tex.
Walker, J. G., Richmond, Va.
Walker, Norvell B., Rchmond, Va.
Walker, Mrs. Stuart W., Martinsburg, W. Va.
Waller, E. P., Schenectady, N. Y.
Walling, Mrs. Willoughgy, Chicago, Ill.
Walton, Capt. C. Cortlandt, Richmond, Va.
Waterman, Edgar F., Hartford, Conn.
Waters, J. S. T., Baltimore, Md.
Watkins, R. Walter, Jr., Baltimore, Md.
Wayland, Prof. J. W., Harrisonburg, Va.
Weddell, Alexander W., U. S. Consul General, Athens, Greece.
Wellford, B. Rand, Richmnd, Va.
Welles, Mrs. Paul T., New York, N. Y.
West, Mrs. H. L., New York, N. Y.
White, Rev. H. A., Columbia, S. C.
White, J. B., Kansas City, Mo.
White, Wm. H., Richmond, Va.
Whitner, Charles F., Atlanta, Ga.
Whitridge, Mrs. Wm. H., Baltimore, Md.
Whitty, J. H., Richmond, Va.
Wight, Mrs. Agnes D., Cockeysville, Md.
Willard, Mrs. Joseph E., American Embassy, Madrid, Spain.
Williams, E. Randolph, Richmond, Va.
Williams, Mrs. F. L., Bristol, R. I.

Williams, Langbourne M., Richmond, Va.
Wilson, Col. Eugene T., U. S. A.
Winston, James O., Kinston, N. Y.
Wise, Mrs. Barton H., Richmond. Va.
Wise, Col. Jennings C., Richmond, Va.
Wise, John C., M. D., U. S. N., Washington, D. C.
Withers, Alfred D., Roane's, Va.
Wise, Rear-Admiral Wm. C., U. S. N.
Woodhull, Mrs. Oliver J., San Antonio, Texas.
Wortham, Coleman, Richmond, Va.
Wright, E. E., New Orleans, La.
Wyatt, Wm. H., Jr., Richmond, Va.
Wynn, Mrs. James O., Atlanta, Ga.
Wysor, Harry R., Muncie, Ind.

Youkum, R. B., Levensworth, Kan.
Young, Mrs. James, Baltimore, Md.
Yonge, Samuel H., Richmond, Va.
Young, Prof. Hugh H., Baltimore, Md.

Zimmer, W. L., Petersburg, Va.

LIBRARIES—Annual Members

Bangor Public Library, Bangor, Maine.
Boston Public Library, Boston, Mass.
Brooklyn Public Library, Brooklyn, N. Y.
Brown University Library, Providence, R. I.

California Society, S. A. R., Los Angeles, Cal.
Carnegie Free Library, Alleghany, Pa.
Carnegie Free Library, Nashville, Tenn.
Carnegie Library, Atlanta, Ga.
Carnegie Library, Pittsburg, Pa.
Carnegie Library, San Antonio, Tex.
Chicago Public Library, Chicago, Ill.
Chicago University Library, Chicago, Ill.
Cincinnati Public Library, Cincinnati, Ohio.
Cleveland, Ohio, Public Library.
Cocke Memorial Library, Hollins, Va.
Colonial Dames of State of New York, New York, N. Y.
Cornell University Library, Ithaca, N. Y.
Cossitt Library, Memphis, Tenn.

Department of Archives and History, Jackson, Miss.
Detroit Public Library, Detroit, Mich.

Fairbanks Memorial Library, Terre Haute, Ind.

Georgetown University Library, Washington, D. C.
Goodwin Institute Library, Memphis, Tenn.
Grosvenor Pub. Library, Buffalo, N. Y.
Hampden-Sidney College Library, Hampden-Sidney, Va.
Hampton N. and A. Institute Library, Hampton, Va.

Handley Library, Winchester, Va.
Harvard University Library, Cambridge, Mass.

Illinois State Historical Library, Springfield, Ill.
Illinois Society S. A. R., Chicago, Ill.
Indiana State Library, Indianapolis, Ind.
Indianapolis Public Library, Indianapolis, Ind.
Iowa Historical Dept. of Des Moines, Ia.

Kansas City Public Library, Kansas City, Mo.

Lawson McGhee Library, Knoxville, Tenn.
Lexington, Ky. Public Library.

Library of Congress, Washington, D. C.
Libraire C. Klincksieck, Paris, France.
Long Island Historical Society Library, Brooklyn, N. Y.
Los Angeles, Cal. Public Library.
Louisville Free Public Library, Louisville, Ky.
Lynn, Mass., Free Public Library.

Maine State Library, Augusta, Me.
Massachusetts State Library, Boston, Mass.
Mechanics Benevolent Association Library, Petersburg, Va.
Michigan State Library, Lansing, Mich.
Milwaukee Public Library, Milwaukee, Wis.
Minneapolis Athenaeum Library, Minneapolis, Minn.

Nebraska University Library, Lincoln, Neb.
Newberry Library, Chicago, Ill.
New Hampshire State Library, Concord, N. H.
Norfolk Public Library, Norfolk, Va.
Northwestern University Library, Evanston, Ill.

Oberlin College Library, Oberlin, Ohio.
Omaha Public Library, Omaha, Neb.
Ohio State Library, Columbus, Ohio.

Parliament Library, Ottawa, Can.
Peabody College for Teachers Library, Nashville, Tenn.
Peabody Institute, Baltimore, Md.
Pennsylvania State College, State College, Pa.
Pennsylvania State Library, Harrisburg, Pa.
Peoria Public Library, Peoria, Ill.
Pequot Library, Southport, Conn.
Philadelphia Free Library, 13th and Locust streets, Philadelphia, Pa.
Philadelphia Law Association Library, Philadelphia, Pa.
Pratt Free Library, Baltimore, Md.
Princeton University Library, Princeton, N. J.

Randolph-Macon College Library, Ashland, Va.
Randolph-Macon Woman's College, College Park, Va.

Southern Baptist Theological Seminary, Louisville, Ky.
State Department Library, Washington, D. C.
Stanford University Library, Cal.
St. Joseph, Mo., Public Library.
St. Louis Mercantile Library, St. Louis, Mo.
St. Louis Public Library, St. Louis, Mo.
Syracuse Public Library, Syracuse, N. Y.

Union Theological Seminary Library, Richmond, Va.
University Club Library, New York, N. Y.
University of California Library, Berkeley, Cal.
University of Illinois Library, Urbanna, Ill.
University of Indiana Library, Bloomington, Ind.
University of Michigan Library, Ann Arbor, Mich.
University of Minnesota Library, Minneapolis, Minn.
University of North Carolina, Library, Chapel Hill, N. C.
University of Pennsylvania Library, Philadelphia, Pa.
University of Virginia Library, Charlottesville, Va.
University of West Virginia Library, Morgantown, W. Va.

Vanderbilt University Library, Nashville, Tenn.
Virginia State Library, Richmond, Va.
Virginia Military Institute Library, Lexington, Va.

Virginia Polytechnic Institute Library, Blacksburg, Va.

West Virginia Department of Archives and History, Charleston, W. Va.

Wheeling Public Library, Wheeling, W. Va.

Wyoming Historical and Geological Society, Wilkes-Barre, Pa.

Yale University Library, New Haven, Conn.

LIBRARIES—LIFE MEMBERS

Boston Athenaeum Library, Boston, Mass.

California State Library, Sacramento, Cal.

Columbia College Library, New York, N. Y.

Library Company, Philadelphia, Pa.

New York Public Library, New York, N. Y.

New York State Library, Albany, N. Y.

Richmond College Library, Richmond, Va.

Washington and Lee University Library, Lexington, Va.

PROCEEDINGS

OF THE

Virginia Historical Society

AT ITS

ANNUAL MEETING

HELD IN THE

HOUSE OF THE SOCIETY

ON APRIL 20, 1920

RICHMOND
OLD DOMINION PRESS, INC., PRINTERS
1920

PROCEEDINGS

OF THE

Virginia Historical Society

IN

Annual Meeting held April 20, 1920

The Annual meeting was held in the Society's House, 707 East Franklin Street, on April 20, 1920, at 4 P. M., with President W. Gordon McCabe in the chair.

The first business of the meeting was the reading of President McCabe's report.

For the first time in many years, this report, always so full of information, of eloquence and of humor, cannot appear. With both hearers and readers it had made a place for itself which was unique, and many who cared little for wholly historical work looked forward eagerly for its appearance.

At this meeting Captain McCabe read only the rough draft of parts of his report. He was so conscientious in his work that he would never complete the report until he had read and reread every page of the Magazine for the year. Delays in printing prevented him from ever seeing the complete Magazine, so his full report was never prepared.

All that can now be done is for the editor of the Magazine to give in brief, dry form, data which our President would have made alive.

Our membership on January 1, 1920 was 702, a loss of 12 from the preceding year. In this connection the writer wishes to pay a hearty tribute to the loyalty of our members.

In spite of long delays in the publication of the Magazine (due to causes beyond the power of the Executive Committee to remedy) almost all of our members showed their devotion to Virginia and Virginia history by refraining from criticism and by prompt payment of dues.

Any general defection during this trying time would, at least, have caused the suspension of the Magazine. Conditions are now better; but we need a hundred or more new members to meet the enormously increased cost of printing.

The President next read, as a part of his report, that of the Treasurer, which was as follows:

Treasurer's Report.

Balance in Bank November 30, 1918		$ 319.94
Receipts.		
Annual Dues	$2,905.18	
Life Members	300.00	
Interest	790.10	
Sale of Magazines	126.50	
Sale of Publications	29.00	
From Savings Bank	133.34	4,284.12
		$ 4,604.06
Disbursements.		
Salaries	$1,408.00	
Wages	360.00	
Postage and Express	103.50	
Sundry Bills	157.62	
Books, Stationery and Binding	6.25	
Printing Magazines	1,340.53	
Insurance	22.50	
Repairs	523.16	
Job Printing	87.87	
Checks Returned	10.00	
To Permanent Fund	133.34	
Coal	41.25	
Interest	.30	
		4,194.32
Balance in Bank November 30, 1919		409.74
		$ 4,604.06

PERMANENT FUND.

34 shares of stock in the Citizens Bank of Norfolk, Va., estimated value	$ 6,800.00
Real estate (6%) mortgages, $1,000.00 $4,500.00	5,500.00
U. S. Liberty Bonds (3½ and 4¼%)	1,600.00
In Savings Bank	1,917.98
	$15,817.98

In accordance with an order of the Executive Committee, the Treasurer presents the following tabulated statement showing the sources from which the Permanent Fund is derived. What is termed the "Society's Fund" comprises the amount the Committee has been able to save from year to year of the ordinary revenues of the Society.

The Virginia Sturdivant McCabe Fund, given by the President of the Society in loving memory of his granddaughter, Virginia Sturdivant McCabe, born February 1, 1906, died August 11, 1919	$ 500.00
The Jane Pleasants Harrison Osborne McCabe Fund, given by the President of the Society in loving memory of his wife, Jane Pleasants Harrison Osborne McCabe, who died November 22, 1912	500.00
The Edmund Osborne McCabe Fund, established in loving memory of Edmund Osborne McCabe (born February 29, 1868, died June 5, 1919), from a bequest left by his devoted mother, Jane Pleasants Harrison Osborne McCabe	500.00
Gift by a member of the Society	500.00
Daughters of the American Revolution Fund	100.00
Byam K. Stevens Fund	750.00
Edward Wilson James Fund	5,567.22
Society's Fund	7,400.00
	$15,817.98

During the past year the Citizens Bank of Norfolk declared a stock dividend of one new share for three old. Under this distribution the Society became entitled to 8 1/3 shares, and bought 2/3 of a share, thus adding nine shares to our previous holdings in that stock .

This is an increase of the Permanent Fund of $2,700.56 over last year. It has been necessary for the Society, in case of extensive repairs to the house costing more than could be paid of the current receipts, to have such repairs made out of the Permanent

Fund. Last year it was necessary to spend $500.00 in making the janitor's quarters habitable. The Committee authorized the Corresponding Secretary and Treasurer, if necessary to meet current expenses, to spend $500.00 from the amount in the Savings Bank. As we have not been able to issue, and consequently have not had to pay for, any magazines since last July, this money has not been called for, but it probably will be, so at present the net amount of the Permanent Fund, not already invested and available for investment is $15,317.98. The Finance Committee is awaiting information in regard to certain rumored additions to the Fund, before making a new investment.

If bookkeeping entries relating to the Permanent Fund are deducted it will be seen that the receipts during the last fiscal year were about $150.00 more than during the year before, and the expenditures, in spite of the great increase in prices, were $258.00 less. This is in part accounted for by the rigid economy practised and in part by the fact, before stated, that on account of printing troubles we have not been able to publish or pay for any magazines since July, 1919. The magazines are now under way and at an early date will call for considerable disbursements.

The financial condition of the Society, when conditions are considered, is very gratifying.

Respectfully submitted,

R. A. LANCASTER, JR.,
Treasurer.

ADDITIONS TO THE LIBRARY.

The additions to the Library in books and pamphlets in 1919 number five hundred and sixty-five (565).

The donors, to whom, as well as to others who have made presents to the Society, our grateful thanks are given, were: Armistead C. Gordon, Robert L. Preston, Prof. W. McNeile Dixon, W. A. Gordon, Jr., John T. Boddie, John C. Collins, O. W. Baylor, Richard C. Jones (Virginia State Forester), Major John D. Guthrie, U. S. A., Judge N. S. Barratt, Mrs. J. A. Johnston, Willis T. Hanson, Jr., Miss Catherine Evans, George Taylor Lee, Dr. J. F. Jameson, P. H. Baskervill, Dr. H. J. Eckenrode, E. A. Hankins, Philip T. Brown, G. C. Callahan, Miss Julia S. Wooldridge, Boutwell Dunlap, M. M. Haywood, Fairfax Harrison, W. Gordon McCabe, Mrs. W. Gordon McCabe, Richmond Chamber of Commerce, Library of Congress, Mass. Commission on Public Records, Illinois Centennial Commission, American Hellenic Society, U. S. War Department, Jewish War History Committee, Richmond Times-Dispatch, Virginia Bar Association, American Bar Association, U. S. Council of National Defense, University of Illincis, Grand Lodge of Masons of Penna., University of Oklahoma, University of California, Smithsonian Institute.

GIFTS.

Three volumes, Blackstone's Commentaries, Oxford, 1770, with autographs of Francis Lightfoot Lee, and book stamp of Arthur Lee. Presented by Milo P. Smith, Cedar Rapids, Iowa.

Photograph of portrait of Washington by Stuart, now at West Point, N. Y. Presented by Major A. E. Potts, U. S. A.

A package of manuscripts, clippings, etc. Presented by Miss L. Peyton, The Plains, Va.

Photostat copies of the Virginia Quit Rent Rolls 1704 (the only one known to exist), 98 sheets. Presented by a member of the Society.

A dressed wax doll and a dressed rag doll (in the costume of the period) over a hundred years old. Presented by Mrs. Wm. Wirt Henry, 812 Seminary Ave., Richmond, Va.

A saucer formerly belonging to the Grymes family of Brandon, Middlesex County, Va. Presented by C. C. Chowning, Urbana, Va.

Framed photograph of Capt. Wilson Miles Cary (many of whose valuable papers are now in our collection). Presented by Fairfax Harrison, Belvoir, Va.

PUBLICATIONS.

The great delay in the publication of the Magazine was due entirely to the impossibility of having printing done. In each case the copy for the Magazine was placed in the hands of the printer (or printers, for we had more than one), in ample time, but in each case they were compelled to take months in completing work which ordinarily would have been done in a few weeks. Vol. XXVII of the Magazine was not completed during 1919, but now has been. A double number (July-October, 1919) was published in 1920. We were not able to publish the index for this volume until the April 1920 number, which was issued late in 1920. Conditions are now improving in regard to printing facilities but the cost of printing and paper has increased so greatly that it will be necessary for us to raise six or seven hundred dollars more than usual this year and next.

The Executive Committee has decided not to raise the dues or materially reduce the size of the Magazine. To meet the need, an earnest effort will be made to obtain at least one hundred and twenty-five new members. All of our present members are asked to aid us.

Our late President's report called particular attention to the departments of the Magazine entitled "Roll of Honor" and "War Notes". These began in July, 1918, and ended in July-October, 1919. The first contains a list of Virginia's dead during the war, and the other an account of honors received, with personal notices, etc. During the period stated we printed, under these two heads, 217 pages.

Necrology.

LIFE MEMBERS.

Mrs. William Liggon Corbin, Philadelphia, Pa.
C. Wiley Grandy, Norfolk, Va.
Mrs. Phoebe A. Hearst, Pleasanton, California.

ANNUAL MEMBERS.

Wilson Miles Cary, Baltimore, Md.
General William R. Cox, Penelo, N. C.
J. J. Doran, Philadelphia, Pa.
Hon. J. Taylor Ellyson, Richmond, Va.
Rt. Rev. Robert A. Gibson, Richmond, Va.

E. T. Lamb, Norfolk, Va.
Mrs. James M. Lawton, New York, N. Y.
C. M. McClung, Knoxville, Tenn.
Capt. Thomas H. Raines, U. S. A.
Douglas H. Thomas, Baltimore, Md.
Richard B. Tunstall, Norfolk, Va.
Benjamin B. Valentine, Richmond, Va.

Whether we regard high character, distinguished service and devotion to the objects sought by this Society, or whether we count numbers lost from our roll of members, it can be said that rarely or never have we had a year with so much cause of sincere regret.

At the close of President McCabe's report he stated that the election of officers and members of the Executive Committee was next in order.

On motion, a nominating committee was appointed. The committee retired and on its return recommended the following gentlemen for election. The vote was taken and officers and members of the Executive Committee, as follows, were elected:

President—W. Gordon McCabe, Richmond.

Vice-Presidents—Edward V. Valentine, Richmond; Lyon G. Tyler, Charles City County; Philip A. Bruce, University.

Recording Secretary—David C. Richardson, Richmond.

Treasurer—Robert A. Lancaster, Jr., Richmond.

Corresponding Secretary and Librarian—William G. Stanard, Richmond.

Executive Committee—Charles V. Meredith, Richmond; Armistead C. Gordon, Staunton; S. A. Longe, Norfolk; Daniel Grinnan, Richmond; William A. Anderson, Lexington; Fairfax Harrison, Fauquier County; J. Stewart Bryan, Richmond; S. S. P. Patteson, Richmond; William H. Palmer, Richmond; John P. McGuire, Richmond; Morgan P. Robinson, Richmond; J. Jordan Leake, Richmond.

After the election of members there was an informal discussion of various subjects of interest to the Society, and then on motion, the meeting adjourned.

THE

VIRGINIA MAGAZINE

OF

HISTORY AND BIOGRAPHY.

VOL. XXVIII. APRIL, 1920. No. 2.

MINUTES OF THE COUNCIL AND GENERAL COURT—1622-1629.

(From the originals in the Library of Congress.)

(CONTINUED.)

A Court held at James Citye the 7th day of May 1627, being present:

Sir George Yeardley, Knt. &c., Doctor Pott & Capt. Roger Smith.

Whereas it appeareth upon the compl't of Ensigne John Uty, by the oaths of John Day(1) & Francis Banks, that Richard Bickley hath resisted & opposed him in his com'and, in denying to take armes & discharge his publick duty, the Court hath ordered that for this his offence he shalbe layed neck & heeles 12 howers & at the Croppe by way of fyne shall pay 200 lbs. of Tobacco

(1) John Utie, afterwards member of the Council, has been frequently noticed in this Magazine. At the Census of 1624-5, John Day, aged 24, who came in the **London Merchant**, 1620, and his wife who came in the same ship, were among Sir George Yeardley's "men" at Hog Island. Francis Banks, who came in the **Gift**, 1623, was one of Edward Bennett's servants at Wariscoyack in 1624. Richard Bickley who had come in the **Return**, was a servant of John Utie at Hog Island.

It is ordered at this court that, in regard Roger Dilk (by his owne confession) hath absented himself from his plantation without the knowledge or leave of his com'ander, contrary to an order of Court, for the space of 8 dayes compleat, that he shall pay (according to that order of court, viz: 25 l. of tobacco for every 24 howers absence) the some of 200 li. of tobacco.

A Court held the 21 of May 1627, being p'sent Sir George Yeardley Knt. &c., Dr. Pott & Capt. Roger Smith.
At this Court was delivered in the last will & testament of Thomas Grub(2), deceased, & proved to be the true will of the said Thomas Grub by the testamonye upon oath of Daniell Lacy, & that the said Thomas Grub was in p'fect sense & memorye at the sealing & deliverye herof.
It is ordered upo' complaint & informacon made by Ensigne John Utye, of the drunkeness & other misdemeanors of Roger Webster(3), that for his fault he shall pay by way of fyne 20 li. of tobacco & put in bond of 300 li. to keepe the good behaviour & to make his appearance at the next quarter court.
It is ordered that wheras it appeares by a bill under the hand & seale of Thomas Mahew(4) for five pounds sterling to be paid unto John Orchard, in com'odityes as they cost in England the first peny, bearing date the ninth of May one thousand six hundred and twenty-sixe, that out of the goods of Thomas Mahew the said debt of five pounds shalbe presently paid (in whose hands soever they remaine) unto the said John Orchard.

Upon the peticon of Bridges & Freeman James Sleight this court doth give them free leave to remove themselves & their goods from Martin Brandon unto some place or plantacon, where they may live more secured.

(2 Thomas Grubb, a joiner, came in the **George** and lived at Hog Island 1624-5.

(3) Roger Webster in 1624-5 lived at Hog Island. In 1632 he was a member of the House of Burgesses for the Glebe Land and Archer's Hope.

(4) A "Mr. Thomas Mahew, gentleman," had in 1637 a commission to examine persons leaving England for foreign parts (**Hotten**).

A Court held the 25th of June, 1627, present:

Sir George Yeardley, Knt., Governor &c
Capt. Smith
Mr. Claybourne.

Wheras Capt. John Martin appeared at this Court to answere unto ye suite of Tho. Gates(5) in the sume of eight hundred waight of tobacco being due by a bond under his hand bearing date the one & twentiethe day of Aprill 1626, the w'ch bond was acknowledged by the said Capt. Martin to be his owne deed and act under his owne hand. It is ordered that Mr Richard Kingsmell, Mr. John Southerne & Randall Smallwood Provost Marshall Shall praise the goods & Chattells of the said Capt. Martin uppon their oathes that soe paim't may be made unto ye said Thomas Gates of the debt aforesaid.

Wheras Wil'm Barnes & Robert Paramore(6) did on Thursday last behave themselves very negligently on their watch, it is therefore ordered that they shall pay three dayes worke a peice in cutting downe & clearing of such shrubbs & low woodes as are before the towne in the feildes. And likewise that Goodman Osborne for the like offence doe give on(e) dayes worke.

James Citty. A Quarter Court held the 2nd day of July 1627, being present

Sir George Yeardley, Knt., Governor &c
Capt. West, Mr Persey
Mr. Doctor Pott, Mr Secretary
Capt. Smyth, Capt Tucker
Capt. Mathewes, Mr ffarrar

The 3th of July 1627

(5) Thomas Gates, who came in the **Swan**, 1609 and his wife Elizabeth, who came in the **Warwick**, 1620, lived in 1624-5 at Pace's Paines, opposite Jamestown.

(6) Robert Parramore, who came in the **Swan**, was in 1624-5, resident at "Pashbehayes and the Main" near Jamestown. The appearance of the land where these careless sentinels were stationed, is still familiar. It was either an "old field,' once cultivated; but now grown up in shrubs, or else it was a tract of woodland from which all the trees had been cut and only undergrowth left. In either case it seems strange that there should have been uncultivated land close to the little palisaded "town". It is possible that the land to be cleared lay across Pitch and Tar Swamp, and did not immediately adjoin the town. "Goodman Osborne," was John Osborne who, with his wife Mary, was living on James City Island in 1624-5.

It is ordered that Capt. Martin shall have three dayes time to sell his goods w'ch are allready prised, that he may make satisfaction unto Tho. Gates of the debt of 800 li. of Tobacco w'ch he oweth unto the said Gates, if not, that the said Gates be satisfyed by ye sayd goods as they are allready prised.

It is ordered that Alice Thornberry for her offence in fighting with Ann Snoode & beating her, whereby just suspision may be had that shee did miscarry a child in the wombe of ye said Anne Snoode & caused abortion, shall receave forty stripes at the whipping post. And that the said Alice Thornbury & Anne Snoode, if they shall brake their good behavior, shall ["& uppon verdict therof"—erased] be whipt three several times in three dayes

At this Court Mrs. Alice Proctor(7) brought in the Inventory of all the goods of her husband Mr John Proctor, deceased, & delivered in the same uppon her oath, & desired a letter of Administration to [be] given unto her, w'ch was accordingly granted.

At this Court Capt. Mathewes did testify on the behalf of Mrs. Alice Procter that Dericke the Dutch Caprenter did proffer to make the one halfe of satisfaction for a wherry or such boate belonging to Mr John Procter, deceased, being left by one Garret—& the said Derricke according to the rate that had before been proffered to the said John Procter by others for ye same.

At this Court there was order given that a letter of Administration should be graunted unto Capt. Samuell Mathewes uppon ye Estat of Robert Lapworth (8) who lately died intestate or w'thout any disposall of his Estate.

It is ordered that Margaret Partin (9) the wife of Robert

(7) For John Procter and Alice his wife, see this Magazine XII, 90-92.

(8) Robert Lapworth, who came in the **Abigail**, lived at the College Land 1624-5.

(9) In 1624-5 "The Muster of Robert Partin" at West and Shirley Hundred, included himself, aged 36, who came in the **Blessing**, 1609, Margaret his wife, aged 36, who came in the **George** in 1617, and their three children, Robert, aged 4 months; Rebecca aged 2 years, and Avis, aged 5 years. Thomas Hale, one of their servants, was 20 years old and had come in the **George**, in October 1623. It would seem that the Partins were old planters of respectability and good-standing, and it is hard to understand, no matter what Hale's crime was, that the mother of three small children should receive such punishment.

Partin of Sherly Hundred for concealing the offence of Thomas Hayle lately executed, & for because she revealed not the same when it first came to her knowledge but did ernestly w'thstand that it should any wayes be made knowne, shall be whippd & receave fortye strypes

ffinis Curiae

A Court at James Citty the 4th day of July 1627, being present

S'r George Yeardley, Kn't., Governor &c
Capt. ffr. West, Mr Persey
Dr Pott, Mr Claybourne
Capt. Smyth, Capt. Tucker
Capt. Mathewes, Mr ffarrar

Bridges Freeman & James Sleight sworne & examined say that Capt. Martin by worde of mouth, did lease unto them some ground to plant at Martin Brandon & that they did covenant to pay him ye rent of two capons or two pulets & were to hold the same untill Christmas next.

At this Court Lt. Giles Allington delivered in uppon his oath an Inventorie of all the estate of Caleb Page deceased.

At this Court it was thought fitt that we should draw out partyes fro' all our plantations & goe uppon the Indians(10) &

(10) This campaign against the Indians (which it may be noted was ordered on a Fourth of July) was one of a series carried on annually for several years after the great Indian Massacre of 1622, which resulted in breaking for a time, the power of the Eastern Virginia Indians. Notices of these annual attacks are in this Magazine XIX, 116, 117, 119, 120, 122, 123. The plan of the campaign was as follows: the people of the College Land, (which included Farrar's Island, then a peninsula, but now really an island through the cutting of the Dutch Gap Canal,) and some adjacent territory in the present Henrico County, and also, probably Coxendale, and other places nearby in the present Chesterfield; and Neck of Land (the present Jones' Neck, on the south side of the river, not far below Dutch Gap) were to attack Taux (or Little) Powhatan, about the present site of Richmond. The commanders were Thomas Osborne, ancestor of the family long resident at Osborne's, Chesterfield county, and Thomas Harris, also ancestor of a large family in Chesterfield, Henrico, Cumberland, Richmond City, &c

Next below, Shirley in Charles City County, Persey's Hundred (now Flower de Hundred), Jordan's Journey (now Jordan's Point) and Chaplain's Choice, all three in the present Prince George, were to attack the Appomattox Indians, living on or near the river of that name and the Weyanokes, living in the present Prince George County. The com-

cutt downe their corne, and further that we should sett uppon them all in one day viz., the first of August next. The plantations of the Necke of land & the Colledge to goe uppon the Tanx Powhatans both the Shirley-Hundred, Jourdaines Journey, Chaplaine's Choise & Persey's Hundred uppon the Townes of ye Wlianoacks & ye Appomatucks, The Corporation of James Citty uppon ye Chicahominies & the Tappahannocs. Warwicke-River, Warrisquoiacke & Newport-Newse uppon the plantation of the Nansamundes Chesapeiacks. Commanders appointed for these services are these, viz: for Tanx Powhatan, Left Thomas Osborne in chiefe, Tho: Harris seconde. ffor Appomattuckes & ye Weianokes, Ensigne Epes & Mr Pawlet & to make choise of their seconds. ffor the Chicahominies Capt. Peirce in chiefe, Mr Harwood seconde. ffor the Tappahannas Capt West in chiefe, Mr Grendon seconde. ffor the Warisquoyacks Capt Mathewes. ffor the Nansamunds, Lt. Tho: Purfury ffor the Chesapeake Ensigne Willoby.

---

manders of this division were Francis Epes or Eppes, afterwards of the Council (some of whose numerous descendants still own land patented by him), and Thomas Pawlett, a great grandson of the first Marquis of Winchester, who was also later in the Council and was the first owner of "Westover."

The people of the Corporation of James City, which included Jamestown as its environs on the north side of the river and various settlements opposite on the south side, were to attack the Chickahominies (whose residence is indicated by their name) and the Tappahannas, living on the borders of the present Prince George and Surry. The commanders of this detachment were William Pierce (later a councillor, and the husband of John Rolfe's widow) and Thomas Harwood, later of Warwick County, where descendants of his name still live. The Commanders against the Tappahannas were Francis West, formerly Governor, a brother of Lord Delaware, and Edward Grindon.

Warwick River, on the north side of the James, and Newport News on the same side at its mouth, together with Warrisquoiacke, (around Pagan Creek, and the present Smithfield, Isle of Wight County), were to attack the Nansemonds, in the river bearing their name, and the Chesapeakes, whose land lay between the Nansemond and the ocean. The commanders here were Thomas Purefoy, later of Elizabeth City County, and Thomas Willoughby, later of Lower Norfolk County, whose family gave the name to the well-known Willoughby Spit. Each of these men were later members of the Council, and each has many descendants. Samuel Matthews, afterwards Governor, commanded against the Nansemonds. Lt Peppet, in his ship, was to lie off the present West Point at the head of York River and make a feint against the formidable Pamunkeys.

And further it is thought expedient that Left. Peppet doe goe in ye good shipp called the [Arke"-erased] Virgin into Pamunkey River & ride to put the Indians in expectation of our coming thither, whilst the aforesaid business is in doeing.

It is alsoe thought fitt that about the beginning of October next there be a sufficient number of men drawne out fro' all the plantations of the Colony to goe to Pamunkey or any other parts to take & spoile as much corne as they shall light on, & to doe what other hurt & damadge to the Indians that they may.

5th of July 1627

At this Court Mrs. Jane Martian(11) ["Bartley"-erased] delivered in an Inventory of the Estate of Left Edward Bartley, deceased, uppon her oath.

The 21th of July 1627

John Passeman sworne & examined sayth that the will of Hugh Hilton(12) dated the 3th day of April 1627, was the true will of the sayd Hugh Hilton and that he was in perfect sense & memorie at the making & the deliverie thereof.

A Court at James Citty the 13th of August 1627, present:
S'r George Yeardley, Knt., Go.
Capt. West, Capt. Mathewes
Doctor Pott, Mr Claybourne
Capt Smyth.

Wheras Alexander George, marchant, late deceased, did as it seemeth by a certain will enclosed & sealed up in a sheete of paper & left amongst his wrightings, appoint Mr Thomas Harwood & Mr Will'm Perry to be overseers of his said will & to take his estate unto their hands, the court hereuppon hath thought fitt, that accordingly the sayd Thomas Harwood &

(11) Lt. Edward Berkeley, who lived at Hog Island, was son of Sir Maurice Berkeley, and grandson of John Berkeley, formerly of Beverstone Castle, Gloucestershire, who came to Virginia in 1621 to take charge of the iron-works and was killed by the Indians in 1622. It has been known that Mrs. Jane Berkeley married, secondly, Capt. Nicholas Martian, afterwards of York County, but not that it was so soon as to be before the presentation of first husband's inventory. This use, however, of funeral baked meats, for a new wedding was common in the colonies.

(12) Hugh Hilton, aged 36 years in 1624-5, who had come in the **Edwin**, May 1619, lived at the Neck of Land in Charles City, 1624-5.

Will'm Perry doe take charge of all the whole estate of the sayd Alexander George & doe give in securitie to be accomptab e for what they shall receave.

Wheras John Hayes, Marchant, deceased about the end of May last, w'thout making any will or Testam't, or any other way disposing of his estate soe as the same remaineth uncertaine & not directly disposed of to any. The Court considering that the said John Hayes addressed himselfe & remained w'th Capt ffrancis West, hath thereuppon thought fitt to graunt the administration of the said estate unto ye said Capt. West, requiring that he doe give a sufficient bond to save the Court harme & as soone as may be to bring in a p'fect inventory of ye same.

A Court at James Citty 27th August, 1627, present:

S'r George Yeardley, Knt., Go. &c

Doctor Pott

Capt. Smyth

Mr. Claybourne

It is ordered that Robert Wright(13) sha l have 12 acres of land in the Iland of James Citty at ye place called the Labour in vaine, & that he have a Patent therof graunted unto him as a part of his divident due unto him for his personal adventure.

Wheras one John Croodeike, mariner, was in March last past unfortunately cast away in a bark about Newports Newes, & dyeing intestate & haveing divers debts of tobacco due unto [him] w'thin this Country, the Court hath ordered that Randall Smallwood shall have a Com'ission of Administration uppon ye sayd estate graunted unto him, & to ye [be?] accountable for ye same unto the widow of the said John Crookdeike in England or to any other to whom it may belonge

James Citty a Court the 3th of September 1627, present:

S'r George Yeard ey, Knt., Governor &c

Doctor Pott

Mr Secretarie

Wheras Philemon Powell, marchant, dceased about the be-

(13) At the Census of 1624-5, Robert Wright, aged 45, who had come in the Swan, 1608, Joane Wright, and two children born in Virginia, lived at Eli abeth City.

ginning of July last past, dying inestate w'thout any disposal of his goods in certaintie [?] haveing divers debts due unto him, the Court hath thought fitt to graunt ye Administration of his estate unto Edward Sharples(14), being the brother of one John Sharples in England who adventured the merchandize & wares that ye said Philemon Powell brought over into the country as is uppon good information very probably conc uded

A Court at James City the 17th of Septmb. 1627, present:
S'r George Yeardley, knt., Go. &c
Doctor Pott
Capt. Smyth
Mr Secretary

Edward Albourne of Shirley hundred sworne & examined sayth, that about the three & twentieth of June last in the morning John Throgmorton(15) being that morning near unto the woods [was] wounded and shott in ye body by th' Indians & afterwards brought into the house, being yet liveing & in perfect memorie, called for Henry Throgmorton his Cosen & tooke him by the hand & sayd Cozin I make you a freeman & all that I have is yours, but the halfe of the house & ground is Edward Albornes and afterwards, about half an hour, being desired to make his will more perfecter, he sayd he gave unto ye wife of Oliver Jenkins the service of his negar for a yere. And further he gave unto his two servants William Edes & Thomas Stent two yeares a peice of their time, And to ye old Cooper Richard

(14) Edward Sharpless, the Clerk of the Council, who was sentenced by the Va. Assembly to have his ears cut off for betraying the secrets of that body was living at Jamestown in 1623; but does not appear in the census of 1624-5. It is stated that only a piece of one ear was actually cut.

(15) At the Census of 1624-5 the muster of John Throgmorton, or Throckmorton, at West and Shirley Hundred, included himself aged 24, who had come in the **William & Thomas**, 1618; Chayne [Cheyney] Boyse, aged 26 years, who had come in the **George** in May 1617, and three servants. Henry Throckmorton apparently came later than 1624. Edward Alborn was living at Flowerdieu Hundred, 1623, but does not appear in the Census of 1624-5. It is probable that these Throckmortons were of the Gloucestershire branch of the family, for Berkeley Hundred near Shirley, had been granted to a company of closely related Gloucestershire men; Sir William Throckmorton, Richard Berkeley, George Thorpe, and John Smith, of Nibley, and a number of their friends and relatives came over.

Andrews he gave after this year all his part & share of the said Richard Andrews his services. And this deponent can say no more in this matter.

Ensigne ffrancis Epes sworne & examined sayth that being present w'th the above named John Throgmorton a little before his death, he, this deponent, desiring him to settle his estate & make a will he answered that for my estate I have allreadie disposed of it unto my kinsman Henrye Throgmorton.

James Citty 10th of Septem. 1627, present

S'r George Yeardley, knt., Go. &c

Capt. West
Doctor Pott
Capt. Smyth
Mr Secretarie

It is ordered that Mr Doctor Pott shall have the ground lyeing behind his house in James Citty together w'th the swamps & fower acres on the other side of the same added & joyned unto his former Patent of 3 acres, w'ch in all amounts unto 12 acres, & to have a patent for ye same, the totall being twelve acres, as part of his own personall divident

It is likewise ordered that Mrs Southey(16) shall have a parcel of ground graunted unto her child Henry Southey, the son of Henry Southey, deceased, who came over in ye Southampton 1622, in the garden near to James Citty adjoyning unto Mr Buck's house

Heruppon it is ordered that Mr Henry Throgmorton above sayd shall have a Com'ission for the Administration on all the estate of the above sayd John Throgmorton graunted unto him. And bring in an Inventorie of all the sayd estate at the next quarter Court & then give in bond to secure ye Court harmless.

The business of Christopher Hall's wife & Wm. Harmms fighting, beating & scolding.

---

(16) Mrs. Southey, was widow of Henry Southey, Esq., of Rimpton Somer!etshire, who died soon after coming to Virginia.

Top—Archer's Hope Creek near its mouth.
Bottom—Confederate earthworks near Archer's Hope Creek, James River in background.

Divers examinations being taken and heard concerning the unquiett life w'ch they the people of Archers Hope(17) had through the scoldings railings & fallings out w'th Amy the wife of Christopher Hall & other abominable contentions lyeing betweene them to the dishonor of God & the breach of the King's peace, the Court hath theruppon ordered that the said Amy shalbe toughed [towed] round aboard the Margaret & John & ducked three times & further that Christopher Hall, John Upton, Robert Hutt, & Will'm Harmm & Amy the wife of the said Christopher Hall & Anne the wife of ye said Robert Hitt shalbe all bound unto their good behaviour & to appear at ye Quarter Court after Christmas.

The will of John Cramnidge brought unto ye Court by Serg. Thomas Crumpe(18).

Elmer Philips & George Saunders sworne & examined doe testifie that the will of John Crannidge brought into ye Court was ye will of ye said John Crannidge & that he was in perfect sence & memory at ye making therof.

James Citty, the 8th of October 1627. At ye Court were present:

Quarter Court] S'r George Yeardley, Knt., Go. &c
Capt. ffr. West, Doctor Pott
Capt. Smyth, Mr Secretarie

It is ordered that Roger Marshall shall have a lease graunted unto him for the terme of ten yeares, of that parcell of land now by him possessed in James Citty Iland containing about eight acres & abutting betweene the lands of Mary Baulie & Thomas Passmore.

---

(17) One who has seen the quiet pine groves and the fields lying on each side of the mouth of Archer's Hope Creek (which takes its rise near Williamsburg and flows into the James), finds it hard to conceive of it as a place where neighbors quarrelled and fought. The little settlement here long ago disappeared. Archer's Hope was first selected as the place for the first settlement; but the water in front was too shoal. The bluff between the river and the creek was fortified by the Confederates and the remains of earthworks are still there. In 1876 a large gun lay close to the edge of the bluff.

(17) For Sergeant Thomas Crump, see this Magazine IV, 75.

A Court at James Citty the 9th of October 1627, present:

S'r George Yeardley, knt., Governor &c
Capt. West, Doctor Pott
Capt. Smyth, Mr Persey
Mr Secretary, Mr Farrar
Capt. Tucker

At this Court Will'm Andrewes of Accomack made petition to have one hundred acres of land granted unto him, abutting uppon ye land of Capt. Wilcox's at ye old Plantation Creeke the w'ch the Court hath condescened unto; provided that he prove that the said hundred acres to be by some meanes due unto him.

Uppon the ernest request of George Graves, it is ordered that he shall have a peice of ground in the Governor's garden behind his house there built, granted unto him.

At this Court Mr Henry Throgmorton delivered in uppon his oath an Inventory of ye estate of John Throgmorton, deceased.

(To be Continued)

PRESTON PAPESS.

(From the originals in the Virginia State Library.)

(Continued)

Col. William Davies(1) to William Preston.

ar Office, Richmond, July 15,-81.

Sir—

Agreeably to the mode of issueing military orders from governent, as directed by the last session of assembly, I have the honor to inform you that from the present situation of affairs to the Southward, it is judged necessary that you immediately put into motion one seventh part of your militia, properly officered, armed and equipt, and direct them by the nearest rout to join the army under General Greene. The present period is a time of exertion, and as the British are putting forth their whole power to have the appearance of, large possessions and great conquests in this country, against the approaching conference for a peace, there cannot be a doubt of the same animation in our parts to confine their pretensions to very narrow limits.

I beg the favor of a return of the strength of your militia, and of the cloathing collected, which I request may be put into the hands of the nearest quartermaster who will forward them—

I have the honor to be very respectfully, Sir, your most obedient Servant

William Davies

[Addressed] Montgomery [Co.]

---

(1) Col. William Davies was the head of the State Board of Was.

Letter from Col. William Davies.

War Office, July 17th 1781

Sir—

I had the honor to communicate to you two days ago an order from the Executive requiring that one seventh part of your militia should be put in motion to proceed to the support of General Greene. Since that time government have judged it expedient to enlarge the number called for. I have it therefore in command from his Excellency the Governor in council to require from your county one fourth part of the militia properly officered, armed and equipt to march to join the Southern army, and to serve their tours of two months, to be computed from the time of their joining it.

Government makes these calls with great reluctance, but the importance of the occasion and the consequences which may attend at the negociations for peace, should stimulate to every exertion. The men destined for the Southward are not to wait till the previous return of those with the Marquis, who will be. discharged without a relief as soon as their two months are out The Law, I understand, has, by an act of the last session made a difference between the pay of those serving in the State and those that march out of it; the former being paid from the time of joining the Army only, but the latter from the time their march begins. I hope this will be some encouragement—

I have the honor to be with great respect

Your most humble Servt

William Davies

(Address) Montgomery, formerly Fincastle

[Endorsement] Col'o Davies Letter

July 1781

Governor Nelson to William Preston.

Richmond 19th July 1781

Sir:

The great superiority of the enemy to the Southward making it necessary to send a Reinforcement to Gen. Greene; Col.

Davies the commissioner of the War Office has orders from the Executive to write to the Lieutenants of the different counties that are to send the Reinforcement. I cannot however forbear requesting that you will interest yourself in a very particular manner with the Militia of your County whose tour it may be to go on this service—Vigorous exertions this campaign will ensure to America what she has been contending for. Our affairs in that quarter look with a pleasing aspect. General Greene has nearly recovered the Southern States, and only wants proper support to finish the campaign with that glory which his extraordinary Conduct & unparell'd perseverance merit.

I am Sir

Y[r] Mo Ob Ser[t]

Thos. Nelson Jr.

Montgomery—

[Endorsement]

Governor Nelson's Letter

19 July 1781

COL. DAVIES TO COL. PRESTON.

War Office July 29, 1781

Sir,

The present situation of the six months men is a matter of serious moment to the public interest, and has a direct tendency totally to destroy, on the part of the militia, all opposition against the ravages of a cruel enemy who avail themselves of every neglect of ours to accomplish the subjugation of this country. The mode of punishment directed by law for delinquencies is undoubtedly a wise one, and is calculated as much for the immediate defence and benefit of the State as for the reformation of the culprits themselves. From a fatal mismanagement in some counties however, it has a directly contrary effect, and instead of adding to our military force, actually weakens it and proves rather an exemption from duty altogether than an obligation to render longer service.

It is difficult to account upon what principle this mischief has been tolerated; it will be ruinous however, if not immediately checked. When a delinquent is condemned to be a six months soldier, he is struck off the militia roll; nobody takes the trouble or thinks it his duty to deliver him to the army; neither Government nor the army know anything of him or of his condemnation, and thus he continues, contrary to every kind of justice, in quiet repose at home, and not only contributes nothing towards the defence of the country, but does essential injury to it, by his example, his conversation, and the toleration he receives. It is the wish of Government, therefore, that an immediate return be made to this office of all your delinquents, and that you employ a sufficient number of your militia for the express purpose of apprehending them, that an end, if possible, may be had to such unjust and dangerous indulgencies. By a law of the last session of assembly any persons apprehending a Deserter and producing a receipt from a field officer of the line of service to which the Deserter belongs, whether continental state or militia, is intitled to an exemption from a tour of militia duty. I hope this will be some encouragement. Posts are established at New London and Staunton where they will be received and incorporated by proper officers.

I am, your most humble Servt

William Davies

Endorsement]

Col'o Davies, July 1781 with form of Returns

BENJAMIN HARRISON TO WILLIAM PRESTON.

In Council, July 23^{d}, 1782.

Sir

I thank you for the trouble you have taken in calling together the Officers of your County and Washington and regulating the militia ordered for their defence. The plan is approved & I hope will answer my expectation & keep the Counties force from the inroads of the Indians.

It is some surprise to me that Col'o Campbell should object to the militia of both Counties being under your command, the proposal came from himself that the person should command but nothing less than his being the man would content him. I shall write to him directing him to conform to the arrangement.

I am

Your most obedient

Humble Servant

Benj. Harrison

Col'o William Preston

[Address] On public service—Colo. William Preston

Benj. Harrison Montgomery

[Endorsement] Order of Council 23 July 1782

WILLIAM DAVIES TO WILLIAM PRESTON.

War Office Aug[t] 1st 1781

Sir,

From the movements of the enemy which have taken place since I had the honor to communicate to you the orders of the Executive of the last month, it has become expedient to suspend the execution of them, so far as relates to the march of your militia to the aid of General Greene. It is, however, necessary that your militia hold themselves in constant readiness to move on the shortest notice when called for. In the meantime, it is not expected you will send any relief to the army under the Marquis, as those who are now with him will be discharged of course, when their times are out.

I must beg your assistance to have the arms and accoutrements of your County put in the best order, and that you will be kind enough to make an exact return, agreeably to the enclosed form.

I have the honor to be

Your most obed. Serv[t]

William Davies

[Endorsement] Col'o Davies Letter Aug. 1-1781 demands returns

William Preston to Governor Harrison.

Montgomery March 15th 1782

Sir

A Letter from Col. Davies Commissioner of the War Office dated the 30th of Jan'y last came to hand about the 15th of Feb'y making a Requisition of the men raised in this County under an act of assembly passed in Octr 1780 for raising this States Quota of Troops to serve in the Continental Army. In April 1781 I had the County laid off into Districts agreeable to that Law & by the first of August the Thirty Eight men called fore from this County were either Recruited or draughted. The Commissioners of the Law not having money to pay the Bounty, the Recruits got Furloughs and the Execution of the Act being suspended the Business remained so untill the Rec^{t} of the above Letter. As many as had not deserted were called together, but as they had not rec^{d}d their Bounty I could not have them marched. I then moved the Court in presence of two of the Commissioners, to levey a sum in specie for that Purpose but the motion was rejected as you will see by the enclosed copy. The Recruits got Furloughs a second time untill I can resceive your Excellency's Instructions herein, which I earnestly beg, as I am altogether at a loss what further steps to take in this matter. I have with much trouble and fatigue endeavour'd to carry this act into Execution and I am apprehensive to little purpose as there is reason to doubt that most of the men will desert before anything effectual can be done.

I would beg leave to lay before your Excellency a Recommendation of field officers in one of the Battalions, which was occasioned by the Resignation of Coll. Ingles whose Infirmities prevented him from serving longer.—I would also entreat your Excellency and the Hon'ble the Council to take into consideration the recommendation of proper Persons to be added to the Commission of the Peace. Such an addition will be extremely useful for keeping good order in this frontier county to which many disorderly People Resort from different parts of this State as well as the Southern States.

I would be much obliged to your Excellency to direct the Commʳ of the War Office to supply me with twenty blank Commissions for Militia Officers, as those he sent me in Jan'y are mostly given out.

I am your Excellency's most Obedᵗ & very h'ble Servᵗ

Wm. Preston

[Address] Public Service to His Excellency

Benjamin Harrison—Governor of Virginia

[Endorsement] Copy of a Letter to the Govʳ March 15ᵗʰ 1782

Col. Davies to Col. Preston.

Colonel William Preston,
County Lieutenant
Montgomery
War Office—

Sir

War Office Apr: 5. 1782
Came to hand the 25ᵗʰ

Yours of the 15ᵗʰ of last month was sent to this office by his Excellency the Governor. Notwithstanding the frequent applications which have been made to various parts of the country for information how far the draft law had been executed; yet we were frequently unable to get the necessary intelligence, from the miscarriage of letters and other accidents. I never knew your county had drafted, till I saw your letter to the Governor, and we must delay the matter till the Assembly meets, unless, indeed, the men are willing to join the army and wait till we can send the money to them, ascertained according to the seale of depreciation.

I have never yet been favoured with a return of the cloathing from your county. I wish some method could be devised to forward them to New London safely packed up and directed to the care of Mʳ Harry Innis.

I have filled up the blank commissions for your field officers. If I can get any more properly authenticated before Mr.

Latham gets off I will send them, tho' the number constantly called for thro' the country would really astonish you: one would think the officers were all deserting the Service of their country, or that an uncommon mortality raged among them.

I have the honor to be with
sincere respect
Your most humble ſerv[t]
William Davies

[Address] Colonel William Preston
County Lieutenant
War Office Montgomery

The Officers commanding & belonging to the Regiment of Militia from Montgomery County in Virginia beg leave to return thanks in behalf of themselves & the soldiers under their Command, to Mr. Bagge & the other Gentlemen & Inhabitants of the Town of Salem, for their polite Behaviour, the hospitable manner in which they received & treated the Troops, & the inconvenience to which they put themselves, to entertain them & to make their stay one night comfortable—

Signed—by order
Wm. Preston

(To be Continued)

VIRGINIA IN 1682.

(Abstracts from Sainsbhry Papers, and Copies from McDonald and De Jarnette Papers, Virginia State Library. From the Originals in the British Public Record Office.)

(Continued)

SIR HENRY CHLCHLEY TO THE KING.

May it please Your Exc^{t} Ma'ty

About a week agoe there happened a strange Insurrection (1) in the heart of this Your Maties Country of which I beseech Your Ma'ty to permit me as in duty bound to give this short account That the people of Gloucester have cut up their own and others growing Tobacco near two hundred Plantations as I am credibly informed to the great prejudice of many Loyal Inhabitants and noe small detriment to Your Maties Interest, there being a great river and about fifty miles of ground between them and mee they committed their outrages three days before ye least intimation of their proceedings at James Citty where I then was with Your Maties Council at a General Court, and about four days before, had prorogued an Assembly which was called and ready to sit before the arrival of Your Maties Commands to the contrary. I presedtly dispatcht Coll. Kemp(2) with orders to raise Foot and Horse forthwith to suppress them by force of Arms which hee effectually executed (with what haste he could) upon the first party hee met is still id quest of the rest, hobe success and humbly beg Your Maties good opinion that my best endeavours shall not be wanting, suppose the Burgesses big with the thoughts of a Cessation and being unexpectedly yet necessarily prorogued by Your Maties Command have blown this coal which hath inflamed the people,

(1) This was the "Plant Cutting" when many Colonists, in desparation at the low price of tobacco, attempted to increase the value by destroying a large part of the growing crop. Much has been published in former numbers of this Magazine in regard to this matter. Sir Henry Chichely was then Lieutenant and Acting Governor.

(2) Col. Matthew Kemp, of Gloucester County.

have wrot at large to Mr. Sec'ty Jenkins. Shall not trouble Your Ma[ties] farther at present but to beg your pardon and your gracious acceptadce of my prayer, That it would please God to protect and bless Your Ma'ty forever Your Ma[ties] most obedient subject and servant Hen. Chichley.
From Middle Plantation May y[e] 8th 1682
[Endorsed] Rec'd 14th June 1682

Sir Henry Chichley to Secretary Jenkins

Right Hon'ble

I am heartily sorry I have occasion to give you so speedy an account of this Country's estate, the people of our County of Gloucester having last week in a tumultuous manner cut of half the Tobacco plants among them some whereof voluntarily destroyed their own and then joined forces and in several parties to the number of twenty or more maugre opposition by the Planters that owned them cut of all plants wherever they came. They had begun three or four days before I had notice of it, being then at a General Court at James Citty, immediately I issued out my Proclamation to that County and soon after to all others to stop their proceedings seconded with a Commission to Coll. Kemp, one of the Council here, to suppress them by force, which with all possible haste hee effectually put in execution taking two and twenty of them in the fact, all w'ch except two more violent and incorrigible than the rest immediately submitted, begged pardon and promised amendment and were dismissed home The two before mentioned were remitted to mee and the Council at James Citty and are now in safe custody I hope my endeavours which shall not be wanting may quench this growing flame. Of the further progress and total quelling of it I shall give Your Honor speedy notice by a ship that I expect will sail ten days hence. The probable occasion as farr as I can yet see of this commotion is briefly thus The Lord Culpeper adjourning the Assembly after w'ch was prorogued till Jan. the last, And the next month Mr. Nat. Bacon(3) by letter to me reciting part of his Lo'ps letter the purport whereof was that an

(3) Nathanial Bacon, Sr.

Assembly should be called some time last month, by which time it was hoped his Lo'p would arrive here and myselfe having not received a sillible to that time from any Publick Minister nor indeed till neer the middle of April about which time Capt. Jeffries arrived with pay for the Soldiers: The beginning of March I issued out Writs for the convening the Assembly I fear unhappily because when I received His Maties Commande not to call them to sit some of them were then on their way to James City and by consequences too late to prorogue them untill met and they big with expectation to enact a Cessation, by the most but not the wisest thought the only expedient to advance the price of Tobacco and being advised by the Council to propose to the House of Burgesses whether they would continue His Maties Soldiers on the Country's pay before their prorogation according to the tenor of His Maties letter by strange pretence they delayed for fower days their answer as will appear by their Journal and ours to bee remitted you by the Secretary here to whom I further referr you at present. They were prorogued with unanimous advice of the Council till the 10th of November next in obedience to His Majesties Command. But before their prorogation, as I since understand, they voted their Journal should be publickly read by their Burgesses when thhe got home to their respective Counties upon the perusal of which it will be easy for Your Honor to observe how the people came inflamed and the Soldiers by abridgement of their pay and some delay occasioned by my necessary presence at the General Court being apter to mutiny than to serve His Matie here, must of necessity in this juncture of time bee with all expeditione disbanded cannot as yet see the bottom nor discover who are chiefly concerned in this tumult nor indeed what will be the issue

It hath an ill face in many respects I can only say for myself your Honor may bee assured I shall manifest my allegiance upon all occasions, submit the whole matter to your prudent consideration and depend upon your generosity for all the just favor can bee shown to Right Hon'ble Your Honor most fatihful & obedient servant Hen. Chichley

Middle Plantation [Endorsed] Rec'd 15 June 1682

May 8th 1682—

NICHOLAS SPENCER(4) TO SECRETARY JENKINS

James Citty May 8th 1682

Right Hon'ble

I have not of late presumed to trouble your Honor with my letters and doe most heartily wish had other matter to signify to Your Honor than the substance of this letter for know the contents will bee as unwelcome to Your Honor as they are grievous to mee to write being now to tell Your Honor the quiet and peace of this His Ma'tye Colonie is not only hazarded by unruly and tumultuous persons but is at present under such sufferings, by a combination of many inhabitants in Gloucester County entering into a resolution to force a Law by their wills that noe Tobacco should be this year planted, the which readily to effect on the first of this month began their evil undertakings First with cutting up their own plants and soe proceeded from plantation to plantation using a forcible way of persuasion by telling the Masters of Plantations where they came if not willing to have their plants cut up they would create a willingness in them by force, and in an hours time destroy as many plants as would well have employed twenty men a summer's tendance to have perfected. These outrages were in progress over three days before the Lieut Governor had any intimation thereof himselfe and the Council being then at James Citty holding the General Court as soon as received advice thereof issued forth-Proclamations whereby to restrain such Riots, tumult, outrages and violences the which to make effectual dispatched Coll. Kemp a worthy gentleman of the Council and Commander of Gloucester Militia with orders to raise such members of the militia Horse and Foot as might be effectual to suppress and reduce the Mutineers whom with his Horse hee surrounded and took every man of them in the very act of destroying of Plants. Two of the principal and incorrigible rogues are committed, the rest submitting and giving assurances of their quiet and peaceable demeanour and behaviour were remitted, hope by this time other parties of the Mutineers may be reduced tho its to be feared the contagion will spread. This day have re-

(4) Nicholas Spencer, Secretary of State.

ceived intelligence that the next adjacent county being New Kent was lately tooke forth committing the like spoyls on plants as in Gloucester County the which to suppress is the like care taken by way of the Militia Horse and Foot or soe many them as may, in this juncture, be admitted to arms. And least the infection should grow, general orders are gone forth to the Commanders of the Militia of each County to provide a party of Horse to be in continual motion, by which vigilancy are in some hopes the growth of these Insurrections and Outrages may be prevented and in it should not write doubtfully did I not know the necessities of the Inhabitants to bee such by their own Commodity Tobacco, soe now sunk to nothing that their low estate makes them desperate and resolve a Law of Cessation of their own making if goe forward the only destroying Tobacco Plants will not satiate their fits to be feared rebellious appetites which if increase and find the strength of their own Arms will not bound themselves.

To add to this unexpected evil His Ma[ties] Soldiers being two companies and just upon the point of disbanding and sensible His Ma[ties] hath been pleased to Command their disbanding on the first of April and noe pay appointed after that day, are so far from being serviceable in this ruly time of assistance from them since their arrival, that their mutinous temper double our apprehensions of evil events. Had not the Ship on which was loaded the Soldiers money been long wind bound and on her passage beyond usual time His Ma[ties] Soldiers had been paid off before these present commotions hapined, the Soldiers' quarters are now accounting for and the Soldiers and Landlords will day after day bee paid off and the Soldiers disbanded and the Country freed of the mischiefs which may be from their mutinous demeanors.

His Ma'ty was pleased to command the disbanding of the two companies if the country would not continue them on the public charge. The Assembly met in five days after the arrival of those His Ma[ties] commande being by writ from the Lieut. Governor Sir Henry Chichley soe appointed near forty days before the arrival of the Ship Concord; by which ship His Ma'ty was likewise pleased to signify His Royal will and Pleasure that noe Assembly should be held or permitted to sit until the 10th of November next, by which time His Excie the Lord Culpeper would be remanded to this his Government by whom His Ma'ty would be pleased to signify his Royal Will and Pleasure to the last addresses of the General Assembly, and that his Lods arrival will be in time for an Assembly the said 10th of November. The Assembly convened by the Lieut Governor being met hee communicated to the Council His Maties commands both as to the disbanding the Soldiers unless continued at the Countrys charge and likewise His Maties Commande that noe Assembly should sit until the tenth of November to both of which that the Council according to their duty might pay and yield all due obedience were of the opinion the Assembly being met tho convened without the advice or consent of any one member of the Council yet should be permitted to set only to advise whether to continue the guards at the Country's charge or not in which proposition the House of Burgesses seemed to spend some days without any other answer then desiring from day to day time to resolve being a point in which to gain time to carry on other imaginations, the principal part of which was a cessation, for which as the assembly was called peculiarly by the unfortunate motions of the over-active clerk of the House of Burgesses Major Robert Beverley soe his influence was noe less in the House when convened. The continuance of the Assembly not being agreeable to His Maties Commande they were prorogued on the twenty seaventh of April to the 10th of November by which prorogation the selfish purposes of some persons were frustrated, most particularly the Clerk of the House of Burgesses who to accomplish his designes of noe Tobacco this year to be planted to advance those great quantities of Tobacco now on his hands has instilled into the multitude as it is vehemently suspected, to justify the right of making a cessation by cutting up of plants; soe that the ground and rise of our present troubles and disorders is from the ill-timed Assembly.

Sir: About ten days hence will sail other ships by them shall be able to speak more positively to our Commotions than at present therefore will now beg leave to close with subscribing Rt Hon'ble Your Honor's most faithful and obedient Servant

Nicho: Spencer

[Endorsed] Rec'd 14 June 1682

REPORT ABOUT COMMOTION IN VIRGINIA.

May it please Yo^{r} Matie

Wee have read three letters from Virginia dated the 8th of May last one being from Sir Henry Chichley Lieut^{t} Govern or of that Colonie to Yo^{r} Matie another from him to the Right Hono'ble Mr. Secretary Jenkins, whereby wee are given to understand that Sir Henry Chicheley having called an Assembly before the receipt of Yo^{r} Mat^{ies} letter forbidding him tocall an Assembly or permit them to sitt without the consent of seaven of the Council, Hee had accordingly with the advice and consent of the said Council permitted them to sit several days pursuant to the directions he had received; during which time they had made divers motions, addresses and speeches tending to Sedition and raising disorders in the Government by a specious pretence of improving the Trade of Tobacco by procuring a cessation from planting and by fomenting other apprehensions which had formerly been a chief occasion of the late Rebellion. After which the Assembly having been prorogued in pursuance of Your Ma'tys commands to the 10th of November next and their Journal having been published throughout the Colony by their order several tumultuous and disorderly people were met together in Gloucester County and had cut up and destroyed the growing Tobacco of neer two Hundred Plantations which riot had noe sooner been supprest by the Militia but another broke out in the next adjacent County of New Kent committing the same spoils on Plants as in Gloucester County. Whereupon the like orders had been given to the Militia or soe many of them as in this juncture might be admitted to take arms for the hindering the further growth and evil consequences of this Insurrection which is very much apprehended by reason of the present necessities and desperate condition of the Inhabitants And wee are further by those letters informed that Robert Beverley, Clerk of the Assembly had not only very much influenced the House of Burgesses in their seditious motions before they were prorogued but had afterwards alsoe ,as it was vehemently suspected, instilled into the multitude the violent means of effecting their end of a cessation by cutting up the growing Tobacco Upon consideration of all which particulars Wee are humbly of opinion that the Lord Culpeper Your Mat[ies] Governor in Chief of Virginia may receive your directions to repair to his Government with all possible speed, in order to find out, by the strictest enquiry, the abettorr and instruments of this commotion, and to put a stop to the further progress of it And that to this end the Frigat intended for Jamaica may bee immediately fitted out for the carrying him to Virginia his Lo'p having declared himself ready to goe thither in case of exigency within a weeks time after notice given him.

And since by the several relations wee have received this Insurrection appears to have been promoted and carried on to the great disturbance of the publick peace of the Colony. Wet cannot but offer our humble advice to Your Ma'ty that soms person who shall be found most faulty may be forthwith pune ished, to the end the dignity of the Government may be pree served and all evil minded men deterred from the like attempt for the future. After which and not before the Governmen- may be directed to consider of and propose with the advice of the Council or Assembly as he shall think fit some temperament in relation to planting of Tobacco and raising the price of that commodity And forasmuch as Robert Beverley Clerk of the Assembly is represented to have been a chief promoter of these disorders Wee humbly offer that the former Instructions given to the Lord Culpeper for the putting him out of all imployment and places of trust may be renewed and forthwith put in execution. Lastly wee take leave humbly to move Your Ma'ty that as there are divers quantities of Your Ma'tys Stores remaining in Virginia which had been sent thither during the late Rebellion Your Ma'ty would be pleased to direct the Lord Culpeper to sell upon his arrival, all such Stores as the Country will buy and to secure the rest for your Ma[ties] service.

All w'ch Etc

Whitehall

14 June 1682

ORDERS ABOUT THE CONDITIONS AT VIRGINIA.

At the Court at White Hall the 17th of June 1682
Present
The King's most Excellent Matie in Council

Whereas the Right Hon'ble the Lords of the Committee for Trade and Plantations did by their Report this day read at the Board humbly represent That by three letters from Virginia dated the 8th of May last one being from Sir Henry Chicheley Lieutt Governor of that Colony to his Ma'ty, another from him to Mr. Sec'ty Jenkins and one from Mr. Nicholas Spencer of Virginia ro Mr. Sec'ry Jenkins they are given to understand That Sir Henry Chicheley having called an Assembly before the receipt of His Mat'ys letter forbidding him to call an Assembly or permit them to sit without the consent of seaven of the council hee had accordingly with the advice and consent of the said council permitted them to sit several days pursuant to the directions he had received during which time they had made divers motions , addresses and speeches tending to Sedition and raising disorders in the Government by a specious pretence of improving the Loade of Tobacco by procuring a cessation from planting and by fomenting the apprehensions which had formerly been a Chief occasion of the late Rebellion. After which the Assembly having been prorogued in pursuance of His Ma'tys commands to the tenth of November next and their Journal having been published throughout the Colony by their order, seferal tumultuous and disorderly people were met together in Gloucester County and had cut up and destroyed the growing Tobacco of near 200 plantations which riot had no sooner been supprest by the Militia but another tooke out in the next adjacent county of New Kent committing the same spoils on Plants as in Gloucester County whereupon the like orders had been given to the Militia or soe many of them as at this Juncture might bee admitted to take Arms for the hindring the further growth and evil consequedces of this Insurrection which is very much apprehended by reason of the present necessities and desperate condition of the Inhabitants.

And that their Lo'ps were further informed by those letters that Robert Beverley, Clerk of the Assembly had not only very much influenced the House of Burgesses in their Seditious motions before they were prorogued but had also, as it was vehemently suspected, instilled into the multitude the violent means of effecting their end of a cessation by cutting up the growing Tobacco. And their Lo'hs having humbly offered it as their opinion that the Lord Culpeper His Ma'ties Governor of Virginia may receive directions to repair to his Government with all possible speed in order to find out by the strictest inquiry the abettorr and Instruments of this Commotion and to put a stop to the further progress of it—His Ma'ty upon consideration thereof was this day pleased to order and command that the Lord Culpeper doe imbarque himself on such of His Ma'ties Frigates as shall be provided for his Transportation to Virginia by the first of August next—And in the meantime that his Lo'p doe prepare himselfe as to be in readiness to goe on board within a week stime after notice in case of any sudden emergency. And their Lo'ps further representing that by the Several relations they had received, this Insurrection appears to have been promoted and carried on to the great disturbance of the Publick Peace of the Colonie.

It was thereupon likewise ordered by His Mat'y in Council according to their Lo'ps advice in this particular That the said Governor doe cause some of the persons who shall bee found most faulty to bee forthwith proceeded against and punished to the end the Dignity of the Government may bee preserved and all evil-minded men bee deterred from ye like attempts for the future. After which and not before the said Governor is hereby Ordered and directed to consider of and propose with the advice of the Council or Assembly as he shall think fit some temperament in relation to the planting of Tobacco and raising the price of that Commodity. And as to Robert Beverley, Clerk of the Assembly who is represented to have been the chief promotor of those disorders it was ordered by His Ma'ty in Council That the Lord Culpeper according to former instructions in that behalf, doe at his arrival cause the said

Beverley to be immediately put out of all employment and places of Trust within the said Colony.

And lastly it is ordered by His Matie in Council upon th Report of the said Lords Committees That the said Lord Culpeper doe upon his arrival give directions for selling such quantities of His Maties Stores that had been sent thither during the late Rebellion as the Country will buy and secure the remainder for His Maties Service.

(To be Continued)

VIRGINIA GLEANINGS IN ENGLAND.

(Contributed by Reginald M. Glencross, 176 Worple Road, Wimfleden, S. W., 19, London, England.)

JOHN BANNISTER, the younger [no place]*
*[no Act bk for 1650]

Dated 4 May 1650. Proved 24 Oct. 1650.
Admon. 19 Dec. 1655.

"Deare Uncle I shall desire you to give these freindes of mine, these small legacies:" To my Cozens, your daughters, 20s. each. To Mr. ARCHBOLD and his wife, 20s. each. To Mr. DEE and his wife, 20s. each. To my cosen, PEASE, 10s. To my cosen BANISTER, 10s. more. To my friend Mr. DELAWNE, the apothecary, 10s. To my friend Mr. SMITH, Haberdasher, 10s. To my friend MATHEW WOOD at my Uncle STANLYES, 10s. To my fellow servant JOANE KIDDER, 10s. To the Pensions of this parish, 40s. To my cozen THOMAS BROCKETT, 10s.

All the residue, unto my uncle desyring him to see that my mother doth not want and that she may continue with my friend Mrs. ARCHBOLD, till her senses be restored again.

I declare this to be my will of I dye before I return into England again.

To my Uncle fowrescore two hundred acres of my land in the Barbadoes, to return to my uncle BANISTER or his heires after his decease.

JERIMIE BUSHER, FRANCIS WHEATELY: Witnesses.

Memorandum that the Testator after the sealing of his will appointed his Uncle JOHN BANISTER his executor.

FRANCIS WHEATLY, JERIMY BUSHER: Witnesses.

Proved 24 Dec. 1650 by the sole executor named.

19 Dec. 1655.
Administration granted to MARY CROSSMAN als BANISTER and MARGARET BANISTER, daughters and executrixes of JOHN BANNISTER, the elder, sole Executor named in this will, to administer the goods etc., of JOHN BANISTER, the younger, deceased, the said JOHN BANNISTER the elder having died. **153 PEMBROKE.**

[John Banister, the naturalist, had travelled in the West Indies before coming to Virginia. He was in Virginia as early as 1678 and died in 1692. A John Banister patented land in Gloucester County in 1653 and Mrs. Elizabeth Banister had grant in the same county in 1679. In the grant a reference is made to her son John Banister, and her deceased husband John Banister. In the fragmentary records of Charles City County, under date, April 9, 1661, in a statement that James Wallis had married the widow of Lieut. John Banister. The testator above may have come from the same English family.]

THOMAS BROADNIX of Ospringe, co. Kent. Gentleman.
Dated 6 Dec. 1650. Adm. 8 Dec. 1654.
To MARY, the now wife of JAMES HAYLES, and to his heirs for ever, my lands called Newes, lying in Burshmosh Parish, near Dym Church, co. Kent, containing, 40 acres, now in the occupation of WILLIAM BRETT of Brensent.
To MARY BRADNIXE, my lands lying in Stirry, co. Kent, and to hir heires for ever, now in the occupation of THOMAS JENNINGS.
To THOMAS BRADNEXE, my kinsman, brother to the said MARY BRADNEXE, my lands lying in Snave Parish in Rushidg Parish and Alstone in Romney Marsh, and to his heirs forever.
To HENRY BRADNEX, my brother in law, £5.
To THOMAS BRADNIXE, the sonne of ANTHONIE BRADNEXE, deceased, £10.
To the poor of the several parishes where my lands lie, £20.
To EDWARD HALES of Faversham, gentleman, brtoher to the said JAMES HAYLES, £20.
To JAMES HALES, and to his heirs for ever, my house and land lying on the parish of Rushidg also one other house with 44 acres of land lying in Bethersden, co. Kent in the occupation of JOHN FARMER.
Sole Executor:—the said JAMES HALES.
EDWARD HALES, SAMPSON KENNETT: Witnesses.
8 Dec. 1654.

Administration to THOMAS BRADNAXE the nephew and legatarie named, JAMES HALES, the executor named being renounced. **410 ALCHIN.**

[This Thomas Brodnix does not appear in the Brodnax pedigree in Berry's **Kentish Genealogies.** Many of the lines are, however, not fully carried down. As is well known, the Virginia line traces to John and Dorothy Brodnax, who appear in Berry's pedigree.]

JOHN COLLYER of Lendon, marchant and Cloathworker. Will 18 December 1649; proved 8 January 1649-50. To be buried in Church or Churchyard of Beddington in Surrey. One third of estate to wife Regina Collyer, one third to my heire Charles Collyer and other third as follows: I forgive my brother Isaack Collyer £500 lent him. To my nephew Isaack Collyer Junior £250, part to set him apprentice. To my mother in law Mrs Anna Senuliano £50. To her daughter my sister in law Mrs Anna Maria £200. To Brother in law Vincentio Malo £200 and what he owes mee upon accompt for charges pictures bought or otherwise only for diet I reckon nothing. To Brother John Knight my interest in the house he now inhabits in Marklane and to my sister Mary his wife £20. To my couzens William and Mary Jurner I forgive twenty five. pounds of what they owe me. To Henry Swift £15. To Mr. Job Throgmorton £50. To poor of Beddington £10. To poor of London £20. To Edward Denny £20. To William Jolliffe I restore of what I had with him £100. Executors: Mr. Job Throgmorton, Brother Isaac Collyer, Wife Regina. My son to be brought up in the English learning and Protestant faith, if my wife leaves England he is not to go with her except with consent of my other two executors. Made in the Hamlet of Wallington in Surrey 18 December 1649 in presence of John Heather, William Blacke. Proved by all executors. **3 PEMBROKE.**

[Edward Lockey, formerly of Virginia, died, without issue, in the parish of St. Catherine Cree Church, London. in 1667. He left a considerable part of his estate in Virginia to his "cousin" Isaac Collier, Jr., son of Isaac Collier. In 1671, Isaac Collier, Jr. was deceased. The inventory of Isaac Collier was recorded in Elizabeth City county in 1675, and the will of Isaac Collier, Sr., proved in York, May 24, 1688. He named his wife Mary and children Charles, Abraham, Thomas and Sarah It would seem from the names that the York county Colliers were of the same family as the testator was. The clue is sufficiently good to deserve further investigation. See **William & Mary Quarterly**, Vols. VII and VIII for notices of the Colliers.]

WILLIAM FARNFOLDE, in the parish of Steaning, in the Countie of Sussex, gent.

Dated 7 Aug. 1610. Proved 8 Nov. 1610.
To the poore of the parish of Steaninge, 40s. To the Churche of Steaninge, 10s. To the Churche of Chichester, iijs. iiijd. To Mr. WILLIAM FARNFOLD, my godsonne, £20. To ANTHONY FARNFOLD, my kynsman, £10. To DOROTHIE FARNFOLD, my brother ANTHONYES daughter, £5. *To SUZAN FANRFOLD, £5. *To MAGDALENE FARNFOLD, £5. *To JOHN FARNFOLD, £5. "Children of Mr. ANTHONY FARNFOLD." To everie one of my sister HARPENYES Children £4 a peece. To ' the sixe of the Youngest" of my brother RICHARDE FARNFOLDS Children, 40s. a peece. To my brother BYNWYNS five daughters, 40s. a peece. To all Sir EDWARDE COLPEPERS Children, 20s. a peece. To my foure sisters a peece of goulde of 20s. a peece. To my "sister ANTHONYES wief [sic], a peece of 20s. To Sir EDWARDE COLPEPER, my baye Gueldinge. To my brother BYNWYN, two Corsletts and Halberds. To ANTHONY FARNFOLD and his heires, one house and barn and all my Lands called Wollies lyeing in the parish of Ashhurst. Residuary Legatee and Sole Executor, my brother ANTHONY FARNFOLD.
WILLIAM FAGGER, WILLIAM BYNWYN: Witnesses.
*All given as separate Items.
Mem of Debts due to me:
of THOMAS TAILO of Steanynge, £7., of HENRY COXE, als Greeneslade, 45s., of Sir EDWARDE BELLINHAM, £20. "Witness of it": JOHN FORDE, PETER SHELLEY and RICHARD FARNFOLD.
of Mr. Doctor TYCHBOURNE, 53s. 4d., of WILLIAM HEATH of Petworthe, £4.
Proved 8 Nov. 1610 by the Sole Executor named. **93 WINGFIELD.**

[In Vol. XXII, p. 399 &c., of this Magazine, wes published the will of Sir Thomas Farnefold, of Gatewicks in Steyning, Sussex, whose son, Rev. John Farnefold, came to Virginia.]

John Gryme of Ightham, county Kent, clearke. Will 21 August 1643; proved 22 March 1644-5. I give my body to be buried in the chancell of Ightham, as neere as possible may be to the body of my late deare wife. I give to the poore of Ightham and of Raynham 20s to each parish, to be distributed among them on the day of my buriall or within one month after my decease. To Mrs. Jane James of Ightham, widdowe, the same ring which was given my be her late husband and my very good patron as the best token I am able to leave her of that thankfulness and dutifull respect which I owe to her and hers. In case she shall depart this life before me, I give the same ringe to Mrs. Anne James, her daughter in law, the wife of Mr. William James, esquire. I bequeath to the said William James Sa;azar one the proverbes, or any other booke (not hereby bequeathed) which he pleaseth to make choyse of out of my library To each of my servantes that hath remained with me the space of one whole yeare and shall remaine soe at the tyme of my decease 10s. To my son Charles Gryme £10 and my tenement called Tibbs, houlden of the manor of Ightham. To my daughter Elizabeth Gryme £50 and Cooper's workes. To my daughter Sara Dawlinge, Smythes workes in two volumes, and my lease taken of Mr. Gossage planted with young trees, adjoining to my tenement bought of Henrie Shoebridge, during her life. After her decease the same shall be annexed to m said tenement. I give her more the use of all the goods, plate and household stuff that were her husband's during her life, she paying 40s. yearly to my executrix towards the education of her daughter Sarah Dawlinge. To my neece Sarah Dawling £10 at 21, and all the said goods that were her father's (by him made over to me by deed of gift) after the decease of her mother. To every of my three daughters (Elizabeth, Anne and Sarah) one bedstead, feather bed and boulster, with all the bedding thereto belonging, the eldest chosing her bed first, the second next and the third last, as they are in age. All the rest of my goods I give to my daughter Ann Gryme, whom I ordain my executrix. And I entreat my loveing cosens William Duckett of Grayes Inne, esquire, Henry Gryme of Charterhouse lane, London, and Richard Bowles, clearke, to be overseers of this my will, to each of whom I bequeath a ringe of 20s price to be bought by mine executrix. As touching my landes, I give to my said daughter Anne two parcells called Downes, containing by estimation 18 acres, with two salt marshes to the same adjoyninge sometimes called Cockell Marsh and Snares Marsh and Downes Marsh all in the parish of Stooke in the Hundred of Hood, county Lent lately purchased by me of George Wilkins late of Stooke aforesaid, gentleman, to hold to the said Anne and the heirs of her body, failing whom to my son Clarke [Charles?] Gryme. To my said overseers I bequeath all that messuage and 3 parcels of land (containing by estimation 7 acres) lying in Igtham aforesaid and lately purchased of Henry Shoebridge deceased, and two parcels of land enclosed called Brownes and Dynes in Ightham aforesaid heretofore purchased by me of William Ferry deceased and others, during the joint lives of Ralph Dawlinge gentleman, and Sarah his wife, my daughter, in trust to bestow the issues thereof at the appointment of my said daughter Sarah and in case she survive her husband I give the premises to my said daughter for her life, with remaynder to my said neece Sarah Dawlinge, except as to Brownes and Dynes which shall remain to my daughters Elizabeth and Anne. But fi my daughter Sarah leave other lawful issue then her said daughter Sarah I give the said tenement and the land called Dynes to such her other issue and Brownes to my said neece Sarah. Witnesses: Thomas Collyer, R. Bowles, Richard Johnson. Proved by the executrix named. **Rivers 56.**

[It is highly probable that Charles, the son of John Gryme or Grymes, the testator, was Rev. Charles Grymes, who was minister of York parish, York Co. Va., as early as 1644. That the son of a country parson should become one in the colonies seems likely. The compiler of these notes thought he had seen, somewhere in **Archaeologia Cantiana**, a reference to the testator, and extracts from the Ightam register, giving the births, of some of his children; but a careful search of the indexes of all the volumes fails to discover the reference. A genealogy of the descendants of Charles Grymes was begun in the April 1919 number of this Magazine.]

ELIZABETH HAM, wife of HIEROM HAM of the Cittie of Bristoll, gent., late wife and Executrix of JOHN OLYVER, of the said Cittie, merchant.

Dated 24 Dec. 1619. Admon. 30 Oct. 1628.

To my daughter, MARY GRYFFITH, one sixteenth part of

the Prysadge lease and to my sonne HENRY OLLYVER the other sixteenth part. To my grandchild, WILLIAM GRYFFITH, the great spruce chest, etc. To MARY GRIFFITH 'my grandchild, my dozen of apostles spoones. To my husband 'JEROM" HAM, £10 yearly.

To my sonne, THOMAS ROWLAND, £10, yearly. If he die then to his children that have no portions left them by their grandmother REDWOOD.

To MARY OLIVER, the daughter of my sonne JAMES OLIVER, £10.

If my sonne HENRY OLIVER, whatsoever is given byt his Will shall remain to his children, JOHN, THOMAS, and HIEROM.

Residuary Legatee: my husband, HIEROM HAM, he to pay, the £100 due to the Chamber for ROBERT ROWLAND.

Executors:—my husband HIEROM HAM and my sonne in lawe, JOHN GRIFFITH.

JOHN SMYTH) Witness.

30 Oct. 1628. Administration granted to WILLIAM GRIFFITH, grandchild, and next of kin, of said deceased, to administer, JOHN GRIFFITH, one of the Executors named, having also deceased and JEROMIE HAM, the other Executor "deferring execution." **92 BARRINGTON.**

[Hierome or Jerome Ham is a name occurring several times in a family of Bristol merchants. A Jerome Ham lived in York Co., Va., and represented it in the House of Burgesses at the session of March 1657-8, and was J. P. 1656. His widow, Sibella, married 2d Mathew Hubard, and 3d William Aylett. On Dec. 7, 1603, Jerome Ham and John Barker were granted reversion of price wine in the port of Bristol for 38 years.]

THOMAS HOTHERSALL of City of London, Surgeon. Will 11 February 1617-18; proved last October 1620. Being bound for East Indies in the good ship Sampson as a master surgeon. A Deed of gift to his uncle Robert Shuttleworth, citizen and merchant taylor of London. Witnesses: Da: Phillipps servant to George Rickner thelder, scrivenor, deceased, Edward Cotton. **SOAME, 92.**

[Thomas Hothersall, of Pashbchay, gent., patented 200 acres at Blunt Point, (Warwick County) 1623. The head rights were himself, his wife Frances, and Richard and Mary his children. He came to Virginia in 1621, in the **Margaret & John**, took part in a great fight with two Spanish ships, and wrote an account of it, in which he describes himself as "late zytisone and grocer of London."]

ANTHONY KEMP, then of Flordon in the Co. of Norff., gent. Dated 9 April 1613. Admon. 26. May 1614.

ANTHONIE KEMP did declare his Will Nuncupative:

"I am heere at board with my Nephew ROUS, (meaning EDWARD ROUS of Flordon, in Co. Norff., Clerk) and am in his debt, and I can not ride myself, for I am an ould man, and therefore I am faine to trowble him to ride for my money to CAMBRIDGE and other places, and now I am going to sojourne at Norwitch where he must be bound to pay for my diett", and therefore, whatsoever that I have shoulde be his.

No Witnesses.

26 May 1614. Administration granted to EDWARD ROUS, of Flordon, Co. Norfolk, Clerk, and principal creditor of ANTHONY KEMP, late of Flordon, aforesaid, Bachelor to administer, no Executor being named. **37 LAW.**

[As has been before stated in this Magazine, it is practically certain (though positive proof has not yet been obtained) that Richard Kemp Secretary of State of Virginia, was the Richard, baptized 1600, son of Robert Kemp, Esq., of Gissing, Norfolk. Secretary Kemp in his will names his brother Edward Kemp, and his nephew Edmund Kemp (the latter then in Virginia). This Edmund Kemp was probably son of Edmund, and grandson of Robert of Gissing. Anthony Kemp, whose will is given above, was probably a brother of Robt. Kemp, of Gissing. A very brief abstract of the will of Arthur Kemp, son of Robert, of Gissing, has been printed in this Magazine, but the one given above is much fuller and more satisfactory. For other notices of this family of Kemps, see this Magazine II, 174-176; III, 40-42; XX, 71-75.]

ARTHUR KEMPE of the parrish of Michael at the Thorne in the city of Norwich, being now (I thanke God) in convenient health. Will 15 January 1644-5 proved 17 May 1645. Not knowing when or how soone some great and dangerous sickness and disease may sease upon me, made as above. I give my body to be decently intered in the same parish where I shall dye, and doe appoint £5 towardes the necessary charges thereof. I give unto the poor of the parish of Flordon 10s, to the poor of the two parishes in Antingham 20s, to the poor of the said parish of Michael 10s. All these sums to be paid into the hand of the churchwardens and overseers of the said parish within three weeks after my decease. Item, I give to four of the eldest children of my brother Edmond £8 apeece, but soe that my executor dispose of it some way for their good. To my neece Dorothy Jackman £6. To my cosen Robert Freeman's wife of Gissing 40s. To the poor of Gissing 10s. To my neece Walgrave 10s. To my neece Elizabeth Kemp 40s. To Mr. Thomas Sair of Bestreete for his great love and respect 40s. To M'ris Bayfeild besides what I owe her 20s. for a ring. To little George Bayfield 10s more. To the servants in Mr. Bayfeildls house 40s. To the woman that keeps me 10s. besides her wages. To my sister the Lady Kempe of Spaines Hall in Eessex whom I desire to be one of my executors 40s, and to my cosen Rowse, whom I desire to be another of my executors 40s. And I desire my said cosen Rowse to see that my cosen Porter, the widdow at Dover, have 40s, which I have owed her this 20 years for her father's library. I give to my cosen Thomas Rowse of Flordon 20s. To every of my elder brother's sonnes 20s for a token of love, and my silver seale to the fowrth sonne. To my cosen Tom Kempe the minister 20s. To Mrs. Elizabeth Sair the elder 10s for a ringe, and to her two daughters 10s apiece. For the overplus of my moneys not disposed, I will that my sister the Lady Kempe of Finchingfeild shall have the dispositng of it where the most need shall be, among my brothers and their children. Item, I will that Doctor Browne shall have the booke in my chamber called Toloseness. I give unto my brother Sir Robert Kempe, all my bookes in my chamber, and those at London I will that my sister Kemp of Finchingfeild shall dispose of to my kindred that are schollers. I will that my clothes shall be given to poore people. Witnesses: Thomas Browne, Geo. Bayfield, Eliz: Fowlsham. Proved by Lady —— Kempe one of the executors, with power reserved for the like commission to —— Rowse. **RIVERS, 63.**

Dorothie Kempe, widow. Will 14 November 1626; proved May 1629. Body to parish church of Wye, Kent., by the shes of my dear husband Sir Thomas Kempe. For all charges £100 and out of which £10 to Dr. Jackson. To my daughter Lady Ann Cutts £150. To my daughter Lady Dorothy Chichely £100. To my daughter Lady Mary Diggs £100

To my daughter Lady Ann Skipwith £100. To Marie Chernock £100. To my son Sir John Cutts £100. To my grandchild Mrs Dorothie Chichely £50. To my grandchild Mr. Thomas Diggs £50. To my grandchild Mr. Wm Skipwith £50. To my son Sir Dudley Diggs £40. To my sister Tompson and Lady Tompson £10 each. To Lady Bowles and Mary Charnock £10 for mourning. To Sir John Cutts Sir Dudley Diggs, Sir Henrie Skipwith and Sir John Tompson my brother Mr Tompson and Sir Charles Boles £4 each for cloaks. To my chambermaid £3. Small legacies to servants for cloaks etc. To my daughter Cutts my wedding ring and my great jewel. To daughter Chichely diamond border, many other jewels given. To Mrs Mary Charnock all my wearing apparel and my Cabinet where my writings lye at Childerley____Gifts to children and grandchildren already referred to____linen at Olentey in Kent at Shelford. To Sir John Cutts the great standard at Shelford. To poor of Olentey £20. To ppoor of Lollworth £3. To poor of Little Shelford £3. To poor of Swansey £3. Sir John Cutts and Sir Dudley Diggs, executors. Witnesses: Jacob Bridgman, Tho: Ady, John Macarnesse, John Collier. Addition—I give £5 to the Steward of my Courts and £4.10s. for a cloake. And £4 to Grisell. All money that remains to my daughter Cutts "This Codicil was annexed to my Lady Kemps last Will—12th March 1626 And was read to her as she appointed and signed with her own hand. Witnesses: James Bridgman, Mary Charnocke, Roda Packe. **RIDLEY, 49.**

[This is quite a notable will as it illustrates the manner in which groups of kinsfolk emigrated from England. Dorothy (Thompson), the testator, married Sir Thomas Kemp, of Ollantigh, Kent, and had issue four children, daughters. They were: (1) Mary, married Sir Dudley Digges, Kt., of Chliham, Kent, and was mother of Edward Digges, Governor of Virginia; (2) Ann, married Sir John Cutts; (3) Dorothy, married Sir John Chichley, of Wimpole, Cambridgeshire, and was mother of Sir Henry Chichley, Kt., Governor of Virginia; (4) Amy, married Sir Henry Skipwith, Bart., of Prestwould, Leicestershire, and was mother of Sir Grey Skipwith, Bart., who emigrated to Virginia. The family of Kemp, of Ollantigh, was one of distinction, and to it belonged John Kemp, Archbishop of York, of Canterbury, and Cardinal, and Thomas Kemp, Bishop of London.]

STEPHEN KENDALL, of Hempstedd cum Eccles, in
Co. Norfolk, singleman.

Dated 12 March 1605-6. Proved 9 Dec. 1611

To the poore of the parish of Hempstedd cum Eccles, xxs.
To every of the Children of my late Sister MARGARETT, the late wife of JOHN LEAME, to either of them, 40s.
Residuary Legatee and Sole Executrix: my Mother DOROTHIE, the now wife of ROBERT RYALL, of Hempstedd cum Eccles.
JOHN SKYNNER, Clarke, STEPHEN KENDALL: Witnesses
Proved 9 Dec. 1611 by the Sole Executrix named. **103 WOOD.**

THOMAS KENDALL of Great Yarmouth, county Norff, marriner. Will 12 March 1618; proved 14 February 1621. To John Kendall my son £20 at 16 years. To Hellen my daughter £5 at 16 years. Residue to be divided among Rose my wife and my four children i. e. John my son to have his part at 16 years as also every of my daughters. To Henry Read and John Lessingham of Great Yarmouth 40s. each and I make them executors. To Alice Stevenson my goddaughter 20s. To Elizabeth Lessingham my goddaughter 20s. Witnesses: James Sheppard, Ri: Mighells, Scr. **SAVILE, 17.**

HENRY KENDALL als Tyndall of Bressingham, county Norfolk gentleman. Will 28 July 1637; proved 24 April 1638 to be buried in church of new Buckenham Norfolk. To poor of New Buckenham £10. To poor of Bressingham and Shelfangeo 40s. each. To 2nd son John Kendall als Tyndall messuage in Shelfanger and Wynfarthinge, lands in occupation of Gylre Banham lands in occupation of William Bagley and Widow Awgar, John West. To eldest son William Kendall als Tyndall £20 per annum and at her decease to his son Richard. To son Edward £200. To 4 daughters Judith, Frances, Mary and Jane £200 each when 20. To sister Katherine Hauers, widow

40s. yearly. Overseer: Loye Aggas gent. Witnesses: Willm Luke, Sam Brigges, John Blumfield, Gregy Wood, John Smith. **LEE, 71.**

[William Kendall, who came from England to Northampton County, Virginia, about the middle of the Seventeenth Century, and became Speaker of the House of Burgesses, in his will, dated Dec 29, 1685, makes bequests to a niece living at North Yarmouth, a nephew, son of his brother, John "living about Brinton," and a brother, Thomas, living in Norwich, all in Norfolk, England. It seems very probable that the testators in the three wills above, were related to him]

ANTHONY LANGSTON of South Littleton, county Worceister Esqre. Will 16 November 1633; proved 28 December 1633 It has pleased God to bless and enrich me with many children. And that no one son shall have preminence I make my wife Judith sole executris. To every of my sons £5 each not as a portion but as a token of my love to them. To my son Francis Langston and heirs the house and land now in occupation of Henry Farmer the younger. To Anne Langston my daughter £800 hoping she will be ruled in marriage by her mother and brethren who love her most. I leave all charitable actions to my executrix not doubting she will have a godly zeal in disposing to the glory of God and to myne and her credit. Residue to my said wife Judith. Witnesses: Henry Langston, Russ Andrews, Fra. Harewell, John Gravison. **RUSSELL, 111.**

[It is possible that the testator was the father of Anthony Langston, who, according to a document in the English Public Record Office, was an ensign in Prince Maurice's regiment, went to Virginia about 1648, returned to England in 1662, and soon afterwards killed a man in a brawl. He was pardoned and became a captain in the navy. He prepared a letter on the condition of Virginia and especially on the need of iron-works, which is among the Egerton MSS., British Museum. Anthony Langston obtained two grants of land in Virginia. The first, to "Mr. Anthony Langston" Sept. 6, 1653, was for 1303 acres on the north side of York River in Gloucester County, adjoinging Mr. Hammond's land. Due for the transportation of 20 persons (names not given.) The other, April 26, 1653, was to "Mr. Anthony Langston" for 1000 acres in New Kent County on the south side of the freshes of York River, adjoining the land of Col. Man. [Mainwaring] Hamond. Due for the transportation of Daniel Rever, Hem. Chiversal,, Elizabeth Andrews, Mary Smith, Elizabeth Kent, William Feild, Mary Creeton, William Davis, Richard Clarke, Richard Crouch, Mary Puckerell, Elizabeth Thompson, Hoell Thomas, Richard Johnson, Mary Clerke, Runberen Davis, Roger Jones, and Robert Bridley.

A little later a John Langston was resident in the same county, New Kent. He took the side of Bacon in his Rebellion, and by act of Assembly June 1680, was disqualified from ever holding office. He had been elected a Burgess for New Kent in this Assembly, but was not allowed to take his seat. In 1704 the name does not appear among the landholders of New Kent or the counties formed from it, but it is possible that John Langston had a daughter or daughters, as Langston appears later as a baptismal name in several New Kent families. John Langston had two grants of land. The first, 1681, to "John Langston" for 1300 acres in New Kent, being the land formerly granted to Hannah Clarke, found to escheat by Marke Workman, Deputy Escheator, and now granted to John Langston. The other, to "Mr. John Langston," Sept. 28, 1681, for 1316 acres in New Kent, adjoining the landsof Sir Philip Honeywood, the river, land patented by Moses Davis, and of John Fleming, Thomas Glass, and James Turner, being the land formerly granted to Mrs. Hannah Clark and found to escheat.

There was a group of loyalists in this section. Sir Philip Honeywood, Col. Mainwaring Hammond and Anthony Langston had been loyalist officers, as had been William Bassett of the same county. Mrs. Hannah Clarke was widow of John Clarke, of York County, who was a son of Sir John Clarke, of Wrotham, Kent, England. She was also the executrix of Sir Dudley Wyatt, a Royalist officer, who died in Virginia in 1651, and was, no doubt, either his daughter or widow.]

William Oprie of Penkergard, in p'ish. of Helland, Cornwall, gent., will dated 17 June 1641. To my son John O. 12d. To my son Edward O. 12d. To my son Richard O. 12d. To my dau. Mary O. 12d. To my dau'r. Jane 12d. To my dau'r Philipp 12d. To my dau'r Emlin 12d. My wife Mary to have use of furniture in my house at P. for her life, remainder to my heirs. My son Thomas O. to have ploughs etc. To my dau'r Elizabeth wife of William Webbs of Landulp(h), gent. 12d. To my son Nicholas O. 12d. To my son Thomas Ol books etc. To my friends Anthony Gregory of Petrockstowe Devon, Clerk, Petherick Jenkin of Lanivet, Cornwall, gent., William Webbe, of Lardulp, gent. & John Courtier of Bridgerule, Cornwall, gent., in fee, my manor of Parke als the Parke p'shes of Egleshayle, Bodmin & St. Kew, Cornwall,messuages etc. in borough of Bodmin, lands in Bodiniell & Cobbleshorne, in p'sh of Bodmin, on trust to raise legacies for sd. four dau'rs M. J. P. & E. & then for son Thomas. Care of sons J. E. & R. & sd four dau'rs to sd. wife, she being their natural mother. Rest of goods to sd. wife & she to be ext'rix. Sd. Trustees to be overseers. Witnesses: Edward Opie, William Lobb, Hugh Bauden, Edward Littleton.
Prob. 23 Oct. 1656 by Marie Opie, relict & ext'rix.

[Thomas Opie, probably from Bristol, came to Virginia and married Helen, daughter of Rev. David Lindsay, of Northumberland County. The will of one of his sons, Thomas Opie, Jr., mariner, of Bristol, was printed in this Magazine, XVIII, 90. One of the descendants of the emigrant Thomas Opie, was the gallant Major Hierome Lindsay Opie (of Staunton, Va.), 116th Infantry, 29th Division, who so highly distguished himself in the World War. As the chief commerical city of the West, Bristol attracted many people of Cornwall and other western counties.]

LAND CERTIFICATES FOR NORTHAMPTON COUNTY

(Con ributed by Judge Thomas B. Robertson, Hopewell, Va.)

The following list of those to whom certificates were issued for taking up land in Northampton County, then including the whole Eastern Shore of Virginia, will show forcefully the rapidity with which the lands were taken up in the county and how the settlement went forward. The lands referred to in the list spread all the way from Cape Charles to upper portions of what is now Accomac County. In addition there are recorded between 1650 and 1660 several deeds to lands given by the Indians. One instance being that of Okiawampe, who styled himself "Great King of the Eastern Shore," deeding land in Occohannock neck. Below are given most of these recorded, some being likely omitted, partly owing to the condition of the book in which they are recorded and a number did not record them for years afterwards. There are, too, a few errors in the names.

At a court holden for Accomacke County the 11th day oc Janyy 1640.

A certificate was granted to Col. Obedience Robins for 2000 acres of land for the transportation of 40 bersons whose names are underwritten:

Thomas Belkes, Simon Lyld, Robert Marriott, David Elvis, Edwd. Carter, Edwd. Smith, Thomas Marshall, Marie Thomas, Thomas Bragley, Thos. Penford, John Blouser, John Drew, John Wheller, Robt. Walterton, A. Densford, Richd. White, Elizabeth Cowld, John Taylor, Richard Holland, Lewis Smith John Gibson, John Parke, Anna Button, Edward Nalden, William Pece, Jane Ffohley, Richard Lyall, John Johnson, L. Ffield, Richd. Pryne, James Sollett, Robt. Mann, Elizabeth Norse, Willm. Lynchbor, Esaw Butterfield, Alex. Larwood William Lawrence, John Browne, Richard Ludson, Martin A Morgan.

At a court holden for Accomack County, Mar. 1642.

A certificate was granted to Henry Weede for five hundred acres of land for the persons underwritten:

Richd. Lacy, Ffra. White, Edwd. Drigg, William Wheeler, Phill Lanseed, Sarvant Mayer, John Bousser, Tho. Beirnham, James Wrenn, William Howson.

Att a court holden for Northampton County Aug. 29, 1642, a certificate was granted to Thomas Savage, Carpenter, for the following:

John Severne Bridgett his wife John Severne Jr. Wm. Stevens Robt. Lattmer Abraham Merigold John Pott Abraham Lagrand Wm. Allogon John Luark

A certificate was granted to William Waters Son & heire of Lt. Edward Waters, Dec'd. for following persons

Edward Waters
Anne Parkson
Antho Brewster
3 men killed at
Massacre Camp Nichols.

William Goute
Theo. Brian
Wm. Warren
John Dyer
John Bowler
4 men cast away with Arnolde Williams

A certicate was granted to Thomas Knight for following

Tho. Adderston
Rich[d] Jones
Thos. Harrison

John Roberts
Percy Terry

A certificate was granted to Wm. Andrews for following

Rich[d] ———
John Zalleman
John Young
Alexander Harrison

Thos. Gaskins
John Lee
Wm. Conner
An. Brower

At court holden for Northampton County 3^{d} day of Jany. 1642-3 A certificate was granted to Capt. Francis Yeardly for 3000 acres of land for transportation of the following persons.

Capt. Francis Yeardly

John Langley	Mary Watkins
Tho. Datre	Henry Leonard
Walter Price	John Lewillins
Ffra. Goldman	Rowland Mills
Jarvis Preschus	John Sherle
Rich^{d}d Swift	John Linch
Roberta Warren	He'y Laugton
Edw. Temple	Wm. Ward
John Featherstone	Tho. Adderstey
——— Kayne	Tho. Jones
Edw. Thorne	Lancaster Lovell
Augustine Moore	Robin Williams
Tho. Butterese	Edw. Bedlen
John Thropp	Wm. Willis
John Turner	Edw. Kensey
Suzanna Neale	Thos. Prince
Hen. Taylor	Pierce Griffin
Rich^{d}d Smith	Rich. Griffin
Myles &ower	John Robtes
John Penner	Rich. Jones
Alice Friser	Ann Lathrine
Margarett Càthner	Anne (negro)
Zama Barls	Wm. Demiss
Anna Thompson	Keo. Miller
Anne Kirkram	John Wortham
Alonzo Bowles	Marmaduke Parkinson
Walter Darby	Charles Atkinson
John Darby	John Chevewell
Robt. Martin	Wm. Bowker

Court held last day of Aug. 1643, Mrs. Harmer right of Mr Charles Harmer for transportation of

Ffwen Jones	John Gold
Lazarus Murring	William Farmer

John, Harrison	Thomas Lewis
Jane Courtney	John Searley
Robt. Swamp	Matthew Cottinge
Thos. Blunt	John Glucke
George Willis	Thomas Gold

Court Oct. 30, 1643 Cert. granted to Mrs. Anne Littleton in right of her father Henry Southy, Esqr. for following

Henry Southy Esq.	Roger Delke	Tho. Lewis
Elizabeth his wife	Tho. Shoare	Robt. Swamp
Henry Southy his child	Valentine Sentell	Roger Marshall
Thomas)	Tynak Woolley	Anne Simes
Mary)Servants	Will Bricklayer	Richd Willows
Elizabeth)		
John Davenport	Alice Dammock	John Rose
Thos Browne	Elleno Paynter	
Margarett Chartier	Sarah Sharley	
	Dynah Glower	

Att court 20 Febry. 1643-4 Certificate was granted to William Uuen^{m} (Munro?)

John Webster	Slaty Hodgkins
Thos. Newton	Geo. Meredith
James Johnson	John Pamwell
Susan Johnson	Edw. Denkins
Joane Grinder	
Joane Longe	

(Same Court)

A certificate was granted to John Dennis for 350 acres for

Richard Pattica	Thos. Long
Charles Wallyrane	Thos. Lother
Barbury Dennis	
Robt. Swanson	
A servant of Capt. Stone	

Same Ct.—A certificate was granted to Edw. Douglass for the following

Edw. Douglass
Wm. Barrett
wife Elizabeth
Wm. Miles
William Pritchett
John Powell
John Browne
John Thomas
Benjamin Bowden
George Holmes
Henry Grasgood
Pelia Nutt
William Gooke
Citwell Long
Rowland Martmore

At a court holden for ye County of Northampto 8th Ffebu'y Anno 1650-1
Present—Coll'o Nath'l Littleton
Argoll Yeardly Esq—
Mr. Obedience Robins
Mr. Edmund Scarborough
Mr. Edw. Douglass

A certificate was this day granted unto Mr. John Custis for six hundred acres of land due unto him by assignment of right from Argoll Yeardly Esq—

Mrs. Ann Yeardley
Wm. Smith
Edw. Sacker
Dante Jackson
Elizabeth ———
Mary Stanfast
Southerd Obbine
Jno. Custis
Elizabeth Roberts
Abrh. Smith
James Stanfast
George Grime
Record at 28th day month Mar. 1651

At Court held in Northampton 28th April 1651, Certificate granted John Robinson for 600 acres of land due by right of the underwritten

Steph. Costen
Eliz. Winn
James Sterrett
Margarett Courren
Eliz. Barnes
Ann Winn
George Smith
John Wilcoxe
Jno. Mundage
Tho. Fitchett
Ann Costen
Wilbur Hawes

Cert. granted Ffarmer Jones for 300 acres for the following Ffarmer Jones Senr and man servant Hanson

Jane Leetra	Sara Jones
Ffarmer Jones Jr.	Robt. Hallowair

Cert. granted to John Johnson for 50 acres of land for transportation of Thos. Wilson.

Cert. granted unto Edmund Scarborough for 3600 acres of land for those underwritten.

Rowland Evans	Joanne Parritt
Jenkin Lleullen	Ann Darby
Edward Evans	Tho. Pitcher
Lewis Rowland	Mary Eddesse
Jno. Jones	Tho. Woodfield
Phill Pemcott	Wm. Skinner
Margaret Tillett	Tho. Hayes
Jester Yeoman	Mary Edgar
Wm. Tomlin	Mary Williams
Nath Smith	Mary Gritheffe
Henry Willis	Jonathan Showett
Susan Foster	Thos. West
Thos. Browne	Margarett Purnell
John Martin	Alice Price
John Surry	Stowell Gladsinger
Walter Wood	Tho. Collers

Ffrancis W. Knight (?McKnight)

Edw. Cowes	Edw. Sermonor	Tho. Cower
Wm. Hollis	Morris Mathews	Nath. Broonfield
Mary Badullor	Edw. Holles	Jane Daniel
Owen Williams	Dorothy Barnes	Jno. Cary
Thos. Shipwin	Domingo)	
James Harris	Servia)negroes	Jno. Jones
Elizabeth Case	Tahania)	
Thos. Browne	John Edwards	Robt. Kinge
Jno. Marrett	Wm. Rinch	Jno. Runney
Jno. Hardwell	Tho. Yeoxill	Wm. Price

Tho. Maior	Ffrancis Wieland	Jno. Owen
Wm. Alesworth	Mary Johnson	Dor'thy Rubie
Hen. Barnes	Lucretia Pott	Rich. Hunsted
Ronald Rich		

Court held 28 July 1651 a certificate was granted to Geo. Clark son of Mrs. Geo. Clarke for 100 acres land for the following

George Clarke Jr.
Elizabeth Clarke

Cert. granted to Wm. Waters for 200 acres for the following

Chas.. Neale	Francis Harris
Arthur Moore	Margarett Bentton

Cert. granted to Michael Painter for 350 acres for

——— Wood	John Rogers
John Martin	Antho. Black
Charles Armstrong	Joseph Karson

Keth Bromfield

20 Sept. 1651 Cert. granted to Sam'l Goldsmith for the following

Alice Clawson	John Long
Jacob Browne	John Harrison
Sam'l Goldsmith	Joanne Goldsmith

Susanna Goldsmith

At a court held for Northampton County the 4th Apr. 1659 a certificate is granted to Doctor Geo. Hack for 1350 acres of land for transportation of 27 persons to this County as follows:

Geo. Nicholas Hack	Margaret Palmer
	a negro
Sopherin Hack	"
Ann Katherine Hack	"
Brian Penaby	"
Benj. Jones	Gilhelinus Varlee
Dorman Nephrininge	William Ffoxey
Mary Nourth	Simon Taylor
Augustine Grisbert	Bridgett Williams

Timothy Blackford	Ann Ffoxry
Rynick Gerritt	Hendrick Volkert
Augustine Harmon	John Gerritte
Cornel^s Hendrickson	Burnard Ramsy

Att. Att a court held in Northampton May 30th 1659 a certifi is granted to Col. Edmund Scarborough for those whose names are underwritten (1500 acres)

John Watts	Alice Roberts	Robt. Ffowkes
Jeffrey Coate	Joseph Hues	Jane Rodgers
Edmund Cantwell	Nicholas Litchby	Ann Lartch
Tho. Stany	John Hapworth	Thomas Warren
Hugh Bowen	Morris Souatt	Henry Robins
Sara Hart	Jane Gethinge	James Hayes
Susan Fflitcher	Thomas Davis	Timothy Jones
Jane Gardner	John Davis	Charles Markworth
Mary Hues	Edward Bamberry	Mary Williams
Sara Gardner	Darby Enns	Thomas Morris

Cert. is granted to Alexander Addison for 10 persons.

At Court held in Northampton Co. 2d Nov'br 1659 Capt. Wm. Andrews is granted a certificate for 300 acres of land due him for bringing into this County six persons as follows

William Bust	Price Dillenger	Hugh Meres
Ffrancis Carlyle	Theren Swan	Jane Maxwell

At Court held Apr. ye 30th 1660 Capt. George Parker is granted a certificate for 300 acres of land for bringing in 6 persons underwritten he having taken no land before.

Mary Thomas	Eliz. Brampton
Philip Swinton	Grace Thompson
Wm. Ramserath	George Beets

At a court holden 30th July 1660 a certificate is granted to Mr. John Wilcocks for ye transportation of 20 persons into this County whose names follow (1000 acres).

Ann Wilcocks	Henry Yardley	George Jenkins
Rose Yardly	Wm. Burton	John Flfoyd

Mary Anery	Arien Ames	Fflorence Pomroy
Cornelius Johnson	John Wilcocks	Wm. Taylor
John Custis	Wm. St. Johns	John Fereby
Wm. Marshall	Mary Barber	Wm. Pryer
Robt. Marklockson	Anne Jeanes	

Court held Sept. 20th 1660, a cert. is granted to John Milby for seven persons namely John Milby, Aron Ramsy, Richard Ackworth, Samarin Milby, Susan Milby, Sam'l Taylor, John Dummon.

At a court held for Northampton 12th Sept. 1660 on petition of Mr. John Michaell for a certificate for 1000 acres of land it is so ordered being due for ye transportation of 20 persons into this County names followeth:

John Michell Sr.	Robert Irish	Mary Teage
John Michell Jr.	Dermon Anderway	Abram Rogers
Lawrence Jacobson	John Fflint	Robt. A. Clew
William)negroes	Rachael Medcalfe	John Jennins
Bundo)	Eliza Braneby	Will Morgin
George Such	John Cameday	Elsie Appue
Thomas Irish	Mary Greenwood	

At a court held 26th Nov. 1660 a certificate is granted Col Obedience Robins for 1500 acres land due him for rights under written

Obedience Robins	John Wood	Robt. Thompson
John Joes	Margaret Waters	Barnabus Brian
John Cousin	Wm. Croment	John Robins
Joseph Aboy	Charles Catlin	Wm. Savage
Christo Massoine	David Walker	John Rogers
Esau Rutherfield	Wm. Eldridge	John Magrove
Thos. Joynes(3 times)	Robt. Mathison	Eliz. Baron
Augustine Hare	Wm. White	John Miller
Martin Kalliamie	William Bromfield	Charles Astin
Rich. Painebeard		

At a court held 13th Decbr 1660 a certificate is granted to Maj. John Tilney for 300 acres of land for the underwritten

Robt. Blaine	Richard Ward	Humphrey Brookes
Ann Watterson	Ann Bryan	Elizabeth Moore

25th Ffeb. 1660 Certificate to John Evans for 400 acres for perons underwritten

Abraham Taylor	Wm. Heinsley	Thomas Turker
Michael Hutton	Henry Stoff	Edw. Sanders
Jane Webb	Joseph Stanard	

Certificate to Timothy Coe for 300 acres

Elizabeth Yorke	Sarah Redder	Jane Coulson
Jane Blay	Anne Smith	Margaret Manes

Certificate granted Robt. Windley for 500 acres

John Truman	Jno. Mill	Robt. Hawkins
Elizabeth Hay	Tho. Grimston	Jno. Harmer
Dona More	John Ellzy	Echo Whitby
	Simon Carrier	

Certificate granted Robt. Berace for 800 acres

Edw. Smally	Thomas Minor	Joseph Hurry
John Smally	Eliz. Reynolds	Bargret Barton
John Knight	Robt. Wright	Miles Gray
Lidia Esterfield	Ffrancis Eston	Eliz. Vincent
	Nich. Smith	
	Eliz. Johnson	
	Jane Williams	
	Ffrancis Eston	

Cert. granted to James Price for 400 acres

John Hill	Mabill Jones	Richd Armstrong
Ffrancis Jones	Hannah Tice	Mary Hepward
Thos. Swindel	Sarah Colue	

Cert. granted to Thos. Leatherbury 600 acres

John Prichard	John Turner	Thos. Booth
John Fisher	Joaner Armitage	Eliz. Glisson
Eliz. Neale	Eliz Wade	Eliz. Wright
Francis Glisson	Henry Jarvis	Jeffry Smith

ORANGE COUNTY MARRIAGES.

(Continued)

1810.

Minister

Leland Blackwell—Anna Burton. Jacob Watts.
Thomas Dickerson—Anna Wood. Jacob Watts.
David Austen—Fanny Williams. Jacob Watts.
Robt. W. Bell—Anne T. Schench. J. Goss.
Wm. Martin—Margaret Snell. J. Goss.
Leonard Baker—Kethorah Robinson. Jere Chand er.

1811.

Edward Breedlove—Haney Hantley. A. Brockman.
Hudson Collier—Betsey Ham. Jacob Watts.
James Rogers—Elizabeth Jackson. Jacob Watts.
Thomas Marr—Sally Harvey. Geo. Bingham.
John Bowen—Sally Seal. Geo. Bingham.
Elisha Turner—Mary Seal. Geo. Bingham.
Henry Wayland—Ara Melone. Geo. Bingham.
John Clee—Catha Price. Geo. Bingham.
Jacob Black—Nancy Cave. Geo. Bingham.
Wm. Reins—Frances Eddins. Geo. Bingham.
May Hainey—Mary Mack Runkle. Geo. Bingham.
John Snow—Jane Burrus. Geo. Bingham.
John Parrott—Fanny Simmons. Geo. Bingham.
Alex. Vinniard—Polly Hensley. John Garnett.
Wm. Blakey—Polly Branham. John Garnett.
David Ballard—Elizabeth Huckstep. Jacob Watts.
Milton Payne—Sarah Burton. Jacob Watts.
Thomas Crenshaw—Nancy Parrott. Jacob Watts.
Christian Kinzer—Mi ly Sutton. R. Jones.
——— Tumely—Patsy Pound. R. Jones.
Thos. Faulconer—Elizabeth Jones. J. Chandler.

Rich[d] Jamar—Betsy Adams. J. Chandler.
Owen Cooper—Mary Mason. J. Chandler.
Wm. Beazeley—Susanna Graves. J. Chandler.
Adcock Carter—Elizabeth Daniel. Philip Pendleton.
William Rennolds—Hannah Jones. James Garnett
Roberson Rall—Mary Ann Clark. James Garnett.

1812.

Willis White, Jr.—Nancy Wayt. Jacob Watts
Alex. Whitelaw—Lucy Chewning. Jacob Watts.
John Burton—Mildred Goodridge. Jacob Watts.
Henry Fackler—Frances Terrell. Jere. Chandler.
John Keeton—Elzabeth Chancellor Jere. Chandler.
Claybourne Duvall—Polly Faulconer. Jere. Chandler.
Geo. Morris—Mary Simmonds. J. Goss.
Nathanl Welch—Mary Mallory. Henry Fry.
Wm. Lee—Sally Terrill. Jere. Chandler.
Elijah Morton—Mary G. Webb. Jere. Chandler.
James Braxter—Sally Payne. Jere. Chandler.
Wm. Montague—Sukey Perry. Jere. Chandler.
Jno. B. Hawkins—Ann Ford. Jere. Chandler.
James Terrill—Susanna Middlebrook. Jere. Chandler.
Obediah Gregory—Nancy Lancaster. Jere. Chandler.
James Humes—Margaret Dodd. Jere. Chandler.
Wm. Caza—Mary Slaughter. John Garnett.
Ephriam Yowell—Polly Eddins. John Garnett.
David Maupin—Jerusha Davis. Geo. Bingham.
Ezekiel Breeding—Betsy Haney. Geo. Bingham.
John Price—Elizabeth Sims. Geo. Bingham.
Michael Sower—Ann Gibbons. Geo. Bingham.
Caleb Norris—Olly Harris. Geo. Bingham.
Wm. Eaton—Elizabeth Duniven. Geo. Bingham.
James Early—Sarah Caw. Geo. Bingham.
John Shiflett—Polly Raines. Geo. Bingham.
Caleb Bush—Lucinda Taylor. Geo. Bingham.
Reuben Sim—Frances Graves. Geo. Bingham.
Wm. Early—Sarah Graves. Geo. Bingham.

John Walton—Rhoda Davis. Geo. Bingham.
George Waugh—Susan Wright. J. Goss.
Michael Walters—Sally McFarland. J. Goss.
John Tay—Elizabeth Sebree. J. Goss.
Wm. Martin—Nancy Fearnyhough. J. Goss.
John Lausly—Catherine Pitcher. Unknown.
Daniel Quisenberry—Mary Rodes. Unknown

1813.

Edward Smith—Sally Bess. Unknown.
Henry Teel—Dicey Read. Unknown.
Alex. Musgrove—Polly Morris. Unknown.
Zachariah Wood—Peggy Clarke. Unknown.
Andrew Newman—Ellander Wright. Unknown.
Thomas Clarke—Catherine R. Jameson. Unknown.
Edmund Terrell—Ann T. Morton. Jere. Chandler.
Braxton Ozborne—Ann Taliaferro. Isham Tatum.
Thomas Nelson—Elizabeth Quesenberry. Jere. Chandler.
Jonathan Atkin—Milly Quesenberry. Jere. Chandler.
Thos. Robinson—Nancy Roach. Jere. Chandler.
John Dixon—Lucy Rumsey. Jere. Chandler.
Geo. Hughes—Polly Harvey. Geo. Bingham.
John Dunn—Susanna Maupin. Geo. Bingham.
Wm. Morris—Sally Roach. Geo. Bingham.
John Sampson—Clarisa Jollett. Geo. Bingham.
Archibald Brock—Sarah Moyers. Geo. Bingham.
Jeremiah Bryan—Franky Long. Geo. Bingham.
Murry Shiflett—Icy Snow. Geo. Bingham.
John Shiflett—Frances Martin. Geo. Bingham.
Joab Early—Elizabeth Thompson. Geo. Bingham.
Geo. Parrott—Elizabeth Catterton. Geo. Bingham.
Benj'n Herndon—Nancy Lucas. Geo. Bingham.
Taverner Riddle—Mary Goodale. Geo. Bingham.
Benj. White—Judith Twyman. Jacob Watts.
John Mitchel —Nel y Wood. Jacob Watts.
John Yowell—Jane Davis. John Garnett.
Benj. Carter—Polly Daniel. Phi ip Pendleton.

Carter Faulconer—Nancy Faulconer. Ambrose Brockman.
James W. Mansfield—Mildred Clark. J. Goss.
Holland Ozbourn—Sally Farneyhough. J. Goss.

1814.

Robt. Stringfellow—Mary Plunkett. John Garnett.
John Walker—Frances Porter. Wm. Mason.
Jonathan Herring—Polly Hill. Wm. Mason.
Thomas Naylor—Jane Walton. Geo. Bingham.
James Walker—Joice Powell. Geo. Bingham.
Isaac Lamb—Elizabeth Slater. Geo. Bingham.
Thos. Harvey—Eleanor Goodale. Geo. Bingham.
Sinclair Cave—Sary Anderson. Geo. Bingham.
Isaac Gregory—Lucy Sampson. Geo. Bingham.
Henry Lee—Fanny Lamb. Geo. Bingham.
William Jameson—Rebecca Maupin. Geo. Bingham.
Joshua Black—Alpha Rains. Geo. Bingham.
Geo. Dunevant—Peggy Haney. Geo. Bingham.
Jonathan Rogers—Frances Twyman. Geo. Bingham.
Michael Eheart—Sarah Eheart. Hamilton Goss.
James Perry—Jane Perry. Jere. Chandler.
Burruss Munday—Elizabeth Crossthwait. I. Goss.
David Whitelaw—Mary Davis. Jacob Watts.
Clifton Rodes—Milly Ham. Jacob Watts.
Newman Faulconer—Maria Newman. J. Goss.
Thomas Mason—Nancy Clark. Jas. Garnett.

1815.

Joseph Wharton—Catherine George. Wm. Mason.
John Bledsoe—Margaret Perry. Jere. Chandler.
Richard Becket—Jemima Kea. Geo. Bingham.
James Goodale—Lucy Riddle. Geo. Bingham.
James Shifflett—Milly Herrin. Geo. Bingham.
Heland Snow—Judah T. Mallory. Geo. Bingham.
James Lankford—Jane Martin. Geo. Bingham.
Francis Catterton—Nancy Clarkson. Geo. Bingham.

John Anderson—Nancy Lower. Geo. Bingham.
Jacob Meadows—Nancy Roach. Geo. Bingham.
Joseph B. Crooks—Kitty M. Hennesy. Jas. Garnett.
Wm. Fisher—Margaret Faulconer. Jere. Chandler.
John Dunaway—Polly Sutherland. Jere. Chandler.
Benj. Quesenberry—Sally Groom. Jere. Chandler.
Valentine Head—Elina Huckstep. Jacob Watts.
Benj. Jones—Elizabeth Whitelaw. Jacob Watts.
Burnes Brown—Nancy Burton. Jacob Watts.

1816.

James Ansel—Frances Estes. Geo. Bingham.
Zachariah Wood—Nancy Estes. Geo. Bingham.
Bennet Shifflett—Polly Shifflett. Geo. Bingham.
Austin Sanderidge—Ann Hall. Geo. Bingham.
Geo. Elliott—Judith Martin. Geo. Bingham.
Edmund P. Walton—Letice Watson. Geo. Bingham.
James Peyton—Anna Huffman. Geo. Bingham.
Austin Snow—Agnes Mallory. Geo. Bingham.
Saml. Bishop—Sarah Via. Geo. Bingham.
Armistead Long—Betty Kendal. Geo. Bingham.
Mitchel Davis—Elizabeth Harvey. Geo. Bingham.
John Davis—Sally Dear. Geo. Bingham.
William Dean, Jr.—Mary Deane. Geo. Bingham.
Wilson Balland—Sarah Goodall. Geo. Bingham.
James Gentry—Nelly Gibson. Geo. Bingham.
Wm. Black—Nancy Sebree. Geo. Bingham.
Jas. Powell—Nancy Shelar. Geo. Bingham.
Jeremiah Jarrel—Lucrecia Sims. Geo. Bingham.
James Coleman—Saluda Snow. Geo. Bingham.
Wm. H. Moyers—Lucrecia Beadles. Geo. Bingham.
Zachariah Gardner—Lucinda Martin. Geo. Bingham.
John Shifflett—Vina Shifflet. Geo. Bingham.
Henry Chambart—Fanny Dawson. Wm. Hawley.
James Wallace—Mourning Oaks. Jno. C. Gordon.
Henry Hill—Matilda Payne. Wm. Mason.
Wm. Boswell—Mary Sleet. J. C. Gordon.

Hugh Faulconer—Elizabeth Faulconer. J. C. Gordon.
Wm. A. Moore—Mary Wright. J. C. Gordon.
Geo. Wallis—Susan Hilman. J. C. Gordon.
Thos. Hawkins—Mary Perry. J. C. Gordon.
Charles Dane—Elizabeth Borton. Jas. Gardett.
Wm. Hancock—Mary Bridenhart. Robt. Jones.
James Blackwell—Elizabeth Burton. Jacob Watts.
Philip Steel—Ann Petty. J. C. Gordon.

1817.

Anthony Thornton—Nancy Twyman. Jacob Watts.
Evan Davis—Polly Hilman. J. C. Gordon.
Lawrence Sanford—Catherine Ford. J. C. Gordon.
Fielding Jones—Mary Johnson. J. C. Gordon.
Roddy Hawkins—Elizabeth Hawkins. J. C. Gordon.
Rich[d] S. Abele—Sarah Hilman. J. C. Gordon.
Larkin Scott—Elizabeth Faulconer. J. C. Gordon.
John White—Lucy Adams. J. C. Gordon.
David Williams—Elizabeth Row. J. C. Gordon.
Micajah Jones—Susan Wright. J. C. Gordon.
John Teel—Nancy Waugh. J. C. Gordon.
Thos. Robinson, Jr.—Sarah Lancaster. J. C. Gordon.
James Wood—Ann Mills. W. G. Hiter.

1818.

Peter R. Johnson—Patsy Alcock. W. G. Hiter.
Benjamin Jacobs—Ann Faulconer. J. C. Gordon.
Bazil Haney—Elizabeth Dean. Geo. Bingham.
John Wyant—Elizabeth Bangler. Geo. Bingham.
Zachariah Crawford—Cibba Rains. Geo. Bingham.
Wm. Sims—Eliza Morgan. Geo. Bingham.
Jacob Madon—Julia Davis. Geo. Bingham.
Mozias Jones—Frances Slaytor. Geo. Bingham.
Fountain Goodal—Peggy Seal. Geo. Bingham.
Richard Shifflet—Nancy Morris. Geo. Bingham.
Wm. Gibson—Elizabeth Morris. Geo. Bingham.

Daniel M. Smith—Frances Stubblefield. Jas. Garnett.
Nathaniel I. Welch—Viranda Newman. Jas. Garnett.

Here ends this Marriage Register:

The record, however, though not in register form, is continued in the clerk's office; too extensive for further insertion herein.

APPENDIX.

It is much easier to "get married" in Virginia now than in the old days, and certainly down to the earlier years of the 17th century the fees were high for that luxury, amounting to nearly three pounds in colonial currency—the governor and the minister receiving the lion's share.

These fees might be commuted in tobacco at ten shillings per hundred, "of the growth of the parish wherein the feme lives." If the groom lived in a different county he had to give bond with security that the fees should not become a charge on the bride's parish, and Thomas Jefferson's marriage bond, preserved in the State Library, is so conditioned. No one could be married but according to the rubric of the book of Common Prayer, and if a female between twelve and fifteen years of age married without the consent of her parent or guardian, or the publication of banns, she forfeited her inheritance. A free person who married a servant forfeited to his or her master a thousand pounds of tobacco or else had to serve the master or owner one whole year in actual service, 3. Hen. **passim.**

The County records in this regard appear to a disadvantage when compared to the other records. The earliest date found is 1772, and, instead of a regular register, there is simply a list of marriages extending through 1779, as set out by the record itself. Then begins, in 1780, a record compiled alphabetically from the marriage bonds down to 1800 inclusive—when a real "marriage register," which however seems not to include all the marriages, appears, which is published in full. The marriage bonds in the period herein embraced were in a penalty of Fifty dollars, and the only condition was that there was no legal impediment to the marriage. The bonds are continued after the "register" begins, but inasmuch as the name of the officiating minister is given in the register, that record has been preferred.

Only one "license" was found that of Robert Brooking and Patsy Russell, issued by James Madison and certified by James Waddel, the "Blind preacher,"

Diligent search has failed to discover any authority in the "senior justice" to issue a marriage license. The signature of the "Blind Preacher" is remarkable for its clearaness and penmanship, and it is with only one l' that he spells his name-

The spelling of the originals have been closely followed, though many of the signatures to the bonds are obscure, and in not a few cases the intending Benedick could only "make his remark."

Marriage Register.

The Marriage Register is not complete, and this record appears to have been kept with less care and diligence than it ought to have been.

It was determined to publish it in the sequence of years, rather than alphabetically, thereby avoiding much detail.

It has been found impossible to determine the denominations of the officiating ministers in each case; when it could be determined positively, the denomination is given, as follows:

Minister—	Denomination—
Nathaniel Sanders	Baptist
Frederick Kobler	
Robert Jones	

Minister—	Denomination—
Hamilton Goss	Baptist
Jacob Watts	
Geo. Bingham	
Wm. Calhoon	
Wm. Douglas	Meth. Episc.
Duke W. Hallum	
Jeremiah Chandler	
Isborn Tatum	
James Garnett	Baptist
Ambrose Brockman (Albemarle Co.)	
J. Goss	Baptist
John Garnett	
Philip Pendleton	
Henry Fry	Meth. Episc.
John A. Billingsby	Baptist
Wm. Mason	
Wm. Y. Hiter	
Wm. Hawley	Episcopal
J. C. Gordon	

NOTES AND QUERIES.

NOTES FROM THE RECORDS OF BRUNSWICK COUNTY.

Deed, 1733, to Batt Peterson of Brunswick.

Inventory of personal estate of Mr. Thomas Godwyn, deceased, 1733 £156.1.2.

Deed, June 6, 1734, from Hodges Godwyn, brother and heir of Thomas Godwyn of Brunswick, deceased, to Robert Munford of Prince George County.

Deed, 1735, to Timothy Rives of Brunswick.

Deed, July 1735, from Cornelius Cargill of Brunswick.

Deed, Sept. 1734, from John Goodwyn of Surry to William Shands of Surry.

Will of Henry Wyche of Brunswick; sons Henry and William, daughter Abigail Brewer (sons Wm. and Henry were under 18), daughter Elizabeth Proved March 4, 1740.

Will of William Maclin, Sr., sons James, William and John; daughter Ann Lanier and her son Thomas Lanier, daughter Judith McKnight. Dated Jan. 29, 1751; proved March 26, 1751.

Will of Sterling Clack; all estate to loving friend, John Lightfoot, Esq., in trust for testator's wife and children; in case of Lightfoot's death, to John Clack and Lewis Parham in trust for same purpose. Dated Jan. 1750. Codicil, dated Jan. 9, 1751. His manor plantation with 1000 acres adjoining and the lands and houses where the Court House stands, to his son Eldridge Clack. Proved March 26, 1751.

Inventory of Thomas Lanier, 1751.

Will of John Lightfoot, 1751 (Printed this Magazine VII, 398.)

Inventory of Walter Campbell (1751 or 1752) including 8 vols. Spectators £1.6; 1 Roy's Wisdom of God 4sh.6d., 2 vols. ye Guardian 8sh. a parcel of books £2.

Will of Samuel Chamberlain, 1752, daughter Elizabeth Lanier &c.

Inventory of Sterling Clack, 1751 (Printed in this Magazine VII, 61.)

Will of Peter Wyche, dated Sept. 29, 1756, proved 1757; sons Henry, George and Drury, daughter Lucy Wyche, daughters Rebecca and Ann Wyche, wife Alex. Wyche.

Will of James Clack, 1757 (Printed in this Magazine VIII, 61.)

Inventory of personal estate of Littleton Tazewell, March 1758, £1341. 0.1.

Will of Metcalfe Dickerson, son Tarpley Dickerson, daughter Betty Dickerson, wife Winifred, dated April 1754, proved May 1758.

Inventory of Sampson Lanier, deceased, 1758.

Will of Joseph Massie, son John, land in Brunswick, daughter Sarah Avent, daughter Amy Avent, daughter Rebecca Wise, Agnes Richardson, son Joseph laid where said Joseph (Jr) lives, sons Thomas and James, daughters Winifred, Lucy, Betty and Frances, wife Elizabeth, granddaughter Sharlott Massie, dated August 19, 1760, proved May 26, 1761.

Will of William Lee, grandson Peter Lee, son William Lee, daughters Elizabeth, Ann, Rebecca, and Amy, wife, William Barror, and Henry Lee executors. Dated Aug. 3, 1759, proved May 1761.

Will of James Maclin, daughter Leah Wyche, granddaughter Elizabeth, brother John Maclin, grandaughter Mary Maclan, son James. Dated March 1767, proved Sept. 1769.

Will of Mildred Willis of "Beddingfieldhall," Brunswick, daughter Sarah Willis, daughter Elizabeth Willis, sons John, Augustine, Francis, Richard and Lewis Willis. Dated Oct. 24, 1769, proved Feb. 27, 1769.

Will of John Willis, gent., of "Bedden Fields Hull" [The name of this place was "Beddingfield Hall."]

All estate to wife, she to divide it among their children. Dated Nov. 7, 1764, proved Jan. 16, 1769.

Will of William Short, Sr., sons William and Jacob, granddaughter Rebecca Abernathy, wife, proved Oct., 1769.

Will of John Nevison, sons John, William, Littleton and Robert, wife Ann. Wife, Allan Love and John Tazewell executors. Dated April 1768 proved Nov. 1769.

Will of Charles Gordon, wife Ann and children. Dated Sept. 1769, proved No. 1769.

Will of John Gordon (x), very sick; wife Elizabeth, son Charles, daughter Mary, dated Feb. 1769, proved Nov. 1769.

Will of Gronow Owen; wife Jona, sons Robert, Richard Brown, Gronow and John Loyd Owen. Dated July 3, 1769, proved March 26, 1770.

Will of Anne Massey, "being old and low of estate and health," son John Massey, son Richard Massey's eldest son, son Richard Massey, daughter Martha Moore, daughter Tabitha Massey, sons William and Hezekiah Massey, daughter Sarah Jones. Dated May 8, 1770, proved Oct. 22, 1770.

Will of Brazure Cocke, wife Frances, son William, son Thomas Cocke's children, daughter Elizabeth Holt, granddaughter Elizabeth Holt, daughter Fanny wife of John Oliver, daughter Mary Anderson, daughter Susanna Coleman, daughter Ann Chich, son James Cocke deceased; daughter Martha Cocke, dated Sept. 20, 1766, proved Oct. 20, 1770.

Will of Nathaniel Edwards, father Nathaniel Edwards, sister Mary Ridley, sister Rebecca Edwards, brother Benjamin Edwards, sister Elizabeth Edwards, brother Isaac Edwards. Dated Aug. 1762, proved Feb. 1771.

Will of Drury Stith, proved Sept. 19, 1770.

Will of William Brodnax, wife Anne, refers to such part of the estate of Stephen Dewey as should appear to belong to the said Wm. Brodnax by Dewey's will, dated June 10, 1762:—Children–Refers to a former will—To brother Edward Brodnax a tract of land now in the possession of Wm. Brodnax of Dinwiddie County, Son-in-law William Evans. John Brodnax [*copy torn], and William Brodnax executors. Dated April 22, 1770, proved March 25, 1771.

Will of Col. Nathaniel Edwards, wife Jane, wife's children by her former husband Henry Haynes, son Isaac Edwards, daughters Anne and Sarah Edwards, daughter Mary Ridley, daughter Elizabeth Willis, daughter Rebecca Jones, son William Edwards. Dated April 29, 1771, proved July 22, 1771.

Inventory of John Nevison, Dec. 6, 1769, £1947.14.2, including 174 vols books, largely divinity, Greek, Latin, &c., valued at £28.6.4.

Will of George Rives, sons Benjamin, William and Francis Rives, wife, daughters Elizabeth Massey, and Ann Peeples. Dated Dec. 19, 1762, proved Jan. 25, 1773.

Inventory of Thomas Harrison, William Harrison administrator £86.6.7, June 25, 1772.

Will of Judith Thweatt, daughter Mary Brown, refers to deceased husband John Thweatt, daughter Elizabeth Birchett, granddaughter Frances Brown, granddaughter Mary Goodwin, son-in-law Wm. Brown, daughter Judith Goodwin, James Goodwin executor. Dated Oct. 12, 1770, proved June 28, 1773.

Will of Robert Read of Essex County, refers to father William Read, deceased,—sisters Ann and Mary Read, brothers John and Lewis Read, sister Susannah Mathis, William, son of James Quarles, Thomas son of James Quarles. Dated Oct. 25, 1766, proved in Brunswick Jan. ,26 1774.

Inventory of Philip Penn, Sept. 1773.

Will of Capt. John Maclin, confirms to son Frederick all property given him same; to sons John and Thomas, son-in-law Matthew Parham, son-in-law James Maclin, son William, daughter Amy Morton, daughter Susannah Maclin. Dated Mune 1771, proved Nov. 28, 1774.

Will of James Harrison, wife, daughters Rebecca and Dolly Harrison Thomas Harrison, wife and Thomas Harrison executors. Dated March 16, 1762, proved May 24, 1762.

Will of Mary Clack, son John Clack, son William Clack, son-in-law Robert Ruffin, refers to deceased husband, grandson Eldridge Clack, dated April 23, 1763, proved May 23, 1763.

Will of Joseph Harrison, daughter Nancy Chappell, son William Harrison, son Daniel Harrison, son Benjamin Harrison, son Simmons Harrison, daughter Patty Harrison, wife Elizabeth. Dated March 8, 1763, proved May 28, 1763.

Inventory of Joseph Harrison, Sept. 1763, £573.19.9.

Will of Col. Henry Embry, wife Martha, son Henry, daughter Mary Embry, granddaughter Mary Embry, daughter of Henry, granddaughter Sarah Embry, daughter of Mary Mariott, grandson Henry Mariott granddaughter Martha Elliott, granddaughter Ermin Embry, grandson Wm. Embry son of Wm. Embry, deceased, date July 14, 1762, proved Sept. 26, 1763.

Will of William Read, dated Dec. 31, 1762, proved Feb. 27, 1764, sons Thomas and Robert, daughter Frances Stone, daughter Catherine Quarles, Elizabeth Read, Susannah Matthews, John, Ann, Mary and Lewis Read, wife Elizabeth, Robert Read and James Quarles, executors.

Inventory of Col. Drury Stith, including 2 pictures £1, 2 maps £1, a fiddle and case £1.10. Total value personal estate £2176.18.7., June 1775.

Will of Harrison Rives, dated Jan. 1776, proved Jan. 1776, cousin Benjamin Rives, brother William Rives' children.

Will of Howell Briggs, wife ,daughter Betsy, nephew Jesse son of Thomas Briggs, Father-in-law Mr. John Quarles.

Will of William Moseley, dated November 1771, proved August 1776 son Levy Moseley, wife, children.

Will of Dr. John Irby, dated Aug. 1746, proved Aug. 1747, wife Anne children.

Will of Sampson Lanier, dated Jan. 1742-3, proved May 1743, sons Thomas, Sampson and Richard, daughter Elizabeth Burch, son Lemuel.

Will of Thomas Lanier, dated Aug. 1745, proved Nov. 1745, sons Jacob, William, Drury and Benjamin, wife Ann.

Will of Ann Brodnax dated Sept. 29, 1788, proved March 23, 1789. son John Brodnax and his daughter Martha Kennon Brodnax, son William Edward Brodnax(among other things gave him the family portraits and, the money due her from his deceased father's estate), grandsons John and William Brodnax Wall, son Thomas Hall Brodnax, daughter Elizabeth Evans, daughter Ann Jackson, daughter Mary Smith, grandsons Henry and William Brodnax Power, John Power.

Will of Gabriel Harrison (x) sons Nathaniel and James, daughter Jane Harrison, dated June 1779, proved Nov. 22, 1779.

Will of William Harrison, dated Nov. 10, 1785, proved Feb. 27, 1786, daughter Ann Marshall, daughter Martha Lashley, sons Henry and William.

Will of Henry Harrison, dated April 14, 1786, proved June 21, 1786, daughter Mary Harrison, sons John and Peter Harrison. Major Binns Jones and Mary Williams executors.

Will of Jonah Harrison (x her mark), dated Aug. 15, 1780, proved Feb. 26, 1787; daughter Jane Cate, son Gronow Owen, son Robert Brown Owen.

Will of Benjamin Harrison, Sr., dated Dec. 29, 1789, proved Jan. 25,-1790, son Thomas, daughter Rita Cooke, daughter Hannar Reas, son

Benjamin, daughter Elizabeth Bainam, daughter Rebecca Hicks, daughter Tabitha Collier, daughter Nancy Hicks, granddaughter Judith Banier, granddaughter Elizabeth P. Hicks, son Theophilus, grandson Robert Harrison, son James.

Will of William Harrison, dated Feb. 9, 1791, proved Feb. 23, 1791, wife Patty, Polly Mayjor Harrison.

Will of Benjamin Harrison (x), dated March 18, 1776, proved, Oct. 27, 1791, brother Nathaniel Harrison.

Will of Mary Lightfoot, dated May 14, 1783, proved Oct. 24, 1785, daughters Patty, Sally, Elmire and Becky Lightfoot, sons Philip an Thomas.

Will of Nicholas Lanier (x), dated April 1788, proved May 1792, son Clement, daughters Sarah Bailey and Mary Crowder, son-in-law Samuel Hudgin.

Will of Richard Clack, dated Jan. 2, 1806, proved Jan. 27, 1806, daughter Eliza Parsons Clack, wife Amy, son Frederick Maclin Clack, six youngest children.

Will of Carter Harrison, dated Sept. 6, 1802, proved Jay 24, 1806 brother James and Benjamin Harisson, refers to deceased father James Harrison.

Will of Daniel Harrison, dated Oct. 19, 1808, proved Oct. 28, 1809, sons John and Richard, daughter Nancy Towns, son Samuel, wife Mary.

Will of William Harrison (x), dated Oct. 1814, proved Nov. 1814, wife Elizabeth, daughters Caty and Nancy.

Will of William Edwards, dated March 1781, proved March 1781, sons Thomas, Nathaniel, Gray, Benjamin and John, grandson James Edwards.

Deed March 1781 from Harmon Harrison and Salley (x), his wife.

Will of Burwell Thweatt, dated Feb. 1781, proved Aug. 1781, Patty Thweatt, daughter of Burwell Thweatt, of Dinwiddie Co., "my mother" Mary Thweatt.

Deed, 1781, from Buckner Stith, of Brunswick Co Va., to Thomas Eaton Esq., of Warren Co., N. C., in consideration of said Thomas Eaton's marriage with Anne, daughter of the said Stith.

Inventory of Philip G. Mallory, 1825.

Deed, 1744, from Benjamin Harrison of Surry Co., and Nathaniel Harrison of Prince George, to John Willis of Gloucester (for £668.1.6, sterling), 3265 acres in Brunswick on both sides of the Three Creeks, also 625 acres on the south side of the little creek of the Three Creeks, also 400 acres or the south side of the Three Creeks, also 130 acres on the north side of Meherrin River, also 201 acres in Brunswick on Uriah's Branch.

Will of Joh Claiborne, dated March 1, 1808, proved Dec. 26, 1808, son James Burnett Claiborne, brother Philip Claiborne and Devereaux Jarrett Claiborne executors.

Will of William Edward Brodnax, dated June 4, 1826, proved March 18, 1831, wife Sarah Brodnax, son Robert all that tract of land he (Robert) lives on on Dan River and Cascade Creek, containing 2664 acres, on his paying £1000 to my estate; to son William Frederick the lands I bought of Frederick Jones, James Robinson and Joseph Winfield and also 1000 acres at the lower end of my Saura Town tract; son Edward Travis the remainder of my Saura Town tract; son Alexander the land I live on, and the land adjoining Joseph Percival's estate, which I purchased of J. Ruffin; also 10 shares in the Roanoke Navigation; to daughter Betty Eppes Wilson all my tract of land in Rockingham County, N. C., bought of Thomas Winsser, also 6000 dollars; daughter Ann Brodnax tract of land bought of Benjamin and Nathaniel Harrison, and also 100 acres of the tract called Thomas Harrison's tract; remainder of said tract to be sold Remainder of estate equally between six children. May 4, 1820.
Codicil; to son William F.; all that tract (Poplar Creek) where he formerly lived, provided he pay my executors 5000 dollars, and also give him all the Saura Town plantation. To Alexander the land purchased of L. Robinson's heirs, and all stocks on plantations given him, and all furniture &c (except the family portraits which I have promised to R. Brodnax). Daughter Anna all work horses on plantation purchased of Benjamin Harrison.

Appraisment of estate of W. E. Brodnax, April 5, 1832

Cash on hand	$8,248.59
Bonds and open accounts	$14,911.12
Land directed by will to be sold	916.50
Negroes not previously distributed (91)	
Stock, and furniture in residence not previously given	635.00
Stocks of all kinds, provisions, plantation implements	755.66
Cotton on hand	125.00

Marriage Bonds.

Thomas Maclin and Julia Edwards, daughter of Lucy Edwards, July 14, 1800.

Edward Pegram and Julia Harper, June 24, 1799.

John Stith of King George, and Susanna, daughter of Lucy Meade, June 24, 1799.

George Feild and Eliza B. Stith, June 15, 1800.

William Harrison and Nelly Holloway, June 5, 1801.

Charles Harrison and Betsy Gladish, May 3, 1801.

Nathaniel Harrison and Rebecca Cooke, May 25, 1801.

Henry Robinson and Mary Clack, Sept. 30, 1772.

Col. John Maclin and Ann Cryer, widow, March 29, 1773.

Timothy Rives and Priscilla Turner, Dec. 20, 1772.

Samuel Garland and Elizabeth, daughter of Nicholas Edmunds, May 27, 1771.

Rolfe Eldridge and Susannah, daughter of George Walker, Nov. 26 1773 (consent of George Walker, witnessed by Courtney Walker).

Andrew Meade, of Nansemond, and Susannah, daughter of Buckner Stith [date omitted, 1773?].

Samuel Edmunds and Betsy Saunders, April 18, 1794.

Robert Harrison and Elizabeth, daughter of Blumer White, Nov. 17. 1794.

Joseph Maclin and Nancy Walker, Aug. 22, 1794.

Thomas Lanier and Polly Vaughan, Aug. 22, 1794.

Burwell Lanier (x) and Elizabeth Pipper, Aug. 22, 1794.

Edward Branch and Sally, daughter of Mary Goodrich, June 24, 1794

Thomas Cocke and Elizabeth Willis, March 21, 1775.

Henry Lanier (x) and Tobitha Eaves, May 25, 1774.

William Cocke and Mary Maclin, March 24, 1772.

Shirley Edmunds and Ermine Simmons, Nov. 28, 1774.

Benjamin Lanier and Elizabeth Parker, Nov. 25, 1771.

Thomas Edmunds and Sarah Eldridge, Nov. 25, 1771.

Benjamin Harrison and Patty Jones, December 1787.

James Blick and Catherine Lanier, Aug. 27, 1787.

Harrison Randolph and Mary Jones, Sept. 7, 1787.

George Woodlief and Katherine Clayton, Sept. 24, 1787.

Nicholas Lanier and Patsey, daughter of George Malone, Dec. 12, 1787.

[Margin of note torn] x x he [or a] in Cocke, and Anne, daughter of Richard Hardy, x x x 17, 1787.

Caddy [?] Harrison and Elizabeth daughter of Arthur Harrison, Jan. 29, 1778.

William Blunt and Ann, daughter of John Gilliam, Oct. 14, 1778.

Roger Mallory, Jr. and Tabitha Baugh, Dec. 24, 1778.

Drury Stith and Fanny, daughter of Allen Love, Sept. 22, 1788.

William Mallory and Sarah Atkins, May 24, 1786.

Richard Clack and Anne Hardaway, Sept. 14, 1786.

William Gray, of Southampton, and Mary, daughter of Henry Ledbetter [date omitted, but 1786 or 1787].

Thomas Read and Nancy, daughter of James Quarles, Feb. 20, 1787.

Benjamin Goodrich and Tabitha Hicks, May 25, 1789.

Clement Read and Clarissa, daughter of Thomas Edmunds, March 27, 1789.

Richard Clack and Amey Maclin, June 3, 1794.

Henry A. Watkins and Ann Edmunds, May 6, 1794.

Edmund Lanier and Patsy Walton, Aug. 26, 1793.

William H. Harrison and Anne Williams, Nov. 25, 1811.

Richard Curd, and Nancy daughter of Benj. Harrison, Oct. 12, 1795.

Richard Eppes and Sarah Mathis, Nov. 22, 1795.

James Wyche, of Albemarle parish, Sussex, and Sarah Maclin, of Brunswick, Jan. 21, 1755.

Matthew Parham, Jr. and Rebecca Maclin, Nov. 25, 1755.

Samuel Dawson, of Amelia, and Martha, daughter of Thomas Jones, Jan. 16, 1756.

Joseph Jones and Ann Jones, widow, May 16, 1756.

Robert Lanier and ——, daughter of John Jackson, Nov. 9, 1754.

John Cook (with consent of his father Henry Cook) and Betty Brown Sept. 25, 1759.

John Nivison and Anne Tazewell, "an infant," June 23, 1757.

Silvanus Stokes and Temperance, daughter of George Clarke, Aug. 24, 1756.

William Clack and Betty Twitty, Oct. 16, 1757.

William Harrison and Ann Major, May 7, 1759.

Henry Taylor, of Southampton, and Temperance, daughter of John Peterson, Dec. 28, 1758.

James Day Ridley and Mary Edwards, Sept. 25, 1758.

Robert Ruffin, of Surry, and Molly Lightfoot, widow, Sept. 6, 1751.

Benjamin Rives and Bethea Rosser, widow, May 1791.

Claiborne Anderson, of Chesterfiled, and Betty Clack, July 24 1753 (consent of Richard Eppes, Anderson's guardian.)

Robert Wynne, of Surry, and Mary Phillipson, Aug. 9, 1753.

William Stith and Catherine Stith, Sept. 14, 1756.

William Maclin, Jr. and Sarah Clack, Sept. 25, 1754.

William Cocke and Sarah Edwards, July 23, 1754.

John Harrison and Cressy Steed, Dec. 14, 1779.

William Thornton and Sarah, daughter of Edward Goodrich, Feb. 16, 1774.

Richard Cocke, and Mary, daughter of Richard Whitehead, May 1769.

Armistead Burwell, and Mary, daughter of Robert Tunrbull, Dec. 10, 1800.

Robert Lanier and Nancy Harrison, Nov. 24, 1800.

John R. Mason and Sarah H. Cargill, Feb. 9, 1799.

William Harrison and Elizabeth Tillman, March 2, 1799.

John Harrison and Dorothy Hancock, Nov. 5, 1799.

Nathaniel Harrison and Martha K. Brodnax, March 25, 1799.

Augustus W. Maclin and Polly James, Nov. 10, 1799.

Wills Etc.

Inventory of Alexander Brodnax, 63 slaves, a parcel of books, &c.

Will of Alexander Brodnax, dated Feb. 1832, proved March 1832, wife Rebecca a plantation in Mecklenburg, called The Hermitage, with stocks etc., for life after her death to his children.

Will of Rebecca A. Brodnax, dated May 1842, proved Oct. 1842, children, Wm. Edward Brodnax, Sally Jones Brodnax, and Alexander John Brodnax, Brother John L. Wilkins, Jr.

HENRY TIMBERLAKE.

(Contributed by A. J. Morrison, Hampden-Sidney, Va.)

Henry Timberlake was no author, but his book should be better known, entitled Memoirs of Lieutenant Henry Timberlake (who accompanied the three Cherokee Indians to England in the year 1762) * * * * * London: Printed for the author 1765. This small volume of 160 printed pages—there is a curious appendix in cipher, the journal of a French officer killed by the Innians—forms the plain statement of services rendered in an irregular way and therefore perhaps charity honored by money award. For at least twenty years after 1762, it must be admitted, the bountiful British exchequer was tempting enough to many Americans.

Timberlake says that he was born in Virgi|ia and received almost as good an education as the country could afford. His father dying when young Timberlake was in his teens and leaving no large estate, the boy looked out for employment as a soldier. In 1758 he was given an ensigncy and a cornetcy in Colonel Byrd's regiment. In 1759 he was with General Stanwix. In 1761 orders came to him at Fort Bird, sixty miles east of Pittsburg, to report for Cherokee business in the Holston river country. Colonel Byrd had been placed in command of this expedition, but at the celebrated Stahlnaker's Colonel Byrd "returned down the country," by which the command devolved on Colonel Stephen." Here is one vexed point made plain. Colonel Stephen kept on with his command to the Great Island of Holston, commonly called Long Island. There a fort was begun and was nearly finished the middle of November 1761 when head men came in from Kanagatucko the nominal King of the Cherokees requesting a peace conference or talk, as the Cherokee styled it. November 19th a peace was fixed up. Then the Indians asked that some officer of Colonel Stephen's family might be sent among their towns down river as a demonstration of good will. The Colonel felt a delicacy about ordering anybody on such a risky errand, so Timberlake volunteered to go. Later, Timberlake having no papers to show in the matter, the Earl of Egremont treated him rather shabbily. Delegations of Indian chiefs had become no novelty in London by the year 1762—General Oglethorpe and others had taken over a good many of them.

Timberlake thought it well to learn the navigation down Holston and up Tennessee to the Cherokee towns. He went from Long Island to Chota by boat. McCormack went along as interpreter and Sumpter as sergeant. Sumpter was of Lieutenant Timberlake's party to see King George upon the throne across the ocean. Getting into the Tennessee River, Timberlake made careful observations and drew off a map which he had printed as the frontispiece to his book —an excellent sketch map from the great Island of Tennessee up as far as Talasse. This chart settles another point neatly and definitely. A little way from the Tellico river stood what was left of Fort Loudoun, on the south bank of

Tennesse. A few miles below stood Chota, the chief town of the Cherokee, and across the river Tennessee, on the north bank, were the remains of a fort, described by Timberlake thus—"a fort built by the Virginians in 1756 and soon after destroyed by the Indians." So the Virginians built their fort opposite Chota, and the South Carolinians built their Fort Loudoun five or six miles down stream. [This Magazine, April 1918, p. 203—"the Question of Fort Loudoun.")

Timberlake smoked amicably and diplomaticaly through the five and more towns up as far as Talasse. Then setting off for Williamsburg by the East Tennessee and Southwest Virginia road (as we say), Ostenaco called also Judd's Friend or the Judge, would not be denied, and Lieutenant Timberlake discreetly took him and two other head men of the towns to Williamsburg and the Governor. At Williamsburg Mr. Horrocks of the College had Timberlake and the three to supper. Ostenaco saw a picture of King George at Mr. Horrocks's and protested that he must go see the King himself. That is how the Lieutenant and the three and Sergeant Sumpter happened to go to London. They got back home before the near year 1764, not very well pleased with their London times. There is more in the book, but the book is small and should be read in full. It is hoped a copy can be found in Virginia.

There was a Henry Timberlake, Colonel of Louisa troops in the Revolution. On examination it appears that Lieutenant Timberlake had been duly recommended to the Board of Trade by Governor Fauquier. See the Governor's Letter of May 1, 1762 in **Journals House of Burgesses** 17 -65.61,. XVII—"I am conscious, my Lords, that such quests are troublesome to His Maj'ty's Ministers, but it appears to me to be of so much moment to the peace and interest of the Colonies, that I hope I shall stand excused for taking this step. The Indians will be accompanied by Mr. Timberlake an Ensign in our Regiment, who has been in the Cherokee Overhill Towns, and is much respected by the Indians; he went from our camp down Holston's River and up the Tennessee and has found it navigable for Batteaus which draw 10 or 12 inches water, all the way, by which we find that we have a good convenience for men, stores, or merchandise into the very heart of their country. He has made a draught of the courses and bearings of the River, a fair copy of which is by my order preparing for Sir Jeffery Amherst." Timberlake had this good map and his book printed off in 1765, when he went to London a second time, partly on a business venture with Mr. Truchaeart of Hanover County. Who was Timberlake's . Mr. Kakoanthropos, the man, he says, that stood so much in his way with Lord Egremont.

NOTES ON THE SHENANDOAH VALLEY OF VIRGINIA.

Volume 3 of **Documentary History of New York,** Albany 1850, contains as its frontispiece "Champlain's May of New France, 1632." This map snows the greater portion of the present Canada, the present New Englann States; a portion of the middle Western States; and the Eastern and Southern States as far south as Albermarle Sound in North Carolina, The Chesapeake Bay with the principal rivers which flow into it is shown. but the names of the rivers are not given.

This map clearly and certainly proves the fact that the Shenandoah Valley of Virginia had been visited, and to some extent explored, as early as 1632, because the course of Shenandoah River is designated. On the map to the junction of that stream with the Potomac at present Harper's Ferry, W. Va.

The Peaked Mountain five east of the present Harrisonburg, Va. is shown on the map, and also the peak which terminates the Massanutten range near present Strasburg, Va.

.On page 18 of the work mentions a table is printed giving the names o f the more important places on the map. Among them Jamestown, Va., and pages 1-18 contain an account of Champlain's expeditions. As he makes no statement to the effect that he visited Virginia in person, it is probable that Champlain gained his knowledge of the Shenandoah Valley from Jesuit Missionaries, the members of which Society are so active at a later time in exploring the Mississippi Valley. And it is highly probable that these missionaries were the first white men to view and explore the Valley of Virginia. Charlesf E. Kemper.

Staunton, Va., Dec. 8, 1919.

Judge John Catron of the United States Supreme Court.

By Boutwell Dunlap.

In the pamphlet lists of Germans and those of German descent who have been distinguished in American history, widely distributed by German propaganda during the war, I never saw a publication which mentioned John Catron, Justice of the United States Supreme Court, 1837-1865, who attained one of the highest political and judicial ranks of any one of German origin in the new world. Another member of the Catrons sat in the United States Senate. It is not frequent a family produces two men, one a United States Supreme Court justice and the other a United States Senator. Nor have the Germans in America, generally speaking, possessed political genius nor been to the fore in political life. Writers on the German element in Virginia seem not to have known or ignored this strain of Catrons. Because of the foregoing and Justice John Catron has been called a native of Pennsylvania by the United States Supreme Court, although in fact a native of Virginia, I select from my notes and collections on the trans-Alleghany movement what I have on his antecedents. My Mss. contains letters from United

States Senator T. B. Catron of New Mexico and other members of the family and a copy of a sworn declaration for a Revolutionary pension under the act of 1832.

Staufle or Stuffle Catron—the first two names being German contractions or Christopher—was born in Germany, probably about 1734. Previous to his coming to America, he lived in Holland. Justic John Catron stated a short time before his death to Mrs. C. C. Childress of St. Louis, an adopted daughter of one of the Catrons, that Stuffle or Christopher Catron lived about thirty miles from Rotterdam.

In 1764, he came with his wife, Susanna ——, and several children, to Pennsylvania. In 1766, he moved to the then Augusta, now Montgomery county, Virginia. Stuffle Catron was the father of at least the following: Peter Catron, Adam Catron, Jacob Catron, Solomon Catron, Frank Catron, Christopher Catron, Crisley Catron, Catherine Catron. Some of the Catrons were out in Dunmore's war. In the 18th century in Virginia, the name was sometimes spelled Kettering, as shown in the case, Pierce's heirs vs. Catron's heirs, before the Supreme Court of Virginia in 1810. Some branches of the family now spell the name Katron and some spell it Cattron.

Peter Catron, son of the immigrant and seemingly the oldest child, was born in 1754 and moved in 1786 to what is now Grayson county, Virginia. In 1804, he removed to Wayne county, Kentucky. His son, Justice John Catron, was born in the now Grayson county, Virginia. On the death of the Justice, memoranda in 70 United States Reports ix, states he was born in Pennsylvania. This is untrue. Justice Catron in 1858 wrote a brother of United States Senator T. B. Catron that he, the Justice, was born in Grayson county, Virginia.

Jacob Catron, son of the immigrant, married —— Goast. Their son, Christopher Catron, born in Wythe county, Virginia, married Famy Jones, daughter of Minitree Jones. Their son, John Catron, born in White county, Tennessee, in 1812, married Mary Fletcher, native of Montgomery county, Virginia, daughter of James Fletcher and Margaret Patterson, and were the parents of T. B. Catron, United States senator from New Mexico.

Peter Catron, father of the Justice, in 1834, applied for a Revolutionary pension. The veteran's sworn declaration made in order to obtain it, recites some of the early Revolutionary movements in Southwest Virginia:

> On this 22 day of January 1834, personally appeared Peter Catron, Before me Roger Oatts a justice of the peace for Wayne County, Kentucky, who is a resident of Wayne Co., Kentucky, aged 80 years old who being first duly sworn according to law, doth on his oath make the following Declaration in order to obtain the Benefit of the Act of Congress passed June 7th 1832. The said Peter Catron states that he was a volunteer as a private malitia man in the State of Virginia Mont-

gomery County for three months in the year 1776, about the last of May or the first of June, the precise time not now Recollected, upon a Draft from the State of Virginia, as he understood. My captains name was Walter Crocket and my Lieutenant's name I think was William Campbell. But, the ensign not now recollected we first met & Rendezvoused on Walkers creek and thence marched and Ranged thro the country from the head waters of Clinch River & Blue Stone, thence over and on the Waters of Sandy River & Guiandotte, principally against the Shawne Indians, in and on the frontiers, all the country on the frontiers in that quarter being forted and Indians very troublesome. But in this tour we had no engagement in our Ranging after the Indians. They in some way eluding us We had no superior officers, our tour being out and the Indians becoming less troublesome we were discharged. By our captain & officers But not in writing. We were almost naked, and suffered much fatigue & Hardship. Having served the said three months tour, some short time after I returned home A call and Draft was again called for By authority of the State of Virginia to protect the people of Houlston from the incursions of the Cherokee Indians who was very troublesome. I again volunteered, I think on the 15 or 16 of July after in 1777 under an ensign his Christian name not now recollected as a private, & Ranged for three months And we marched Ranged & scoured the country rom the head waters of Houlston & Clinch Rivers Backwards & forwards in constant service. In this tour we had no engagement—But requently saw the sign and hail of the Indians who were thought to be pretty thick. Having actually served our three months tour provisions hard to get, the Indians less troublesome, we were discharged by our ensign the officers. But not in writing and we returned home much fatigued.

In the month of January or February the year 1878 [sic] the day not now distinctly recollected But some short time before the Treaty volunteered as a Ranger from the State of Virginia and from the County of Montgomery as a private from a call of the State of Virginia under Captain John Stepehens under a call for three or 6 months tour this Deponent does not know recollect which But he is inclined to think for 6 months tour, Having no General officers we first rendezvoused at the head of Reed creak, and marched and Ranged in a Direction to a fort on Clinch River called the Rye cove, and then we were stationed guarding In the fort a considerable time, we then ranged in a Direction to the Cumberland gap. We ranged to Martins Station in Powels va lley we were then met by another company of Ranger's under Captain J. Martin we then Ranged and Marched back to the Rye cove, where we were first stationed where we found the Indians had killed several persons, just before our return. Shortly after a Treaty, was about to take place Between the Cherokee Indians & Governor Preston & Col. Shelby, our company of Rangers, was ordered and Marched to the Treaty on long island on the Houlston River, and we remained there on guard until the Treaty was made, several other companies meeting there. After the Treaty was made, we were all discharged in our company but not in writing by our Captain. & we returned home to the County of Montgomery in the State of Virginia, Having actually served six months in this tour amounting to 12 months in my three tours for which I Respectfully claim compensation. as a private under the aforesaid law of Congress. The said Peter Catron knows of no person in this country now living, by whom he can prove his aforesaid Revolutionary services. & the said Peter Catron cannot Read the English Language, am old & infirm was born in the year 1754 in Germany, came to Pennsylvania, with my Father Stuffle Catron in the year 1761 and in the year 1766 removed to Montgomery county State of Virginia and remained there untill the year 1804 and then Removed to Wayne county Ky. where I now live and have lived about 29 years * * * * * *

NOTES FROM PRINCESS ANNE COUNTY.

(Concluded from xxiv. 416.)

Will of Sampson Trevethan, of the town of Plymouth, Cornwall, gent. dated May 17, 1726, proved Oct. 1, 1729. To be buried in the parish church of Madderne. Legatees: wife Katherine (including £400 due him on a mortgage by James Keigwyn, of Mousehole in said county) and after her death to his two daughters he left in Virginia, Mary and Ann Trevethan. To wife a messuage in Madderne called Shoals House. To William Gwavas Esq. and Gregory Trigwitha, tanner, both of Penzance, all the rest of his estate, in trust to pay his debts, &c, and to pay his daughters Mary and Ann £200 each. All lands &c in Lynhaven parish, Va., to his two daughters.

Will of Ann Trevethan, Jr., of Lynhaven parish, Princess Anne Co., dated Dec. 25, 1735, proved May 5, 1736. Cousins James, Daniel and Elizabeth Tennant, cousin Mary Ann Thouroughgood, loving mother Ann Trevethan, mother and friend Anthony Moseley, executors.

Deposition of Ann Trevethan, aged about 60 years, taken July 5, 1738. She was intimately acquainted with Mr. Jonas Cawson, late of Norfolk County, deceased, and was at the celebration of a marriage between him and a certain Abigail Church. A minister of the Church of England performed the ceremony. They had several children, viz.: Keziah, Christopher, Argal, Ann, Abigail, and Jonas. He died 1726, and his son Keziah died about 1732, and also Christopher Cawson and eldest son and said Jonas made a will.

Deposition of Mrs. Abigail Cawson als Whiddon, aged about 50 years. Taken July 5, 1738. She was married to Jonas Cawson about 29 years ago by Rev. Mr. McMioner, then minister in Norfolk County, that Keziah their first born died in 1732. She had heard the said Jonas Cawson speak of his native country, Old England, saying he was born in Lancaster in England, and he told her that he expected an estate to fall to him from his father and mentioned it in his will.

Deed [partly mutilated], 173-, between Thomas Bolithoe, of Cornwall, heir at law of the deceased John Bolihoe, late of —[Va, to John Nicholas and Yates his wife in consideration of her dower [1738.]

Will of Francis Thoroughgood, of Princess Anne, dated Feb. 13, 1740, proved April 1, 1741. Wife Amy, eldest son John, nine children (not named.)

Deed, Aug. 21, 1745, between John Thoroughgood, gent., and Anthony Walke, Gent. John Thoroughgood had married Margaret Walke, Oct. 13, 1743, and became entitled to certain property said Anthony Walke gave his daughter.

Deed, Dec. 15, 1745, from Thomas Walke, and Mary Ann his wife, to Adam Thoroughgood, conveying 230 acres of land, being land left by Robert Thoroughgood, the elder, to his son Thomas (father of the said Mary Ann Walke) she being the only child of said Thomas Thoroughgood, from whom she inherits said land.

THE LOVELACE FAMILY AND ITS CONNECTIONS

By J. Hall Pleasants, Baltimore, Md.

(Continued)

VII. Sir William Lovelace[7] (John[1], Richard[2], William[3], William[4], William[5], William[6]). He was baptized February 12th, 1583-4, at St. Alphege, Canterbury. He is usually known as "Sir William Lovelace of Woolwich", where one of his residences, possibly acquired through his wife, was located, although he is styled in his will and in his *inquisition* as "Sir William Lovelace, the younger, of Bethersden", and would, of course, have succeeded to Lovelace Place had he have outlived his father. He was knighted by James I at Theobald's, 20 September, 1609. (*Shaw's Knights of England;* ii; p. 148). He married, apparently as early as 1610, Anne the daughter of Sir William Barne, knight, of Woolwich, Kent, by his wife Anne the daughter of Edwin Sandys, Archbishop of York. Both the Barne and Sandys families took a very active part in the colonization of Virginia, and will be considered later in separate sketches. Sir William Lovelace[5] was a member of the Virginia Company and an incorporator of the second Virginia Charter, 1609 (*Brown's Genesis of the United States:* pp. 213, 939).

Sir William Lovelace[7] was a soldier by profession, although the assertion in a letter of Charles I that he "had served about forty years in ye warres" is obviously an exaggeration, as he was only forty-three at the time of his death. From some Latin lines preceding *Lucasta* by his son Richard Lovelace[8], the poet, it appears that he had served with distinction in the Low Countries (*Poetical Works of Richard Lovelace; Hazlitt Edition;* p. xiv). It is stated definitely both in the letter of Charles I reproduced below, and in *Hasted's Kent* that Lovelace fell at the Groll. As his *inquisition post mortem*, a full abstract of which follows, states that he died 12 August, 3 Charles I [1627], there is no question that he was killed at the last siege of the Groll* in Holland. England and

*Emphasis is laid upon the evidence that Sir William Lovelace was killed at the siege of the Groll, 12 August 1627, because it is stated in another connection that he was "slain at the siege of the Burse." In a *calendar of inquisitions, temp. Henry VIII to Charles I,* in the Heralds College, compiled and annoted by Sir Charles Young, Garter King of Arms, and now being published in *The Genealogist* (1915; xxxi; 276) occurs the following: "Sir William Lovelace, knt., slain at the siege of the Burse [1628]". As the year of death is incorrectly given here, and as the original *inquisition* contains no reference whatsoever to the place of death, the compiler of the *calendar of inquisitions* has obviously added from some other source the statement in regard to the Burse. The writer has not only been unable to find any confirmation of this statement, but has been unable to locate a place of this name in Holland, or to find any reference to such a siege. It seems quite possible, however, that some minor engagement at a place bearing such a name may have taken place in connection with the operations about Groll.

SIR WILLIAM LOVELACE, of Woolwich
Father of Ann (Lovelace) Gorsuch.

Holland as members of the Protestant Alliance were then at war with Spain, and Lovelace fell only a few days before the stronghold of the Groll was recaptured by the allies from the Spaniards. Among the Egerton MSS. in the British Museum (No. 2553; folio 50-B) is a very interesting letter from Charles I to the Governor of Sutton's Hospital, London, later known as Charterhouse School, apparently written early in 1628, endorsed "For one of Sir William Lovelace's Sons". This letter, a copy of which follows, has been published in the *Gentleman's Magazine* (1884:-ii; p. 462):

From His Majesty to ye Governour of Sutton's Hospital

Whereas we are given to understand that Sir William Lovelace after he had served about forty years in ye warres, and was slaynte at ye last siege of Grolle, and his fortune most depending upon ye warres left his lady ritch only in great store of children, and she most humbly beseeching us to bestow one of our places in Sutton's Hospitall upon one of his sonnes, Wee are pleased to grant his request. Wherefore our royal pleasure is that ye Lord Archbishop of Canterbury, and others ye governours of ye said Hospitall doe take orders that Thomas Lovelace his son may be admitted ye said house in our prime place at yr next thereon.

Given under our hand this day in ye fourth yeare of our reign
[Charles Rex]

From the will of Sir William Lovelace[5] and the *inquisition post mortem* upon his landed estate, and from the will of his widow Lady Anne, here reproduced for the first time, many facts of interest are learned. As Sir William Lovelace was outlived by his father he never came into actual possession of Lovelace Place, although the *inquisition* specifically states that the "remainder" was vested in him, subject to the life interest of his father. From the *inquisition* we also learn that the tenure of Lovelace Place was held by the Lovelaces "of the Archbishop of Canterbury as of his Manor of Bethersden by fealty." Reference is also made in his will and in the *inquisition* to other lands held by him in Bethersden and to sundry lands in Shoulden, Chart Magna, Shidonhurst and Canterbury in the county of Kent. How he actually came into legal possession of these various properties during his father's lifetime, except in the case of the Shoulden lands which he acquired by purchase, is somewhat uncertain. It seems most probable that they had been made over by indenture to him by his father prior to July 15, 1622, the date of his will, as his father makes no mention in his will, dated 6 October, 1629, of any lands whatsoever, disposing only of personal property. On the other hand any lands belonging to the elder Sir William[6], in regard to which he died intestate, would of course have passed by law to the issue of his only son Sir William, deceased. Those which the grandfather had held by the "custom of gavelkind of Kent" would, however, have been equally divided among all his grandsons, while those held by entail, as Bethersden Place, would all have passed to his eldest grandson Richard, the poet. As no property in Woolwich is mentioned in the will or *inquisition* it seem probable that his residence there was of a temporary character, and with his wife's family, the Barnes.

Sir William Lovelace[7], the younger, had by his wife Anne Barne eight children, five sons and three daughters who reached maturity, and whose names are known. As neither the parish register of Bethersden nor of Woolwich covering this period are in existence, the exact dates of baptism or birth of most of the children cannot be determined. Anne was certainly the eldest child; Richard the poet was the eldest son and became the proprietor of Lovelace Place. The wills show that Thomas, Francis and William were respectively the second, third and fourth sons. The *inquisition* shows that Joan was the "child to be born" named in Sir William's will, dated 15 July, 1622; Elizabeth, not named in her father's will, was the youngest daughter, and Dudley, or as he styled himself, Dudley-Posthuums, was the youngest child and born after August 12, 1627, the date of his father's death. It will be noted that the only children named in the *inquisition* are those who under their father's will were to receive land or legacies chargeable against land. The *inquisition* settles a point of no little general interest—the exact date of birth of Richard Lovelace, the poet. All biographical sketches of him state that he was born in 1618, although none give the month and day. The *inquisition* now enables us to show that this date is incorrect, and to fix the date of his birth definitely as December 6, 1617.

The portrait of Sir William Lovelace[7] which is reproduced here is from a photograph of the painting in the Dulwich Gallery (Gallery No. 365-panel 25x21 inches). An excellent copy in oil of this same portrait is in the collection of Mr. Walter deC. Poultney of Baltimore. It is interesting to note that this portrait,as well as those of his father and grandfather are referred to in his wife's will. Lady Lovelace's will also shows that she was at one time in the Low Countries. His widow Lady Anne Lovelace married, January 20, 1630, at Greenwich as her second husband Jonathan Browne, Doctor of Laws. Browne matriculated at Gloucester Hall, Oxford 13 October, 1620, aged 19, and received the degree of B. C. L. 1624-5, D. C. L. 1630 and L. L. D. He held the following preferements: rector of Shelly, Essex, 1621; rector of St. Faith's, London, 1628; rector of Hertingfordbury, Herts, 1630; canon of Hereford Cathedral, 1636; dean of Hereford Cathedral 1636; canon of Westminster Abbey, 1639. He outlived his wife and died December, 1643, and his will (undated and unregistered) was proved 8 April, 1645 (*Oxford Wills; Prerogative Court of Canterbury;* 1645). A copy of this will in the possession of the writer shows that he had a daughter Anne Browne who had married prior to 8 April, 1645, Herbert Croft, S. T. P. The will of "Dame Anne Lovelace, now the wife of Jonathan Browne, of London, Doctor of Laws", dated 16

May, 1632, and proved by her husband, 22 May, 1633, of which a full abstract will follow, makes bequests to "my daughter Anne Browne". The date of marriage, 20 January, 1630, of Jonathan Browne and Anne (Barne Lovelace as given by Crisp (*Visitation of England and Wales; Notes vii* 121), may be incorrect, for unless Anne Browne married Croft at a very early age, it is hard to see how she could have been a daughter by Anne (Barne) Lovelace, as the wills indicate she was.

The will of Sir William Lovelace, dated July 15th, 1622, disposes of sundry family manors and lands, which his father, who did not die until 1629, had doubtless already legally settled upon him. The will of Sir William Lovelace the younger of Bidersden [Bethersden], co. Kent, knight, dated 15 July, 1622, was proved 23 June, 1628, in the Prerogative Court of Canterbury (*1628; Barrington 60*). The following is an abstract

I Sir William Lovelace of Bidersden, co. Kent, Knight, appoint my wife Anne Lovelace and Thomas Twisden of Wie, co. Kent, esq., guardians of my children, and I make the said Thomas Twisden my executor with my wife. I give to them all my lands whatsoever in Bethersden, Holden [Sholden], Chart Magna, Shidonhurst and Canterburie, till my eldest son Richard Lovelace attain his age of 24, when he shall enter therein. If he die before that age, I give them to my second son Thomas, and in the event of his death, to my third son Francis at 24. I give to my said two younger sons all my lands in the parish of Sholden, co. Kent, which I purchased of Sir Peeter Manwoode. To my daughter Anne Lovelace, all my stock and adventure in the East India Company, with all the profits thereon to be paid her at her age of 21 or marriage. To the child to be born to me £200 if a son, £300 if a daughter, to be paid out in lands. I give to the said Thomas Twisden my embroidered scarf, with all my horses, swords and arms whatsoever.

(signed) William Lovelace.

Witnesses: Thomas Aton, Ric. Tucker.

Proved 23 June 1628 by Anne Lovelace, the relict, the other executor being dead.

The *inquisition post mortem* upon the estate of Sir William Lovelace[7] taken 9 August 1628 (*Court of Wards and Liveries–Inquisitions Post mortem;* 77; p. 128), has never been previously published, and contains most intersting data. It will be noted that the *inquisition* does not mention the younger children, William, Elizabeth and Dudley who were not born at the time their father's will was made, 15 July 1622, and were not provided for under its terms, but does mention Joan who was "the child to be born to me" of the will.

Sir William Lovelace the younger of Betherisden, co. Kent, Knight. Inquisition taken at the castle in Canterbury 9 August 4 Charles 1 [1628]. The said Sir William was seised of the wood or woodland called Lamberden Wood, containing about 100 acres, in Betherisden;a farm or messuage, & 18 acres of land in Bethersiden in the tenure of Thomas Bird; inclosed land there called The Parke (about 70 acres), in the occupation of George Trusse; a messuage & 30 acres of land there in the tenure of James Wills; a tenement there called Loders House, in the tenure of Andrew Loder; 15 acres called Hunt's Lands, in the tenure of ——Loder, widow; a messuage and 60 acres called Carpenter's Farm, in the tenure of ——Howard; a messuage & 50 acres called Barboddenden, in the tenure of Thomas Waterman; 30 acres called Burthouse lands, in the tenure of ——Gadsby; a messuage & 50 acres called Elites Farme, in the tenure of the said George Trusse; tenements in the occupation of ——Carpenter, widow, Thomas Witherden, Richard Long, Thomas Ellis, John Wilverden, Stephen Austen and John Howlet, all in Betherisden; a messuage in the parish of All Hallows, Canterbury, in the occupation of John Jorden; 2 messuages and 40 acres of land in Betherisden, lately purchased of the heirs of Thomas Blechenden, in the occupation of John Holmes and George Morris; a messuage called "le Mazondien house, keepers house or warriner's house" in the Downes in the parish of Shouldon, co. Kent, and 50 acres of land called Sandhilles and Outgroundes, lying between the sea and the marshes there, late in the tenure of Christian Hurlstone and Ezekiel Barbar, and afterwards of ——Brooke; marshes heretofore called "le Nethermarshe" in Shouldon, late belonging to the dissolved house called "le Mazondew" of Dover, & now called the Mazondew marshes, containing about 60 acres. At the time of his death and eversince, his father, Sir William Lovelace, Kt; was and is seised of a capital messuage and 30 acres of land in Betherisden, now in the occupation of the said Sir William Lovelace the father and George Trusse.

By their deed dated 18 February 18 James I [1620] the two Sir William's granted to John Blechenden, citizen and mercer of London, an annuity of £20 payable out of all the premises, at the south door of the parish church of Tenterden, beginning in the year 1623. The interest of the said John Blechenden in the said annuity has been conveyed to Sir John Hales, Kt., heir apparent of Sir Edward Hales, baronet. The will of Sir William the son is here recited. He died 12 August 3 Charles I [1627]. Richard Lovelace, his son and heir, was then aged 9 years, 8 months, 3 days at the time of the death of his father. The chief messuage in Betherisden, in the occupation of his father for his life, with remainder to the deceased Sir William, is held of the Archbishop of Canterbury as of his manor of Bethersiden by fealty and a rent of —— Dame Anne Lovelace, his widow, is still living. Thomas Twisden named joint guardian with her of his children by the will of the said Sir William, died at Wye, co. Kent, 1 August 1 Charles I. His sons Thomas and Francis Lovelace survive. After the date of his will, his wife Anne bore a daughter Joan, who is now alive.

The will of Anne, widow of Sir William Lovelace, dated 15 May, 1632, proved 22 May, 1633, in the Perogative Court of Canterbury (*1633. Russell*, 51). The following is an abstract:

I Dame Anne Lovelace*, now wife of Jonathan Browne of London, Doctor of Laws. Whereas the wardship of my son Richard is granted to me by his Majesty's Court of Wards till his age of 21, I give the same to the said Jonathan Browne and to Miles Barnes, M. A., my brother with power to sell underwood for the payment of the debts of my late husband Sir William Lovelace and myself. The £100 which Sir William Lovelace owed to my uncle Francis Barne, esq., which he always promised to give me at his death, shall be given to my daughter Elizabeth Lovelace. My said trustees shall obtain a new lease from Sir Robert Honeywood, Knight, of the manor of Bethersden, co. Kent; and out of the profits thereof they shall pay £300 apiece to my daughters Elizabeth and Joane, and my son Dudley Lovelace. I give to my son Richard my furniture for a bed of black velvet, with cushions, chaires and carpets, etc., as the same is wrought in colours by his grandmother, the Lady Lovelace, and my best suit of diaper and which I made in the Low Countries, and a pair of fine Holland sheets, and a black gilded cabinet, which was his fathers, and all the furniture those goods and implements of household standing in his chief house at Bethersden, and the pictures of his father and myself, and of his grandfather, and my wedding ring which was his father's. To my sons Thomas, Francis and William Lovelace, £20 apiece for their maintenance till their age of 21, to be paid yearly out of the lands called Sholden, co. Kent, which my late husband purchased of Sir Peter Manwood, Knight. To my daughters Elizabeth and Joane, and my son Dudley, £20 apiece in like manner out of the lease of Bethersden. To Anne Gorsage, my daughter my third suit of diaper which I made in the Low Countries, etc. To each of my younger children a ring enamelled, at 16. To my daughter Anne Browne, my scarlet velvet petticoat, my diamond ring, etc. To my husband Jonathan Browne, my cabinet of black ebony. To my brother Miles Barne, £2 and a ring, etc. If my husband continue housekeeping and keep my younger children, he shall have the use of all my linen, etc; otherwise it shall be sold, towards the payment of my debts and the portions of the said Elizabeth, Joane and Dudley. To my brothers Sir William Barne, Knight, Robert Barne and George Barne, and to their wives, 20s. apiece to make them rings; and the like to Mr. Richard Juxon, Daniell Gorsage and his wife, and my sone Gorsage. To my two men servants, a mourning cloak apiece, and to

*This is an example of the custom of the time, which permitted a woman who had made a second marriage, to retain the name and title acquired from her first husband, if his rank was higher than that of her second husband.

my three maid servants, serge for mourning gowns. I make the said Jonathan Browne and Miles Barne my executors.

(signed) Anne Lovelace.

Witnesses: Robt. Barne, Tho. Grent, Jo. Smyther.

Issue of Sir William Lovelace[7] (John[1], Richard[2], William[3], William[4], William[5] ,William[6],) and his wife Anne Barne:

1. Anne Lovelace[8]. She was apparently born not later than 1611 as she married as early as 1628 the Rev. John Gorsuch of Walkern, Herts. *The Visitation of London;* 1633-1635 gives the wife of the Rev. John Gorsuch as "Anne da of Sir William Lovelace of Kent, Kt." (*Harleian Soc. Publ.* xv; 327). She received under her father's will, dated 1622, "all my adventures in the East India Company with all the profits to be paid to her at the age of 21 or marriage". By her mother's will, dated 1632, there is left to "Anne Gorsage my daughter my third suit of diaper which I made in the Low Countries". She went to Virginia, probably about 1650 and soon after the death of her husband, with her younger children and died there (*Va. Mag.* xxiv; 90). Letters of administration were issued in England, 2 June, 1652, to "Daniel Gorsuch son of Anne Gorsuch, late of Weston, co. Hertford, but deceased in parts beyond the seas, widow" (*Prerogative Court of Canterbury Administrations 1652*). She had issue by her husband Rev. John Gorsuch, eleven children whose fortunes and descendants have been traced by the writer in the preceding volumes of this magazine; viz.: (i) Daniel; (ii) John; (iii) William; (iv) Katharine married William Whitby; (v) Robert; (vi) Richard; (vii) Anna married 1st Capt. Thomas Todd, 2nd Capt. David Jones, 3d Capt. John Oldton; (viii) Elizabeth married Howell Powell; (ix) Charles; (x) Lovelace; (xi) Frances) Of these, Katharine, Robert, Richard, Anna, Elizabeth, Charles and Lovelace settled in Virginia or in Maryland, married, and with the probable exception of Robert, left numerous descendants (*Va. Mag. xxiv-xxvii*).

2. Richard Lovelace.[8] Poet and cavalier. Born, 9 December 1617, at Woolwich, Kent. The exact date of his birth, as shown in the *inquisition* upon his father's estate, has not been previously known, all biographical accounts simply giving the year 1618. He attended Charterhouse School, London, and received the degree of M. A. at Gloucester Hall, Oxford, 1636, when he "retired in great splendour to the court" of Charles I. He served as ensign and then as captain in the Scottish expeditions, and on his return took possession of Lovelace Place at Bethersden and his other estates. As one of the justices of Kent he was selected to present to the House of Commons the celebrated Kentish petition for the restoration of the king to his rights, for which he was committed in April 1642, to Gatehouse Prison, London, where he wrote his most celebrated poem *To Althea from Prison.* He joined Charles at Oxford in 1645 and after its sur-

COL. RICHARD LOVELACE, Poet
Brother of Ann (Lovelace) Gorsuch.

render he formed a regiment for service under Louis XIV. He was wounded in 1648 at Dunkirk, and returned to England, where he and his brother Captain Dudley Lovelace were imprisoned at Petre House. Here he edited his poems which were published in October 1649, under the title *Lucasta, Epodes, Odes, Sonnets, Songs, etc.*, Soon afterwards he was released from prison, and the last ten years of his life, his resources exhausted and his health broken, were spent in London, where he died April 1658. He was buried at St. Bride's. He had sold Bethersden Place in 1649 to Richard Hulse. His brother Dudley Lovelace edited a second collection of Richard's poems, which he published in 1659 as *Lucasta: Posthume Poems of Richard Lovelace, Esq.* He did not marry. The statements by Berry, Hazlitt and others that he did have been shown by Pearman to be erroneous. (*Archaeologia Cantiana:* x; 215). Lovelace is said to have been strikingly handsome, although his portrait at Dulwich Gallery is disappointing. His fame as a poet rests largely upon the lyric *To Athea from Prison* in which occur the lines,

Stone Walls doe not a prison make,
  Nor iron bars a cage;
Mindes innocent and quiet take
  That for an hermitage;
If I have freedom in my love,
  And in my soule am free
Angels alone that sore above
  Enjoy such liberty.

and upon the poem *To Lucasta Going To The Warres*, which ends with the lines,

Yet this inconsistancy is such,
  As you too should adore;
I could not love thee, dear, so much,
  Lov'd I not Honour more.

3. Thomas Lovelace[8]. Born about 1619 or 1620 as he is referred to in his father's will as the second son. He apparently went to Charterhouse School, [Sutton's Hospital], London. He was an active royalist, but does not seem to have had a military career. A poem by him to the memory of his brother Richard appears in the posthumous edition of the latter's poems. He was with his brother Francis in New York when the latter was governor of that province. He appears there as a member of the governor's council in 1671, was an alderman of New York City in the same year, and was appointed captain of the Foot Company of Staten Island in 1672. He appears in 1672 as one of the commissioners appointed to strengthen the defenses of Fort James, and in 1672-3 as a justice of New York city. He was one of the messengers sent on board to confer with the Dutch

admiral when New York surrendered to the Dutch in 1673, and was for a short while detained as a prisoner of war. His estates were confiscated and he was ordered to leave the province, but managed to postpone his departure until New York again passed into the hands of the English. He owned a plantation on Staten Island known as "Lovelace Farme", which he occupied until his death which occurred in 1689; and appears as a sheriff of Richmond County in 1684 and 1685. He was married and had at least one child, a son William, who was buried with great ceremony at Fort James in 1671; there were possibly other children. He was survived by his wife Mary, whose family name is not known, Lovelace Farme finally passing after his death to a niece Mary, the wife of Ellis Duxbury of the Barbadoes and later of New York. The identity of this niece has not been determined. The writer has traced the career of Thomas Lovelace and the history of his plantation "Lovelace Farme" in considerable detail in the *New York Genealogical and Biographical Record* (July 1920; li; 188-192) to which the reader is referred for fuller data, and for the authorities upon which the above statements are based.

4. Francis Lovelace[8]. Colonial governor of New York 1668-1673. The question of the identity of Governor Francis Lovelace of New York has been a matter of dispute, the governor until recently having been thought to be a son of Richard, first Lord Lovelace of Hurley, Berks. (see a note by the editor in the Va. Mag. xvii, 288-291). The writer has recently contributed a paper to the *New York Genealogical and Biographical Record* (July 1920; vol. li; 175-194) establishing beyond question that Governor Lovelace was the son of Sir William Lovelace of Bethersden, and has presented there all the known facts of his life, to which the reader is referred for further details.

Francis Lovelace[8], the third son of Sir William Lovelace[7], was born between 1620 and 1622. Under his father's will he received jointly with his brother William lands in Shoulden, Kent. He was furnished by his brother Richard Lovelace, the poet, with money and men for the royalist cause, serving with the title of colonel in the civil wars and as governor of Carmarthen Castle during its siege in 1644 and 1645. He was in Virginia in 1652 when he was selected by Governor Berkeley to carry the news of the surrender of the colony to Charles II, then on the continent. We find him soon afterwards with Charles during his exile on the continent, with whom he remained until shortly before the fall of the commonwealth, when he returned to England, and was arrested and imprisoned there in 1659 for his royalist activities. He was appointed deputy governor of Long Island, and in 1668 became governor of New York, holding this position until New York was captured by the Dutch July 30, 1673. His private fortunes were ruined by the confiscation of his property by the Dutch Council and on his return to England the Duke of York brought about his political ruin on the ground that the loss of the province was due to the fact that the governor was absent from his post at the time of the Dutch attack, although it was conclusively shown that had he been present Fort James was entirely inadequate to withstand the attack of the strong Dutch fleet. Lovelace was imprisoned in the Tower and his property was confiscated. He does not appear to have been actually tried, and was released April 26, 1675 on account of ill health. He died the latter part of the year at Woodstock, Oxfordshire, his estate being administered upon by his brother Dudley, 22 December 1675. He is referred to in the administration entry as a bachelor.

5. Joane Lovelace[8]. She was the second daughter, and was born in 1622 or early in 1623, as the *inquisition* upon her father's estate shows that she was "the child to be born to me" mentioned in his will dated 15 July 1622. Her name sometimes appears as Johanna. She married Robert Caesar. Lodge in his *Life of Sir Julius Caesar*, 1827 (p. 54) states that Robert Caesar, who married Joane daughter of Sir William Lovelace, was the son of Sir John Caesar, knight, of Willan, Herts, and that by her he had issue three daughters (1) Anne (died June 23, 1739), wife of Sir John Payntz of Iron Acton, Gloucester, (2) Julianna married Thomas Sage of Butley, Sussex, (3) Johanna (died December 15, 1694) wife of John Rampayne. Robert Caesar, his wife Joane, and two of his daughters are said to be buried in St. Catherine's Church near the Tower. Richard Lovelace's poem *Paris's Second Judgement—Upon the Three Daughters of My Dear Brother Mr. R. Caesar* (Hazlitt edition, p. 221) must have been written while the three sisters were still mere children. "Joan Caesar, alius Lovelace, wife of Robert Caesar and sister of Dudley Lovelace" was appointed Dudley's administratrix, May 10, 1686, and the same day was also appointed (to succeed Dudley) administratrix of her brother Francis Lovelace's estate (*Prerogative Court Canterbury: Admns*, 1686 & *Admn. Act. Book*. 1686, fol. 76d.).

6. William Lovelace[8]. He was the fourth son and apparently the sixth child, and was born between 1623 and 1627, as he is not named in his father's will, but is in that of his mother. He espoused the cause of the king and was killed either in 1644 or 1645 at the siege of Carmarthen, Wales. His brother Richard's poem *To His Deare Brother Colonel F.*[*rancis*] *L.*[*ovelace*]*—Immoderately Mourning My Brother's* [*I. e. William's*] *Untimely Death in Carmarthen*, commemorates the event. It will be recalled that Francis Lovelace[8] was in command of Carmarthen Castle. Nothing further has been learned about William. It seems improbable that he married, although there is a remote possibility that he did and that a certain unidentified Francis Lovelace, elsewhere referred to, (*New York Geneal. & Biog. Rec.* lvi

179), who died in Maryland in 1684 and who was of the Behersden, line, was a son.

7. Elizabeth Lovelace[8]. The third daughter, and apparently the seventh child, was born between 1624 and 1626. She is named in her mother's will but not in that of her father. *The Visitation of Berkshire 1664* (*Harleian Soc. Pub.* lvi; 221) shows that Elizabeth, the daughter of Sir William Lovelace of Bethersden, Kent, knight, married [about 1650] Daniel Hayne of Kintbury Eaton, Berks, the son of Thomas Hayne of Auborne, Wilts, and his wife Katherine Gorsuch, the daughter of Daniel Gorsuch of London, and that at the time of the visitation, March 23, 1664, Daniel Hayne was 37 years old and then had issue (1) Daniel, age 10, (2) John, (3) Katherine, (4) Ann, (5) Elizabeth, (6) Frances, (7) Mary. From this it is seen that Daniel Hayne, the husband of Elizabeth Lovelace[8] was a nephew of the Rev. John Gorsuch, the husband of her sister Anne Lovelace[8]. The writer has obtained an abstract of the will of Daniel Hayne, the elder, of Wallingtons, Parish of Kintbury, co. Berks, gent., dated 3 April, 1663, and proved 11 May, 1687, by his son Daniel Hayne (*Prerogative Court of Canterbury Wills; Foot, 63.*) This will names his wife Elizabeth his sons Daniel, John and Thomas, and his daughters Katharine, Anne, Elizabeth, Francis and Mary. The testator names his father Thomas Hayne, gent., deceased. He provides that his son Thomas be sent to Cambridge, and is afterwards to study law at the Inns of Court, and that his sons Daniel and John be sent to Oxford. Sentence was pronounced by the court, 7 May, 1687, in a suit between Daniel Hayne, only son of the deceased, and Anne Chokke, minor, by John Longland, her guardian, legatrix in a pretended will dated, 1 September, 1686, in which the latter will is declared invalid, and that dated 3 April, 1663, upheld. No attempt has been made to carry down the Hayne lines.

8. Dudley Lovelace[8]. He was the youngest son and was doubtless born in 1627, soon after his father's death, as he styles himself Dudley-Posthumus Lovelace. He was furnished with money by his brother Richard to study "tactics and fortification" in Holland. He was an ardent royalist. He served as captain in his brother Richard's regiment under Louis XIV, he and his brother Richard being imprisoned in Petre House on their return to London in 1648 on account of their royalist sympathies. He was with Charles II during his exile on the continent. He appears in 1659 as the editor of the second part of his brother Richard's poems: *Lucasta, Posthume Poems of Richard Lovelace, Esq.; London,* 1659. He was in New York early in 1670 with his brother Governor Francis Lovelace, and appeared there as a member of the governor's council, president of a commission to grant lands at Esopus and to define the boundaries of

Hurley, and also on a commission to survey Staten Island, and was commissioned as lieutenant of the Troop of Horse of New York City. He owned a plantation on Staten Island and is usually referred to in the records as Captain Dudley Lovelace. He was one of the three officers in charge of Fort James at the time of the surrender and was sent to Europe as a prisoner by the Dutch commander. He is constantly referred to as the brother of the governor in the colonial records, and was the administrator of the latter's estate in England. The administration upon the estate of "Dudley Lovelace late of London, but dying at Newington, Butts, co. Surrey, was granted May 10, 1686, to his sister Joan Caesar, Mary Lovelace the relict renouncing". The surname of his wife Mary is not known, nor is it known certainly whether Dudley Lovelac left childrer, this point and all the known facts of his life being discussed by the writer in greater detail in a sketch of Governor Francis Lovelace in the *New York Genealogical and Biographical Record* (*July 2920;* li; 192-4).

(To be Continued)

This concludes the sketch of the Lovelace family proper. This will be followed by sketches of certain families from which the Lovelaces are decended, beginning with the Aucher family of Bishopsbourne, Kent.

---

*GRYMES OF BRANDON ETC.

(Continued)

12. BENJAMIN[3] GRYMES, was born Feb. 19, 1725, died about 1776, He removed to Spotsylvania County, and settled on a plantation named "Smithfield." He was presiding Justice of the County and represented. it in the House of Burgesses at the Sessions of Nov. 1761, Jan. 1762, Nov. 1762, Nov. 1766. March 1767. March 1768, May 1769, Nov. 1769, May 1770. and July 1771. On Aug. 13, 1755, Benjamin Grymes of Spotsylvania Co. gent, and Betty his wife, sold to John Champe, of King George Co.; merchant, for £3103 Currency, 1750 acres in Spotsylvania Co. where said Grymes lived, also 700 acres in Spotsylvania, lots in the town of Fredericksburg, and 51 slaves. On May 9, 1758, John Champe, and others, executors of William Woodford, deceased, sold to Benjamin Grymes, 6300 acres in Spotsylvania, called Massaponnax lands. In 1758 Benj. Grymes and Anthony Bacon, of London, who had been concerned in shipping tobacco, dissolved partnership. On Feb. 5, 1767, Benjamin Grymes, of Spotsylvania Co., gent., and Priscilla his wife, conveyed to Hon. Presley Thornton, Esq. and William Fitzhugh, Esq. to indemnify them from loss on account of various sums they have or may advance to

*The statement (xxviii, 96) that, 20, John Randolph Grymes died without issue is incorrect. He had issue: (a) Wyndham, died unmarried; (b) Arianna, married 1st in Middlesex Co., Feb. 6, 1802, William Curtis, married 2nd Peter Kemp; (c) Mary Beverley, born at Brampton, England, married 1st, 1809, Robert West, of Gloucester County, 2d Peter Francisco.

said Grymes, the tract of land where the furnace stands, 1650 acres also a tract of land purchased by said Grymes of Wm.Woodford, 1600 acres; also tract purchased of Williams and Tompkins, 500 acres; also the tract of land given the said Grymes by his father, Hon. John Grymes, Esq., deceased, upon Mattapony River, 1900 acres; also a tract of land whereon the forge stands, purchased of Rice Curtis, 400 acres; also tract purchased of Joseph Herndon, 250 acres; also tract purchased of the executors of William Waller, deceased, 250 acres; also lots and houses in Fredericksburg, forges, furnaces, slaves, stocks, vessels, goods, etc. On Aug. 15, 1770, Benjamin Grymes of Spotsylvania Co., Esq., in his own right and as executor of Hon. Philip Grymes, Edq., Hon. John Tayloe, of Richmond Co., Esq., in his own right, and as executor of Hon. Presley Thornton Esq., Joseph Herndon, of Spotsylvania Co., gent., sold to Thomas Poole, for £1250 current money, a forge called Grymes' Forge, with bellows, plates, etc., and 800 acres of land. On Aug. 9, 1775, the executors of Hon. Peter Randolph, late of Chatsworth, Henrico Co., conveyed to Walker Taliaferro of Caroline Co. for £800, 2000 acres in Spotsylvania Co., which had been bequeathed to Benj. Grymes, by his father, Hon. John Grymes, Esq., deceased; and which said Benj. Grymes, had, in 1775, mortgaged to Peter Randolph to indemnify him for going security for a debt said;Benj. Grymes owed Hon. Wm. and Thomas Nelson Esqrs., and had not paid.

Benjamin Grymes was a man of great energy and activity and had so many and varied business interests that at his death his estate was greatly involved and he was perhaps insolvent. He was a planter, merchant, tobacco exporter, a speculator in lots and houses, and an iron manufacturer and miner. He died before 1777 and though his will is referred to in deeds it is not in Spotsylvania County. He married 1st, Sept. 11, 1747, Elizabeth (born April 3d, 1731) daughter of Henry Fitzhugh, of "Eagle's Nest," and 2d Priacilla, daughter of Philip Rootes, of "Rosewall", King and Queen County.

Issue: [1st m] 27 Benjamin[4]; 28 Mary, married 1st, Peter Randolph, of Henrico Co., 2d Col. Richard KidderMeade, aide to Washington in the Revolution. She was mother of Rt. Rev. William Meade, Bishop of Virginia. (2d m.): 29. Mildred, (will proved Sept. 2, 1822, in Spotsylvania) married 1st Reuben Thornton, of Caroline County, 2d Major Peter Dudley, of Spotsvylania Co.: 30. Lucy Rootes, died unmarried, 1817; 31. Charles[4], born ——, died 1831. He may have been Mr. Charles Grymes of Va., Midshipman U. S. N. In 1819, Charles Grymes who had been in the Navy, married Jane, daughter of Thomas Whiting, of Gloucester Co., and had a daughter Mary, who married Lewis Burwell, of the same county; 32. Ludwell[4]; 33. Randolph[4]; 34. Anne, married William Wedderburn.

15. Ludwell[3] Grymes, was born April 26, 1733, and died before 1795. When a young man he removed from Middlesex to Gloucester, and later

in life to "Burlington," Orange County, where he died. He married, in 1756, Mary, daughter of William Dawson, D. D., commissary of the Bishop of London, President of William and Mary College and member of the Council. On May 18, 1771, Ludwell Grymes, of Orange County and Mary his wife, sold a lot in Fredericksburg. Ludwell Grymes appears to have died intestate. In 1795 there was recorded in Orange Couty. an account of John D. Grymes, administrator of Ludwell Grymes. Mrs. Mary Grymes' will was dated May 15, 1787, and proved in Orange, June 23, 1787. The will mentions Hannah Grymes, her son John Grymes; legacies to Mary Maury, daughter of Rev. Walker Maury, and Mary, daughter of William Maury. She frees certain negroes at the age of 22 years and enjoins each "legatee to teach or cause to be taught each negro respectively to read," and the General Assembly to be petitioned in case there is any difficulty as to their manumission.

Ludwell[3] and Mary (Dawson) Grymes had issue: 35. John Dawson. In Spotsylvania Co., April 5, 1783, John Dawson Grymes, mariner, gave a power of attorney to John Dawson, of Caroline County, to sell land in Henry County, formerly Lunenburg, which was conveyed Aug. 10, 17C4, to said Grymes, Thos. B. Dawson, and said John Dawson, by John Dawson, dec'd. of Caroline County. In 1795 he was acting as his father's administrator. The compiler has no further information in regard to him: 36. Mary, born in Williamsburg, August 26, 1753, married Rev. Walker Maury on May 7, 1777, and died Sept. 23, 1789; 37. Elizabeth, born in Gloucester Co., 1765, died in Robertson Co., Tenn., March 31, 1852, married Rev. William Moore; 38. Hannah (?)

10. Phillip Ludwell Grymes, of "Brandon," was born in Christ Church Parish, Middlesex, April 5, 1746, baptized May 9, 1746, and died May 18, 1805. He was a member of the House of Burgesses for Middlesex Co. at the sessions of May 1769, Nov. 1769 and May 1770. In the next year he vacated his seat by accepting the office of sheriff. He was a member of the House of Delegates for the same county 1778 and 1802-3, was chosen a member of the Council of State 1803. He had been educated at Eton, along with his brother, John Randolph Grymes. Following is a copy of the will of Philip Ludwell Grymes.

"In the name of God, Amen, I, Philip Ludwell Grymes of Brandon in the Parish of Christ Church and County of Middlesex, do ordain and publish the following to be my last Will and Testament, hereby revoking all other Wills heretofore by me made.

Imprimis I desire that my body may be buried, among my Relations, in the church yard of this Parish with Christian decency: but without Pomp or much Ceremony. Item it is my Will that all my just debts, and those of my lately departed son be honestly paid. Item I give unto my wife Judith Grymes, all her Rings, Jewels, Gold Watch and other Paraphernalia, my Post Chaise and Harness, and any four Horses belonging to me, that she may choose, to drive therein, forever.—Item I lend unto my said wife, Judith Grymes, the use of my Plantation and Mansion House tlled Brandon, the outhouses, Stables, Gardens, Orchards and appurenances thereunto belonging; also of all my Plate, Household and Kitchen nm ture during term of her natural Life—ItemIt is my Will that after my Debts and those of my son above mentioned, together with the Legacies herein after bequeathed are paid or appropriations for the payment thereof be made, then all the Residue of my Eestate both real and personal (except the before mentioned Plantation and Mansion House called Brandon with the other property in the two former clauses of my Will bequeathed to my said wife, Judith Grymes) be divided by my Executor and Trustees herein after mentioned into two equal moieties or parts that my said executors and trustees allot one equal moiety or part thereof to my said wife Judith Grymes, to be held by her (in addition to the property before given or lent to her) to her own use and behoof for and during the term of her natural life: and it is to be understood that the above provision made by me for my said wife is to be in lieu of any claim of Dower—Item I do devise the other moiety or equal part of my said estate both real and Personal to my said Executors and trustees hereinafter mentioned and their heirs forever, in trust for the sole use and behoof of my daughter Jane Sayre for and during the term of her natural Life; and after her decease to be equally divided along the children of the said Jane living at her death and their heirs forever. Item I do also devise to my said Executors and trustees and their heirs forever that other equal moiety or Part of my Estate both real and Personal, together with all the other property both real and personal above by me lent to my said wife Judith Grymes for her life, after the death of my said wife to be by them held in Trust for the sole use and behoof of my said daughter Jane Sayre for and during the term of her natural life, and after her death to be by them equally divided among the children of the said Jane Sayre living at her death, and their heirs forever. Item If my said daughter Jane Sayre should die without lawful issue then I give unto Samuel William Sayre her husband, and to his heirs forever, one half or equal moiety of that equal moiety or Part of my estate which I have above in the first instance devised to my executors and trustees in trust for my said daughter Jane Sayre, and all the rest of my Estate both real and Personal I give to be equally divided among the children of my Brother Benjamin Grymes, and their heirs forever. Item I give unto my faithful manager William Wood, one hundred Pounds to be paid to him by my said Trustees and Executors in twelve months after my death, as a small memorial of his Integrity and good services.—Item I direct my Executors and Trustees herein after named to take from my different Plantations, after the crop is finished Twenty Negroes and deliver them to Francis Page, and also to assign to him that Bond which is executed by Grief Green and others to me for the third payment for my Mecklenburg

property, which Negroes and Bond I give to the said Francis and his heirs forever. Lastly I do appoint my worthy Friends Ralph Wormeley, Senior, of Rosegill, Nathaniel Burwell senior and Junior of Frederick my nephews Robert Nelson of York ["and Philip Grymes"—erased] and Mann Page of Gloucester Executors of this my last Will and Testament and trustees to execute the trusts above mentioned—I desire that all questions doubts or disputes touching the premises or which may arise touching the true meaning or exposition of this my last Will, may be finally decided by the opinions and judgment of my said Trustees or the major Part of them—I further desire that my Estate may not be appraised—In teste: ——— that the above is my true last Will and Testament I have hereto subscribed my name and affixed my seal and also published the same as my last Will and Testament this twenty third day of April 1805 in the presence of Philip L. Grymes.
The words "Living at her death interlines between the 1 & 2 line on this page before publication.
Ariana M. Curtis
Elizabeth Page
Dorothy Churchill
William Wood
Jules B. Pollard

This 16 of May the three words, "and Philip Grymes" the pen ran over by Mr. Gryme's position order & signed by me by his Injunction
Ralph Wormeley

Test—F Page
Eleanor Wormeley
Dorothy Churchill

At a Court held for Middlesex County, at the Courthouse in Urbanna, on Monday the 24th day of June, 1805,—This last Will and Testament of Philip Ludwell Grymes, Gentleman, deceased, was produced in Court by Ralph Wormeley Senior—Esqr. and the same was proved by the oaths of Ariana M. Curtis, Dorothy Churchill, and Jules B. Pollard three of the witnesses thereunto, and the memorandum indorsed thereon was proved by the oaths of Eleanor Wormeley and Dorothy Churchill two of the witnesses thereto, whereupon the said Will and memorandum were admitted to record, at the time of the probate thereof Philip Grymes tendered to the Court a Bill of exceptions, which were received, signed and sealed by the Court & ordered to be entered on record, and which are in the words following (Vizt) "The last Will & Testament of Philip L. Grymes being produced in the Court of Middlesex County, for proa bate & having been regularly proven, the Witnesses to the obliteration of the words Philip Grymes were introduced to prove the same, whereupon Philip Grymes moved the Court to suppress s'd evidence until a summons had issued to all the Parties having any interest under s'd will, and the trustees therein named, to require of them to show cause, if anything could, why the Will sho'ld not be proven without any regard to the obliteration afores'd, and he, the said Grymes be permitted to take out letters testamentary of the Estate of the Testator which summons was decreed to the s'd Grymes & the evidence received & s'd obliteration being proven to have been made by the direction of the Testators was ordered to be * * * * [word obliterated] to which opinion of the Court the s'd Grymes excepts and prays that his exceptions may be signed, sealed etc.

Thos. Healy (seal) Thos Mense (seal) Wm Segar (seal) Henry Hefferman (seal)

Teste

O. Cosby CC."

In 1808 his slaves were appraised. The following list gives the names, ages, valuation, and the plantations on which they lived.

In obedience of an order of the worshipful court of Middlesex, Thomas Healy, Churchill Blakey and Elliott Muse qualified by oath, viewed and valued the slaves of Philip L. Grimes, dec'd at the following prices and places, viz.:

Gloucester Plantation.—George, 60, $10.00; Bridget, 55, $20.00; am 30, $100.00; Nelly, 20, $80.00; Hannah, 2, $20.00; Rose, 70, $9.00;P her daughter, 18 and child Caty 1, $100.00; Caty 20, and child Jefferson 1 $100.00; Rhoda 36 and child Judy 1, $80.00; Jenny, 14, $70.00; Bob, 8, $15.00; Rose, 6, $30.00; Ned, 30, $100.00; James, 24, $100.00; George, 16. $80.00; Peter, 14, $70.00; Ralph, 45, $80.00; Essex, 14, $70.00; Hardy, 21, $90.00; Prince, 16, $80.00; Beck, 15, $75.00; total valuation $1,439.00.

Kemps Plantation.—Frankey, 16, $80.00; Harry, 55, $50.00; Peg, 45, $45.00; Rachel 22, and child Jesse, 3 months, $95.00; Henry, 5 years, $25.00; Ester, 3, $15.00; Billy, 18, $80.00; Peg, 12, $60.00; Sarah, 10, $45.00; Billy, 7, $38.00; Molly, 1, $12.00; Charles, 17, $100.00; Ben, 15, $80.00 Edmund, $35, 95.00; Sucky, 55, $30.00; Mall, 24, $100.00; Venus, 20. $100.00; Matt, 1; Sucky, 9, $40.00; Isreal, 6, $35.00; Mary, 45, $35.00; Molly 24 and Betty 1, $90.00; Bob, 3, $15.00; John 13, $60.00; Anna, 10, $45.00; Charles, 6, $35.00; Manuel, 30, $100.00; Tom, 60, $35.00; Billy, 40 $20; total valuation $3,005.00.

Mill Plantation.—Cromwell, 30, $100.00; Lucy, 30, $30.00; Reubin, 9 months, $10.00; Nelly, 7, $35.00; London, 6, $35.00; Sally 25 and Isbell, her child, 1, $95.00; Prince, 8, $35.00; Robin, 6, $35.00; Bluff, 3, $20.00; Scilla 20, and George, her child 7 months, $95.00; Jackson, 3, $20.000 Jenny 18, and Judy, her child, 1, $95.00; Bella, 55, dept; Toby, 18, $100.00; Grace, 15, $70.00; Henry, 10, $60.00; Tom, 30, $100.00; Jackson, 26, $100.00; Jenny, 86; Ben, 55, $50__.; London, 16, $80.00; Fanny 40, and child Nelly, 2, $70.00; Pattey, 18, $80.00; Caesar, 16, $80.00; Sucky, 12, $60.00; Fanny, 9, 45.00; Amos, 5, $30.00.

Old House Plantation.—Frank, 45, $80.00; Sarah 30, and Charles her child 1, $90.00; Sucky, 15, $75.00; Godfrey, 12, $75.00; Grace, 10, $50.00; Davy, 9, $40.00; Menba, 7, $30.00; Frank 4 and Philip, $40.00; Cymon, 60, $50.00; Mary, 60; Nancy, 27, $80.00; Villa, 22, $100.00; Tom, 16, $90.00; Rose 26 and child Topmark, 1, $95.00; Hagin, 6, $35.00; Charles, 4, $20.00; Menba, 60, $20.00; Peg 28 and child John 6 months, $90.00; Tamer, 7, $35.00; Dolly, 3, $20.00; Tamer 22 and child Sally, 9 months, $95.00; Caesar, 3, $20.00; James, 50, dept., $30.00; Billy, 45, $75.00; John, 55, $50.00; Criss 17 and child Sam 1, $95.00; Walker, 27, $100.00; Moses, 22, $100.00; Bluff, 45 crip., $20.00;

Pinetop Plantation.—Cromel, 35, $75.00; Billy, 40, $75.00; Venus, 36, $50.00; Billy, 3 months, $10.00; Susanna, 20 years, $30.00; Tom, 18, $90.00; Zena, 14, $60.00; Sally, 13, $60.00; Boss, 10, $45.00; Frank, 9, $40.00; Beverly, 7, $35.00; John, 3, $20.00; Sampson, 28, $100.00; Minter, 27, James 1 month, $90.00; Bob, 7 years, $45.00; Cromel, 5, $25.00; Venus, 2½, $15.00; Daniel, 36, $80.00; Mildred 24, Betty 1½, $95.00; Cloe, 5, $25.00; Ned, 20, $100.00; Agathy 20, Philip 2, $95.00; Lucy 20, Clary 3 months, $90.00; Nashe, 4 years, $20.00; Samuel 18 months, $12.00; Jenny 56, $30.00; Jenny 15, $75.00; Rose, 13, $60.00; John, 45, $60.00; Tangy, 36, $80.00; Samuel, 46, $60.00; Rose, 58, $30.00; Susanna, 90, ; Susannah, 8, $45.00; Hannah, 7, $35.00; Harry, 75.

Brandon Estate.—Dolly, 40, $45.00; Martha, 13, $60.00; Fanny, 11, $50.00; Robin, 9, $45.00; Colly, 5, $25.00; Creson, 3, $20.00; Frank, 36, $60.00; Jackson, **smith**, 60, $75.00; Ben., **street**, 52, $60.00; Isabella, 50, $36.00; Venus, 11, $45.00; Daniel, 6, $35.00; Scipio, 41, $80.00; Betty, 30, $60.00; MEagary, 9, $40.00; Areana, 7, $35.00; John, 5, $25.00; Scipio, 2, $15.00; Essex, 55, $60.00; Frank, 23, $100.00; Charles, 35, $80.00; Peter, 22, $100.00; Susanna, 30, $75.00; Sarah, 8, $45.00; Fanny, 6, $35.00; Rosellar 2, $20.00; Clara, 14, $60.00; Sally 35, child Nelly ½ year, $90.00; Jane, 16, $80.00; Sucky, 14, $75.00; Robin, 12, $70.00; Henry, 9, $60.00; Jenny, 53, $40.00; Grace, 37, $80.00; Feorge, 14, $75.00.Marcus, 9, $45.00; Cyrus, 7-$35.00; Billy, 60, defec., $20.00; James, 40, $75.00; Jack, 38, $80.00; Ned, 50, $60.00; Beck, 50 fdeec., $20.00; BetMy 22, Ned 1, $95.00; Joyce, 3, $20.00 Areana 25, Mary 6 weeks, $95.00; Bob, 3, $20.00; Fanny, 4½, $25.00;; Jenny, 29, $75.00; Grace, 45, $40.00; Caty, 19, $80.00; Sarah, 90; Civiah, 90; Lucy, 25, $80.00; Amos, 45, $80.00; Bob, 36, $90.00; Bluff, 36, $90.00; Anthony, 49, $60.00; Ben, 29, $100.00; Aaron, 23, $100.00; Dick, 24, $100.00; Rachel, 55, $40.00; Phillis, 60, $30.00; Letty, 20, $80.00; Mary' 16, $75.00; Billy, 18, $80.00; James Hoecake, 45 car, $100.00; Sam, 30 Dc, $120.00; John, 25 Dc, $120.00; Sam, 18, $100.00; Tom, 45, $80.00; Philip, 15, $85.00; Abram, 20, $10.000; Ralph, 18, $100.00; Juba, 90, 0; Peg, 80, 0; Edmund, 12, $60.00; Moss, 10, $50.00; Marcus, 14, $75.00; Jane, 80' invalid.

Elliott Muse, Tho. Healy, Chuc. Blakey. At a court held for Middlesex county in Urbanna on Monday the 27th day of June 1808, this appraisement of the negroes belonging to the estate of Philip L. Grymes was this day returned and ordered to be recorded—

Teste Tho. Muse

The foregoing is a true copy of a writing recorded in the Clerk's Office of Middlesex County, Virginia in Will Book No. 2, pages 402-403-404.

C. W. Eastman,
Clerk.

Philip Ludwell Grymes married 1st Sarah, daughter of Attorney General John Randolph (a sister of this brother J. R. Grymes' wife) and had no issue. He married secondly, May 27, 1773, Judith, daughter of Ralph Wormeley, of "Rosegill," Middlesex County. In addition to children who died young, they had issue, 39. Jane, married Samuel William Sayre, July 23, 1804, and died at "Brandon," Jan. 1, 1806. S. W. Sayre was son of Stephen Sayre, a native of Long Island, who removed to London, became an eminent merchant, a Whig leader in the City, and one of the sheriffs. His ardent Americanism brought him nearly to imprisonment in the Tower at the beginning of the Revolution. Stephen Sayre and his wife died at the residence of his son in Virginia in 1818.

(To be Continued)

William Gordon McCabe

A BRIEF MEMOIR

BY

ARMISTEAD C. GORDON

Member of the Executive Committee of the Virginia
Historical Society

RICHMOND
OLD DOMINION PRESS, INC., PRINTERS
1920

WILLIAM GORDON McCABE

WILLIAM GORDON McCABE

William Gordon McCabe was born in Richmond, Virginia, August 4, 1841, and died there June 1, 1920. There he spent a large part of his life; and to the historic city, rich in memories of all that has been Virginian, he gave a loyal and lasting affection.

He was the son of the Reverend John Collins McCabe, D. D., also a native of Richmond, and a friend of Edgar Allan Poe during his editorship of *"The Southern Literary Messenger,"* to which Dr. McCabe was a frequent contributor.

His record as a soldier of the Confederacy, whose fortunes he espoused when a lad at the University of Virginia and followed until Johnston surrendered to Sherman at Greensboro, had its prototype in that of his great-grandfather, James McCabe, an officer of the Revolution, who served the Continental cause with conspicuous gallantry throughout the period of the war, and who had led his men in the column under Montgomery, through a driving snow storm, in the assault on Quebec in December, 1775, and caught in his arms his dying commander as he fell.

If it was from his Revolutionary progenitor that Gordon McCabe, as his friends all called him, inherited some part of his military tendencies and talents, so from his father, Dr. John Collins McCabe, appears to have been transmitted to him a measure of that passionate pursuit of letters,—"the noble and simple presentation of things noble and simple"—which was an essential feature of his long career.

Dr. McCabe, a militant churchman, born November 12th, 1820, after studying medicine, entered the Episcopal ministry, and served at various times many churches, notably those at Smithfield and Hampton, Virginia. He was an indefatigable student and literary man, loving books and the investigation of old records, a poet, an essayist and an antiquarian. When the great civil conflict of the 'Sixties began, Dr. McCabe resigned a parish charge in Maryland, entered the Confederate service as chaplain of the 32nd Virginia Regiment in the Peninsula, and afterwards became chaplain-general to the military prisons in Richmond. He survived the Confederacy, and died in Chambersburg, Pennsylvania, in 1875.

During his youthful association with his father, to whom he was devoted with the singular attachment which illustrated his domestic life and his many friendships, young McCabe breathed in an atmosphere of books and reading and good talk; for the clergyman encouraged his son's literary instinct, and had a fine library; and he entertained in his hospitable home a multitude of friends and visitors, who were representative of the best in the social life of the Virginia of that day. From him the boy learned first, what he always kept foremost in school and army and university and at the teacher's desk: "to ride, to shoot and to speak the truth"; and, for a close second, he cherished a love of literary things. He was accustomed to say that among the earliest memories of his childhood was that of lying face downward on the floor, propped upon his elbows, with an open volume between them, too big for him to hold, reading untiringly; and he would insist with great earnestness that no one ever caught "the divine fire" of letters, who had not begun to "follow the gleam" after some such early fashion.

His mother was Sophia Gordon Taylor, a great-granddaughter of George Taylor, signer of the Declaration of Independence, for whose civic story he felt and exhibited great filial and patriotic pride.

Sophia Gordon Taylor was sprung on the distaff side from the emigrant, Lewis Gordon, who was an influential citizen of Easton, Pennsylvania, and who came of a line of Galloway Scots that has adorned Border ballad and legend and history with the romance and adventure of "The Gay Gordons" of Earlston, Lochinvar and Kenmure. Of this Scottish strain in his veins he was very proud; and to those bearing the name or inheriting the blood it was his delight to declaim, with the fervor and stirring intonation that went with whatever he recited or read aloud, the ballad-lines which enshrine the memory of the Jacobite Viscount William Gordon of Kenmure, who lost his head on Tower Hill, after "The 'Fifteen":

"Here's Kenmure's health in wine, Willie,
Here's Kenmure's health in wine!
There ne'er was a coward o' Kenmure's blude,
Nor yet o' Gordon's line."

One of the grandsons of Lewis Gordon, of Easton, was William Lewis Gordon, a distinguished officer in the United States Navy, who for gallantry in the War of 1812 with Great Britain was voted by the Commonwealth of Virginia a sword of honor. William Gordon McCabe was named for this sailor grand-uncle who had adopted Sophia Gordon Taylor after the death of her mother.

The first ten years of his life were spent at Smithfield, Isle of Wight County, Virginia, where his father was the rector in charge of the parish whose history goes back to 1632. This was the time when he began to read the big books on elbows; and here was first kindled the enthusiasm for "what is fine in human kind, that ruled his choice of books" and lasted him through life.

The following six years he spent at Hampton, where Dr. McCabe was rector of St. John's Church, in a parish hardly less ancient and rich in historical associations than that at Smithfield, where as early as the year 1667, the parish records tell of "the new church of Kickotan." Here he attended the Hampton Academy, and received instruction at the hands of its scholarly principal, the late Col. John B. Cary, whose daughter, Gillie Armistead, became his second wife. At Hampton Academy, where he was a pupil for two years, he made a distinct impression on both school and teachers as a youth of uncommon intellectuality, of great eagerness to learn, and of unwearying industry; and when he left its walls he carried with him its highest honors, having won its gold medal twice and been its "valedictorian" upon his graduation in 1858. At this time he was already "as packed with energy, as fiery in hope," as he continued to the winter of his age; and his lasting possession of these qualities even unto his end, keeping him always youthful in spirit, gave for those who knew him best a finer interpretation and a nobler meaning to the Greek apothegm that "whom the gods love die young."

After his graduation from the Hampton Academy he was private tutor in the family of the Seldens of Westover; and there, in the midst of associations dedicated to exalting memories of much that was finest in the story of Colonial Virginia, we see him inaugurating his career as a writer of distinction with contributions to *"The Southern Literary Messenger,"* beginning with a poem of unusual merit from a youth, written in 1858: "To my Alma Mater: Academia Hamptoniensis," and signed "An Old Boy," which was published in the July, 1859, number. This was followed by a series of historical essays and poems and stories, which were printed in the *"Messenger"* from time to time during his University career, and even while he was a soldier in the trenches.

One can but believe that these early years at Smithfield and Hampton and Westover, lived in an atmosphere of inspiring memories and associations, and in constant contact with the highminded and cultivated gentlemen and gentlewomen of a golden age in Virginia, exercised an unconscious influence in fixing for him that lofty attitude toward life which struck the minds of his acquaintances with its loyalty, its manliness, its buoyant courage, its love of letters and of friends, and its indefinable charm of interest in the movement of the world.

An incident of this contact with high thoughts and fine idealisms is in a little story of simplicity and generosity and loyalty, which he never tired of telling. One day, when riding with a neighbor of the Seldens, a prominent country doctor, who had once known affluence, but was then in reduced circumstances and compelled at an advanced age to return to the practice of his profession in order to support his family, the old gentleman drew rein, and pointing with his riding switch to where the James River "low-grounds" lay golden with the ripening harvest as far as the eye could reach, said to him:

"All these acres were once mine. I lost them by endorsing for a friend and neighbor. He was a noble gentleman, and had he ever been able, he would have repaid me every cent."

In the autumn of 1860 he entered the University of Virginia. Here his time was short, for on the night of the 17th of April, 1861, the day when the Virginia Convention dissolved the Commonwealth's association with the other States of the Federal Union, he set out with "The Southern Guard," a military company of fellow students, for Harper's Ferry, and remained thenceforward a soldier of the Confederacy, until the sun had set on the long and heroic struggle.

Of the incidents of his life as a soldier, there is no room to write here. Entering the service as a private, he became in succession first lieutenant and captain of artillery. From Harper's Ferry to Appomattox and Greensboro, he served through the gigantic campaigns of that array of "tattered uniforms and bright muskets," "which for four years carried the Revolt on its bayonets," with a constancy, a fidelity and a devotion that were unexcelled. The details of his service would fill a narrative of hard-fought battles, of weary marches, of suffering and self-denial, of gallant and enthusiastic courage, of unfaltering purpose, of pride and exultation in dearly won victories, of uncomplaining fortitude in defeat. But no shadow of regret, no thought of apology ever crossed his quenchless spirit, when time had made plain the ineffectuality of it all. From Appomattox until death he championed with eloquent tongue and busy pen the cause he had fought for in "Our War," whose events remained always outlined before his memory with the clear simplicity of some immortal legend.

In the years "after the War" he made many warm friends among the best of those who had once been his foes; but to them he yielded not even a tacit surrender of his convictions. And they in turn, won by his genuineness, his enthusiasm, his loyalties, if unconvinced by his accurate knowledge, his ready wit and quick resourcefulness, accorded to him the ungrudging recognition of his sincerity. "To the kindest soul who ever cussed or killed a Yankee," wrote one of these Northerners on a photograph which he gave him.

He loved to think and to read and to talk of the Confedcracy and of the heroic deeds of its defenders; and in later life he numbered among his closest associates many who had been of its civil and military leaders. His enthusiasms about it extended in unexpected directions. "I have been trying for months to find the name of the man who wrote 'The Barefooted Boys'," he once said; and then he repeated with indescribable expression the lines of the poem, telling

"How the South on a time
Stormed the ramparts of hell
With her barefooted boys."

He was never satisfied until he got at the bottom of any question concerning the war, and either proved or disproved it; whereupon his catholicity of spirit rested satisfied with the incontrovertible conclusion. He was as eager and as interested in his demonstration in the press that "All quiet along the Potomac" was written, not by a southerner but by a northern woman, as he was to prove by meticulous evidence that Whittier's "Barbara Frietchie" was based on an alleged incident that never could have occurred. He ranked, with those competent to judge, as a military critic of high order, and his "Defence of Petersburg" is regarded as a war classic. Among some of his most notable articles published in the English periodicals were papers on questions arising out of the War. He held Lee and Jackson and Stuart and their compeers in adoring memory; and he taught his little grandchildren, in his afternoon drives with them along Monument avenue in Richmond, reverently to salute, as he himself never failed to do, Mercier's noble equestrian statue of the great Confederate Commander. In his letters to his friends allusions and references to the Confederacy and to incidents of the struggle repeatedly occurred; and when he gave them books that bore in any direction upon its story, it was his pride and delight to write on the flyleaf of the volume, in the fine Oxford hand that marked the scholar and man-of-letters: "From W. Gordon McCabe, formerly Captain of Artillery, Pegram's Battalion, A. P. Hill's Corps, A. N. V."

Yet with all his unforgetting loyalty to old memories, he was none the less loyal to the later duties and obligations of the highest citizenship under a reconciled and restored Union. No one took a larger or more eager interest in the success of the Allies and America in the World War, in which his youngest son, a colonel in the United States Army, served with distinguished gallantry; but he regarded with scant respect the idea that it was a war "to make the world safe for democracy," —holding rather that it was fought in defense and vindication of the honor and the interest of the American Republic, as "Our War" had been fought for constitutional liberty, and for homes and hearthstones.

In October, 1865, he opened "The University School" at Petersburg, Virginia, and continued it there until he removed it in 1895 to the larger field of Richmond. One of his former pupils, on the occasion of the presentation in 1903, two years after the school was finally closed, to the University of Virginia by his "Old Boys" of a portrait of its "Head Master," painted in London by the celebrated artist, Walter Urwick, described him as he was when he began his career as school-teacher:

"Well do I remember him; a small, live, wiry, active man physically, almost a boy in appearance; full of life, enthusiasm, mental activity, accomplishments and ability; deeply interested in his work, with the highest ideals upon all subjects, and with rare power to maintain discipline and conduct his school, the latter doubtless due to his experience as an officer in the army; a disciplinarian in the school-room, yet a player on the baseball nine of his older boys; and in and out of the school always recognizing and treating each boy as a gentleman, and out of school as his equal and companion." In his annual school-catalogue his announcement of the school's discipline was as concise as its enforcement was invariable: "The discipline is strict. The honour system—(honor spelled always with the *u*, after the English fashion)—obtains entirely in the management of the school, and the only punishment for deviation from that system is expulsion." To his pupils he taught, as for himself he held,

"That Life may go, if Honor stay";

and "the honour system" soon developed the honor habit in them. During his long experience he sent forth from the school many of whom he had made scholars, but he sent out very many more of whom he had made gentlemen.

In a letter of his to Charles Foster Smith, reproduced in a paper on "Southern Colleges" in the *"Atlantic Monthly,"*—in which a place among the best is accorded McCabe's University School,—he wrote:

"I announced to the school that I should take every fellow's word as being as good as my own, and that in all matters touching personal honor a boy should be treated as any other gentleman; but if after such consideration on my part, he in any way forfeited his word, or even tampered with it, that he should not associate with me, nor with his honorable fellows. I drew the big fellows very closely to me. I was 'pitcher' on the school 'nine,' and was happy one day when I accidently overheard a boy say to another, as a knot of them were discussing some point of honor: 'Well, I think any fellow who would tell McCabe a lie is a dirty blackguard'."

The scholarship of the University School was of the highest; and from its doors went into the Universities and the world a host of young men, who later became eminent as teachers and professors and ministers and lawyers and physicians, and who illustrated in their subsequent careers its lofty standards of learning and of life. Here his most significant work was done, and from it he derived the rich reward of a modest satisfaction in the conscious impression of his own personality upon the youths who had come under his tutelage. "The Old Man," as they called him, always felt that he had done his part by "the Boys."

During this school-period he was constantly busy with his pen, and achieved enviable distinction as scholar and editor and author. He contributed essays and papers of recognized merit to leading magazines and newspapers; and the foremost English periodicals, such as *"The Saturday Review," "The Acad-*

emy," and *"The Oxford and Cambridge Review"* gladly welcomed his articles on literary and military topics. He edited dictionaries and cyclopedias, and the writings of classical authors, he was "literary adviser" to great publishing-houses, he wrote Latin Grammars, and won fame among classical scholars as a Latinist "of exact and penetrating scholarship"; he collected and edited books of ballads; his multifarious knowledge and boundless energy found outlet in many directions in the world of letters; while he gave evidence of his ability and stirring eloquence as a speaker in a wide and versatile series of occasional addresses and speeches.

He was a poet of no ordinary gifts, and his poems, for the most part written in war-time and characterized by a lyric fire and genuine poetic expression, have found a place in the leading authologies of America. In his later years, while President of the Virginia Historical Society, he gave in his annual "Reports" a long line of biographies of members of the Society who had died during his incumbency, which are unusual in their literary character, and as distinctive within their limits for charm of style and sureness of touch as are the gentle "Essays of Elia"—"a well of English undefyled."

He was *"intus et in cute,"* the finest type of the Virginian of his generation, saturated with the history of Colony and Commonwealth, and carrying at his fingers' ends the innumerable details of their story. In his great library, teeming with first editions and with autographed volumes, the gifts of many friends who were writers throughout the English speaking world, his wonderful collection of "Virginiana" held first place; and his delight in adding to it ceased only with his end. His collection of manuscripts was no less remarkable than his books; and among them are hundreds of personal letters written to him by many of the foremost authors and soldiers and statesmen of America and England.

Space fails for even a bald and austere catalogue of the societies, associations and organizations of which he was a member, and in most of which he held high official position. He was President of the Westmoreland Club of Richmond, where a generous and lavish Virginian hospitality has long abounded; of the "Society of the Sons of the Revolution in Virginia"; of the "Society of the Cincinnati in Virginia," and of the "Society of the Signers of the Declaration of Independence"; and for several of them he was historiographer or historian-general. Among these organizations in which his distinction as scholar and soldier and orator gave him place, his affections and interest were most strongly centered upon the "Virginia Historical Society," of which he long held the office of President,—a position that he occupied at the time of his death. In its congenial work and its eminent accomplishments he had a constant pride, and on it he bestowed his continuing devotion, his latest activities and many generous benefactions.

His collegiate and University degrees included that of Master of Arts, *honoris causa,* from the venerable College of William and Mary in Virginia, which also conferred on him the degree of Doctor of Laws; that of Master of Arts, *honoris causa,* from Williams College, Massachusetts; and the Doctorate of Letters from Yale.

For his own *alma mater,* the University of Virginia, which confers no honorary diplomas, but which had given him the incommunicable decoration of soldiership among her students, and of scholarship upon her rolls, he felt an abiding affection; and he served her loyally as student, as alumnus, and as official Visitor.

But after all else is said of his honors, his illustrious friendships, his scholastic and literary achievements, and his varied experiences of life, it was the personal human side of him that was his most meaning and attractive possession. He had a genius for friendship. Wherever he went, whether to private home or club, in America or in England, his coming was hailed with delight by those who greeted him. His knowledge of what was best in books and in people, his charm as a talker, his unchallenged gift as a story-teller, his winning and kindly humor, his "keen sense of language and its imperial influence on men," the spell of his cheerfulness and ancient courtesy,—every grace and attraction that sprung from a fine sincerity, a generous sympathy, a warm heart, and a noble intellectual independence, won for him a wide range of associates and friends among both gentle and simple.

In his domestic life he was all that husband and father could be in affection and unselfish devotion. His first wife, who was the mother of his children, and in every thought and deed his "helpmeet," was Jane Pleasants Harrison Osborne, whom he married April 9, 1867, and who died November 22, 1912. As elsewhere stated, he married, second, March 16, 1915, Gillie Armistead Cary, who had been, in his boyhood, his junior schoolmate and youthful companion, and who survives him.

He had travelled much and in many lands, and had many intimate friends among the most intellectual men and women of his time; and he was cosmopolite in the variety of his interests, his experiences and his acquaintanceships.

He lived a busy and useful and generous life; and left wherever he passed unforgettable memories in the hearts of those along the way who learned to know him; and he died—after exceeding the allotted span of the Psalmist—as he had wished to die: not lingering, but quickly, as they who pass in battle. He never grew old in thought or feeling; and his pursuits, his enthusiasms, his freshness of outlook upon life, were only quenched in death.

So, as R. L. S. wrote of his preceptor, Fleeming Jenkin, "he passed; but something in his gallant vitality had impressed itself upon his friends, and still impresses. Not from one or two only, but from many, I hear the same tale of how imagination refuses to accept our loss and instinctively looks for his reappearing, and how memory retains his voice and image like things of yesterday."

(NOTE.—This paper was prepared at the request of the Executive Committee of the Virginia Historical Society.)

THE

VIRGINIA MAGAZINE

OF

HISTORY AND BIOGRAPHY

VOL. XXVIII JULY, 1920 No. 3

VIRGINIA QUIT RENT ROLLS, 1704

During the colonial period all land owners in Virginia paid to the King an annual "quit rent" of one shilling for every fifty acres. The list of the land owners and the amount each owned was prepared by the sheriffs of the various counties and delivered to the Receiver-General, who collected the quit rents and transmitted the lists, with his accounts, to the English government.

It is singular that, as lists must have been sent annually, only one, that of 1704, has been discovered. The Library of Congress had a copy made of the original in the British Public Record Office, and that used here is from a photostat copy of the one in the Library of Congress.

It is not certain that all of the persons named in these lists owned the lands in fee simple. There are some indications that persons renting or leasing lands may have been charged with the payment of the quit rents. For instance one of the Cary family of Warwick County died after 1704, bequeathing a certain tract of land. It does not appear on this roll in his name, but does appear in the names of two of his sons.

Either the grantees of many large tracts of land bought to sell in smaller tracts (and this did often occur) or, else persons not holding by an absolute fee simple title were charged with the quit rents on the land they occupied. A study of one of the county rolls in connection with the county records, wills, deeds, etc., would be of interest.

It can be readily seen that this quit rent roll is of considerable interest and value. Unfortunately it does not include the counties between the Rappahannock and Potomac to their headwaters. These counties were Lancaster, Northumberland, Westmoreland, Richmond and Stafford. The quit rents for this section—the Northern Neck—were paid to the proprietors, the Culpeper and Fairfax families successively.

The amount derived from quit rents gradually increased. In 1684 it was £574 and in 1751, £16,433. This revenue was usually donated by the Crown for the uses of the colony.

For notices of the subject see P. S. Flippin's "Royal Government in Virginia," 233-235; P. A. Bruce's "Economic History of Virginia in the Seventeenth Century," 556-563, and references given by them.

At this time Henrico included the present Henrico and Chesterfield and westward, on both sides of the James River as far as the settlements extended. The Huguenots, just coming to Manakin Town, are not included.

[Endorsed] Virginia

Copy of the Rent Rolls of the Sev[ll] Countys in Virg[a] for the year 1704 referred to in Col. Nicholsons Lres of the 25 July last.

Recd 8 October

Read

705

M. 61 Entred C. fol 365

A True and Perfect Rent Roll of all the Lands held of her Maj[tie] in Henrico County, Aprill 1705

A

	ACRES
Andrews, Thomas	396
Ascoutch, [Ascough] Mary	633

Archer, Jno.	335
Adkins, Jno.	125
Archer, Geo.	1738
Aldy, John	162
Akins, James, Senr	200
Asbrook, Peter Senr	200
Akins, James, Junr	218
Allen, Kidd	99
	4106

B

Byrd, [Wm] Esqr	19500
Bolling, Robt.	500
Bolling, John	831
Bevill, John	495
Branch, X.^{to} [Christopher]	646
Blackman, W^m	175
Bridgwater, Sam^{ll}	280
Bowman, John, Junr	300
Bowman, Edwd	300
Branch, Benj^a	550
Brown, Martha	893
Bullington, Benj^a	100
Bowman, Len.	65
Bullington	144
Bevell, Essex	200
Baugh, John	448
Baugh, James	458
Burton, Isaac	100
Bottom, John	100
Bayley, Ab'^{r}	542
Brooks, Jane, belonging to Wm Walker, New Kent	550
Braseal, Henry	200
Brazeal, Henry Junr	300
Burton, Robt	1350
Burgony, John	100
Branch, James	555

Burrows, Wm Wm Blackwell, New Kent	63
Branch, Thomas	540
Bailey, Thomas	251
Branch, Matthew	947
Burton, W^m	294
Bullington, Robt	100
Broadnax, Jno. J C C [James City Co.]	725
Beverley, Robt.	988
	33590

C.

Cheatham, Tho.	300
Cox, Batt.	100
Cox, John	150
Cox, George	200
Chamberlaine, Maj^r Tho.	1000
Childers, Ab^r, Senr	368
Cannon, John	108
Cox, W^m	300
Childers, Ab^r Junr	100
Clark, W^m	333
Clark, John	300
Cox, $Rich^d$	300
Cardwell, Tho.	350
Croydall, Roger	200
Cock, W^m	1535
Cock, $Rich^d$ Senr	2180
Childers, Philip Senr	50
Childers, Philip	300
Childers, Tho.	300
Carter, Theo.	75
Cock, Capt. Thomas	2976½
Couzins, Charles	362
Clerk, Alenson	604
Cock, James	1506
Curd, Edwd	600

Cock, Richd	C C C [Charles City Co.]	476
Cock, John		98
		15171½

D.

Dison, Nicholas	150
Dodson, Wm	100
Douglas, Charles	63
	313

E.

Edwd, Tho.	676
Entroughty, [Enroughty] Derby	200
Ealam, Robt.	400
Ellis, John	217
East, Tho. Senr	475
East, Tho.	554
East, Edwd	150
Epes, Capt. Fra.	2145
Evans, Charles	225
Ealam, Martin	130
Epes, Isham, Epes, Fra. Junr each 444½ Acres	889
	6061

F.

Field, Peter Major	2185
Farrar, Capt. Wm	700
Farrar, Tho.	1444
Farrar, Jno.	600
Fowler, Godfrey	250
Ferguson, Robt.	230
Ferris, Wm	50
Franklin, James Senr	250
Franklin, James Junr	786
Ferris, Richd Senr	550
Farmer, Henry	100
Forrest, James	138

Forrest, John	150
Fetherstone, Henry	700
Farloe, John Sen[r]	100
Farloe, John Jun[r]	551
Faile, John	240
	9024

G.

Gilley Grewin Arrian [Gilligrew Marin, or Gilly Gromarin]	2528
Gee, Henry	435
Good, [Goode] John Sen[r]	600
Gaithwaite, Sam[ll]	50
Gaithwaite, Ephraim	163
Granger, John	472
Gill, John	235
Good, [Goode] Sam[ll]	588
Gower, James, Grig's Land	500
	5571

H.

Hill, James	795
Holmes, Rich[d]	100
Harris, Tho.	357
Harris, Tim[o]	250
Hill, Rosam[d]	1633
Hobby, Lawrence	500
Hatcher, John	215
Haskins, Edw[d]	225
Hatcher, Edw[d] Sen[r]	150
Hunt, Geo.	200
Hughs, Edw[d]	100
Hancock, Sam[ll]	100
Holmes, Thomas	50
Hambleton, James	100
Hutchins, Nich[o]	240
Hatcher, Benj[a] Sen[r]	250

Hatcher, Wm Junr	50
Hobson, W^m	150
Hatcher, Wm Senr	298
Hatcher, Henry	650
Hancock, Robert	860
Harris, Mary	94
Hall, Edwd	184
Herbert, Mrs.	1360
Hudson, Robt.	281
	9242

J.

Jones, Hugh	934
Jefferson, Thomas	492
Jones, Philip	1153
Jorden, Henry	100
Jamson, John	225
Jackson, Ralph	250
	3154

K.

Kennon, Eliz^b	1900
Knibb, Sam^ll	209
Knibb, Soloman	833
Kendall, Rich^d	400
	3342

L.

Liptroll, Edwd	150
Lewis, W^m	350
Lester, Darius	100
Ladd, W^m	70
Ligon, Eliz^b Widdo	
Ligon, Mary Wid^o	1341
Laforce, Ren. [or Rene.]	100
Lockett, James	50
Lownd, Henry	516
Lockett, Benj^a	104

Ligon, Rich^{d}	1028
Ligon, Hugh	150
	3959
M.	
Mann, Robt.	100
Matthews, Edwd	330
Mosely, Edwd	150
Mosely, Arthur	450
	1030
N.	
Nunnally, Rich^{d}	70
O.	
Osbourn, Tho.	288
Owen, Tho.	68
	356
P.	
Perkinson, John	622
Perrin, Ann	500
Pleasants, John	9669
Parker, W^{m}	100
Parkins, Nich^{o} Senr	500
Pledge, Jno.	100
Powell, Robt	150
Peice, John	130
Pleasant, [Pleasants] Jos.	1709
Porter, W^{m}	305
Peirce, W^{m}	175
Peirce, Francis	312
Paine, Thomas	300
Portlock, Eliz^{t}	1000
Pew, Henry	350
Pattrane, Fra.	778
Pride, Wm Senr	1280
Polland, Thomas Senr	130
Perkinson, Seth	50

Puckitt, Wm	192
Puckitt, Tho.	300
Pattison, Joseph	500
Porter, John	100
Polland, Tho junr	235
Polland, Henry	235
Puckitt, John	215
	19937

R.

Robertson, Geo.	1445
Ragsdale, Godfrey	450
Rawlett, [Rowlett] Peter	164
Russell, Charles	200
Rowlett, Wm	200
Rowen, Fra.	148
Robertson, John	415
Rouch, Rachell	300
Robertson, Thomas	200
Russell, John	93
Royall, Joseph	783
Redford, John	775
Randolph, Coll. Wm. including 1185 Acres in Swamp	9465
	14648

S.

Steward, Jno Junr	902
Scott, Walter	550
Soane, Capt. Wm.	3841
Stanley, Edwd	300
Scruggs, Charles	400
Sewell, Wm	59
Smith, Humphrey	40
Sharp, Robert	500
Stovoll, Bartho	100
Sherrin, Widdo	75
Steward, Daniell	270

Smith, Obadiah C C C [Chas. City Co.]	200
Stowers, Wid^{o}	200
Sarragin, Stephen	120
	7557

T.

Tancocks Orphans	1230
Trent, Henry	224
Turpin, Thomas	491
Turpin, Philip	444
Turpin, Tho.	100
Turner, Henry	200
Taylor, Tho.	475
Tanner, Edwd	217
Traylor, Edwd	100
Totty, Tho.	260
Traylor, M^{rs}	730
	4471

V.

Voden, [Vaden] Henry	100

W.

Woodson, John	4060
W^{ms}, Robt.	300
Woodson, Robt. Junr	1157
Ward, Rich^{d}	300
Watson, John Senr	1603
Walthall, W^{m}	500
Walthall, Henry	832
Whitby, W^{m}	215
Watkins, Henry Senr	100
Webb, John	100
Watkins, Tho.	200
Woodson, Rich^{d}	180
Woodson, Wid^{o}	650
Williamson, Tho.	1077

Webb, Giles	7260
Wood, Tho.	50
Watkins, W^m	120
Watkins, Jos.	120
Watkins, Edwd	120
Ward, Seth	700
Wood, Moses	100
Wilkinson, Jos.	75½
Wilkinson, John	130
Worsham, John	1104
Womack, Ab^r	560
Willson, John Senr	1686
Willson, John Junr	100
Walthall, $Rich^d$	500
Wortham, [Worsham] Geo.	400
Wortham, [Worsham?] Charles	90
Womack, W^m	100

W	24489½
V	100
T	4471
S	7557
R	14648
P	19937
O	356
N	70
M	1030
L	3959
K	3342
J	3154
H	9242
G	5571
F	9024
E	6061
D	313
C	15171½

B	33590
A	4106
Totall	165814
Out of which must be deducted these sev[ll] quantities of Land following viz: Tancockes Orphans Land	1230
Allens Orphans Land	99
	1329
An Acct. of Land y[t] hath been concealed	
John Steward Jun[r]	2
Tho Jefferson	15
Tho Turpin	10
Hen Gee	10
Steph Sarrzen	10
M[r] Lownd	1
James Atkin Sen[r]	32
Matt Branch	10
James Franklin	360
James Hill	50
Rosemond Hill	33
John Bullington	44
Benj[a] Lockett	4
John Russell	23
Charles Douglas	13
Coll Randolph Carles [Curles] Swamp Land	1049
	1669

The Q[t] Rent being 162719 Acres

MINUTES OF THE COUNCIL AND GENERAL COURT

From the Originals in the Library of Congress.

(CONTINUED)

A Court at James Citty the 10th of October, 1627, present:

S'r George Yeardley, Knt. Gov. &c

Capt. West	Mr. Secretarie
Doctor Pott	Capt. Tucker
Capt. Smyth	Mr Farrar[1]
Mr. Persey	

Whereas there remaine certaine of the *Duty*[2] boyes whose first seaven yeares of service as apprentises expired in May last past, & were from that time to begin to serve other seaven yeares as Tenants for halves, the Court hath ordered that the sayd boyes shall for the sayd time of seaven yeares as Tenants for halves, serve S'r George Yeardley, Knt. now Governor, & that he have the benefitt of their service or to make composition w'th them for the same as they will agree w'th him. And this the Court doth the rather order in regard that all the

[1] William Farrar, or Ferrar, who was born 1594-5 and came to Virginia in the ship *Neptune* in 1618. He was a Commissioner (Magistrate) for the Upper Parts, a member of the Council from 1623 to 1633 and probably until his death, which occurred some time before June 11, 1637. It was once believed that he was a son of Nicholas Ferrar, Sr., of London, but this is an error. He was possibly the son of John Farrar, Esq., of London (of the Farrars, or Ferrars, of Eawood, Yorkshire), who in his will dated April 24, 1628 (this Magazine XXII, 398), made bequests to his son, William, then out of England.

[2] These were 50 London boys sent to Virginia in 1620, in the ship *Duty*, to be apprenticed to planters.

Tenants belonging to ye place of Governor are now freed & noe meanes remaining for the maintenance of the place.

Uppon the request of the Governor to the Court in the behalfe of serg't Richaard Popeley[3] it is ordered that sixteene hundred pounds weight of tobacco be this yeare paid unto him out of some of those fines that are now dew unto ye Publique whereby the estate of ye said Popely may be relieved & in some sort restored, he being a man that hath both heretofore & is still ready to doe good service to ye Colony. And haveing for this yeare given his attendance uppon ye Governor & being to continue in his employment until the spring.

It is ordered that Robert Wright & Andrew Rawleigh[4] shall have a lease for ten yeares of that parcel of land lately belonging unto Thomas Grubb, Joiner, of James Citty Island and by his will given unto them.

At this Court were read & heard divers examinations touching Will'm Garret the servant of Mr. Abraham Persey, his lewd behavior w'th Katherine Lemon his fellow servant, and the Court after full examination & debate uppon the matter, doe not find as yet sufficient cause to punish the said Will'm Garrett any farther then for that fault for w'ch he hath allready been punished by Mr. Persey.

A Court at James Citty the 11th of October, 1627, present:

S'r George Yeardley, Knt. Governor &c
Capt. West in pomerdino

Doctor Pott	Mr. Secretary
Capt. Smyth	Capt. Tucker
Mr. Persey	Mr. Farrar

[3] Richard Popely, who was born in 1608 in the parish of Wolley, Yorkshire, owned, later, 700 acres at the Middle Plantation (Williamsburg). In 1624-5 he was living on the plantation of Rev. Jonas Stockton at Elizabeth City, and is stated, in the Census, to have come in the *Bona Nova* in 1620.

[4] Andrew *Railey* was living on James City Island 1624-5. Thomas Grubb, who came in the *George* was an inhabitant of the same place.

Whereas there was a controversy pursued in Court between Beniman Sim's & Joan Meatheart his servant by him brought over into this Country w'th an interest to make her his wife and for that uppon some dislike between them about the beginning of May last past, it was agreed that the sayd Joan Meatheart should serve the sayd Beniman Sim's[5] for the terme of two yeares then next ensueing as by the testimonyes of Richard Brewster & Steven Barker doth appear, The Court hath ordered that the said Joan shall performe the sayd time of service for two yeares, shee being put to serve the same unto Mr. John Gill & he to pay unto ye said Beniman in consideration thereof one hundred weight of Tobacco & to deliver him one man servant as soon as any shall arrive here by any shipping for the terme of three yeares.

It is ordered that John Phillips & Joan White for their offence in com'itting fornication, whereby the said Joan hath had a bastard, shall be whipped at ye Post at James Citty & receive 40 stripes a piece. And farther that Mr. Persey doe take such course as they may be separated and not suffered to come together.

Susan Wilson sworne & examined sayeth that about two months after that Steven Tailor had been put out to service unto Allen Kineston by Mrs. Doctor Pott, the sayd Kineston brought home to the Doctor's house the sayd Tailor being verie lame, And then Mrs. Pott in her husband's absence tooke the said Tailor into her house uppon the said Kinestons intreaty, hee saying that he would pay whatsoever it would cost.

Steven Tailor being examined sayeth that he himselfe being sicke & brought home to Doctor Potts his house, by his master, Allen Kineston,[6] hee heard ye sayd Kineston to say I pray take him in, & whatsoever costs & charges he is at I will pay for it.

---

[5] Benjamin Simms, or Syms, was afterwards the founder of the first free school in Virginia, the Syms Free School, Elizabeth City County, still existing in part, in the Syms-Eaton Academy at Hampton. In 1624-5 he was aged 33 and lived at Basse's Choice.

[6] Allen Keniston, who came in the *Margaret & John*, lived at Pashbehays, 1624-5.

The Court having taken into their consideration danger w'ch might ensue to ye Colony by those Indians[7] of the Carib Islands w'ch were lately brought into ye Country by Capt. Sampson, & haveing admonished the said Capt. Sampson to consider w'th himselfe what profitt he could make by the said Indians, & to devise w'th himselfe so to dispose of them, as that they may prove noe discom'oditie to ye Colonie. The said Capt. Sampson hath returned his answere to ye Court that he knoweth noe way or means to dispose of those Indians, but delivereth them wholy upp unto our hands to dispose of them as we shall please, The Court hereuppon having had full & large deliberation of this matter, & being likewise given to understand by good information that the said Indians have run away and hid themselves in the woods attempting to goe to ye Indians of this Country as some of them have revealed & confessed, And for that they have stolen away divers goods, & attempted to kill some of our people as by good probability wee are informed, And for that especially they may hereafter be a means to overthrow the whole Colony, have adjudged them to be presently taken & hanged till they be dead.

A Court at James Citty the 12th of October 1627, being present:

Sir George Yeardley, Knt. Go. &c

Capt. West	Mr. Persey
Doctor Pott	Mr. Secretarie
Capt. Smyth	Capt. Tucker
Capt. Mathewes	Mr. Farrar

The voiadge of going to Pamunkey was taken into consideration.

---

7 The Caribs, originally resident in Guiana and on the lower Orinoco, and on the Windward and other islands in the Caribbean Sea, were a cruel, ferocious and warlike race, who long fiercely resisted the Spaniards. It would be interesting to know how Capt. Sampson got his cargo. Their character was well known to all who frequented that sea and it would be known that an attempt to capture them for sale as slaves would be a most risky venture. It is probable that Sampson had been paid to carry away a lot of captured Caribs and drop them where he chose, so that it would be far enough to prevent their return.

It was the opinion of the Court that Capt. Mathewes[8] should doe his best indeavor to procure such a number of volunteers through the whole Colony, as may be sufficient to go to Pamunkey or uppon any other Indians our enemyes, And that after notice by him given to ye Court there shall be a Comission granted unto him to authorize him for the proseqution of that voiadge.

A Court at James Citty the 13th of October 1627, being present:

Sir George Yeardley, Knt. Governor &c

Capt. West	Mr. Persey
Doctor Pott	Mr. Secretarie
Capt. Smyth	Capt. Tucker
Capt. Mathewes	Mr. Farrar

The Court being informed that divers planters at Accawmacke doe intend at the old plantation Creeke and at Magety Bay on that shoare to erect some new plantations and to seat themselves in such sort as may be both inconvenient & dangerous, uppon full & large deliberation concerning the same, have resolved in noe sort to permit such their planting, but rather to keepe them, as much as may be, seated closely together, & rather more especially to indeavor the full planting of ye Forest[9] then any other place.

At this Court Mr. Abraham Persey put in a bond of one Samuell Kennells,[10] deceased, in suite againste John Barnet who hath marryed the wife & relicte of ye said Kennell, And the Court hath adjudged the said Barnet shall pay the debt of the said bond, viz. the sume of three hundred pounds of tobacco, unto Mr. Persey, for that the wife of ye said Kemmell

---

[8] Captain Samuel Mathewes, afterwards Governor.

[9] The "Forest" was the country between the James and the York.

[10] Samuel Kennell was in John Lauckfield's "Muster", at Elizabeth City in 1624-5. He was then aged 30 and had come in the *Abigail* in 1621. John Barnett, aged 26, in 1624-5, who had come in the *Jonathan* in 1620, lived at James City 1624-5.

did w'thout any order by Court given Administer & put away all the estate of the said Kemmell, And this is ye opinion of ye Court, notw'thstanding that ye said Barnet marryed her w'th-out and goods of ye said Kennell's.

(To be continued)

VIRGINIA IN 1681-82

(Abstracts by W. N. Sainsbury and Copies in the McDonald and DeJarnette Papers, Virginia State Library).

(Continued)

Order for Lord Culpeper's Departure.

At the Court of White Hall the 17th of June 1682
Present
The Kings most Excellent Matie in Council

Whereas His Matie upon information of the disorders and Tumultts lately arisen, and carried on by several Inhabitants within this Colony of Virginia hath thought fit in order to the suppression thereof, to command the Lord Culpeper His Ma'ties Governor in Chief of that Colonie to embarque himselfe for that place by the first of August next and in the meantime to prepare himselfe in case of any sudden emergency as to bee in readiness within a weeks time after notice to repair to his said Government. It was Ordered by His Maty in Council that the Rt Honoble the Lords Commissioners of the Admiralty doe forthwith give directions for the immediate equipping one of His Matye Frigates such as they shall judge fittest, to be in readiness within the time above mentioned for transporting the said Lord Culpeper to Virginia.

Order for Lord Culpeper's Departure.

At the Court of White Hall the 13th of July 1682
Present
The King's most Excellent Matie in Council

Whereas the Right Honoble the Lords of the Committee of Trade and Foreign Plantations did this day acquaint His

Ma^{ty} in Council that upon consideration of the present state of affairs in Virginia they had on the Sixth of this Instant signified to the Lord Culpeper the necessity of his making himselfe ready to embarque on the 15th Instant on Board the Frigat intended to transport his Lo^{p} to Virginia. His Ma^{ty} in Council is hereby pleased to Order that the Lord Culpeper doe not fail to embarque himselfe on Saturday next being the 15th Instant in pursuance of the directions signified unto his Lo^{p} by the Committee.

Report Concerning Virginia.

At ye Committee of Trade & Plantations Friday the 21st of July 1682

Present

Lord President	Earl of Aylesbury
Duke of Ormond	Earl of Conway
Earl of Craven	Earl of Halifax
Earl of Bath	Lord Visco^{t} Hyde
Earl of Clarendon	Mr. Godolphin

The Lords of the Committee of Trade and Foreigne Plantations agree most humbly to represent to His Ma^{ty} That in consideration of the present state of affairs in Virginia which are in very much disorder to the great prejudice of His Ma^{tye} Authority and Revenue His Ma^{ty} would be pleased to appoint some fit person who may be forthwith sent to that Government with such powers and Instructions as shall be necessary for His Maties Service.

Order in Regard to Frigates Going to Virginia.[1]

At the Court at White Hall the 13th of July 1682

present

The King's most Exct Ma^{ty} in Council

[1] It is evident that the English Government was disturbed by the plant-cutting commotions in Virginia and feared a repetition of Bacon's Rebellion.

Whereas the Right Hono^{ble} the Lords of the Committie for Trade and Plantations did this day represent unto His Ma^{ty} the present state of Affairs in Virginia. It is upon consideration thereof hereby Ordered in Council that the Right Hono'^{ble} the Commiss'^{rs} of the Admiralty doe give Instructions to the Captain of the Frigat designed to carry the Lord Culpeper to Virginia that hee remain in that place with the Frigat under his command in case of an actual Rebellion And that the Captain during such Rebellion may receive his directions from the Lord Culpeper or the Commander in Chief for the time being

And it is His Maties further pleasure that the said Commiss^{rs} doe send Orders to the Captain of the Norwich Frigat now at Jamaica That hee call at Virginia in his return home and that in case of an actual Rebellion there at the time of his arrival and not otherwise he may be ordered to follow such directions as shall be given him by the Lord Culpeper touching his stay there and prosecution of His Maties Service for soe long time as the said Commissioners shall think convenient in such case who are likewise to direct the said Captain to take on board, upon his departure from that place all such ammunition and Stores of Warr as the Lord Culpeper or the Commander in Chief of Virginia for the time being shall think fitt.

Order Concerning Military Stores in Virginia.

At the Court of White Hall the 13th of July 1682
present
The King's most Excell^{t} Matie in Council

Whereas it was this day represented to His Matie by the Right Hono^{ble} the Master General of the Ordnance that a considerable quantity of Ammunition Arms and other Stores of Warr, sent to Virginia during the late Rebellion are yet remaining there It is hereby Ordered by His Ma^{ty} in Council That soe much of the Stores as are necessary for His Maties Service may be kept in some place where they may bee secure And that if any part of the Stores shall appear necessary for the use of the Inhabitants they may be sold to such persons and at such reasonable rates as the Governor or Commander in Chief for the time being with the advice of the Council shall agree for and that the money for which they shall be sold be forthwith transmitted to the Office of the Ordnance and an acct thereof be turned into the Exchequer as is usual in like cases as alsoe that the remainder of the stores that shall be found not absolutely needful for that Plantation bee immediately sent home in the Norwich Frigat. Whereof this Right Hono^ble^ the Lord Culpeper and all other persons whom it may concern are to take notice and to proceed accordingly.

Order That No Governor Depart From His Government Without Leave.

That in August 1682 was delivered to my Lord Culpeper an Authentick copie of an Order of Council dated the 3rd of November 1680 commanding that noe Governor of His Maties Plantations doe come into England from his Government without leave from His Matie in Council first obtained, Which Order is Entered in the Book of Plantations in general—page 82.

No King's Ships to Lade Merchandize in the Plantations.

7th of Feby 1682

It was ordered that the several Governors of His Ma'^ties^ Plantations in America doe not permit any of His Ma'^ties^ Ships coming within their respective Jurisdictions to lade any Goods or Merchandises whatsoever or give any Instructions contrary to the Standing Instructions of the Navy And that they doe not upon any misdemeanor or accident hap'ning on board any of His Maties Ships call any Court Martial for the Tryal of the Offenders but take depositions of the fact and transmit the same hither in order to their Tryal for the same.

ORDER ON PETITION OF RICHARD BULLER.

[Richard Buller,[2] merchant, of London, petitions the King for the restitution of certain deer skins seized in Virginia. On March 2d, 1682, the King in Council gave order, which recited the fact that certain deer skins and other goods belonging to him had been seized in Virginia on board the Dolphin, of London, as forfeited by virtue of a recent act passed there prohibiting the exportation of such commodities. The matter was referred to the Lords of Trade and Foreign Plantations. On March 21st that body advised that due time was not given in Virginia for notification of the act and that, as the forfeited goods were vested in the King, that the goods be restored to the petitioner.]

SECRETARY SPENCER TO THE COMMITTEE OF TRADE AND PLANTATIONS.

May it please your Lordships

I humb'y present unto your Lordships the Journal of the last Assembly and as its my duty your Lo'ps will alsoe herewith receive the Acts that Session made and passed. I humbly suppose the time spent (or rather mispent) in long debates between the two Houses, of no other moment than that of the Clerk of the House of Burgesses, as alsoe their positive desires and motions to have members of the Council conjoined with their committees will not pass your Lord'ps reading without animadversions thereon.

And as the matter represents itselfe the Lt. Gov'r and Council may bee censured, therefore humbly begg leave to inform your Lord'ps great sums of tobacco were to be raised for ye paying off the four Garrisons two years in arrear—which, to-

---

[2] Act III of the session of the General Assembly of March, 1680, forbade the exportation of deer and calf skins on account of the need of leather in Virginia. The seizure of Buller's goods was made in December, 1682, and Governors Culpeper and Effngham each held that the seizure was proper. The latter stated that Buller's agent, John Herbert of Prince George County (who had a son, Buller Herbert) confessed that he was trying to evade the law.

gether with the unhappy circumstances the Government lay under by the late tumults and meetings in Plant Cutting daily threatening fresh Iruptions contracted a great charge and noe standing revenue to discharge the same, nor by any ways or means to be effected but by ye ord'^ry^ course of a Assembly raising Tobaccos by the pole; neither in that juncture was the peace and quiet of the Government soe intirely quieted and settled as to offer at fresh hazards which the House of Burgesses made use of and from ye same raized an expectation of gaining their floaty desires in which all circumstances considered; hope may receive your Lordships favorable opinion.

And I begg leave to assure your Lo'^ps^ tho' it has been and is ye great care of the Government to prevent such impositions, yet it is hardly possible for the Government to avoid such streights not having a Fund wherewith to discharge the constant necessary charges thereof but by an Assembly, the convening of which by the Burgesses brings in the Countys they represent, is often found to exceed the whole public charge of the Government which formerly was provided for by a Law[3] impowering ye Governor and Council to raise a levy on y^e^

[3] Spencer's letter shows the illiberal feeling which had animated some Virginians since the Restoration. Before 1660 the General Assembly repeatedly declared that it alone had the right to levy and disburse taxes. In March 1623-4 (Hening, I, 124), February, 1631-2 (ib. I, 171), September 1632 (ib. I, 196), March 1642-3 (ib. I, 244), this claim is clearly and positively made. The Articles of Surrender to the Commonwealth of England, March 12, 1651, acknowledged this right. At the session of March, 1660-1 (ib. II, 21), an order of the Governor (Berkeley) and Council imposing a duty of five shillings on each barrell of provisions exported was confirmed by the Assembly and ordered to be continued until the end of the next July. The action of the Governor and Council was an innovation probably held justified by the emergency; but it was evidently considered that the approval of the Assembly was needed. The influence of the Restoration was farther shown in Virginia, as it was in England, by another act of the same session (ib. II, 24). The Assembly authorized the Governor and Council in September, 1662, and for three succeeding years, to levy a tax of not more than 20 lbs. of tobacco per poll. This dangerous departure from popular government was repeated in an act of March, 1661-2, (ib. II, 35). On Nov. 9, 1667, however, Berkeley desired to send two councillors to sit with the Burgesses when the levy was laid; but they replied that it was their privelege alone, to which the Governor "willingly assented." In November, 1682, (ib. II, 507), the levy was laid by the General Assembly and this continued to be done throughout the Colonial period.

people not exceeding thirty pounds of Tobacco pr pole for answering and satisfying public charges. That Law revised or a Power of the like nature would enable the Govern-or a Power of the like nature would enable the Governor and Council to maintain and keep up the Dignity of the Government and free the Inhabitants of the charge of too frequent Assemblys.

And to the intent all interests may therewith be satisfied. It is humbly proposed the account of the whole summe soe raised with all its Articles of Payments bee produced to the next General Assembly manifesting for what use the Tobacco was raised and how disposed of.

Upon the closure of the Assembly his Ex'^{lle} the Lord Culpeper whom if wee had been soe happy to have enjoyed at the first meeting thereof, his Lo$^{p's}$ great prudence and knowledge in Government would have allaied all heats and fitly tempered matters and expedited the affairs thereof for His Majesty's Service. The disorders in plant cutting are well settled and at the next General Court which is at hand some of the most notorious plant cutters will by due course of Law bee proceeded against, there will be a full meeting of the Council and what Orders will there pass shall transmit to your Lo$^{p's}$ together with all Orders of Council since my last return. And in the interim humbly begg your Lo$^{p's}$ favorable acceptance of the zealous endeavours of service from R^{t} Hono^{ble}.

Your most humble & most obedient servant,

Nicho. Spencer.

James City
March 20th 1682/3
Received May 21, 1683.

Letter from the Clerk of the Virginia Assembly.

To the Right Hono^{ble} the Lords Committees of His Ma^{tles} most Hono^{ble} Privy Council. For Trade and Foreign Plantations

Right Hono^{ble}

In obedience to your Lo'^{ps} commands to the Clerk of the Assembly of Virginia for the time being to send home to your Lo'^{ps} a Journal of the Assemblys proceedings, with copies of the Votes, Orders, Bills and Laws I have transmitted to your Lo'^{ps} a copy of the Journal of the House of Burgesses at the Assembly begun at James Citty the 10th day of November 1682, together with Copies of the Acts and publick levy and proportion thereof for payment in the several countys in this Country the like whereof I have delivered to His Ex^{cle} the Lord Culpeper which hee was pleased to say should bee sent by some Ship soon after the rising of the said Assembly and I shall take care that Duplicats shall be sent to your Lo^{ps} by the next conveniency

Right Hono^{ble}
Your Lo^{ps} most Humble and most devoted
Servant Thomas Milner Clerk
to the Assembly

Received June 7, 1683.

SECRETARY SPENCER TO THE COMMITTEE OF TRADE AND PLANTATIONS.

May it Please your Lo^{ps}

With my last to your Lo^{ps} of the 20th of March 1682/3 I humbly presented your Lo$^{p's}$ the Journal of the last Assembly and all Acts then made and passed and in pursuance of my duty I herewith transmit to your Lo^{ps} all Orders of Council which have passed since the 9th of May 1683 by which your Lo^{ps} will receive an account of all Political occurrences in this His Ma'^{ties} Government which at present (I thank God) is in a peaceable and quiet condition all former disorders of plant cutting being by the prudent management of his Ex'^{cle} the Lord Culpeper composed and settled and to deter others futurely from the like attempts examples have been made of two of the most notoriously active mutineers the last Summer in plant destroying who have deservedly suffered death for the same. One more condemned for the same who, being a very young fellow and ill seduced, and since having given all outward assurances of a hearty and sincere repentance his Ex'^{cy} hath though fit to suspend the execution of the sentence of death passed upon him untill His Maties pleasure shall bee therein further known. Our only Commodity Tobacco having the last Winter a pretty quick market hath encouraged the Planters vigorously to go on this year with the same, of which there is the greatest probability of an early and plentiful crop as I have known. His Ex'^{cy} having well setled all affairs and noe other prospect but of their soe continuing, His Ex'^{cy} takes this opportune time to make a Voyage for England to render His Ma'^{ty} and Your Lo$^{p's}$ the present state of His Ma'^{ties} affairs in this Government in whose absence according to His Maties Commission of Instruction to His Ex'^{cy} the Lord Culpeper the Government resides in a President and Council, whom cannot doubt but will according to their duty to His Ma'^{ty} with all care and due circumspection keep up and maintain this His Majestys Government. Your Lo'^{ps} will receive from his Ex'^{cy} the Lord Culpeper so full and significant an account of all Affairs that for me to enlarge on the Same would give your Lo^{ps} an unnecessary trouble therefore humbly begg leave without further enlargement to conclude that I am

Your Lo^{ps} most humble and obedient
Servant

Nicho. Spencer

James Citty
May 29th 1683
Received June 19, 1683.

CULPEPER'S PATENT AS GOVERNOR FOR LIFE FORFEITED.

[On Aug. 2, 1683, a Commission was appointed to enquire whether Lord Culpeper had forfeited his patent. On Aug.

the matter was tried "Apud le Court House proacto S'te Clements Ducor in Comt. Midd" and it was found that on account of his absence frim his government without leave, he had forfeited his patent.]

VIRGINIA GLEANINGS IN ENGLAND

Contributed by Reginald M. Glencross, 176 Worple Road, Wimbledon, London, S. D. 19, England.

Extracted from the Consistory Court Records of the Diocese of Gloucester.

CHAMBERLAYNE, EDWARD PYE.

Abstract of Will of Edward Pye Chamberlayne of the Boyce in the parish of Dimock Co Gloucester Esquire
I give unto my Son Thomas the sum of two hundred pounds An the rest of my personal estate & money of my Grove I have lately sold I give &c to be equally divided between my younger children namely my said Son Thomas, Deborah, Anne Elizabeth and Mary I give to my said younger children, Thomas Deborah Anne Elizabeth and Mary the sum of one thousand two hundred pounds to be equally divided between them charged and payable out of all my manors messuages lands tenements and hereditaments within the said parish of Dimock to be paid as soon as my elder son shall come to the age of 21 years for non payment of which said sum as aforesaid my Will is my Son Thomas & daughters Deborah Anne Elizabeth & Mary or survivors shall enter in & upon all said manors &c until sum of £1200 shall be paid & satisfied
I appoint my Mother Yem & my Wife Executors
Will dated 14 April 1729

E Pye Chamberlayne

Witnesses
James Wingod Peter Thomas John Cam
Proved 12 May 1729 by Dorothy Yem & Elizabeth Chamberlayne the Executrixes

THOMAS CHAMBERLAYNE OF CITY OF BRISTOL (*sic P. A. B.*) merchant

Will dat. 2 Mar. 1748 £1,000 which Ann my daur. will be entitled to after my death by virtue of settlemt on marre. with my late wife dec.; to sd daur. her late mother's watch etc. To my brother Richard C., grocer, Stephen Nash, woollen draper, John Harmer, merchant, all of Bristol, George Roberts of Leiston co. Hereford, gent., & George Smith of Kentchurch, co. Hereford, yeom., all my lands & two copyhold messuages called Nokes Court *als.* Newhouse & Cookes meadow part of the manor of Killpeck, Heref., which I have surrendered to uses of Will, in fee, in trust for sd. daur. at 21 or marriage, for life, remr. to her sons successively, in tail, in default to her daurs. equally, in tail, in default, one quarter to my nephew Edward Pye C. son of my sd. brother Richard C. in fee; the other three quarters to my nephews & neices Edward Pye, Thomas, Ann, Elizabeth & Mary C. sons & daurs. of my late brother Edward Pye C. dec., in fee. To sd. trustees £10 each for mourning. Rest of personal este to sd. trustees in trust to pay to my sister Mary C. so long as she live unmarried £10 a year, rest for sd. daur. for life & then among her children, but if none, to pay £3,000 as my daur. may appoint, £500 to my sd. sister, £300 a piece to my neices Mary & Elizabeth C. (daurs. of my late brother William C. dec), one quarter of residue to sd. Edward Pie C. son of the sd. Richard C., & the other three quarters to sd. Edward Pie, Thomas, Ann, Elizabeth & Mary C. sons & daurs. of sd. Edward Pie C. dec. sd. Trustees to be exors. in trust & guardians of my daur. till she be 21 or married. Witnesses: James Duffet, Geo. Adderley, Thos. Blackwell.

Prob. 13 June 1749 by Richard Chamberlayne, Stephen Nash, John Harmer & George Roberts, e. the exors. Power reserved to Geo. Smith the other exor. *Lisle* 76.

[Following a suggestion by the annotator of these "Gleanings", that Elizabeth Chamberlayne, niece of Edward Pye, and mother of Edward Pye Chamberlayne the elder, was the same Elizabeth, widow of Thomas Chamberlayne, of London, merchant, who was dead in 1682 (see wills and notes in Vol. XXVI of the Magazine), members of the family authorized a brief investigation in England. No will of this Thomas Chamberlayne was found; but he was probably the Thos. Chamberlayne, of Stepney, Middlesex, whose widow, Elizabeth, qualified as his administratrix, Sept. 16, 1674.

Mr. Glencross found the following in a chancery suit; Chamberlaynes *vs.* Kidley. The plaintiff was Edward Pye Chamberlayne, the elder. His son, William Chamberlayne of Virginia, had a posthumous daughter, Ann Kidley Chamberlayne, named for his mother.

Chanc. Proc. B. & A. bef. 1714 Ham. 265, 20

Dec. 1693

Answer of Thos. Batoon & Anthony Wallinger 2 of the Defts. to Bill of Edward Pye Chamberlayne.

They believe Compl. was Edward Pye's nephew & godson, that sd. E. Pye was a planter in Barbadoes & that he placed Compl. with Richard Howell & Richard Guy, 2 other Defts. in Bill, in Barbados. Do not know if sd. E. Pye advised Compl. to marry Anne Kidley (now Compl's wife) nor that Richard Kidley made proposal mentioned. Sd. E. Pye was owner of Lordship of Dymock & of manor of Boyce. Never heard sd. E. Pye say that Mrs. Whitaker had a writing to sd. other Defts. in trust for Compl.

Chanc. Proc. B. & A. before 1714. Ham. 265, 46.

29 May 1693

Edward Pye Chamberlayne of the Newhowse co. Heref. gent. son & heir app. of Elizabeth C. widow the only daur. & heir of Margaret Somors dec. who was sister & heir of Edward Pye heretofore of Barbadoes & late of the Boyce in prsh. of Dymock, Gloucs. merchant dec., orator. Sd. E. Pye, orators great uncle was for many years a merchant in Barbadoes & acquired much estate & having no child he bore affection to orator, his godson & provided for his education. He told Richard Howell esq & Richard Guy esq. both now of London & late of Barbadoes that he intended to make orator his heir but kept it private from fear of orator becoming extravagant. Orator sent to Barbados under sd. Howell & Guy. Sd. E. Pye procured orator to marry one Anne Kidley spr. one of the daurs. of Richard K. of Bromley, Herefs. esq. Sd. E. Pye proposed that the Newhowse &c. (£20 a year), Cookes meadow (£8 a year) etc, etc, in Herefs. lands in Gusmound, Monm. shd. be settled on orator. Sd. Mr. Kidley promised to settle on his daur. Anne an estate at St. Waynards called Reddican worth £40 a year. Orator on 29 Oct. 1689 married the sd. daur of Mr. Kidley & sd. orator has had by her several children, 2 sons being alive. Sd. E. Pye was owner of manor of Dymock, Gloucs. & capital messe. there called Boyce which he had purchd. from Mr. Sergt. Leyes dec. value £300 a year. Sd. E. Pye made a lease of his property to sd. Howell & Guy in trust for orator & sd. Mr. Whitaker who lived at the Boyce with sd. E. Pye had the writing. Sd. E. Pye on 10 Feb 1690 signed his will in presence of William Winteer esq. Richard Hill the elder & younger gentlemen all of Dymock viz. I. Edward Pye late of Barbados, merchant, now of Boyce in prsh. of Dymock Gloucs. to my kinsman Edward Edward Pye Chamberlaine of the Boyce in prsh. of Dymock Gloucs. esq.; orator, sheweth that Edward Pye esq. late of the Boyce afsd. dec. orator's uncle having no children of his own & having an estate of £600, having bred & educated orator, about Aug. 1689 proposed a marre. betw. sd. orator & Anne, daur. of Richard Kidley of Bromley, co. Heref. gent. who had no other children but 2 daurs., it was agreed that if marre. took place he would settle on orator, his wife & issue his farm called Penvoirs, Herefs. & sd. R. Kidley should similarly settle his farm called Reddicar in prsh. of 8 Waynards, Herefs. As latter farm was more valuable sd. E. Pye was to deliver goods to sd. R. Kidley to use of sd. orator etc. also £107 10s & this was done & a schedule made. Orator then very young. Some time after marre took effect sd. E. Pye about 168 [—] made his will & (pursuant to an unwritten agreemt.) devised to orator in fee the rest of his estate & orator hoped sd. R. Kidley would have paid sd. £107 but he delayed & orator having expectations did not press him. Orator now has discovered that sd. R. Kidley has settled all his real estate on his other daur. or one of her children after his decease. Orator now asks for sd. £170 with intt.

Chamberlain vs. Kidley, Chan. Proc. Ham. 270|59.

The following pedigree is derived from the papers in this suit. At the time the said suit was brought several of Edward Pye Chamberlayne's children had not been born. It is hoped that same member of the family will have farther investigation made in England.

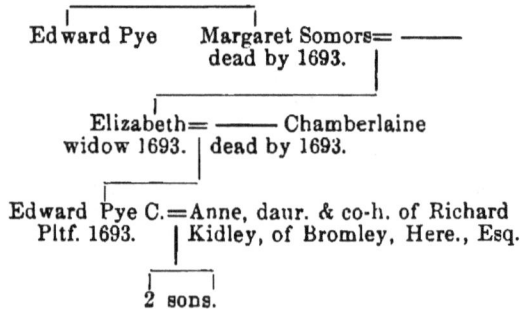

Edward Pye   Margaret Somors= ——
dead by 1693.

Elizabeth= —— Chamberlaine
widow 1693. | dead by 1693.

Edward Pye C.=Anne, daur. & co-h. of Richard
Pltf. 1693. | Kidley, of Bromley, Here., Esq.

2 sons.

The wills given above are those of two of the brothers of William Chamberlayne of Virginia.

William Clopton thelder of Groton, county Suffolk, gent Will 1 November 1640; proved 27 November 1640. To my wife all customary lands in Groton holden of William Hobart Esq as of his Manor of Lynsey. And all customary lands holden of John Sampson Esq as of his Manor of Lillesey cum Sampsons Hall in Carsey And all my Customary lands holden of Isaac Appleton Esq in Groton aforesaid in tenure of Henry Samford and Jerom Lamberde to her for 18 years, and after expiration to my son William and heirs for ever. Whereas I and my said son William by indenture 27 October last granted to John Sampson the younger and Robert Sampson gentlemen my manors of Chastlynes Chipley and Saundefords my freeholds in county Suffolk to hold for 18 years at a certain rent set forth in said Indenture which said lease was made for raising portions for my younger sons and daughters The said leases shall in convenient time set over to my said wife the said premises. My wife possessed in Trust shall raise portions for my younger children. For every one of them (except my youngest son) £200 apeece. I am seized of one copyhold tenement and lands in Lynsey now in tenure of Robert Pinson the custom of which Manor is that it descends to the youngest son. My executor shall pay to my youngest son £160 and if my son William observe obligations then the said premises to my said son William and heirs. I desire that my executrix continue my son Walter at the University of Cambridge until one year after he shall have taken his degree of Master of Arts. My loving wife Alice Clopton sole executrix. Witnesses: Richard Doggett, Henry Sanford, Ro: Simpson. *Coventry*, 146.

[The emigrant of the Clopton family of Virginia was William Clopton, who was born about 1655, and was living in York County, Va., in 1682. Later he removed to New Kent County. His sons were Robert, William and Walter, and he had a grandson Waldegrave Clopton. William Hammond, Gent., of Ratcliffe, England, by will July, 1732, left lands in Essex, England, to his uncle William Clopton, of Virginia.

William Clopton, of Castleton in Groton, Suffolk, 1636, married Margaret Waldegrave, and had three sons, William, Walter and Waldegrave, and several daughters, one of whom was Thomasine, who married John Winthrop, Governor of Mass. This William Clopton, of Groton, is probably the testator above, though he must have married a second time, as he names his wife Alice. It is probable that William Clopton, of Va., was a grandson of the testator. A genealogy of the Virginia Cloptons was published in Dr. Lyon G. Tyler's *William and Mary Quarterly*, Vols. IX and X.]

JOHAN FOOTE of Tedbourne St. Mary, county Devon., widow. Will 27 December 1647; proved 2 September 1653. I bequeath unto Agnis Westcott, daughter of Anthony Westcott, £20. To Anthony, son of said Anthony Westcott of Tedbourne aforesaid, £1. To Peter Ware, my son in law, one shilling. To Mary Ware, daughter of the said Peter, 10s.

To Jane Ware, her sister, 1s. To Margarett Foote, daughter of Humfrey Foote, my son, 1s. All the residue of my goods not bequeathed I give unto Anthony Westcott, my son in law, whom I make my executor; and I desire Robert Poope of Holcombe Bornell and Giles Westcott of Whitston to be my overseers, to whom I give 1s. apiece for their pans. The mark of Johan Foote. Witnesses: the mark of Thomas Ponsford; Will. Squier. Proved by the executor named. *Brent,* 181.

WILLIAM FOOTE of the parish of Pinnock, county Cornwall, gent. Will 1 August 1652; proved 19 July 1653. I bequeath to my wife Margaret two of my best chests, a dozen of pewter dishes of the best sort, my brewing kettle, my best riding nag or mare, the side saddle with its furniture, half a dozen of silver spoons, my little silver cup gilded, two of my best cows, etc. and £10, on condition she give security for the payment of £70 to my brother Mr. Simon Foot and our cousin Mr. William Symons (whom I make my executors) within 3 months after her marriage with any other person. I give her more one bedstead which now standeth over the hall at Boturnell. I give to the poor of the parish of Veryan 20s., to the poor of Pinnick 6s. 8d. To my daughter Elizabeth £300 at her age of 21 or marriage. To Margery Robbins, my mother, one gold ring. To my brother one birding gun. To my uncle Sumons, in token of my love, my best silver spoon. To my cousin William Symons my small gold ring with a signet on it. To John Clarke the younger my best serge suit. To each of my servants 5s. All the rest of my goods to my son William Foot at his age of 21. If both my children die under age, I give all my goods, to my said brother Symon, he paying my wife £100 if she be then alive. (signed) William Foote. Witnesses: William Cothler, the mark of Christopher Luke. Proved by the executors named. *Brent,* 347.

[Richard Foote, the emigrant to Virginia, was son of John Foote, Gent., and was born at Cardenham, Cornwall, August 10th, 1632. A pedigree of the Virginia family was published in Numbers 1 and 2, Vol. VII, of this Magazine. The testators, especially William Foote, of Pinnock, were doubtless relations.]

PRESTON PAPERS

(From the originals in the Virginia State Library)

John Watkins to William Preston.

War Office May 5th 1782

Sir

I now inclose you the order for powder which Colonel Davies mentions in his last to you; and which was neglected to be sent by Mr. McGavock—

I am, Sir

Your most Obdt Sert

John Watkins

[Address]

Colonel William Preston

Montgomery

[Address]

Capt. Pearis

Wm Davies Lt

William Lewis to Co. Lt. Montgomery Co.

War Office May 6. 82

Sir,

In consequence of the invasion of the frontiers, his Excellency in council has thought proper to direct that all the six months men from the frontier counties should be returned to their respective settlements, and serve the remainder of their time out in their counties. You will therefore be pleased to give the men, of which a list is enclosed, such a length of furlow for the men to take care of their families, as you may think proper, after which you will order them on duty.

I am Sir,

Your most Obdt Servt

William Davies

[Address]

County Lieutenant

Montgomery

Field Officers for Montgomery and Washington Counties.

Montgomery Courthouse, July 2d 1782

At a meeting of the Field Officers of the Militia of Montgomery and Washington Counties in conformity to instructions received from His Excellency the Governor bearing date 15th day of June last: to concert and settle some proper plan for the defence of both counties—Present

William Preston; Walter Crockett; Joseph Cloyd; Daniel Trigg; John Taylor, Jr.; Abraham Trigg: Field Officers for Montgomery County.

Arthur Campbell; William Edmondson; Aaron Lewis; James Dysart: Field Officers of Washington County

and

Major Patrick Lockheart, District Commissioner—

It is the unanimous opinion of the Board of Officers That the 200 men permitted to be drawn out by His Excellency the Governor, for the defence of the frontier have divided the same into the following Districts viz.

On New River in the neighborhood of Capt Pearis 30 Men. Sugar Run 20, Capt. Moore's Head of Blue Stone 25, Head of Clinch 25 Men—

In Washington at Richlands 20, Castle Woods 30, Rye Cove 20, Powell's Valley 30 Men. The extent of the different Districts. From Capt. Pearis to Sugar Run 10 Miles to Capt. Moores Head of Blue Stone 30 to Capt. Maxwells, Head of Clinch 16 Miles, which is nearest the Washington line. To Richlands 24, to Castle Woods 30, to Rye Cove 28, to Powells Valley Fort 26 Miles in all 164 miles We find the greatest difficulty in making any provision for the support of those men while on duty as there is no specific tax brought into the places appointed for that purpose in either of the Counties. The Officers have therefore recommended it to Major Lockheart the District Commissioner to purchase 200 bushels of Corn in Montgomery County at the most convenient places to where the Militia are to do Duty at three Shillings per Bushel being the current price, and an equal quantity in the County of Washington for the use of the Troops and at the most convenient places at the current prices there, which we are convinced will be a great saving to the State as the Transporting of grain from Botetourt, where there is some belonging to the Publick on hand, to the several Districts where the Militia are to do duty, will be attended with a very great expense the distance being from sixty to One hundred and sixty miles. To procure what further supplies of provisions that may be necessary it is to be an instruction to the Commissioners of the District to instruct the different County Commissioners and Commissaries of Specifices to deliver or facilitate the delivery of provisions to a Commissary of the Troops for each County to be appointed for that purpose or to the order of the Commanding Officers. To which may be added a Warrant to each Commissary to impress agreeable to the Invasion Law as objections have been made to that part of the Governors instructions ordering the direction of the Militia of both Counties, while on duty, under that of the County Lieutenant of Montgomery who lives upwards of 180 miles from Powells Valley and not less than 90 miles from the Richland District in Washington which renders it impossible and useless for him to have these men under his direction for which reason he declines that part of the Command. Let it therefore be humbly recommended to His Excellency the Governor to alter that part of his orders by giving the Superintendance of the Troops in each County to the Commanding Officers of the same as it will save the expense of a Field Officer being on Duty which otherwise would be necessary; and the Defence of the Frontiers will in all probability be better Conducted.

The Board of Officers are unanimously of opinion that the Counties of Montgomery and Washington will provide the number of men ordered for their Defence without calling on any of the neighboring Counties for assistance unless there is a real occasion to do so on some emergency; or on the approach of a large body of the Enemy.

They also beg leave to suggest that the usual manner the Indians conduct their attack on our Settlements makes it necessary that a proper number of Scouts be employed in each District to discover their approaches for which reason it has induced the Officers to direct that two be employed in each District for the immediate safety of the Inhabitants.

Signed by Order

Wm Preston

[Endorsement]

Proceedings of the Board of Officers at Fort Chiswell, 2 July 1782.

Instructions to Colonels Crockett and Cloyd.

Fort Chiswell July 3^d^ 1782

Sir

The Board of Officers appointed to meet at this Place have directed that a Company of Militia be raised immediately and sent to the Frontiers of this County & to be stationed in the following manner to wit at Capt. Maxwells twenty five men & an equal number at Capt. Moores. In consequence of this resolution you will please to appoint an Active discreet Captain, to take the command of this Company as also two Lieutenants and an Ensign.—The Captain and Ensign to command at Maxwells & the two Lieutenants at the other place. These men are to continue ranging the Woods as much as in their power. Two Scouts or Spies are to be sent from each of these Districts & to be under the Direction of the Officers at the respective Stations. You will please to instruct the Officers to be very alert and active in their duty, to keep up good Discipline amongst their men and to be extremely careful to keep exact accounts of the receiving & issuing provisions & that the greatest Ecconomy be used as well with regard to Provision as ammunition.

This Company must be raised & kept out of the upper Batallion by Drafts or Enlistment untill the middle of October: I would earnestly recommend it you to endeavour to have the men engaged for the whole time as it will save a great expense to the State and better answer the purpose of defending the Frontiers.

I beg that no time may lost in carrying this Business into Execution as the safety of Numbers depends upon it.—If anything extraordinary happen in those Districts be pleased to inform me thereof.—Should you be informed of the approach of a large Body of the Enemy you will please to take the most prudent and hasty steps to repell them.—The Field Officers and Captains in your Batallion are hereby required to give you every possible assistance in executing these Orders.

WILLIAM DAVIES TO WM. PRESTON.

War Office Aug 15—1782

Sir

I have never had a certain opportunity of acknowledging your favor of the 6th of last month, for which I am thankful to you—

His Excellency informs me he has himself signified to you his approbation of the measures you have concerted with the advice of the field officers of your County and Washington, and is satisfied with the propriety of your observations for declining the Superintendency in both,

I am sensible of the difficulties which will unavoidably occur in this Business, but would observe to you that many of these difficulties arise from the real mis-conduct of the public agents. You represent, and I am sure with justice, that transportation will be hardly accomplished for want of public horses: I must inform you however, that a certain Evan Baker of Washington was largely entrusted by the Government with the purchase of a large number of horses and other things for the Western defence—but that man has never yet been brought to account, though various applications have been made to him, and tho' there is great reason to believe he retains many of these stores in his possession, or applies them to his own advantage. I must request the aid of your influence to bring this man forward a little, that he may settle his account of the distribution of horses and so forth, with Major Lockheart. I have been told a large number of horses were also purchased by Mr. Maddison. Possibly he may have several by him yet—

With most sincere wishes for the permanent security of your County, I remain Sir, with most respectful esteem,

Your very obedient Servant

Col. W. Preston William Davies

[Endorsement]

Col. Davies Letters—Aug. 15—1782

(To be continued)

VIRGINIA STATE TROOPS IN THE REVOLUTION.

(From State Auditor's Papers, now in State Library.)

(Continued.)

	Ditto paid John Dandridge for a Gun furnished by William Finnie	2	5	
	Ditto paid Martin Haekins for a Gun furnished the service	2	15	
	Ditto paid Ditto for Forage furnished the Troops at Hampton	72	12	2
	Ditto paid Ditto for Rum furnished Ditto	286	3	4½
	Ditto paid Ditto for Express hire		16	6
	Ditto paid Charles Judkins for pay his Company of Militia	252	19	10
	Ditto paid Ditto for William Simmons for Sundries to a Powder Escort		18	4
	Ditto paid Jane Robe for a Horse impressed & lost in the service	20	17	
23	Ditto paid Robt. Anderson for pay of his Company M Men	199	5	
	Ditto paid Wm. graves for Carter Burwell, fodder furnished the Army	3		
1776	To Cash paid Thomas Cary for Col'o Harwood for the pay of			

February 23	several companies of Militia called into service..........	92	14	5
	Ditto paid Ditto for balance of pay & Provisions to the said Militia	48	2	3
	Ditto paid Ditto for Hire to the Army	7	10	6
	Ditto paid Ditto for rectify an Error in his Militia pay roll..	1	8	
	Ditto paid James Cocke for 2 Guns furnished the public service	4	10	
	Ditto paid Ditto for Mrs. Randolph Fodder furnished the public service	2	5	
	Ditto paid Jacob Cunes for a Gun furnished the Army....	2	15	
	Ditto paid Timothy Leste for Guns 2 Ditto	6	10	
	Ditto paid Cole Digges for Fodder furnished the Public Service	40	15	
	Ditto paid Andrew Leith for Sundry Arms furnished Ditto	59	10	
	Ditto paid Samuel Harwood for pay & Provisions as a Major to the Battallion of Minute Men in Elizabeth City......	38	5	
	Ditto paid Pleasant Cocke for pay of himself & Company of the Prince George Militia called into Service	19	4	
	Ditto paid Ditto for William Allison for pay of his Company Militia	15	2	2
	Ditto paid Ditto for Penjamin Harrison Provisions to said Militia	26	6	
	Ditto paid William Johnson for William Farrows for Wagon hire to the Army...........	33	10	

	Ditto paid Andrew Leitch Advances for different Companies M. Men............	300		
	Ditto paid William Badget for Lewis Burwell for Wood to the Army..................	8	8	
	Ditto paid David Griffith 2 Months pay as Surgeon to the Prince William Batallion...	30		
	Ditto paid Griffin Fauntleroy for 2 Guns furnished the Army	5		
	Ditto paid William Shepherd for Express hire	3	13	
	Ditto paid Wiliam Lewis for Provisions furnished Captain Johnson's Company.........	12	16	10
26	Ditto paid John Clayton for a Gun furnished the Army..	4		
	Ditto paid Adam Craig for George Reed for a Gun to the Army	3	18	
	Ditto paid Elias Peay for 2 Guns furnished Ditto	7		
	Ditto paid Clesley Jones for 2 Guns furnished Ditto......	6		
	Ditto paid Anthony Digge for a Horse impressed & lost in the Service	15	7	
	Ditto paid William Elson for Express hire to the Public...	4	4	6
1776				
February 26	To Cash paid Thomas Browne for Mrs. Gibbons for Sundrys to the Army	2	9	7
	Ditto paid James Jarvis for Express hire to the public.....	4	8	9
	Ditto paid James Davidson for a Rifle Gun to the Army....	5		
27	Ditto paid J. Tazewell for Richard Bland for a Muskett to Ditto	6		
	Ditto paid Dickerson Shield for a Gun furnished the Army..	1	5	

	Ditto paid Bartlett Field for Wood furnished the Army by Thomas Wooten	14		
	Ditto paid Ditto by John Fielde for Wood furnished the Army	8	10	
	Ditto paid George Aubrey for Ferdinand O. Neal for Waggon hire..................	26	13	8
28	Ditto paid William Pearson for Shoes furnished for Public use	1	16	
	Ditto paid Robert Combs for Waggonage to the Public..	31		9
	Ditto paid William Hinnkin for Foddero furnished the Army	8	8	
	Ditto paid John Piggit for Fodder furnished for use of Army	8		8
	Ditto paid Theo. Bland for pay of a guard at City Pt.......	17	16	8
	Ditto paid Robbert H. Hove for his pay from 26th December last	27	5	3
	Ditto paid Richard Cooke amount of his Waggon hire for public use	31	10	
	Ditto paid Ditto for trouble & expense in issueing provisions Etc	20		
	Ditto paid James Wall for Waggonage to St. Hampton Battallion	29	10	
29	Ditto paid John Ellis for William Ellis for Waggon hire..	7	10	
	Ditto paid Theo. Bland for Archibald Cary for Necessaries furnished the Army......	156	2	10
	Ditto paid Shady Kelly for his trouble in mounting cannon..	2		
	Ditto paid Thomas Harris for his Service as Public Armourer..	7	14	
	Ditto paid Ditto by a former order for Ditto	4		
	Ditto paid George Brown for a Muskett & Bayonett to the Public	4	5	

March 1	Ditto paid Tully Roberson for wood furnished the Troops..	12	12	
	Ditto paid Ditto for Cap^n Frederick Boush for Pay & Necessaries furnished his Company Militia M. Guard...........	90	1	8
1776				
March 1	To Cash paid George Slaughter for 1 months pay of his Company	176	10	
	Ditto paid Ditto the Balance of his recruiting Account	29	10	
	Ditto paid John Camp for 5 Rifles Purchased for use of the Public	27	10	
	Ditto paid Ditto for balance of Cap^n Thorntons recruiting money	20	10	
	Ditto paid Ditto for Thomas Camp for Waggon hire to the Public	4	10	
	Ditto paid William Johnson his Pay as Adjutant from 26th December last	27	10	1½
	Ditto paid George Burwell for 297 bushels Salt furnished the Public	59	8	
	Ditto paid William Lawrence for a Gun furnished the public Service	2	15	
	Ditto paid Henry Brown for Fodder furnished the Army..	33	17	
	Ditto paid Thomas Lester for a Gun furnished the public Service	2		
2	Ditto paid David Lowe for Provisions to the Culpepper Batallion	4	11	4
	Ditto paid John Pendleton for Express Hire to the Public...	2	10	
	Ditto paid Thomas Wills for Ferriager on account of the Public	4	4	7
	Ditto paid Henry King for Repairing Public Arms	1	10	1

	Ditto paid Simon Loughlin for Provisions furnished a guard		18	
	Ditto paid Landis Patterson for Expenses as a Messenger on Public Business	6		
	Ditto paid Peter Royster his pay & Expenses on Duty as Captain	22	13	8
1776 March 3	To Cash paid George Brook for use of Ambrose Jefferies for making Hunting Shirts to Cap^{n} Gregory's Smiths Company	3	3	
	Ditto paid Samuel Boush for Wiliam Smith for Fuel Etc. Furnished the Troops at Great Bridge	175	3	10
4	Ditto paid Thomas Nelson for Lead furnished the Army....	28	19	2
	Ditto paid Cuthbert Hubbard for House rent for public use	2		
	Ditto paid Samuel Newell for Expenses in the public Service	2	2	3
	Ditto paid Ditto to John Howe furnished	1	5	
	Ditto paid Paul Carrington for Issac Reed for Purchasing Arms	121	1	6
	Ditto paid Ditto for use of Charlotte County for Ammunition	37	6	5
	Ditto paid Ditto for Col^{o} Cole for the Carriage of Salt Peter....	5	7	6
	Ditto paid John Brent for recruiting Expenses & Arms furnished the public	64	5	
	Ditto paid Thomas Walker for Jo. Calvert for Sundrys to the Hampton Troops	21	10	
	Ditto paid Ditto for Benjamin Isabell as Quarter Master to Ditto	18	4	8
	Ditto paid Smith & Bressie for Wood furnished Ditto	23	19	9

	Ditto paid Samuel Boush for Horse Hire		10	
	Ditto paid Cornelius Deforest for 2 Rifles furnished the public	10		
	Ditto paid William Stauard his pay as Quarter Master......	9		7½
4	Ditto paid Robert B. Chew his Pay as Quarter Master Serjeant	5	19	4½
	Ditto paid Charles Tomkies for Guns and Necessaries to his Com^y	286	8	10
	Ditto paid Samuel I. Cabell pay his Company to 28 Feby last..		90	9
	Ditto paid Ditto for Math Swook for a Drum and Fife........	4		
	Ditto paid James Johnson pay of his Comp^y to 28 Feby. last..	151	7	
	Ditto paid Arth Smith for balance of my Recruiting Acct. & Pay of my Company to 28 Feby. last Inclusive	127	9	8
	Ditto paid William George for Guns & Necessaries furnished Captn Woodsons Company of the 9th Regiment	100	4	9
	Ditto paid Ditto for Provisions furnished said Comp^y	29	3	1½
	Ditto paid William Lumpkin for a Gun furnished Cap^n Andersons Company	3		
	Ditto paid John Ross for a Gun furnished the Army	2	15	
5	Ditto paid Thomas Massie for the pay of his Company to the 28th Feby. Inclusive	116	1	8
	Ditto paid William George for Provisions to Capt Woodsons Co^y	17	3	1½
	Ditto paid Paul Carrington for Micajah Watkins for Rifles furnished Captain Cocke's men	137	19	11

Ditto paid Ditto for Math^{l} Ferry for Arms furnished the Halifax Reguars	169	14	10½
Ditto paid Ditto for William Ferry for Cartage of Gun powder	2	8	
Ditto paid Ditto for Wright Bond for Waggonage	21	3	3
Ditto paid William Cabell for Wm Pollard for Provisions furnished the Amhurst Company of Regulars	23	9	
Ditto paid Ditto for Hugh Rose for Provisions to said Comp^{y}	10	15	
Ditto paid Ditto for John Nicholas for Ditto	2	9	3
Ditto paid Ditto for John Barrett for a Rifle	4		
Ditto paid Ditto for John Morrison for a Rifle	4		
Ditto paid Ditto for Balance of Bounty Money	2		
Ditto paid David Low for Repairing Guns to Cap^{n} Smith's Company	4	13	9
Ditto paid M. Carrington for 2 guns furnished the Cumberland Compy	7		
Ditto paid Ditto for his Ration & Forrage to First March	4	4	4½
Ditto paid Hutchins Burton for Captn Samuel Hopkins for Blankets Hunting Shirts & Pay of his Company to 28 Feby	92	9	
Ditto paid Archibald Gowan for 4 double fortifyed 6 pounders	75	18	9
Ditto paid James Donald for John Turner for Rugs furnished Captain Pleasants Company	15	11	4½

Ditto paid John Mayo for Pro-

	visions to Capt[n] Cabells Company	7	13	4
6	Ditto paid Samuel Newell for Charles McFaddin a Soldier for Provisions furnished himself	1	5	
	Ditto paid Capt. James Barron for pay of his Company of Militia for the month of Nov. last	117	12	
	Ditto paid Ditto for the Pay of his Company of Militia to the 28th January	113	13	4
	Ditto paid Ditto for the Pay of himself & Men for Board the Boat Liberty to the 25th February	75	11	6
	Ditto paid Ditto for Capt. Richard Barron for pay of himself & Men for Board the Boat Patriot to the 25 February..			
7	To cash paid Capt[n] Charles Fleming for pay of his Company to the 1st Inst.........	99	19	
	Ditto paid Ditto for William Mosely for Arms purchased for the Public	27	16	3
	Ditto paid Ditto for Arms furnished the Public Service...	14	10	
	Ditto paid Ditto for recruiting expenses & Bounty Money..	20	10	
	Ditto paid Gregory Smith for Arms Purchased for the Public	76	3	6
	Ditto paid George Brown as a Manufacturer of Salt Petre..	5		
	Ditto paid William Stokes for a Rifle Gun	5		
	Ditto paid Ditto for Waggon Hire and other Public Expenses	7	12	6
	Ditto paid Ralph Faulkner for the Bounty & Expenses in recruiting his Company.......	92	10	

(To be continued)

ORANGE COUNTY MARRIAGES

Contributed by W. W. Scott.

(Continued)

Benj'm. Hawkins—Sally Scott.
James Hawkins—Betsey Coleman.
James Hawkins—Elizabeth Rector.
Pleasant Hunter—Jane Harris.
John Hestand—Zantipey Nowel.
Benjamin Jacobs—Sarah Martin.
Gabriel King—Hulday Biggers.
William Lee—Polly Simco.
Jeremiah McDaniel—Rachel Brooks.
John Padgett—Nancy Beckham.
Thomas Phipps—Polly Montague.
Merry Raines—Ammy Floyd.
Michael Roberson—Polly Williams.
Richad Robertson—Elizabeth Collins.
Weedon Sleet—Patsey Petty.
Wm. Smith—Mary Porter.
John Smonts—Polly Fleek.
Benj. Spicer—Catty A. Snell.
Benj. Stephens—Agnes Spicer.
John Stone—Elizabeth Burton.
Luke Thornton—Sarah Steet.
David Willet—Polly Baughan.
James Yates—Sally Hansford.
Letestine Wright—Mary Lindsay.
Larkin Wright—Lucy James.

1800

Wm. P. Bailey.
Absalom Brightwell—Wimlfred Pines.
Robt. Coleman—Sarah Ceman.
John Dalton—Polly Earles.
John Gaines—Joanna Sanders.
Thos. Gaines—Milly Row.
Joshua Gear—Jane Watson.
Benj. Grady—Catherine Adams.
Jacob Graves—Fanny White.
R. Graves—Marian Marquess.
Leroy Hamilton—Sukey Blunt.
John Harris—Milly Price (widow.)
John Hardy—Elizabeth Felix.[d]
Wm. Harvey—Alice Wood.
Armistead Hughes—Sally Chisham.
James Hutchinson—Catherine Dear.
Thomas Jenkins—Elizabeth Quarles [?].
Robt. Jones—Mary Herndon (widow).
St. Clair Kirtley—Ann Pannill.
Geo. Lee—Katy Foster.
Moses Linton—Nancy Peed.
Nathaniel Moore—Sally Adams.
Elijah Page—Sally Sisk.
James Padggett—Phillis Bescom.
David Parsons—Elizabeth Clark.
Reuben Powel—Elizabeth Ballard.
Rich'd Reynolds—Lucy Finnel.
Reuben Sanford—Nancy Wallace.
Daniel Simpson—Elizabeth Jones.
John Sleet—Frances Wright.
Oswald Smith—Loice Quisenberry.
John Snow—Elizabeth Lower.
Thos. Sorrille—Elizabeth Clee.
Leonard Styers—Elizabeth Wolf.
Edmund Taylor—Nancy Thornton.
Geo. Thornton—Nancy Webb.
Geo. Walters—Nancy Harvey.

James Williams—Sally Thompson.
Armistead York—Joanna Hilman.
Lawrence Young—Catherine Martin.

1801

Minister.

Ezekiel Ludas—Catherine Ahart—Jacob Watts.
Thomas Blackerly—Elizabeth Herring—Jacob Watts.
John Bradley—Saley Huncock, Robt. Jones.
Sam'l. Grady—Catey Mountague, Jere Chandler.
Elijah Page—Nelly Sisk, Jacob Watts.
John Straw—Catherine Walters, Jacob Watts.
Thos. Boyer—Patsey Thompson, Jacob Watts.
Fielding Powell—Susannah Ballard, Jacob Watts.
James Taylor—Sally Wood, Jacob Watts.
Elijah Lucas—Nancy Brockman, Jacob Watts.
John Humbleton—Sally Rippett, Jacob Watts.
Wm. Silvey—Mary Atkinson, Jacob Watts.
Henry Ancil—Nancy Baegley, Jacob Watts.
Reuben Clark—Martha Clark, Isham Tatum.
Johnathan Kirtley—Theodosia Anderson, Geo. Bingham.
Dan'l. McClary—Katy Picket, Geo. Bingham.
Washington Pollard—Elizabeth Thornhill, Isham Tatum.
John Vims—Betsey Beazeley, Isham Tatum.
Aaron Gentry—Polly Ogg, Isham Bingham.
Zachary Henry—Lucy Kirtley, Isham Bingham.
Lewis Bailey—Lucy Mahony, Isham Bingham.
Martin Crawford—Susanna Lamb, Isham Bingham.
Nelson Keaton—Edna Davis, Isham Bingham.
Josiah Morris—Suckey Shiplett, Isham Bingham.
Eason Fitzgerald—Mary Self, Isham Bingham.
Jonathan Geer—Sarah Frackwell, Isham Bingham.
Elijah Morris—Elizabeth Geer, Isham Bingham.
Ransom Geer—Polly Lamb, Isham Bingham.
Jonathan Harvey—Margaret Ross, Isham Bingham.
Walter Jones—Sally Freeman, Isham Bingham.
John McClumer—Jennie Estes, Isham Bingham.
William Allen—Elizabeth Wallace, minister unknown.

Armistead York—Joanna Hilman, Nath'l Sanders.
John Wright—Catey Faulconer, Nath'l Sanders.
Edmund Peacher—Lucy Hilman, Nath'l Sanders.
Moore Bragg—Jenny York, Nath'l Sanders.
James Mackeny—Patsy Sent, Nath'l Sanders.
Benjamin Hume—Elizabeth Taliaferro, Fred'k Hukler.

1802

Benj. Hawkins—Polly Bickers, Fred'k Hukler.
Thomas Watkins—Frances Moseby, Robt. Jones.
Thomas Arnold—Peggy Sandford, Robt. Jones.
Henry Clarke—Nancy Grasty, Nath'l Sanders.
Thomas Bush—Liddy Breedwell, Nath'l Sanders.
James Lovell—Elizabeth Harvey, Hamilton Goss.
Hezekiah Wood—Sally Bradley, Hamilton Goss.
James Hunt—Susannah Darnele, Hamilton Goss.
Saml. Mahanes—Elizabeth Brockman, Hamilton Goss.
William Bradley—Polly Marshall, Hamilton Goss.
Henry Herndon—Lucinda Wood, Hamilton Goss.
Kallan Durrett—Elizabeth Thompson, Robt. Jones.
Elias Faulconer—Polly Newman, Robt. Jones.
Jas. C. Melton—Mary Taylor, Robt. Jones.
John Stowers—Sally Herndon, Jacob Watts.
John Beazley—Lucy Porter, Jacob Watts.
Bazel Hale—Lucia Maiden, Geo. Bingham.
James Hensley—Elizabeth Maiden, Geo. Bingham.
Benj. Tinder—Nancy Terrell, Nath'l Sanders.
Reuben Sleet—Frances Mallory, Nath'l Sanders.
Elijah Hambleton—Polly Barge, Nath'l Sanders.
Reuben Twyman—Drucilla Cowhard, Wm. Calhoun.
Alex. Bradford—Hannah Burton, Wm. Carpenter, Jr.

1803

Peyton Keith—Sally Petty, Jas. Garnett.
Willis Kirtley—Mary Presley Thornton, Jacob Watts.
John Collins—Elizabeth Kirtley, Geo. Bingham.

Aaron Gentry—Peggy Ogg, Geo. Bingham.
Abner Cave—Betsy Sims, Geo. Bingham.
Belfield Henry—Elizabeth Kurtley.
Abner Lowry—Nancy Lowrey, Geo. Bingham.
Valentine Beazley—Franky Powell, Geo. Bingham.
James Moore—Nancy Jones, Nath'l Sanders.
Reuben Terrell—Catey Gaines, Nath'l Sanders.
John Donathan—Polly Eluck, Nath'l Sanders.
Alex. Newman—Lucy Sleet, Nath'l Sanders.
Wm. Bell—Fanny Borton, minister unknown.
Henry Beach—Delilah True, minister unknown.
Wm. Gibson—Betsey Carty, Nath'l Sanders.
Rodney Hawkins—Alice Chamberlaine, Nath'l Sanders.
James Dodd—Nancy Cash, Nath'l Sanders.
Allen Elliste—Percilla Gaines, Nath'l Sanders.
James Bradley—Elizabeth Willis, Nath'l Sanders.
Wm. Jacobs—Polly Martin, Nath'l Sanders.
John George—Elizabeth Long, Nath'l Sanders.
James Stubblefield—Polly Backman, Nath'l Sanders.
James Dawson—Nancy Hughes, Nath'l Sanders.
Alex. Hughes—Elizabeth Mitchell, Nath'l Sanders.
Robt. G. Lane—Polly Whitelaw, Wm. Douglas.
Yelly Moore—Elizabeth Brown, Robt. Jones.
Benjamin Porter—Patesey Newman.
John Boston—Sarah Mosely, Robt. Jones.
Jesse Wheeler—Catey Cash, Robt. Jones.
Wm. Moore—Susan Day, Robt. Jones.
Benjamin Hawley—Frances Edwards, Robt. Jones.
James Cramb—Mary Wood, Robt. Jones.
Wm. Tyler—Mary Ann Herndon, Nath'l Sanders.
Charles Cappage—Lydia Wayt, Jacob Watts.
John Stone—Judith Parratt, Jacob Watts.
Wm. Piper—Elizabeth White, Jacob Watts.
Thomas Morris—Elizabeth Acree, minister unknown.
John Wine—Rachel Eheart, minister unknown.
John Rogers—Lucy Darnell, minister unknown.
Valentine Johnson—Elizabeth Cave, minister unknown.

1804

John Mallory—Frances Morton, Nath'l Sanders.
James Clark—Sally Payne, Nath'l Sanders.
Wm. Moore—Rebecca Smith, Nath'l Sanders.
John King—Cynthia Row, Nath'l Sanders.
Geo. Martin—Fanny Sisson, Nath'l Sanders.
Wm. Paggett—Ann Clarke, Nath'l Sanders.
Thos. Chapman—Elizabeth Early, Geo. Bingham.
Thomas Marshall—Nancy Ancell, Geo. Bingham.
Nath'l Clark—Nancy Hall, Geo. Bingham.
Valentine Winslow—Ann Beadles, Geo. Bingham.
Wm. Graves—Peggy White, Hamilton Goss.
Jacob Medley—Fanny Head, Hamilton Goss.
Augustine Grimes—Polly White, Hamilton Goss.
Philip P. Barbour—Frances T. Johnson, Hamilton Goss.
Jonathan Taylor—Lizzy Ann McDaniel, Hamilton Goss.
Wm. Acree—Rebecca Morris, Hamilton Goss.
Rill Darnell—Polly Ahart, Hamilton Goss.
Thomas Bell—Silah Milburn, Wm. Calhoon.
Wm. Lands—Elizabeth Herring, Geo. Bingham.
Isaac Vernon—Nancy Patterson, Geo. Bingham.
Robt. Ancell—Frances Pearson, Geo. Bingham.
Preston Collier—Eliza Haney, Geo. Bingham.
Jno. Goodale—Sally Davis, Geo. Bingham.
Rich Austin—Mary Snow, Geo. Bingham.
Henry Marshall—Eleanor Wood, Geo. Bingham.
Francis Abrahams—Jerten Mallory, minister unknown.
Osburn Henley—Martha Winslow, minister unknown.
Joseph Hubbard—Diana Durrett, minister unknown.

1805

Gerard Banks—Ann Davis, Geo. Bingham.
Thomas Price—Elizabeth Dehoney, Geo. Bingham.
Joel Anderson—Lucy Reddish, Geo. Bingham.
James Bailey—Nancy Mallory, Geo. Bingham.
Murryman Stevens—Ann Gregory, Fred'k Kubler.

Joel Bickers—Roxanna Atkins, minister unknown.
John Payne—Elizabeth Mallory, Hamilton Goss.
Ebenezer Sprig—Nina Sanford, Jas. Garnett.
Joseph Hilman—Susanna Abele, minister unknown.
James Hancock—Elinor Hancock, Robt. Jones.
Benjamin Herndon—Mary Stephens, Robt. Jones.
Aaron Quisenberry—Henrietta Reynolds, Robt. Jones.
Richard Cane [Cave?]—Maria Porter, Robt. Jones.
Juniper Smoot—Rebecca McClone, Wm. Douglas.
Jesse Shearman—Sally Breeding, Geo. Bingham.
Minister.
Wm. Smith—Nancy Morris, Geo. Bingham.
Levi Wiles—Charlotte Marshall, Geo. Bingham.
James Harris—Sally Estes, Geo. Bingham.
Richard Beckett—Nancy Thornhill, Geo. Bingham.
Reuben Terrell—Susanna Morton, N. Sanders.
Thomas Lowry—Nancy Dedman, N. Sanders.
James Fisher—Fanny Mason, N. Sanders.

1806

Peter Lower—Judith Ham, Geo. Bingham.
James Snow—Jenny Harvey, Geo. Bingham.
John I. Fant—Fanny James, N. Sanders.
Geo. Herndon—Sarah Teel, N. Sanders.
Moses Robinson—Fanny Jones, Jas. Garnett.
Wm. G. Waggoner—Lucinda H. Hansford, Jas. Garnett.
Benjamin Davis—Jane Jones, Wm. Douglas.
William Tullock—Nancy Whitelaw, Wm. Douglas.
Peter Marsh—Lucy Walker Jollett, Wm. Douglas.
Lewis Harrison—Nancy Harrison, Wm. Douglas.
Jesse Wood—Nancy Page, Wm. Douglas.
Congress Phillips—Elizabeth Farneugh, Jacob Watts.
Wm. Barton—Ann Goodridge, Jacob Watts.
James Mozings—Mildred Clements, Robt. Jones.
James Bookman—Milly Turner, Robt. Jones.
Robert Cave—Lucy Bradley, Robt. Jones.
Wm. Kinney—Fanny Beal, Robt. Jones.

Reuben Morris—Sally Acree, Robt. Jones. Minister.
John Wright—Nancy Wright, N. Sanders.
Wm. Bennett Webb—Martha Lancaster, N. Sanders.
Mainyard Jacobs—Nancy Straghan, N. Sanders.
Richard Cave—Lucy Shelton, Wm. Douglas.
Joseph Snell—Elizabeth Mansfield, Wm. Douglas.
Rich. Wood—Tabitha Cox, Geo. Bingham.
Elijah Davis—Elizabeth Jones, Geo. Bingham.

1807

James Wood—Sarah White, Jacob Watts.
Anthony Twyman—Sarah Davis, Jacob Watts.
Catlett Madison—Winny Routt, Robt. Jones.
Richard Rawlings—Lucy Herndon, Robt. Jones.
Isaac Walters—Elizabeth Pence, Robt. Jones.
John King—Frances Yates, Robt. Jones.
Elijah Hawkins—Elizabeth Scott, N. Sanders.
Wm. S. Berry—Rachel Row, N. Sanders.
Washington Fletcher—Elizabeth Payne, N. Sanders.
John Oakes—Joanna Graves, N. Sanders.
Alex. Moore—Lucy Ford, N. Sanders.
Geo. Proctor—Fanny Grady, N. Sanders.
Walker Rumsey—Polly Camike, N. Sanders.
John Walters—Margaret Hamilton, R. Jones.
James Johnson—Nancy Quisenberry, R. Jones.
Wm. Danise—Jane McCalley, R. Jones.
Thos. B. Adams—Judith Burnley, R. Jones.
John Wallis—Nancy Randel, R. Jones.
Nicholas L. Wood—Nancy Key, Wm. Douglas.
James Clark—Eliza Graves, R. Jones.
Robt. M. Beadles—Sarah Winslow, R. Jones.
Reuben Blakey—Polly Lother, Wm. Douglas.
Killis Rogers—Mary Ham, Geo. Bingham.
Reuben Collins—Fanny Riddle, Geo. Bingham.
Alex. Hawkins—Anna Scott, Nath'l Sanders.
John Grady—Sally Procter, Nath'l Sanders.

Wm. Fletcher—Deliah Sullivan, Nath'l Sanders.
Geo. French Strother—Sally G. Williams, Isham Tatum.
Joseph Bates—Cincy Oliver, Jacob Watts.
Loudon B. Bruce—Milly Estes, Geo. Bingham.
Willis Lamb—Rebecca Slater, Geo. Bingham.
Benj. Anderson—Mary Miller, Geo. Bingham.
James Blakey—Nancy Branham, Geo. Bingham.
John Austin—Gestina Burrus, Geo. Bingham.
Ambrose Hall—Elizabeth Marr, Geo. Bingham.
Charles Thornton—Martha Ogg, Geo. Bingham.
James Garnett—Frances Chiles, Robt. Jones.
Thomas Morris—Sally Wright, Robt. Jones.

1808

Abner Lee—Sally Lee, Nath'l Sanders.
Alexander Wright—Betsey Jones, Nath'l Sanders.
Jacob Bell—Martha H. Taliaferro, Isham Tatum.
John Walton—Agnes Snow, Geo. Bingham.
Joseph Braden—Polly Neale, Geo. Bingham.
John Lambe—Polly Watson, Geo. Bingham.
Larkin Taylor—Elizabeth Hume, Geo. Bingham.
John Fye—Catherin Baughen, Geo. Bingham.
Christian Miller—Elizabeth Beazeley, Geo. Bingham.
Thomas Gibbons—Lucy Dubord, Geo. Bingham.
Joseph Rogers—Burlinda Newman, Robt. Jones.
John Gilmore—Sarah Minor, Robt. Jones.
Philip Barbour—Peggy Poge, Robt. Jones.
John Veatch—Nancy Cooper, Robt. Jones.
Minister
Thornton Tucker—Elizabeth Bickers, Robt. Jones.
Kendall Brent—Polly Burton, Jacob Watts.
John Allen—Sarah Head, Jacob Watts.
Benjamin Rogers—Mary Lain, Geo. Bingham.
Geo. Aary—Elizabeth Shipplett, Geo. Bingham.
Philip Frederick—Betsey Baughen, Geo. Bingham.

1809

Cynthia Mallory, Robt. Jones.
John Evans—Nancy King, Robt. Jones.
Aquila Gilbert—Fanny Newman, Robt. Jones.
Charles Stevenson—Susanna Hancock, Robt. Jones.
John Rickham—Rebecca Hancock, Robt. Jones.
Joseph Eddins—Nancy Davis, Jacob Watts.
Elley Rucker—Mary Burton, Jacob Watts.
Nicholas Whitelaw—Elizabeth Beazley, Jacob Watts.
Tandy Collins—Ann Beazley, Jacob Watts.
George Goodridge—Fanny Burton, Jacob Watts.
Isaac Sims—Nancy Catterton, Geo. Bingham.
Wm. Sampson—Sally Jollett, Geo. Bingham.
Charles Hicks—Judith Watson, Geo. Bingham.
John Jackson—Polly Herndon, Geo. Bingham.
Wm. Melone—Mary Wayland, Geo. Bingham.
Isaac Burk—Jane Miller, Geo. Bingham.
David Goodale—Tabitha Clark, Geo. Bingham.
Geo. Quick—Mildred Reins, Geo. Bingham.
Thos. Watts—Sarah Head, Geo. Bingham.
Thompson Lloyd—Sarah Mowbray, Geo. Bingham.
Valentine Riddle—Betsey Goodall, Geo. Bingham.
John Morris, Jr.—Sucky Colleris, J. Goss.
William Anderson—Lucy Hawkins, Jere Chander.
Thomas Thompson—Frances Robinson, Jere Chander.
Minister.
Blifield Rucker—Nancy White, Ambrose Brockman.
Nath'l. Breedlove—Elenour Mitchell, Ambrose Brockman.
Broddus Breedlove—Nancy Duval, Ambrose Brockman.
John Twyman—Peggy Wayt, Jacob Watts.
Cypress Hensley—Catey Thompson, Jacob Watts.
John Thomson—Julia Pierce, Jacob Watts.
Garland Quinn—Helen Smith, Jacob Watts.
Wm. Newman—Lucy Faulkner, Robt. Jones.
Wm. Arnall—June Martin, Robt. Jones.
Robt. Taylor—Fanny King, Robt. Jones.

(To be Continued)

LETTER FROM JOHN BANISTER[1] TO ELISHA TUPPER, GUERNSEY

Virginia July 11th 1775.

Sir

I had the Pleasure to receive your letter by Cap^{n} Maingey on the Lord Chatham; and have literally complied with its direction respecting the Shipping & Consigning your Tobacco. Hearing that Cap^{n} Maingey's Ship was about to be lengthened, I had purchased between fourty & fifty Hogsheads of Tobacco, hoping for some further Commissions, towards the Completion of her Load; but at a Meeting of the Merchants last Month and about two days before Maingey's arrival I disposed of the Tobacco, fearing to risque it on my hands any longer, when the Price had risen so high as 27/7½. a Price at which I could most readily have sold yours, and the rest designed for Maingey's Load.

The early arrival of your Commission afforded me the utmost Pleasure as it enabled me to save 17½ per Cent, on two hundred Pounds, and fifteen on the last drafts, besides at least fifty shillings a Hogshead in the Purchase of the Tobacco. There are usually at the time the Courts are held for legal Proceedings, in April & October general Meetings of the Merchants, for the Payment of money, Negotiation of exchange $\&^{c}$. at these Meetings the Bills on England $\&^{c}$ are principally disposed, & the Price of Exchange is exceedingly fluc-

---

1 This letter from the British Public Record Office (C. O. 5/158) has been sent us by E. Alfred Jones, Esq., of London, the author of the well known work on old American communion plate. It was written by Col. John Banister, of "Battersea" near Petersburg. He was afterwards a Colonel in the Revolutionary Army and a member of Congress. For an account of the Banister family see this Magazine XI, 164, 165.

tuating from various causes, as scarcity of Money high Price of, & demand for the articles made in the Country, particularly Tobacco. These Meetings used to be regularly held four times a year, but they are now only general in April sometimes June, in Octo^r or November; At these meetings it is usual for Merchants to sell Bills & provide money for the Purchase of Tobacco. Last November, at W^ms burg, the exchange between this and England rose to 35 per C^t, owing to the extreme avidity with which Bills were sought after in order to remit to England. A Fortnight had not elapsed before the rise of Tobacco, & the fall of exchange became obvious. The Moment I received your letter, about the 10th of december, authorising me to draw for the Purchase of the Tobacco, I set about the disposal of the Bills as fast as I could see an opportunity, of either getting money for them, or applying them to my own use. The Event amply justified this Proceedings, as in a few days after I got 32½ per C^t for your first Bills, no Bills would command money at 25 per C^t, in this Place, I therefore sent 200 Ster^l to Phripp & Bowdoin who luckily procured 30 per Cent. at Norfolk. The Commissions from Mr de Jersey Agent for the Ship, not arriving till February, the Scene became extremely changed. Bills had been constantly falling, Tobacco continually rising during the whole time, untill Tobacco had reached 24/Ster^l and Bills were reduced to 15 per Cent. I do not know how far these Gentlemen may be satisfied with the Purchase I have made for them, but if they reflect upon the Tobaccos having been purchased @ 3/6 per Cent under the Price current when their last Bills were sold, I hope they will do me the Justice to think, I have not been an unprofitable Agent, as at the Rate I sold my own Tobacco, & their's was much better, they would have been gainers exclusive of Commission at least £200 upon the Purchase. A Continuance of the Intercourse between yourself and the other Gentlemen of your Place, commenced thro your kind Influence in our Behalf, I had hoped would have been mutually beneficial, and of long continuance; but Reasons of a political nature forbid a commercial Intercourse with G. Britain, & the substituting Force instead of Reason prohibits, by Act of Parliament, & naval Force, our Trade with all the rest of the world. This Interruption I hope will be temporary & that a Revival of our Correspondence will immediately succeed to a Reconciliation with the Mother Country; When this may happen God only knows, as things are brought in the Massachusets Bay, to the ultimate Resort for Justice by an appeal to the Sword. There never was a Country in any age more oppressed, than that of N. England. The Blockade of Boston continued now more than a year has totally & finally ruined that Place, & in the general Wreck many large Fortunes laid out in Improvements, are gone to Ruin; and all this because the People of that Country will not submit to despotic sway.

About the 17th of last April, the first Hostilities commenced by an attempt in the Regulars to seize and destroy a Magazine which had been deposited in the Court house, at Concord. This the Regulars effected, but the Consequence may be Evils of the most fatal kind.

The accounts of this action are variously related, according to the Party they come from. The Provincials swear the Regulars fired on, and shed the blood of the Country People first, on the other hand the Regulars with equal Pertinacity, declare the *Rebels, as they are now called* gave the first fire. Be that as it may it remains unquestioned that the Regulars seized the Property of the People in plunder [ing and [cut off] the Court h e]. Will not such Conduct justify Resistance?

The Congress have now appointed Col. Washington, General of the Army at Boston, with orders to act defensively, hoping that Administration will at length relent, and stop the further Effusion of human Blood, already too much wasted in a Cause the most Iniquitous, that ever disgraced the annals of any Country. This Contest originated with the enaction of a Law imposing Stamp duties, in America, with which a Compliance was utterly impossible from the scarcity of Gold & Silver Coins in which alone a payment was to be received; but this was not our objection to the operation of the Law.

We held it fundamentally wrong, against the Genius of our Constitution, & against common right, that any Person should impose a Tax upon others, of the Burthen of which he did not himself participate. The numerous and just Complaints against the oppression of this act produced its repeal before a single instance of its Execution had been submitted to; but it was repealed from its inexpediency & not from its being essentially wrong and unconstitutional. Here the latent assertion of the right was discernible. But it became quite apparent in the declaratory Act by which the Parliament claimed a right to tax, and by Law to bind America in all cases whatever. This you will easily see struck at the Foundation of American Liberty, inasmuch as the Parliament claimed an unlimited Right of legislation including of course that of taxation, & therefore the unlimited disposal of American Property. Upon the arrival of this Law it was warmly protested against in this Country, by way of Petition to the King, Memorial to the House of Lords and Remonstrance to the Commons; the Language of these several addresses was respectful, 'tho spirited, and contained a detail of American Rights, from the Beginning of its Settlement, to its Charters in Confirmation of the Settlers Rights as Englishmen, & pointing out a form of Government as Colonists, shewing plainly that the Right of Legislation & therefore taxation was inherent in us as Englishmen & confirmed by Charter, that these Priviledges had been often recognized by our Kings, who had often sent over the Forms of Laws to be considered & passed here, by the Assemblies, which had been returned with emendations and additions, as best suited the Circumstances of the Country, for their Completion by the royal Concurrence. The Colonists further alledge that the acts of Navigation for monopolising & restraining their Trade, were productive of immense gain to the Parent State, & by confining the Colonies to the Trade of G Britain only, had a manifest Tendency to keep them dependant, & the Mother Country opulent & Powerful. That if the Parent State insisted on a monopoly of our Trade, she should desist from the claim of taxation, on the contrary, "say the Colonists," let us have a free trade to all the world & we will readily pay a Proportion of the expences of Government, but do not by insisting on both exact from us double taxation. From that time they have with uniformity proceeded in a Plan to establish a new System of Government in America unknown to the Constitution, and at length the article of Tea, on which a Duty had been reserved as a Precedent of Arbitrary taxation, was sent in large Quantities to Boston, to gather on it a tax of Parliamentary imposition, supposing that this w[d] fix on that People a submission to the asserted right of Parliament to tax America, but the People resisted in a riotous manner the landing the Tea, & in the end threw it overboard. This w[d] be called in London, in Paris, & indeed I believe in Turkey nothing but a Riot, but what is the Consequence—a British Parliament, for this Trespass, determin[d] to punish indiscriminately the whole Town, involving innocent & guilty in one common Ruin. And to give a Sanction to any oppression which Power might choose to inflict upon them, three Acts of Parliament passed that August Legislature, for blocking up the Harbour, & inderdicting all kind of Commerce, another for altering their Charter & subverting their Constitution, and a third for authorising the apprehending & carring for Tryal to G. Britain any Persons committing capital offences; and to enforce these Laws a fleet & army was sent to invest by Sea & Land this devoted Town. These Violations of the rights of a Sister Colony, alarmed all the rest, in such a manner, as that their common oppressions effected that Junction which nothing else could have done, & established the firmest union, & closest attachment to each other. This dictated the Necessity of sending Delegates from each Colony to form at Philadelphia, a Council for the good of the whole Continent. Among many other things calculated for general Safety this eminent Body of disinterested Patriots, came to a Resolution to forego the advantages for themselves & Constituents of any commercial Intercourse with G. Britain, untill her Justice should induc her to restore to the Americans their violated rights, but that this might be productive of as little Injury as possible to our Connections in G. Britain, the Period for retaining our Exports was deferred 'till the 10th of the ensuing September in order to give the Merchants an opportunity of sending out the last Crop of Tobacco. The near approach of the time limited for non exportation, has produced many Speculations in Tob° to the great augmentation of its Price, both here & in England and indeed as no Tobacco will probably be shipped from hence next year, unless an accommodation should take Place, it will no doubt dictate to you and my other Friends in Guernsey the Propriety of not parting with the Lord Chatham's Cargoe, but at a very considerable Profit, which surely is to be made by yours as it is laid in at 5/. & the last commissioned Tob° @ 3/6 per Cent, under the Price which is, & for some time past has been given, very eagerly, for this Commodity. To return to the Affairs of America. The Plan of a Commercial opposition to the encroachments the Parliament had made upon the Rights of the Subject, here, had been adopted in this Colony more than twelve Months past, and confirmed by the Gen[l] Congress, in September last, with a little variation as to time, in expectation of its engaging the People of England in our favour, and we are told it has in some Measure had that effect, but we have feeled no good from their Petitions and Reasonings in our favour. The Parliaments refusal to grant any redress this Session, & resolving to proceed by force against the northern Colonies, induced them to prepare for their defence, after having patiently suffered for almost a year, every Insult, & Irritation from an Army & Navy in and about the Town; The Action at Concord & Lexington I have mentioned, it was bloody the troops began it, & the People defeated & persued them into Cha[s] Town, near twenty miles from the Place where the Action began; Since this Action the Provincials 12 or 15,000 strong have been posted near Boston & the neighbouring Towns, to watch the motions of the King's Troops. The Contiguity of the two Armies has from that time 'till the 17th of June occasioned several Skirmishes. On that day it seems an action of considerable Moment did happen, but as the accounts are vague & uncertain I cannot form any certain Conclusion as to the Event, but I believe the Regulars sustained a greater loss than the Provincials, but keeped the ground. Other accounts again say that the Regulars lost 1000 Men which I deem next to an impossibility. I believe the Provincials had the advantage. There probably will be some bloody Battles this Summer, and before it expires Lord Sandwich may be convinced that the Americans are not such Poltroons as he, in the House of Lords, thought proper to represent them. Upon the whole, what can G Britain gain by a Conquest of her Colonies I will venture to affirm neither Honor nor Profit. Had she been content to have governed her American Subjects upon liberal Principles, she would in a little time have derived immense Benefits from their increase in Trade & Population, & would in the Course of Commerce alone have experienced a Source of Wealth, which by War Desolation & Exaction she can never acquire. Is it not shocking to think of the King's Troops burning Charles Town, for the advantage of attacking the Provincials under cover of the Smoak. I certainly must have tired you with Politicks; 'tho I have treated this Subject in so general & concise a Manner that you have merely the outlines but I send by Capt. Maingey the News Papers for two or three Weeks back. If an opportunity should occur to New York or any part of the Continent I should be happy to hear from you. By our non-Exportation agreement G. Britain will lose a Remittance of at least one Million from this Country, our Wheat particularly is the finest Crop that has been recollected & the quantity great beyond any Instance heretofore; if Capt. Maingey's Commission for wheat and flour could have been executed I should have had pleasure in a Complyance with the Terms, as it is so very easy for me to do it, & so much in my way, to do it advantageously as I always buy & therefore the purchase of a Ship Load would be unperceived & would add nothing to its Price, whereas in other Instances, it generally augments the Price, by giving an Alarm of a great foreign demand. This in future you may please mention if in your way to my advantage. The Price of your Tobacco being 1/6 per Cent under that of the other Gentlemen's pray explain to them, as I have fully accounted for it to you, from the early arrival of your Orders. Had the last Orders, from Mr de Jersey for the 125 Hogs^ds^ come to hand one Month later the Tob^o^ would have cost them 27/6. I wish you that Tranquility & Happiness, which we Americans must be strangers to for some time. I am under the highest Sense of your civility & favours, with regard y^r^ mo. obliged

& obed^t^ Servant

J. Banister for himself

&

Phripp & Bowdoin.

[Endorsed] To

Elisha Tupper Esqr

Guernsey.

By Capt Maingey
in the Ld Chatham
Q: D: C.

NOTES AND QUERIES

VIRGINIA HISTORICAL SOCIETY

The following circular, prepared by the Executive Committee of this Society early in November, 1920, explains itself. As this note is written (Nov. 26) we are glad to report that a very encouraging beginning has been made in securing new members. The Committee intends that the canvass shall continue and asks the aid of all members and friends of the Society. We have felt for years the need of larger funds.

Since the statement of last year, quoted in the circular, bequests received or soon to be in hand, have increased the endowment fund to $18,000.00.

The income of the Society in the past has averaged $4,000.00. If, from an increased membership, or (a more permanent addition) from an increased endowment, we could have $6,000.00 a year, the work of the Society would be greatly aided.

With this increase the affairs of the Society would have to be administered in a careful and economical way, but it would enable us to insure the publication of the Magazine, would permit us to employ a very much needed Assistant Secretary and Librarian, and to keep our building, library and collections in much better order and make them of greater value and interest to members of the Society and visitors to our home.

"THE VIRGINIA HISTORICAL SOCIETY.

This Society was organized in 1831 with Chief Justice Marshall as the first President.

From that date until the present time it has done a great work in the preservation and publication of source material for Virginia history. For twenty-seven years it has been publishing the Virginia Magazine of History and Biography. The value of this publication (which is sent to all members without additional charge) is best shown by the use historians have made of it.

Like other historical societies of the Eastern States, ours has no State support, but is dependent upon the dues of members, sales of publications and the income from its endowment, now about $14,000.

Though the Society has never been able, on account of its small income, to meet fully the ideals of its members, it has, through careful and economical management, been able to continue its admirable work, and even to have a small surplus at the end of each year.

Now, however, the great increase in the cost of printing leaves us with a possible deficit of six or seven hundred dollars, if we continue our Magazine as it now is.

As the Magazine is the most important work of the Society, our Board is determined that its volume shall not be lessened by great reduction in size. We have also come to the conclusion that it is not advisable to raise the dues.

Gifts to the endowment fund would be the most permanent form of aid, and we shall be glad to receive these; but we think the quickest form of relief is to secure a considerable number of new members.

The dues of annual members are $5.00, and of life members $50.00. Each class receives the Magazine without additional charge.

Those who may become members will not only be aiding us in a most valuable work, but will receive, for their dues, full consideration in the Magazine."

The Virginia War History Commission.

We are gratified to be able to announce that an arrangement has been made between this Society and the Virginia War History Commission by which the latter organization, beginning with the January, 1921, number of our Magazine, will have a 32-page supplement in each number as long as the Commission may deem necessary. These supplements will contain accounts of the progress of the Commission's work and much other matter of great value and interest in regard to Virginia's part in the World War.

War Notes.

During the Fall of 1920 two Virginians received the Distinguished Service Cross for service in the recent war.

The first was Captain Ewart Johnston, of Winchester, who commanded Company L, 116th infantry, composed largely of Lynchburg men, in the Meuse-Argonne offensive and in the Alsace sector. The decoration was "for extraordinary heroism in action during the attack on Malbrouck hill and Consenvoye woods, north of Verdun, France, Oct. 8, 1918. Captain Johnston led his company through heavy machine gun and artillery fire in the attack to his objective. Upon reaching a position scheduled for a passage of the lines he located a strong enemy position. Upon his own initiative he led his company in a bayonet attack and captured about 200 prisoners."

The other was Lt. Col. Jennings C. Wise, formerly of Richmond, now of Washington, D. C.

The citation accompanying the award of the war cross was as follows:

"Award of distinguished service cross. By direction of the President under the provisions of the act of congress, approved July 9, 1918 (Bul. No. 43, W. D., 1918), a distinguished service cross was awarded by the war department to the following named officer:

Jennings C. Wise, lieutenant-colonel, 318th infantry, Eightieth division. For extraordinary heroism in action during the Meuse-Argonne offensive near Nantillois, France, on Oct. 4, 1918. Lieutenant-Colonel Wise, then major, while gallantly leading his battalion in the attack was painfully wounded by a shell fragment. He refused to be evacuated, but continued to successfully command his battalion in advance against strong enemy resistance until his battalion was relieved on Oct. 7. Residence at appointment: 'Garrallan,' Richmond, Va."

Roll of Honor—Correction.

(See this Magazine XXVII, 244)

Lt. Edward Walker, of the American Red Cross, died from typhus fever at Kavalla, Macedonia, March 3, 1919. His home should be given as Blacksburg, Virginia; and his mother is Mrs. A. C. Walker, Weyers Cave, Virginia.

Mineral Lands in Albemarle County.

Albemarle County. Deed Book No. 1, page 164. 25 Mar. 1748.

John Warren of St. Annes Parish am bound unto James Warren of the same, James Warren the younger of Lunenburg County, Betty wife of Matthew Whittle, Sarah wife of Charles Caffrey, Eleanor wife of John Rucker and Grace Warren, the four last named being of St. Annes parish Albemarle County in the sum of £1000 to be paid in equal proportions to the said James Warren, Betty Whittle, Sarah Caffrey, eleanor Rucker and Grace Warren their attorneys executors or assigns to which payment I bind myself my heirs forever.

The condition of this obligation is such that if the above bounden John Warren shall pay or cause to be paid unto the above James Warren, Betty Whittle, Sarah Caffrey, Eleanor Rucker and Grace Warren six eighth parts in equal proportions one eighth to each of the neat product of all mines and minerals that now are or hereafter shall be discovered on a tract of two hundred and seventy six acres of land surveyed for the said John Warren on the North side of Buffalo Ridge in the aforesaid Parish of St. Annes in Albemarle County the charge of working the said mines and minerals and the sum of £200 only excepted During the term of their natural lives and shall afterwards for the space of one thousand years to be completed and ended from the death of the survivor of them the said James Warren, Betty Whittle, Sarah Caffrey, Eleanor Rucker & Grace Warren pay or cause to be paid yearly and every year at the day of the Feast of St. Michael to the heirs of the aforesaid James Warren, Betty Whittle, Sarah Caffrey, Eleanor Rucker and Grace Warren lawfully issuing from their bodys the above mentioned proportion of one eighth part of the clear or neat produce of the aforesaid mines and minerals to the heirs of each of them according to their parent stocks then this obligation to be void and of no effect otherwise to remain in full force and virtue.

Witnesses: John X Warren, his mark
Joshua Fry
John Harvie
John Caffrey

At a Court held 13 February 1749 this Bond was Proved by Joshua Fry and John Harvie two of the witnesses. [Contributed by Mrs. Augusta B. Fothergill.]

NOTES FROM THE RECORDS OF RICHMOND COUNTY—

(1) Deed for 300 acres formerly conveyed by Mr. Aumaree [Amory] Butler to Mr. William Underwood as marrying the sister of said Mr. Butler, and now made over to him by exchange with Mrs. Elizabeth Coumbs as the thirds of lands belonging to her, and with her consent, to William Underwood, Jr., John Coumbs and William Coumbs, said William Underwood, Jr. (x) sells his share to William Thomas, of Washington parish, Westmoreland County, Dec. 11, 1692.

(2) Deed from Joseph Bickley of Rappahannock County, conveying 100 acres on the north side of Rappahannock River. His wife, Mary, joins in the deed, March 30, 1692.

(3) Deed from Alexander Doniphan and Margaret his wife for land she inherited from her father (George Mott), 1693.

(4) Deed from John Fosaker, of Rappahannock County, for lands granted in 1670, from John ——— [copy torn], the last being her father, Sept. 1693.

(5) Deed from William Barber, of North Farnham parish, Richmond Co., to John Newton of Copley [Cople] parish, Westmoreland, land on Totuskey Creek.

(6) Deed, Sept. 27, 1693, from Arthur Spicer and Elizabeth his wife, daughter and heiress of Thomas Jones, deceased.

(7) Dec. 7, 1704, attachment granted to William Barber, sheriff of Richmond County, against the estate of Katherine Henderken.

(8) Suit by William Barber and Joyce his wife *vs* Samuel Sanford, Dec. 7, 1704.

(9) Sept. 11, 1705, certificate to Capt. William Barber to obtain grant of 250 acres.

(10) Deed from Charles Barber and Frances his wife, to Austin Brockenbrough, conveying 240 acres, Nov. 1, 1709.

(11) Deed from Charles Barber and Frances his wife, Sept. 4, 1710, conveying 50 acres in Richmond county, formerly granted to his father, William Barber, deceased, and by him bequeathed to the said Charles Barber.

(12) Deed Oct. 3, 1710, from William Barber and Joyce his wife, of Richmond County, to their son Samuel Barber, conveying 426 acres, 300 acres of which was purchased by Thomas Robinson, grandfather of said Joyce, in 1656.

(13) Deed, Dec. 3, 1723, from Charles Barber to Thomas Barber, conveying 300 acres in Richmond County on Totuskey Creek, formerly belonging to William Barber, father of the said Charles Barber.

(14) Deed, 1699, from William Barber and Joyce his wife, to Rawleigh Travers, conveying land on Totuskey Creek.

(15) Deed, July 7, 1697, from Elizabeth Gardner, widow, of St. Mary's County, Maryland, daughter and heiress of John Weire, late of Rappahannock Co., deceased, conveying 2502 acres in Richmond Co., granted to John Weir, June 6, 1666.

(16) Deed, 1698, from Charles Cale to William Downing, conveying land patented by Thomas Stephens and left to Charles Cale by his brother Nathaniel Cale.

(17) Deed, June 5, 1699, from Edward Bray, of Richmond Co., nephew and heir of Richard Bray, late of said county, deceased, to John King, of Bristol, merchant.

(18) Deed from William Woodbridge to Morris McCathlin [Maclathlin], conveying land given Elizabeth Woodbridge, now wife of said McCathlin by her father Paul Woodbridge, deceased. Dec. 10, 169—.

(19) Deed, July 20, 1720, from Francis Kenner to his brother Matthew Kenner.

(20) Will of Job Webb; Cousin John, son of my brother Thomas Webb, Counsin John, son of William Berry, Cousin Sarah Berry and Elizabeth Webb, dated Jan. 16, 1720, proved Feb. 15, 1720-21. (Possibly a Northumberland Co. will noted here by mistake).

(21) Deed, January 6, 1756, from William Barber and Elizabeth his wife to Samuel Barber, 231 acres in Richmond County, where said William Barber now lives, being the same land devised to the said William Barber by his father, Charles Barber, deceased.

(22) Deed, April 29, 1756, from Ann Barber and her son Thomas Barber, 114 acres to Charles Jones.

(23) Deed, Sept. 3, 1756, from Ann Barber and Thomas Barber, executors of Thomas Barber, gent., deceased, in pursuance of his will, make conveyance to George Grayden.

(24) Deed, May 26, 1792, from Samuel Barber and Katherine his wife, and William Barber and Elizabeth his wife, of Culpeper County, conveying 80 acres in Richmond County, to George Northen.

(25) Deed, Jan. 4, 1747, from Thomas Barber and Ann his wife.

(26) Deed, June 7, 1736, from Thomas Barber, as sheriff of Richmond County.

(27) Deed, Oct. 3, 1768, from Wm. Barber and Elizabeth his wife, and William Barber, Jr., and Elizabeth his wife, conveying 80 acres on Totuskey Creek, to Griffin Garland.

(28) Deed from James Orchard to William Barber, of Richmond County, conveying 533 acres in Richmond County on Rappahannock Creek [date omitted in note].

(29) Deed, May 4, 1692, from Sarah Suggett, widow, to William Barber, Sr., of Richmond Co., and Rawleigh Travers, Sr., of Northumberland County.

(30) Deed, June 6, 1763, from Charles Barber and Mary his wife, to William Smith, conveying the land where said Barber lives.

(31) Deed, Nov. 14, 1763, from William Barber to his son William Barber.

(32) Bond, June 5, 1764, from William Barber, of King George County, gent., to John Woodbridge, of Richmond County, in penalty of £500 current money, to secure said Woodbridge, who, some time before was security for said Barber as tobacco inspector at Totuskey.

(33) Deed, May 4, 1715, from William Barber, gent., of Richmond Co., to Charles Lewis and Mary his wife, eldest daughter of said Barber.

(34) Will of Thomas Barber, of Lunenburgh parish, Richmond Co., dated Dec. 8, 1753, proved May 6, 1754, ——— wife, son and daughters; Wife, son Thomas, Mr. Ajalon Price and Samuel Barber, executors.

(35) Division of estate of Thomas Barber, Jan. 8, 1757, between Thomas, Betty, Ann, Catherine and Lucy Barber.

(36) Will of Samuel Barber ——— my Aunt Lewis, Mary wife of Charles Beale and Sarah wife of Charles Mortimer (my mother's and grandmother's rings), William Brockenbrough, William Mins, Samuel Kelsick, Younger Kelsick. Dated Oct. 10, 1760, proved May 4, 1761.

(37) Will of Mary Kelsick ——— son Richard Kelsick my land in Culpeper, if he should return to Virginia from which he has been absent several years. If he does not return, to Sir Jonathan Beckwith, to sell for the benefit of the following persons: My son and my four daughters, Ellenor Barnes, Isabella Barber, Elizabeth Younger and Rebecca Beckwith. Rest of estate to be equally divided between my daughters. Dated Aug. 15, 1784, proved July 7, 1794.

(She was daughter of John Smith of Richmond County, who left her property by his will dated 172—).

HALL END, POLESWORTH, WARWICKSHIRE, ENGLAND

GENEALOGY.

THE CORBIN FAMILY.

The following pedigree of the Corbin family of Warwickshire and Staffordshire (here altered from chart to narrative form) is given in the visitations and county histories. It should be borne in mind that frequently the correctness of statements as to the earlier generations, in such genealogies, is very doubtful.

Robert[1] Corbin, als. Corbion was the father of Robert[2] Corbin who gave lands to the Abbey of Talesworth between 1 and 7, Henry II, A. D. 1154-1161. He was father of William[3] Corbin, who was father of Hamon[4] Corbin, who was father of William[5] Corbin. The latter had a son Thomas[6] Corbin, living *temp.* Edward I, who married Felicia, daughter and heir of John Lulley (9 Edward II).

Thomas[6] and Felicia Corbin were the parents of William[7] Corbin, of Birmingham, who married Edith, daughter of —— Frebody (she remarried Robert le Heigge).

William[7] and Edith Corbin had issue: 1. William[8] Corbin, of Kings Swinford in the county of Stafford, 6 and 34, Edward III, 1332-1360, who married Felicia, kinswoman of Sir John Sutton, of Dudley, Knight, 15 and 30, Edward III; 2. Thomas[8], 19, Edward III (who had several children); 3. Edith, wife of Robert le Rider, of Dudley.

William[8] and Felicia Corbin had a son Henry[9] Corbin, 8 Richard II, and 8 Henry VI, 1384-1430, who married Margery, daughter and heir of John Day, of Gornehall or Gornishall, Co. Stafford, 8 Richard II; a widow in 9 Henry V and 8 Henry VI.

Henry[8] and Margery Corbin had a son William[10] Corbin, 8 Richard II and 9 Henry VI, 1384-1430, who married Margery, daughter of —— Blunt, Knight.

William[10] and Margery Corbin had issue: 1. Thomas[11], 9 and 22, Henry VI; 2. John[11], 9 and 20, Henry VI, married (1st), 3 Henry V, Katherine (and had no issue), and (2nd) Elizabeth, daughter and heir of William Everdon, 9 Henry VI, 1430.

John[11] and Elizabeth Corbin had a son Thomas[12] Corbin, 31 Henry VI and 4 Edward IV, who married Joanna, daughter and heir of —— Holbach, widow, 14 and 18 Edward IV.

Thomas[12] and Joanna Corbin had a son Nicholas[13] Corbin, seized of Hall End and other lands in the county of Warwick (*Jure ux-*

orio), 1 Richard III and 14, Henry VIII, who married Johanna, daughter and coheir of William Sturmy .

Nicholas[13] and Johanna Corbin had issue: 1. Richard[14], 14 and 25, Henry VIII, 1522-1533, married Anne, daughter of Thomas Ramsey of Hitcham, Co. Bucks. She remarried Edward James; 2. Alice, wife of ——— Bastard, of the City of London, Gent. 14 Henry VIII; 3. ———, wife of ——— Benton; 4. ———, wife of ——— Whorwood.

Richard[14] and Anne Corbin had issue: 1. Thomas[15], 2 Edward VI, died *Circa* 1584, married Ann, daughter of William Reppington, of Annington, married 31 Henry VIII, died 1606; 2. John[15], married Ann, daughter of ——— Chapman, of London; 3. William[15], 3rd son; 4. Ann, wife of Thomas Brickwood, of Pilcewell, Co. Leicester.

Thomas[15] and Ann Corbin had issue: 1. George[16] Corbin, of Hall End, 1615, died 25 Sept. 1636, and was buried in the Chancel of Kingswinford, married Mary, daughter of William Faunt, of Foston, Co. Leicester, died 1614; 2. Edith, wife of Thomas Wright, of Coton, Co. Warwick, died 1627; 3. Florence, wife of ——— Billingsley, died 1598; 4. Anne, wife of Anketill Bracebridge, of the Cliffe, in Co. Warwick.

George[16] and Mary Corbin had issue: 1. Henry[17], born 25 March 1592, died unmarried 1619; 2. Thomas[17], of Hall End, born May 24, 1594, died June, 1637, buried at Kingswinford, married Winifred, daughter of Gowen Grosvenor, of Sutton Colfield, Co. Warwick, married 1620; 3. Jane, wife of James Prescott, of Warwick, died 1632; 4. Anne born 19 Feb. 1593, wife of John Hawkins, of Rock Hall, Co. Warwick.

Thomas[17] and Winifred Corbin had issue: 1. Thomas[18], of Hall End, eldest son, born April 1624, married 1645, Margaret, daughter of Edmund Goodyer, of Keythorp, Co. Oxon. (and had an only daughter and heiress, Margaret, born April 11, 1657, married William Lygon, of Madrasfield, Co. Worcester. Her descendant and representative is the present Earl Beauchamp); 2. George[18], 2nd son, died in the West Indies, married Abigail, daughter of George Cayspill, of New Kirk near Ypres in Flanders (and had an only son, Thomas, who married, but died without issue in the East Indies, and a daughter, who married but died without issue); 3. Henry[18], 3rd son, of the County of Middlesex in Virginia, died 8 Jan. 1675, and buried there; married 25 July 1645 (*sic*) Alice, daughter of Richard Eltonhead, of Eltonhead, Co. Lancaster. She remarried Capt. Henry Creek of London and died about 1684. (For notice of Henry Corbin and genealogy of his decendants, see later); 4. Gawin[18], 4th son, died at Yelverton, Norfolk, Feb. 25, 1709, and was buried there, married Grace Smith, of Derby; 5. Lettice, married Thomas

Okeover, of London, son of Thomas Okeover, of Okeover, Co. Stafford.

Garvin[18] and Grace Corbin had issue: 1. Thomas[19], only son, died unmarried at 31; 2. Mary, married Sir Richard Leving, of Pewick, Co. Derby, Knt. and Bart., sometime Attorney and Solicitor General in Ireland. She living 1715; 3. Lettice, married Roger Borough, of London, 1st wife, and died 1685; 4. Felicia, married Thomas Rant, of Yelverton, Norfolk, and was living in 1715.

(To be continued)

GRYMES OF BRANDON, &C.

(Continued)

21 CHARLES[5] GRYMES. Little is known of him. A Charles Grymes married, in 1773, Ann Lightfoot, of York County, and a Charles Grymes probably the same, married Dec. 10, 1777, Mary Hubard. He probably lived in Gloucester County about 1798.

22 BENJAMIN[5] GRYMES, of "Vaucluse", Orange County, married, Oct. 8, 1773, Sarah, daughter of Peter Robinson, of King William County. He apparently made no will. That of his widow is of record in Orange County.

Will Book 7:516. Will of (Mrs.) Sally Grymes, dated 1827, codicil 1831, prob. 1832. Son Peyton Grymes, executor; my eldest daughter Mary L. Bayly and her female children; my three unmd. daughters Lucy, Hannah F., & Sarah Berkeley Grymes. My daughter Elizabeth Pope Braxton.

(Note—Mary L. Bayly was wife of George B. Bayly.)

They had issue: 40. Philip[6], married, May 10, 1804, Sarah R., daughter of William Steptoe, of "Hewick", Middlesex County, and had one child, who died young (Mrs. Sarah Steptoe Grymes, married 2nd, William Burke); 42. Thomas[6], married ——— Wormeley, and died without issue; 43. *John Randolph*[6]; 44. *Peyton*[6]; 45. Elizabeth, married Carter Braxton, of King William County; 46. Mary, married George B. Bayly; 47. Judith, married Peter Cottom; 48. Lucy, died unmarried; 49. Hannah, died unmarried. Her will is of record in Orange County: Will Book 13:387. Will of (Miss) Hannah F. Grymes, dated July, 1875, prob. Feb., 1876. My niece Harriet Grymes, wife of my nephew Benj. A. Grymes; * * * my great-niece Betty Braxton Grymes, dau. of my nephew Peyton Grymes * * * my great nephew Horace G. Taliaferro * * * my niece Mary Lester Grymes * * * my niece Nelly Grymes * * * my great-nephews Peyton Taliaferro, Edwin C. Taliaferro, & Philip P. Taliaferro."

50. Sally Berkeley, died unmarried. Her will is of record in Orange County: Will Book 13:233. Will of (Miss) Sally Berkeley Grymes, date 1863, codicil 1865. "My nephews Wm. P. Braxton; Dr. Horace G. Taliaferro; my nephews Robert P. Grymes & Peyton Grymes * * * my niece Lester * * * my nieces Kate & Nelly Grymes * * * my niece Lucy N. Taliaferro * * * my niece Molly C. Grymes * * * nieces Kate, Harriet, & Nelly Grymes." 51, Susan, died unmarried.

(We are indebted to Rex. B. L. Ancell for abstracts of Orange County wills).

27 BENJAMIN GRYMES[4], of "Eagles Nest", King George County. A partition deed, dated Jan. 27, 1800, recorded in King George County, recites that William Fitzhugh, of Fairfax County, by his will left to his [great] nephews William F. Grymes, Benjamin Grymes and George N. Grymes, two tracts of land in King George County, called Eagles Nest and Somerset, and also directed that said lands should be divided between said nephews; by this deed the lands are divided as follows: lot No. 1, to William F. Grymes, 676 acres; lot No. 2, to Benjamin Grymes, 676 acres; lot No. 3, to George N. Grymes, 676 acres. Benjamin[4] Grymes was 1st Lieutenant in Grayson's Additional Continental regiment Jan. 18, 1777, and later was a Captain. He is stated to have served in Washington's guard. He married Ann, daughter of John Nicholas, of "Norborne", Dinwiddie County. He died about 1803. Issue 52. *William Fitzhugh*[5]; 53. *Benjamin*[5]; 54. *George Nicholas*[5]; 55. Lucy Fitzhugh, married, January 2, 1804, A. B. Hooe, of "Barnesfield", King George County; 56. Martha Carter, married John Stuart, of King George County.

43 JOHN RANDOLPH[6] GRYMES was born in Orange County, Va., in 1786, and died in New Orleans, Dec. 4, 1854. He removed to Louisiana in 1804, served as a volunteer aide to General Jackson at the Battle of New Orleans and was complimented in dispatches to the War Department; was for many years a very eminent lawyer, and was Attorney General of the State, U. S. District Attorney and member of the State Constitutional Convention. He took part in two duels and was severely wounded in one of them. Mr. Grymes married Mrs. Suzette Claiborne (nee Bosque) widow of Governor W. C. C. Claiborne and had issue: 57. Medora, married Samuel Ward of New York; 58. *Edgar*[7], married ———, of Pittsburg, Pa., and had no issue; 59. Dr. Alfred, married twice in New York and had children; 60. Athenaise, married F. von Hoffman, German Consul at New York.

44 PEYTON[6] GRYMES, of "Selma", Orange County, was born 1791, and died 1878. He married Harriet (Shepherd) Dade, widow

of Dr. Frank Dade. Following is an abstract of the will of Dr. Grymes:

Will Book 13:436. Will of Peyton Grymes [son of above]. Date 1877, prob. 1878. "My two daughters Nellie & Mary Lester; [both died unmarried: B. L. A.] my son Peyton Grymes; my four sons Benj. A., Wm. S., Robert P. & John R. Grymes. My grandson Horace G. Taliaferro."

Peyton[6] and Harriet Grymes had issue: 61. Lucy Nelson, married Dr. Horace D. Taliaferro; 62. *Peyton*[7]; 63. *Robert Page*[7]; 64. *Benjamin Andrew*[7]; 65. *William Shepherd*[7]; 66. *John Randolph*[7]; 67. Nellie, died single; 68. Philip Meade[7], died single at Galveston, Texas; 69. A. Pope[7], died single at Galveston, Texas; 70. Mary Lister.

(To be continued)

THE LOVELACE FAMILY AND ITS CONNECTIONS

By J. Hall Pleasants, Baltimore, Md.

(Continued)

AUCHER OF OTTERDEN AND BISHOPSBOURNE, KENT, WITH NOTES ON CORNWALLIS, WROTH AND RICH.

The Aucher family is connected with the Lovelaces through the marriage of Elizabeth, daughter of Edward Aucher (1539?—1568), Esq. of Bishopsbourne, Kent, with Sir William Lovelace (1561—1629), the elder, of Bethersden. Through this Aucher marriage the

Lovelaces also trace their descent from the families of Cornwallis of Brome, Suffolk, of Wrothe of Enfield, Middlesex, of the barons Rich of Leez, of Diggs of Barham, Kent, and of St. Leger of Otterden, Kent, and of Hawte of Hawte Court, Kent. There is said to be a pedigree among the *Hasted Manuscripts* in the British Museum which traces the descent of the Auchers from "Walter Fitz-Auger, a noble Briton, who flourished at the time of the Conquest", and from Thomas Fitzaunger, who possessed the manor of Losenham, Kent, in the time of King John [1199-1216]. A roll of arms in the time of Henry III [1216-1272] and of 6 Edward I [1277] includes Henry Aucher with the same arms as were used later by the Auchers of Losenham and Otterden (*Archaelogia Cantiana;* xv;3). Sir Thomas Fitz Aucher founded in 1241 at Losenham the Carmelite Priory of St. Mary's (ibid. xiv;311), and in 1253-4 "*Thomas filius Alcheri* [Aucher] held one-fourth of a knight's fee of the Prior of Leeds and one-fourth of a knight's fee in Losenham of Radulpho de Sancto Leodegario [Sir Ralph St. Leger] (ibid. xii;222).

The pedigrees of this old Kent family as usually presented in such standard works as *The Visitation of Kent 1619* (*Harl. Soc.* xlii;180), *Berry's Genealogies; Kent* (222-3;287), *Hasted's Kent* (*2nd ed.* v;535-7) and *Burke's Extinct and Dormant Baronetages* (*2nd ed.;* 27-9), begin, however, with Nicholas Aucher[1], said to be sixth in descent from Walter Fitz-Auger *temp.* the Conqueror. The writer has made no effort to verify these pedigrees prior to John Aucher[1] (died 1502), great gread grandfather of Elizabeth (Aucher[9]) Lovelace, but beginning with this John[5], stated in his will to be the son of Henry Aucher[4], he has been able to secure original evidence in the form of wills, inquisitions and other contemporary documents, which afford independent verification of much of the latter portion of these pedigrees, and which seem to be of sufficient interest to publish, presenting as they do much which has never hitherto been printed, and correcting several errors, especially in regard to marriages, which exist in the so-called standard pedigrees. Where in the earlier portions of the pedigree the several authorities cited above show variations, *The Visitation of Kent, 1619*, unless other authorities are cited, has been followed. In the fifteenth and sixteenth centuries the name appears in contemporary records variously as Aucher, Awcher, Auger, Alcher, Awger, Ager and Agger. The most notable progenitor of the family is Sir Anthony Aucher (1500-1557), who although conspicuous in political and military affairs in the reign of Henry VIII, Edward VI and Mary, and Marshal of Calais at the time of its capture by the French, has for some reason escaped the notice of all modern biographers.

The Aucher arms are: Ermine, on a chief azure three lions, rampant, or. Crest: A bull's head erased gules armed or.

I. Nicholas Aucher[1]. "Son of the Lord of Losenham" in Newenden, Kent, and possessor of lands in county Essex. He held certain manors in Mayham Magna and Losenham, Kent, early in the fourteenth century (*Archaeologia Cantiana;* x; 140). Married a daughter of ——— Oxenbridge of Bread [Brede] in Sussex. He was succeeded by his eldest son:

II. Henry Aucher[2] (Nicholas[1]). "Of Losenham in the time of Edward III [1327-1377], milites." Henry Aucher was assessed upon sundry manors held by him at the knighting of the Black Prince in 1346, and then appeared as possessing the following manors in Kent: one-quarter of a knight's fee in Losenham formerly held by Nicholas Aucher of Ralph St. Leger; one-quarter of a knight's fee in Mayham Magna formerly held by Nicholas Aucher of John Malmayns; and one-half of a knight's fee in Mayham Magna held jointly with Stephen Forshame (*Archaeologia Cantiana;* x; 139, 140). He married a daughter of "John Diggs of Berham [Barham], Kent, armiger." (For pedigree of Diggs of Berham, see *Harl. Soc.* xlii; 64-5; *Berry's Genealogies; Kent;* 142-3). He was succeeded by his son:

III. Henry Aucher[3] (Nicholas[1], Henry[2]). Of Otterden, Kent, milites. He married twice. By his 1st wife Isabella, daughter of ——— At Towne of Throwley [Throwleigh], Kent, he had issue (1) Thomas Aucher[4] of Losenham and (2) Robert Aucher[4], ancestor of the Auchers of Westwell. By his 2nd wife Mary [or Joane], daughter and heiress of Thomas St. Leger* he acquired the Manor of Otterden. *The Visitation of Kent, 1619,* states that he and his second wife are buried near the High Altar of Otterden church. By his second wife Mary St. Leger he had issue a son (3) Henry Aucher[4]—see IV:

IV. Henry Aucher[4] (Nicholas[1], Henry[2], Henry[3]). Of Otterden, living 19 Henry VI [1440]. The manor of Otterden was acquired through his mother Mary [or Joane] St. Leger, daughter and heiress milites. He married twice. By his 1st wife Isabella, daughter of ——— Boleyn by whom he had issue two sons (1) John Aucher[5]—see V, and (2) Henry Aucher[5]; it may have been this Henry Aucher

* The line of St. Leger of Otterden as given in *Hasted's Kent* (2nd ed. v; 535) begins with Ralph St. Leger of Ulcomb, Knight of the Shire of Kent, 51 Edward III [1377]. His second son Thomas St. Leger of Otterden, Sheriff of Kent, 20 Richard II [1396], died 10 Henry IV [1408], and is buried under the High Altar of Otterden Church. The latter's daughter Joane [the *Visitation* gives Maria!] married Henry Aucher of Otterden. The descent of Thomas St. Leger, father of Mary or Joane Aucher is given somewhat differently in the St. Leger pedigree in *Berry's Genealogies; Kent* (p. 287).

who married Eliza, daughter of Sir John Gulford (*Archaeologia Cantiana;* xiv; 5).

V. John Aucher[5] (Nicholas[1], Henry[2], Henry[3], Henry[4]). Of Otterden, Kent. *The Visitation of Kent, 1619,* and *Burke* state that he married *Alice* Churche, which is an error as regards the Christian name, for his will names his wife *Margaret,* and the will of his son James while referring to his uncle Thomas Churche, names his father John Aucher and his mother *Margaret.* John Auger is named among "The Gentils of Kent Anno Regni Regis Henry 7" [1485-1509] (*Archaeologia Cantiana;* xi; 395). It is stated in *Burke* that John Aucher died April 23, 1503, and that he and his wife *Alice* are buried in the north chapel of parish church at Otterden, but his will proves that this date is incorrect and that he died between 18 July and 26 October, 1502.

John Aucher's[5] will shows that some time before his death he had conveyed by a "feoffement" to Henry Horne, esquire, and others [as trustees] all of his lands in Kent. His will provides that immediately after his death his "feoffees" [trustees] make over an estate in all the lands which had formerly belonged to his father Henry Aucher (subject to an annuity of forty shillings to be paid to his wife Margaret) to his eldest son James Aucher, with reversion in event of the latter's death without heirs, successively to his sons William, John and Marcus, and then to his next heirs. The lands thus conveyed included his manor of Otterden with the advowson of the Otterden church, and certain other lands in the parishes of Otterden, Statesfield, Moulston and Bordesfield, with a special provision that if there were no heirs of his body lawfully begotten, the manor and advowson of Otterden were to pass to the "right heirs of Thomas Seyntleoger [St. Leger] esquire now dead." It will be recalled that his grandfather Henry Aucher[3] had acquired Otterden through his second wife who was the daughter of Thomas St. Leger. He further provides that his other lands, which he apparently had not inherited from his father, and which included the manor of Moulston and the advowson of the Moulston church, and the manor of Little Frognall, also known as Rollings, should go to his wife Margaret during her life, subject to annuities to be paid to his younger sons William, John and Marcus, the manor and advowson of Moulston finally passing to his eldest son James and the manor of Little Frognall to his second son William. No daughters are named in the will. He had doubtless provided for them at the time of their marriage. The two daughters named below are given in the *Visitation* and in *Burke.*

The will of John Auger [Aucher], the elder, of Otterden, dated

18 July, 1502, was proved in the local Archdeaconry Court of Canterbury, 26 October, 1502, by the executors (Vol. VIII; folio 11).

I, John Auger theldard [the elder] of the pishe of Ottreden Kent gentyllman by my will dated the xviii day of July 1502 desire my body to be buried in the Chureyerd of our Lady before the Imager ther. I bequeath to the high Auter of the same churche for my tithes forgotten iii s. iiii d. I bequeath a cow pce of viii s. orelles [or else] viii s. for the said cowe at the discretion of my executors for to fine a lampe brenny ing before the Sacrament of the Hugh Auter of Ottre den aforesaid. I bequeath 200 lbs. of shyngill to be made and leyed upon the repation of the said churche of Ottreden ther (sic) moost nede is at my cost and charge. I bequeath to the house of the Holy Trynte of Motynden iii s. iiii d. to pray for my soule and all cristen soules. Also to every of the house of Freers [friars] in Canterbury iii s. iiii d. to pray for my soule and all cristen soules. Also I bequeath v marks for an honest prest to syng in Oxenford for my soule and all my frends soules by the space of a hole yer. Also I will my executors fynde a preste imedialye aftre my decease to synge a Trentall of Masses in the church of Ottreden aforesaid. Also I bequeath a wedre [wether] sheepe of iii yer age to fynde Judas light. Also I bequeth to Margarete my Wif all the hole instuff of my householde only to be at her disposition w'out any other ptyner [partner]. The Residue of all my goods and catall I geve and bequeth to Margaret my Wif and James Aucher my Son whome I make my Executors.

Second Part of Will of John Aucher of Ottreden theldar gentillman made the 12th day of August 1502 Upon a feoffement by me made to Herry Horne Esquire and other of all my maners lands and tent's in the Countie of Kent.

First I will that my feoffees imediately aftre my decease make estate of and in my manor of Ottreden wt the avoson of the churche ther and all other lands and tente in the pishes of Ottreden, Statesfeld, Monketon and Bordesfeld which sometyme were Henry Auchers my fadre to James Aucher my eldest Son and to his heires for ever the said James and his heires paying yerely to Margaete my Wif xl s. And if the said James die wtout heires lawfully begotten Then I will the said manor advoson lands and tente should remayne to William Aucher my second son and to his heires for ever And for defaute of such heires of the said William lawfully begotten I will the said manor advoson lands and tene should remayne to John Aucher my son and to his heires for ever And if the said John Aucher wtout issue lawfully begotten die then I will the said manor advoson lands and tente should remayne to Markis Aucher my youngest son and to his heires for ever And for defaute of heires of the said Marks body lawfully begotten then I will the said manor advoson lands and tente wt the appurtennes holly should remayne to the next heires of my body lawfully begotten. I will the said manor of Ottreden wt the advoson holly should remayne to the right heires of Thomas Seyntleoger [St. Leger] esquire now dede for evmore. I also will that Margaete my wife anone aftre my decease should have my maners in Monketon and Little Frognale otherwise called Rollings during her life she paying yerely to every of William, John and Markys my sons, xxvi s. viii d. And aftre the decease of the said Margarete I will the said maner of Monketon wt the advoson of the churche of Monketon and other apprtennes to the said James Aucher my eldest son & his heires for ever he paying to John Aucher and Markys Aucher my sonnes xx s. li d. to be equally divided betwene thaym at the rate of v marks yerely. I will imediately after the dethe of the said Margaerte my wif my feoffes grantt severally to eyther of John Aucher and Marcus my sonnes an annuytie of xxvi s. viii d. by yer to be had to them and their heirs out of the said maner called Little Frognall for ever at the feest of Eshe and Saynt Michill tharchangell and in defaute of payment with power for them to distrayne And aftre these grannts sufficiently prformed the said man'r of Little Frognall otherwise called Rollings wt the lands thereto pteyning to the said William Aucher my son his heires and assigns for ev . This Witnesseth Richard Sharpe Sir John Byn pson [parson] of Ottreden James Dunstone and Thomas Wever.

John Aucher[5] by his wife Margaret Churche had issue (1) James Aucher[6], eldest son and heir—see VI, (2) William Aucher[6] d. s. p., (3) John Aucher[6] living 1509, and (4) Marcus Aucher[6] (*The Visi-*

tation and *Burke* incorrectly give his name as Marmaduke; the latter states that he married a daughter of ——— Gilboe), (5) Jane Aucher[6] married Tho: Corbett, (6) Elizabeth Aucher[6] married Tho: Barham.

VI. James Aucher[6] (Nicholas[1], Henry[2], Henry[3], Henry[4], John[5]). Of Otterden, Kent, esquire. *The Visitation of Kent, 1619*, states that he married Alice the daughter of Tho: Hill, and that after his death she married James Hardres. *Burke* states in one place (*Extinct and Dormant Baronetages*, p. 28) that she was the daughter of Thomas Hills, Esq., of Eggarton, near Godmersham, Kent, and that her second husband was James Hardres, of Hardres, Kent, and again in another place (p. 242) that she was a daughter of *Robert* Hill. This remarriage of the widow, the writer has been unable to verify, although Mabel, the widow of her grandson Edward Aucher[8] of Bishopsbourne did marry Richard Hardres of Hardres. See also *Visitation of Essex, 1612*, (*Harl. Soc.* xiii; 211). It is probable that she was really a member of the Hilles or Hillys family prominent in Eggerton, Kent. James Aucher died January 6, 1508-9, and is buried in Otterden church near his father. His will, an abstract of which the writer has been able to secure from the probate records, dated January 1, 1508-9, was proved April 9, 1509 (*Prerogative Court of Canterbury Wills; 13 Bennett*).

> Will of Jamys Aucher of Oterynden, 1st January 1508 [-9]. I give my body to be buried in the chapel of our Lady the Virgin within the parish church of Oterynden, to the re-edifying, garnishing and reparation of which chapel I bequeath £10, to bestcwed in such form as my wife knoweth my mind. To the use of the high altar and high chancel of the said church 40 s., and to the reparation and expedient works of the body of the church 20 s. To the Abbot of Boule, to the use of the image of the crucifix called the Roode of Grace there, 20 s. To the Abbot of Feversham, to pray for my soul 13s. 4 d. I bequeath all such sums of money as ben owing unto me of me fee in the monastery of St. Augustine besides Canterbury, that I may there be prayed for, to the use of the building of the said monastery; and I will that my best ring be fixed upon the shrine of St. Augustine thereto abide. I bequeath to Mr. Dean of St. Paul's to pray for me, of his charity, 66 s. 8 d. To Mr. Garrard, late charity priest of Sheryngton's chantry, as well to pray for me as in recompense of all griefs and other occasions by suits or otherwise between the priests of the said chan-

try and me lately had, 66 s. 8 d.; and to the said Mr. Garrard, if he be there chantry priest or such other as shall be in the day of St. Andrew next coming, in the said form and intent, 66 s. 8 d.; these last three sums to be paid out of the debt to be paid to me in November coming by the said Mr. Garrard and others. To my brother William Aucher, with that I have paid him before, £6. 13 s. 4 d. to pray for my soul and with condition to enseal such writing and all other things do for the surety of the said priests of Sheryngton's chantry for the lands that I lately recovered against them in Tenterden, as shall be advised by the counsel of the said priests. To my brothers John and Marcus Aucher in the same form and condition 66 s. 8 d. To the said William Aucher my best gown, so that hė cause a trental of masses and other suffrages thereto belonging to be said for me at the place besides the chapel of St. Stephen in Westminster called Scala Celi; and to my brother John my second gown, and to my brother Marcus my third gown on the like condition. To my uncle Thomas Churche, my coat, so that he cause to be said in the same place 5 masses, parcel of a trental, with the suffrages. To Mr. Dr. Wodroffe 40 s.; and to Mr. Docter Churche 20 s.; to pray for me. To George Hilys to pray for me and to be aiding to my wife 20 s. To an honest priest to celebrate divine service in the church of Oterynden for the space of two years, for my soul and for the soul of Sir Richard Guldeford, knight, John Aucher my father, Margaret my mother, Thomas Corbett and Margaret, late the wife of Gervase Horne, 20 marks. To the Friars Minors of Cantebury called Observants, 10 s. To the Black Friars and the Austin Friars there, to each house 40 d. to pray for me. To the marriage of Susanne my daughter, if to be perceived of my daughter's good and chattels. All the residue of my goods to Alice my wife and Anthony my son, whom with Mr. Roger Churche, Doctor of Law, and John Hales, I ordain my executors; and Mr. Edward Guldeford, George Guldeford and the said William Aucher and George Hillis overseers. As touching my lands and tenements, my feoffees shall accomplish in everything in the agreement between Sir John Bynne, parson of Aterynden [Otterden], and me for his new mansion and garden set on the end of the churchyard of Aterynden for an obit to be observed for ever, as by the papers in the custody of John Hales may appear. If my wife lives til my son Anthony be 20 years of age, he shall have yearly out of my land during the life of his mother 10 marks; and my wife shall have all my lands and tenements except the said mansion and garden and the said 10 marks, finding my said Anthony to school and learning by the discretion of the said Mr. Dr. Churche and John Hales. If both my children die within age without lawful issue, all the lands and tenements that were my fathers shall remain according to his last will, and all my other lands to my next heirs according to the laws of the realm of England. Witnesses: James Dergng, John Hert, William Aucher, John Aucher, Marcus Aucher, George Hillys.

Proved 9 April, 1509, by Alice the executrix named, the said Anthony refusing, with power reserved, etc., for the other executors.

James Aucher[6] left issue by his wife Alice (Hilles?) (1) Sir Anthony Aucher[7], knt.,—see VII, (2) Susanne Aucher[7], unmarried 1 January, 1508-9; not traced.

VII. Sir Anthony Aucher[7] (Nicholas[1], Henry[2], Henry[3], Henry[4], John[5], James[6]). Knight of Otterden and Bishopsbourne, Kent. He was probably born about 1500. Although conspicuous in public affairs, both civil and military, in the reigns of Henry VIII, Edward VI and Mary, no biographical sketch of him has ever been published as far as the writer can learn. He inherited the manor of Otterden, the Aucher ancestral seat, from his father. His *inquisition* shows that he purchased the manors of Bishopsbourne and Hautsbourne [Shelvingbourne] 1 June, 2 Edward VI [1548] from Thomas Culpeper, esq., of Bedgebury, who had acquired them through his wife Anne, daughter and heir of Sir William Hawte [Haute]. The statement made by Philipott (*Villare Cantianum; 1659;* p. 89) and repeated by *Hasted* in his *Kent*, that he purchased these manors from Sir Thomas Culpeper in 34 Henry VIII [1542] is therefore incorrect.

He first came into prominence through the active part which he took as one of the agents of Henry VIII in the suppression of the monasteries. He is said to have been receiver for Kent, Surrey and Sussex in the late thirties for carrying out this work. The published series of *Letters and Papers of Henry VIII*, the *Calendar of State Papers—Edward VI and Mary*, and the *Acts of the Privy Council* for this period abound in references to him. Under date of 1538 he appears as one of "the gentlemen of My Lord Privy Seal's to be preferred with the King's Service" (*Letters and Papers of Henry VIII, 1538;* ii; p. 497). In the published state papers he appears between 1536 and 1558 variously as Controller of the Works of Dover, Paymaster of the Works of Dover, Chief Victualler of Boulogne, Joint Master of the Tents, and during the latter part of the reign of Henry VIII and in the opening years of the reign of Edward VI as Master of the Jewel House of the Tower of London. February 22, 1546-7 "Anthony Aucher was dubbed Knight of the Carpet by the King [Edward VI], on Tuesday after the Coronation, being Shrove Tuesday" (*Shaw's Knights of England;* ii; p. 59). The office of the Master of the Jewel House he seems to have held for several years during the latter part of his life. He also held the important military positions of Marshal of the fortress of Calais and Governor of the town of Guisnes. The exact date of his appointment to these posts is not known, but he was Marshal of Calais during the siege, and was killed at the time of its capture.

The French commenced operations against Calais and Guisnes in the late autumn of 1557. Lord Grey the then governor of Guisnes and English commander of that stronghold, late in November, 1557, reports to the Queen that "having with me Mr. Aucher marshal of Calais" and other officers, he led an expeditiou for the destruction of the French outpost at Bushing, surrounding there about forty of the enemy in a church with a force of some two hundred English "footman harquebuziers". Upon their refusal to surrender without a struggle, Grey rejected a later request for a parley, blew up the church and put all the survivors to the sword, justifying this act of wanton cruelty on the ground that the rules of war forbade the defence of a fort not rationally defensible! (*Froude's History of England; New York; 1866;* vi; pp. 457-9).

December 1st, Lord Wentworth in command of Calais reports that he sent the marshal of Calais [Aucher] with a troop of horse to attack a force of the enemy which was trying to cut off the English from the bridge, but that when the marshal realized the size of the opposing force he "took a very honest retire" (*Calendar of State Papers; Foreign; 1553-1558;* pp. 348, 354-6). The resistance of the small English garrison at Calais, numbering not over eight hundred men, against an army of thirty thousand under the Duke of Guise was, of course, perfectly hopeless, Calais falling January 7, 1558, and Guisnes with its garrison of only a thousand men just two weeks later. Sir Anthony Aucher was killed at the siege of Calais. Philipott, the Kentish historian, writing about the middle of the seventeenth century of the manor of Lyminge in Kent owned at one time by Sir Anthony Aucher, says:

"Henry the eighth in the thirty sixth year of his Reign [1554], granted it to Sir Anthony Aucher, who after, in the Reign of Queen Mary, was slain at Callis, whilst he endeavoured to make good that City, and the English interest together, by a noble and generous Resistance against the Furious Impressions and Onsets of the Duke of Guise, and the French Army, when he pressed upon with a straight and vigorous Siege." Philipot adds that the manor of Lyminge remained in the Aucher family until sold by a descendant, a later Sir Anthony, to Sir John Roberts in the first half of the seventeenth century (*Philipott's Villare Cantianum;* p. 222). The rector of Bishopsbourne, the Rev. F. Evelyn Gardiner, has been kind enough to send the writer a copy of the inscription upon an old memorial tablet to the memory of Sir Anthony Aucher and his son Edward and their wives in the chancel of Bishopsbourne church.

Sr ANTHONY AUCHER. K^t^
MARESCHALL OF CALLICE
GOV^or^ OF GUISNES
MASTER OF THE
JEWELHOUSE
IN THE TIMES OF HENRY Y^e^ EIGHT
EDWARD Y^e^ SIXT & QUEEN MARY
SLAIN AT Y^e^ LOSS OF CALLICE
1558
AFFRA CORNWALLIS HIS WIFE
EDWARD AUCHER THEIR SON AND
MABEL WROTH HIS WIFE
SHE WAS BURIED 1597

(To be continued)

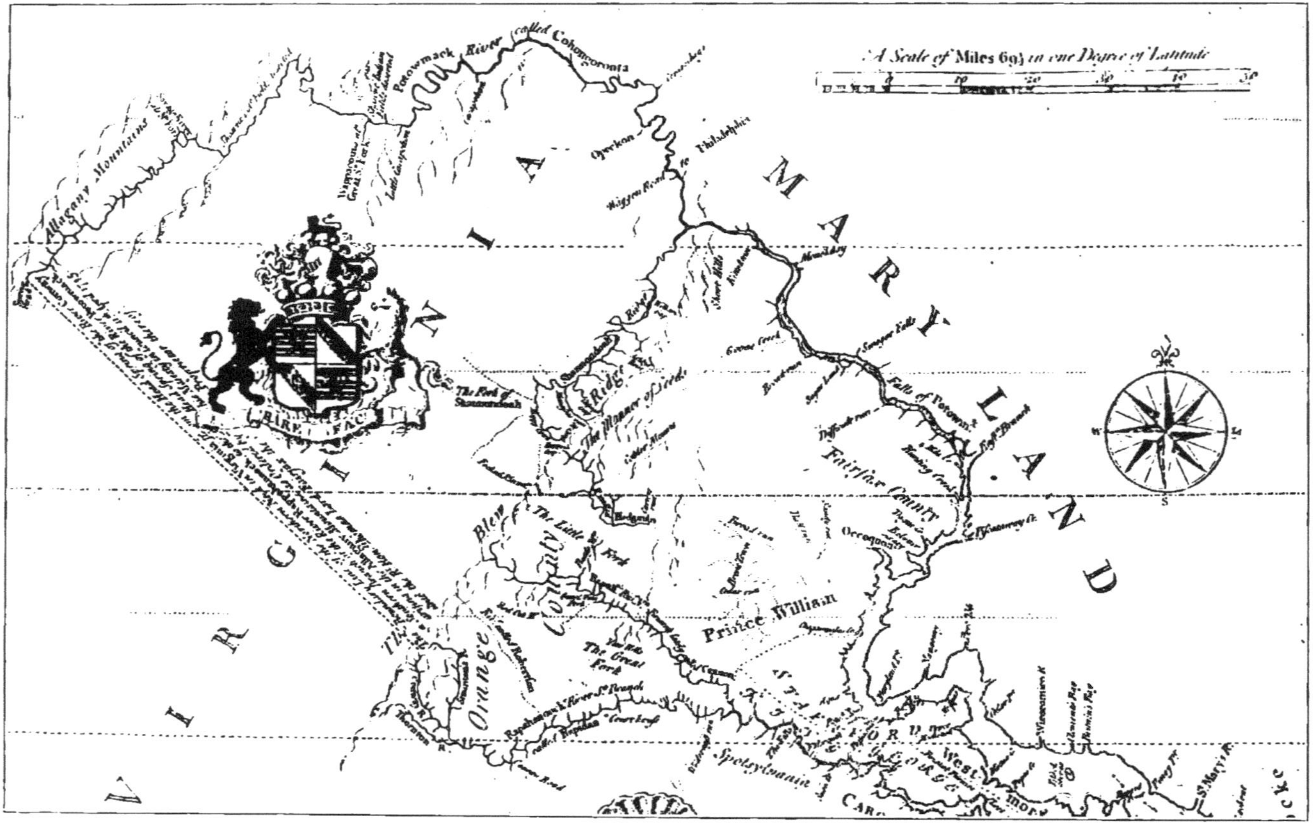

THE NORTHERN NECK OF VIRGINIA

THE

VIRGINIA MAGAZINE
OF
HISTORY AND BIOGRAPHY

VOL. XXVIII OCTOBER, 1920 No. 4

DOCUMENTS RELATING TO THE BOUNDARIES OF THE NORTHERN NECK

From the Originals in the British Public Record Office.

Contributed by Charles E. Kemper.

[By a series of grants from the Crown beginning in 1650, by Charles II, then in exile, the Northern Neck, that is, the country between the Rappahannock and Potomac to their head-waters, was granted to various individuals. Finally the titles all became vested in Thomas, Lord Culpeper, and to him, on Sept. 27, 1688, James II, made a new grant for all the country "bounded by and within the heads of the Rivers Tappahannock alias Rappahannock and Queenough or Potomac River". This great property descended to Culpeper's daughter and heiress, who married Lord Fairfax, and, in 1722, to her son Thomas, Lord Fairfax, who afterwards removed to Virginia.

Long controversies were carried on between the proprietors of the Northern Neck and the Government of the Colony of Virginia representing the Crown, as to the true "heads" of the two rivers. As it flowed through country more accessible to settlement from the East, the question of the Rappahannock seemed at the time to be the most important. There was a long contest as to whether the South branch (the Rapidan) or the North branch of the Rappahannock was the true head. The matter was finally left to a joint commission representing the Crown and Lord Fairfax.

After careful surveying and the taking of much evidence, the Commission made a report in 1736. This report was taken to England and a final decision given in favor of Fairfax. In the matter of the Rappahannock it was decided that the true "head" was the Conway River, a branch of the Rapidan.

Under the construction finally given to the Culpeper-Fairfax grant it included the present counties of Northumberland, Lancaster, Richmond, Westmoreland, Stafford, King George, Prince William, Fairfax, Loudoun, Fauquier, Culpeper, Madison, Page, Shenandoah and Frederick in Virginia, and Jefferson, Berkeley, Hardy, Hampshire and Morgan in West Virginia. For additional information see this Magazine XV, 392-399 and authorities there cited.

The map[1] accompanying these documents is a reduced copy of the upper section of the map giving the boundaries as finally settled. We are indebted to Mr. Fairfax Harrison for a photographic fac-simile of the original in the Library of Harvard University. The lower section of the original map comprises the Northern Neck below the head of tidewater. To reproduce the whole here would make it so small as to be of little value.

[1] This map is listed as No. 169a in Swem's *Maps of Virginia* and is noticed in Phillip's *Virginia Cartography*, p. 46. It appears from Col. Byrd's papers relating to the settlement of the Northern Neck Boundaries (which are reproduced at length in Wynne's edition but not in Bassett's) that the Byrd commission and the Fairfax commission each made a separate map (Wynne II, 122, 132). The Byrd map was drawn by Wm. Mayo (Wynne II, 116, 122) and that seems to be Swem's No. 161. This Harvard map is undoubtedly the Fairfax map, in a second state, to show the line of the award of 1746. It is the same as Swem's No. 169 and, if so, where does Swem get his authority for attributing it to Peter Jefferson and Robert Brooke? A comparison of this map with Fry and Jefferson's map of 1751 shows that whoever drew the Harvard map knew much more of the local topography (of Fauquier e. g.) than did the authors of the Fry and Jefferson map of 1751, and it seems unlikely therefore, that Peter Jefferson ever had much to do with the Harvard map. (F. H.)

The documents published below were procured by Mr. Kemper from London as material for his study of the history of the western portion of Virginia. The readers of our Magazine have already been under a heavy debt of obligation to Mr. Kemper for his exceedingly valuable notes to the series of articles entitled "The Westward Movement in Virginia" (published in vols. XI and XII) and as collaborating with Dr. Hinke in editing the diaries of the Moravian missionaries who travelled through the western portion of the Colony, which was one of the most valuable contributions ever made to the Magazine.

We have other valuable papers from Mr. Kemper which will be published at an early date.]

Letter From Governor Gooch, 1729[2].

My Lords

I have not had the honor of any Commands from your Lordships by any of the Ships come hither this year = my last Dispatch was by the Randolph of London in which were conveyed the Council Journals and other publick Transactions to that time, of which I herein inclose a Duplicate. With this your Lordships will receive the Journals of the Council from the first of Aprill to the 12th Instant, together with the Accompts of the Revenue of Quit Rents and two shillings per Hogshead ending in Aprill, and the Returns of the Naval Officers.

Sometime after my Last a number of Negroes, about fiftenn, belonging to a new Plantation on the head of James River formed a Design to withdraw from their Master and to fix themselves in the fastnesses of the neighbouring Mountains: They had found means to get into their possession some Arms & Ammunition, and they took along with them some provi-

2 Besides the discussion of the boundaries of the Northern Neck, this long letter from Governor Gooch to the English authorities, contains a good many other matters of interest. Among them are: a negro plot, training of the militia, a notice of the neighboring Indians, a plague of caterpillars, the services of the chaplain (Mr. Fontaine) with the Virginia and North Carolina boundary commission, the Tobacco trade, and the freeing of a negro in return for his making public his secret cure for venereal disease.

sions, their Cloaths, bedding and working Tools; but the Gentleman to whom they belonged with a Party of Men made such a diligent pursuit after them, that he soon found them out in their new Settlement, a very obscure place among the Mountains, where they had already begun to clear the Ground, and obliged them after exchanging a shot or two by which one of the Slaves was wounded, to surrender and return back, and so prevented for this time a design which might have proved as dangerous to this Country, as is that of the Negroes in Jamaica to the Inhabitants of that Island, Tho' this attempt has happily been defeated, it ought nevertheless to awaken us into some effectual measures for preventing the like hereafter, it being certain that a very small number of Negroes once settled in those Parts, would very soon be encreas'd by the Accession of other Runaways and prove dangerous Neighbours to our Frontier Inhabitants. To prevent this and many other mischiefs I am training and exercising the Militia in the several Counties as the best means to deter our Slaves from endeavouring to make their Escape, and to suppress them if they should; and as the Establishment I made of an Adjutant to discipline the Militia is much to the satisfaction of the People, and like to prove very useful towards their safety and Defence, I doubt not your Lordships will approve of that part of my conduct, for, it is to this new Regulation of the Militia, and the good disposition of the Officers I have now appointed to instruct those under their Command in the exercise of Arms that we owe the present peace with our tributary Indians; who sometime before were become very turbulent and ungovernable, but are now so submissive, how long that temper will continue I can't say, that one of the great Men of the Saponie Nation having killed an Englishman, tho' the murder was committed when he was drunk, which they look upon as a just excuse, because, as they say, a Man is not accountable for what he did while he is deprived of his reason. Yet they readily delivered him up to justice upon my first message, and he has been since tryed and executed without any sign of resentment from that Nation altho' he was in much esteem among them. I had ordered some of the Nation to be at the tryal, who did attend, and by an Interpreter were made to understand that the Proceedings in the Court against Him were the same as in the like case they would be against a White Man, and indeed so it hap'ned that there was one try'd and executed with Him.

The eagerness of the Inhabitants to take up Lands amongst the great Western Mountains, has renewed a Contest, which for a long time had layn dormant touching the Right of granting the Lands on the Head of Rappahanock River. the Proprietor of the Northern Neck claims the same by virtue of his Grant; and I find former Governours made no scruple to sign Patents for Lands as far as the most Northern Branch of Rappahanock River: But for my better direction therein, I have now before me a Letter from your Lordships dated March 26th 1707 the twelfth Paragraph of which I am governed by and intend now to answer, "in being very watchful that his Majesty's Lands be not invaded under any pretence of a Grant to any Proprietor". agreeable hereunto, I have absolutely refused the suspension of granting of Patents, notwithstanding the remonstrances of the Proprietor's Agent; but proposed that the Case should be fairly stated and determined according to the genuine Construction of the Proprietor's Charter, which 'tis agreed shall be prepared and transmitted to your Lordships for that purpose. In the meanwhile, to give your Lordships a clearer Idea of the Lands in controversy, I herewith send a sketch of that part of the Country which lies near and amongst the Mountains, watered by Streams which fal into the Rivers Rappahanock and Potomack, and which are insisted on to be within the Northern Neck Grant as head springs of those two Rivers, the Draught is not offered to your Lordships as accurately done: But by it your Lordships may please to observe, that the River Rappahanock, which from the Bay of Chesapeak is navigable to the Falls, is about tenn Miles above the Falls divided into two Branches, and those again about thirty Miles upwards divided into other Branches, and so the nearer they approach the Mountains into other lesser Streams, so that it is scarce possible to distinguish which of them ought to bear the name of a River. Here it is that the Lands now in dispute ly: But as the last Grant made in 1688 to the Lord Culpeper, which is the most extensive, describes "the Territory to be bounded by and within the first Heads or Springs of the Rivers Rappahanock & Potomack, the courses of the said Rivers from the first said Heads or Springs as they are commonly called and known by the Inhabitants, and description of those Parts"—it seems a doubt whether the Proprietor can claim any farther upon these Rivers than what was called Rappahanock and Potomack Rivers at the time of the Grant; and that was only as far as they are Navigable, for above that there was then no Inhabitant: or at most, whether the Grant shall extend any further than the River Rappahanock continues one entire Stream. For since the River is formed by the confluence of two lesser ones not discovered till long after the Proprietor's Charter, and those of such equal bigness as to render it doubtful which of them deserves the name of Rappahanock River; and since there cannot be two Rivers of the same name, and as neither of them is described in the Grant, with submission to your Lordships, it seems to me the most natural construction of that Charter, to fix its limits at the confluence of those two Rivers, where Rappahanock is first formed, and from thence runs in one continued Stream into the Bay of Chesapeak; And as Potomack River is the boundary between the Province of Maryland and the Northern Neck, and the first fountain of that River laid down in the Charter of the Former, and the first Head or Spring thereof as the Boundary of Both to the Westward; I must still presume to say, that wherever the Proprietors of Maryland and of the Northern Neck agree to fix the first Fountain or Spring of Potomack River, a line drawn thence to Rappahanock River must terminate the Northern Neck Patent; and then all the Lands lying westward of that remains still in the power of the Crown to grant. But if on the other hand all the Lands which ly on any of those Rivulets or Brooks which fall into Rappahanock or

Potomack Rivers be allowed to belong to the Proprietor of Northern Neck as his Agent pretends, the King will then have very little more Land to dispose of in Virginia. For your Lordships may please to observe by the enclosed Draught that one of the Branches of Potomack River which is now known by the name of the River Shenundo, runs through and paralel with the great ridge of Mountains, and is said to have its source near Roanoke River; So that almost the Tract which is now called Virginia is encompass'd and bounded by that River, and the Proprietor instead of being circumscribed by and within the Head of Rappahanock will extend his Bounds upwards of Sixty Miles to the Southward of it, which can never be imagined, I think, to have been the intention of the Crown, nor agreeable to the words of the Charter. Seeing therefore my Lords it is of importance to his Majesty with respect to his Revenue of Quit Rents, and of no small concern to the People of Virginia, who are very averse to the taking up of Lands under a Proprietor, I thought it my duty to let your Lordships thus far into the Merits of this Case by way of Advance, that if it be thought necessary I may receive your Lordships Opinion and Direction therein before the matter comes to be stated between Me and the Proprietor's Agent, which I apprehend will require some time to adjust, because I shall not easily agree to Facts of the truth whereof I am not perfectly convinced.

As the Journal of Council and Proclamation herewith sent mention the dreadful apprehensions this Colony again lay under from the Caterpillars; it is fit that I should now inform your Lordships, that by the peculiar favour of Heaven that danger is now over without any other consequence than the destruction of some Orchards and Timber.

I forgot in my last among the Allowances for the Gentlemen employed in running the Boundaries to mention that of a Chaplain whom I appointed to attend that Service, and who deserves his Majesty's consideration when the Payment of that Work shall be ordered. It was very necessary that a Clergyman should be sent out with such a number, when they were to pass through a Country where they could not have the oppurtunity of attending the Public Worship; and the Report that Gentleman made to me sufficiently proves how well he answers my purpose in sending of him; for he Christened above an hundred Children, a great many adult Persons, and preached to Congregations who have never had publick Worship since their first Settlement in those Parts; such is the unhappy State of those poor Inhabitants who possess the borders of our neighbouring Province, in which, there is not one Minister.

I have herewith sent your Lordships a List of the Military Officers in this Province; and as soon as the severel Troops and Companies are adjusted, I shall transmit the List of their officers and number of Men.

As the state of the Tobacco Trade calls for a speedy Remedy, as well to prevent an apparent Loss to his Majesty's Revenue, as a great Blow to the Manufacturers of Great Brittain, if the Planters discouraged from making of Tobacco by the lowness of the Price, should be driven to the Necessity of laying that aside, and should provide themselves with their own Cloathing from the Materials this Country affords, since their Tobacco will no longer supply them; what immediately follows is part of a Letter I have sent by this conveyance to the Duke of Newcastle, in compliance with what I promised his Grace in a former Letter, of which I sent your Lordships a Copy.

"It is evident that the Duty have (sic.) and is a strong temptation to Many to contrive all possible ways of defrauding the Crown by running the Tobacco in Great Brittain: and the success they have had therein, has likewise given occasion to buying up all the mean and trash Tobacco, purchased here by Agents and Sailors who well know how to dispose of it without paying any Duty. And this sort of Traffique has encouraged the Planters to cure a great deal or all of their Trash, which otherwise must have been thrown away. Thus is the Market for the good Tobacco damp'd by the fraudulent importation of the Bad, and the fair Trader and honest & industrious Planter greatly discouraged.

I have taken some pains to find out a Remedy for this great Evill, and to that purpose have consulted divers of the principal Inhabitants of this Province as well Merchants as others, and find it generally agreed that the only effectual means to prevent the Abuse which long since crept into this Trade, will be to bring all the Tobacco under a strict examination by sworn Officers, before it be allowed to be ship'd of for Great Brittain; that all that is found Bad be destroy'd and None exported but what is really good and Merchantable, and that an Acc[t] of the true weight of every Hogshead or Cask shall be transmitted to the Commissioners of his Majesty's Customs, by which the fraudulent Practice of breaking open of hogsheads and running of the Tobacco may be more easily detected and prevented. I now send to your Lordships also, the Heads of what I humbly propose for the improvement of the Tobacco trade, hoping that when your Lordships have consider'd them, they may be approved and immediately put in Practice, either by obtaining his Majesty's Letters Mandatory to the Governors of Virginia & Maryland to pass them into Laws, or, which would be much more efficacious, an Act of Parliament to put all the Tobacco made in the Plantations under the Regulation therein proposed; for it must be confess'd that though the judicious and honest part of the People here are well inclined to these measures, there are too many of a different Character, who are ready to oppose everything that is not suited to their narrow Conceptions and private Views. If these proposals are thought by your Lordships to deserve encouragement, and to pass in the Parliament, there is one thing not mention'd that must be provided for, and that is, the Nomination of the Officers to inspect the Tobacco, who must be Men of Character & Understanding in that Commodity, which may be left, unless your Lordships shal order otherwise, to the Appointment of the Governours, who must also ascertain their Sallarys in proportion to their Trouble; for some Places where

Storehouses must be built, will have much more Tobacco brought to them than others.

What I have to add I hope will not be unacceptable, since 'tis to inform your Lordships that upon the Bruit of many wonderful Cures performed by a Negro Slave in the most inveterate Venerial Distempers, I thought it might be of use to mankind, if by any fair Method I could prevail upon him to discover to me the Means by which such Cures were effected, which the Negro had for many years practiced in this Country, but kept as a most profound Secrett; as the Fellow is very old, my endeavours were quicken'd lest the Secrett should dye with him: therefore I immediately sent for him, and by good words and a promise of setting him free, he has made an ample discovery of the whole, which is no other than a Decoction of the Root and Barks I have sent over to a Phisitian, that the Colledge may have the opportunity what effect it will have in England; and I flatter myself, by the Ingenuity of the Learned in that Profession, it may be reduced into a better draught than he makes of it, which they tell me is nauseous enough. the difference of Climate may probably cause a difference in its operation; but there is no room to doubt of its being a certain Remedy here, and of singular use among the Negroe's who are frequently tainted with that Disease, (for I made a tryal of the things by the hands of a Surgeon here, before I purchased his freedom, the whole charge of which costs the Government about £60 ster) and is well worth the Price that has been paid for it, since we know how to cure Slaves without the aid of Mercury, who were often ruined by the unskilfulness of the Practitioners this Country affords. At the worst my Lords I hope it will be deemed a laudable Attempt, and be an encouragement for one of Dr Ratcliffe's travelling Phisitians to take a tour into this part of the World, where there are many valuable discoveries to be made, not to be mett with in France or Italy.

It is so long since we received any Advices from England, and those of the latest date speaking with great uncertainty as to Peace or War, I thought it absolutely necessary to lay an Embargo to the end of this moneth: this may possibly raise a Clamour, especially if things are quiett among those Merchants whose Ships were ready to sayle sooner; but I did it my Lords to give an oppertunity to the most valuable Ships to form a Fleet for their greater Security, and not doubting but by that time in case of a War, Convoys would be order'd for them. But his Majesty's Ship the Ludlow Castle is oppertunely arrived here, and intends to accompany them in their Passage Home. And it happened very luckily that this Embargo was laid in time, since we have been alarmed by a Spanish Privateer's being upon the Coast, by the Deposition sent me from Hampton as follows

The Deposition of John Pitts Master of the Sloop Dolphin of Bermuda, Who says that he sayled from Bermuda the 31st day of May last in the Sloop Dolphin burthen twenty five Tonns, no Guns & five Men, that on the eight of June following He saw in the Lat. of 37^{d}:18^{m} about 12 leagues East from Cape Charles a large Sloop which gave him Chase and fired two Guns at Him and pursued him till Night; that he believes him to be a Spanish Privateer and that he is now lying off the Cape, and further this Deponent saith not.

taken & sworn to before me Signed John Pitt
this 9th day of June 1729
Wilson Cary
Naval Off:

I have nothing more to trouble your Lordships with at present, but to repeat the Assurance with which I am

My Lords
Your Lordships Most faithful and most obedient
humble Servant William Gooch.

Virginia
W^{ms}burgh June 29th 1729

My Lords

The Military List I could not get compleated for this Conveyance.

Endorsed Virginia
L[r] from Major Gooch
L[t] Governor of Virginia
dated y[e] 29th of June 1729.
Rec[d] 28th August
Read 2[d] Septem[r] 1729
R. 120

Governor Gooch's Letter In Regard to the Boundaries of The Northern Neck, Maryland and Pennsylvania.

(Record Office, London. B. T. Virginia. Vol. 20. S. 32. Letter from Major Gooch. Feb. 8th 1732/3.)

My Lords.

I have the honour of Your Lordships of the 13th 7ber, with the papers your Lordships were pleased to send in Relation to the Pretensions of the several Proprietors of Pensilvania, Maryland and the Northern Neck, to the Lands lying Westward of the G[t] Mountains of Virginia

In my letter of the 29th of June 1729 I gave your Lordships a true state of the Dispute between the Crown and the L[d] Culpeper as to the Construction of his Grant: and I then humbly offered my opinion for determining that matter at Home, and I am still of opinion that the best and most effectual way to do it, must be either by a Tryal in Westminster Hall, or by the Arbitrament of Persons deputed, by the King and L[d] Fairfax, for that Purpose, since by viewing the Mapp I sent your Lordships and comparing it with the Grant of King James the 2[d] to L[d] Culpeper, and considering how far the Rivers Rappahannock and Potomack were then known, a true judgment may be formed what was the Intention of the Crown, and what ought to be the Boundarys conformable to that Intention and until such determination be made either by a legal Decision or Compromise. I am humbly of opinion that appointing Commissioners here will prove a fruitless Labour and Expence.

It is to be noted My Lords that the Rivers Rappahannock and Potomack took their Names from the Indian Nations inhabiting their respective Banks, and that the Places where these Indian Towns stood, when Virginia was first seated, and continued while there were any Remains of those Nations, are below the Falls of both Rivers, and where they are Navigable. What denomination Rappahannock had above its Falls, or the several Rivers had which form it, doth not certainly appear, tho' 'tis more than probable the Indians had other names for them; for that part of Potomack River which has been lately discovered and settled above its Falls is known and called by the Indian Nations that have most commonly frequented it, by the name Cahongarooten, as all the other Rivers which fall into it are called by their several distinct names. So that if according to L[d] Culpepers Grant nothing Passes by the names Potomack or Rappahannock Rivers but as they were known and called at the time of its Date, my L[d] Fairfax can claim no farther Westward than the Falls of each River, or at the farthest where those Rivers begin to be one stream. But if His Majesty out of his more abundant Bounty, thinks fit to allow that Grant to extend up to the Head Spring of that River which forms the North Branch of the Rappahannock, then the Bounds must be runn from thence to the River Cahongarooten, where from the same Meridian the head Spring of Rappahannock lyes in, and consequently must be Bounded by the ridge of Mountains, as your Lordships will see by the Mapp; and then L[d] Fairfax will have an extent of Territory upwards of Two Hundred Miles in length, and in some places thirty Miles broad; and His Majesty be at liberty to Settle a Barrier between this Colony and the Lakes, upon which the security of this and the other Provinces greatly depend.

L[d] Fairfax's Agent here has laid down such strange Pretensions, as never, in my opinion, can be reconciled with the words of the Grant: They will have it that because the head Springs of both Rivers are mentioned in the Grant, His Lord-shipp is not to be Bounded by the head of Rappahannock, but is to comprehend all the Rivers that fall into Potomack, wheresoever their Head-Springs or Sources take their Rise; and therefore because the River Shenanto or Sherando falls into Cahongarooten, they will have all the lands on that River as far South as the Borders of N° Carolina, and from thence all the Lands Westward and Northward to the Source of Cahongarooten to be within their Bounds, which would extend that Grant, confined plainly by the words of it between the two Rivers Rappahannock and Potomack, upwards of one hundred Miles beyound Rappahannock to the Southward, and above that distance to the West, and so to extend North behind Maryland, intersecting the Province of Pensilvania.

Your Lordships will hence Perceive how impracticable it is for Commissioners here to determine a Controversie so perplexed, and how unequal any Commissioners here are like to prove for such a Task, where the Foundation, the Letters Pattent of the Crown are deemed altogether uncertain; and neither the King was informed what he Granted, nor could the Pattentee know how to describe what he asked and would now extend his Claim beyond what ought to be allowed, or it can be supposed the Crown intended to bestow.

I have enlarged the more fully, My Lords, on the Claim of L[d] Fairfax, because until that is determined, there is no occasion for His Majesty to interest himself in the dispute concerning the Boundarys of Maryland or Pensilvania: for if the Northern Neck Grant is judged as extensive as the Proprietor's Agent would have it, I know no Lands His Majesty hath to dispose of beyound the great Ridge of Mountains. Shenando, as laid down in the Mapp, runs paralel with that Ridge from the extremity of our Southern Boundary. Cahongarooten is said to have its source beyound the fortieth Degree of North Latitude, and intersecting the Boundarys of Pensilvania runs on the West of Maryland, till it falls into Potomack River properly so called,—and the many Rivers which fall into Cahongarooten from the West, are said to interlock with the branches of the Messissippi So that the Lands in Virginia which are in the Power of the Crown to Grant, are entirely cut off, and seperated from that which ly (sic) contiguous to the Lakes, by this extraordinary Claim under the Grant of the Northern Neck

But since my Lords I can never suppose that such a Construction of the Northern Neck Grant will be allowed, and that your Lordships may receive all the Information I can give, I shall go on and state the difference between Virginia and L[d] Baltimore; His Lordship's Province of Maryland is bounded on the South, from the Sea, to Watkins's Point (which is not laid down in the Mapp I sent, but your Lordships may judge it to be on the South side of that River I should have said the South side of the Mouth of that River which runs out of Cheseapeak Bay into the Eastern shore) and thence cross Cheseapeak Bay to the South side of Potomack River (which River is in his Lordship's Grant, tho' in His Majesty's Instructions 'tis called a pretended Right, and I am thereby directed to assert His Majesty's Right) and so that River continues the Limit between His Lordship and Virginia. On the North his Ldshipp is bounded by a West line (where they are to sett out is not yett, as I hear, agreed upon, 'tis conjectured about Delaware River or Sasafras River, but that is not material) which is to extend as far Westward as the true Meridian of the first fountain of Potomack; by which, my Lords it is evident that the first Fountain of Potomack was then supposed to be somewhere to the South of that line, otherwise it would have been more properly expressed, by extending that line Westward till it intersected Potomack River, and so have made that River the Western Limit, as well as it is the Southern of his Lordship's Grant. Hence I think it clear, my Lords, that neither in the Grant to Maryland, nor that to my L[d] Culpeper, Potomack River was ever imagined to extend so far as the River Cahongarooten doth and if L[d] insists on that as Potomack, and if it be true that its Source takes its Course from the North-east, as it is generally reported, then a line drawn from that Meridian to Potomack River, properly so called, will cut off a large Tract now inhabited under Grant from L[d] Baltimore as part of his province: and some People here are so confident of this, that they have Petitioned me for Grants of large Tracts of Land there as belonging to Virginia, which Petitions are referred till the Boundarys be settled. Others argue that by the first Fountain of Potomack, his Lordships West line can extend no farther than till it falls on the first River on its Course, which emptys itself into Potomack, of which it seems there are many on that side of Cahongarooten, as well as on the other, and they pretend to know that River called Cahongarooten Conneichiga† [by another hand, F. P. transcriber.] is that which the line between Maryland and Pensilvania will first intersect, and have their eye upon Lands on the Westside of that River as undoubtedly in Virginia; in which case Lord Baltimore will lose less, and have his Limits sooner ascertained, than by tracing Cahongarooten to its Source, and then running a South line from thence according to his Charter

The Grant of Pensilvania is the only one whose Western limit is capable of being reduced to a certainty consistent with the Description mentioned in the Letters Patent: and if the Proprietors of that Province and L[d] Baltimore shall agree to run the line of Division between them, and to measure as far as that extends, the rest of the five Degrees of Longitude, which is the extent of Pensilvania, may with small Expence and no Dispute be measured and fixed so as no Controversy may arise hereafter.

Since therefore, My Lords, there appears such uncertainty in the Description of the Boundarys of these Proprietary Grants, made without due Information or Knowledge of what was intended to be Passed to the several Patentees; and since the Proprietors are neither like to agree amongst themselves where their Boundarys are, nor how they Interfere, nor seem to be contented with what may reasonably be supposed the Crown granted them; it is high time to take some speedy Measures to put an end to these Disputes, and the rather since there is now a View of having great numbers of foreign

† For the Alteration vide Major Gooch's letter to the Secr'y dated . . . July [in another hand].

Protestants to seat these Frontiers, and thereby prevent the French, an oppertunity if lett slip, perhaps may never be retrieved.

But I cannot leave this Subject without representing to your Lordships that the erecting new Provinces and Governments will be attended with many Inconveniences: such as the weakness of an Infant Settlement to support itself; the difficulty of bringing Foreigners to the knowledge and under the Subjection of the English Laws, where they are left to themselves and not Incorporated with an English Government; the disputes that may arise concerning their Boundarys, if a Tract of Land should be Granted them, the true Limits whereof cannot be with certainty described, besides many others which 'tis needless to trouble Your Lordships with.

I should rather, if your Lordships will give me Leave, advise if they are to be Settled within the Limitts of Virginia, that His Majesty would leave it to the Government here to assign them lands proportionable to their Number, and to Grant them distinct Patents, with exemption for seven or tenn years from Payment of Quitrents, and such other ease in the manner of taking and cultivating as His Majesty shall think reasonable for their Encouragement; and care may be taken here that no more Land than is already entered for on the back of the Mountains will be granted to any other Person whatsoever till they have their full complement assigned them, all which I submitt to your Lordships better judgment.

My Lords, I have made all the Inquiry I can into the matter sett forth in Mrs Jones's letter, and can only find, and I am perswaded 'tis all that is in it, that one Dr Watkins and some other necessitous People have imposed upon some Gentlemen of Estates, and drawn them into buying Shares of a Silver Mine they pretended, at first, they had found on the back of the Mountains, tho' they afterwards reported it near Sasquehannah River in the Province of Maryland, and having showed something which they affirmed to be silver oar, it proved to be only antimony, and the Gentlemen concerned are now convinced it is a Cheat put upon them for which they paid in advance about £20 p man. However I shall have a watchful eye over them, and if I can discover any appearance of a Royal Mine shall give speedy notice of it to Your Lordships

I am, My Lords, Your Lordships
most dutiful and most faithful humble Servant
William Gooch.

Virginia
Wmsburgh
February 8th 1732/3
This comes by a ship to Leverpool.

[Endorsed] Virginia.
Lr from Maj'e Gooch Lieutent Govr of Virginia, dated ye 8th of Feby 1732/3 giving a large State of the dispute about the Boundaries between that Government and ye Northern neck Maryland & Pensylvania, occasioned by a Petition for a New Settlement on the back of the Great Mountains, and about a pretended Silver Mine found there.

Reced 25th May 1733
Read Septem 16 : 1734
S:32.

Report of The Commissioners to Settle The Boundaries of the Northern Neck.

(From a document in the Library of Congress)

[Incomplete]
We shall now take notice of the Principal Matters contained in their several Reports together with the Proofs and Grounds upon which they proceeded.

The Commissioners appointed by the Lieutenant Governor of Virginia in behalf of the Crown in their Report say,—

"That they took their Survey of the Main Branch of the

River Potowmack (called Cohongoronton) from its Confluence with *Sharando* and so upwards beyond the Blew Mountains to its first Spring Head, and of the River Rapahannock from its Fork, pursuing both North and South Branch to the Spring Heads likewise and found the North Branch to be wider at the mouth than the South by 3 Poles Nine Links. That they can find no evidence that the Fork of Rapahannock was known at the time of Lord Culpeper's Grant. That Lord Fairfax has produced no evidence to support his Pretension to the South Branch. But they, the said Commissioners, offer some in support of his Majesty's which are chiefly arguments, inferences, and deductions drawn partly from the sense of the Legislature in Virginia and partly from Grants of the Crown. They thus pursue their account of the river Potowmack and refer to the Deposition of Thomas Harrison[3] taken upon oath before them "That the Falls of Potomack were not known fifty years ago". They further say "That the Lands at or near the falls were not granted till 1709, and that it was not known that the River runs through the Mountains till several years after, That the River loses its name at the Confluence and is called by the Indians as it goes higher up *Cohongaronton* and *Sharando,* and conclude "That the Fork may not therefore be improperly called the Head", which opinion they endeavor to corroborate by saying "That as the Head of Potowmack stretches beyond the Blew Mountains and that of Rappahannock reaches no higher than those mountains they could not be intended as Boundarys by the Grant of King James since the one reaches Two Hundred Miles above the other".

They conclude their Report by Stating four several Boundaries for the Lord Fairfax's Grant and mention what quantity of land each of those Boundaries contains.

"The first from the Fork of Rappahannock to the Fork of Potomac containing 1,476,000 acres of Land.

---

[3] Thomas Harrison, whose deposition was taken in 1736, was born in 1665 and died in 1746. He lived at Chappawamsic, Stafford County, to which his father Burr Harrison had come in the Seventeenth century. For an account of the Harrison family see this Magazine XXIII and XXIV.

"The Second from the head of Hedgeman River to the Fork of Potomac containing 2,030,000 acres of Land.

"The Third from the Hedgeman River to the Head Spring of Cohongoronton containing 3,872,000 acres of Land.

"And the Fourth from the head of Conway River to the Head Spring of Cohongoronton including the Great and Little Fork of Rapahannock containing 5,282,000 acres of Land.

The Papers referred to in their Report are

1st, The Governor's Commission to them which was *to Examine, Settle and Determine*

2nd, Lord Fairfax's to them which is only to *Survey and Report,*

3d, Lord Fairfax's Commission to Messrs Carter, Beverly and Fairfax, which was *to Survey and Report only.*

4th, Deposition taken upon oath of John Taliaferro[4], Francis Thornton and William Russell, who severally declare there were no Inhabitants on either side of the river so high as the Falls even so late as the year 1707.

5th, A General Map of the Delineation of the Courses of the Rivers from the Parts where they began their survey up to their respective Spring Heads.

6th, A Copy of a Grant from the Lord Culpeper to Mr. Brent and others in 1686 of Land *to be laid out six miles distant at least from the Main Rivers of Rappahannock and Potowmack* which being laid down in their map as taking its Distance from the North Stream they quote it to shew that

---

[4] John Taliaferro, son of Robert Taliaferro, the emigrant, was a justice of Essex County, Sheriff, Lieutenant of Rangers against the Indians and, in 1699, member of the House of Burgesses. He married Sarah, daughter of Major Lawrence Smith, of Gloucester County, and had ten children.

Francis Thornton (born Jan. 4, 1682) settled at Snow Creek near the present Fredericksburg about 1702. He was a Burgess for Spotsylvania in 1723 and 1726, and was ancestor of the Thorntons, of "Fall Hill", Spotsylvania, and others.

In 1724, William Russell, of Drysdale parish, King and Queen County, bought 614 acres in Spotsylvania from Loyd and Chew, and, as of St. Georges parish, Spotsylvania, sold the same tract in 1725. On Dec. 1, 1730, he (William Russell, gent.,) bought the interest of George Hume in two land grants of 6,000 and 10,000 acres. In 1755 he lived in Culpeper County. He was the father of Brig. General William Russell, of the Revolution.

the Original Patentee always understood the North Branch to be the main branch.

7th, Governor Nott's Grant to Henry Beverly, Esqr. of 1920 acres in Essex County, ten Miles above the Falls of Rapahannock in November 1705.

8th, Two Grants from the Governor to Robert Carter, Esqr. for Land in the Fork of Rapahannock twelve Miles and more above the Falls in January 1717.

9th, Two Grants to Philip Ludwell, Esqr. from Lady Culpeper of 5860 acres above the falls in June 1709.

10th, Henry Willis's Patent for 3,000 acres of land in the Little Fork of Rapahannock from Governor Carter in February 1726.

11th, The Deposition of Thomas Harrison, who declares upon oath that the falls of Potomac were not known Fifty years ago, dated in June 1737.

12th, Letters Patent from King Charles the Second to the Earl of St. Albans and others.

13th, Letters Patent from King James the Second to Lord Culpeper.

The Commissioners for the Lord Fairfax in their Report give an account "That the Dispute between the Crown and the Lord Fairfax being which is the Main River of Rappahannock the North or the South Branch as appears by the order of the Governor and Council of Virginia in 1706 to which they refer, as also which is the first Head or Spring of Potowmack, they have Surveyed and Measured up the River Potowmack from the Mouth of Sherando and that of Rappahannock from the falls to their respective Heads or Springs, and are of opinion that a Line run from the *first Head or Spring* of the South or Main Branch of Rappahannock to the *first Head or Spring* of the River Potowmack is and ought to be the boundary line determining the said Tract or Territory of Land commonly called the Northern Neck, They refer themselves to the evidences produced by the King's Commissioners (quoted in the other report) that the two Branches of Rappahannock were always called the North and South

Rivers, not North and South Fork, and that the name of Rapidan was given to this latter by Col. Spotswood when Governor, as also to a Declaration of one Mr. John Talliaferro that the Heads or Springs of the said two Branches were known in 1682, and to their own Surveyor's Report in proof that the South Branch was the Widest. They say their own Surveyor made a mistake in going up Conway instead of Thornton river, which they have caused to be dotted in token of the Lord Fairfax's claiming it.

The papers referred to in the above Report are—

1st, The Order of the Governor and Council of Virginia in 1706 directing a survey to be made of the two branches of Rappahannock to see which is the Main Branch. This order is referred to by the Lord Fairfax's Commissioners to obviate the objections made of the Forks never having been claimed by the Proprietors or their agents.

2nd, The evidences produced by the King's Commiss[rs] of which We have already given your Lordships an account.

3rd, A Declaration of John Taliaferro. This Declaration is annexed to the above mentioned order of 1706 and is only a copy and not upon oath. It contains that *about Twenty-four years ago he in company with Colonel Cadwallader Jones had been at the Heads or Springs of the said two branches and that in his judgment and that of the company with him the South Branch was the biggest and headed* in the Mountains.

4th, The Surveyor's Report, which ascertains that the South Stream was twenty-one Miles longer than the other.

MINUTES OF THE COUNCIL AND GENERAL COURT, 1622-1629

From the Originals in the Library of Congress.

(Continued)

A Court at James Citty. the 15th of Octob: 1627 being present
Sr George Yeardley Knt Gouernor &c.
And all ye Councell.

Ensigne George Thomson[1] sworne & examined sayth that in May 1626, being in a boate wth Mr Mayhew & Capt Nicolas Martiau at Kecoughtan comeing from aboard a shipp, they fell in talke about ye two Kings of England & ffrance, & Mr Mayhew sayd that the King of England was King of ffrance & that the King in ffrance was but the ffrence [French] King & then Capt Martiau seemed to be very angry & sayd that if the English-King were King of England, then ye ffrench-King was King of ffrance: and then ye said Capt Martiau putting his hand to his brest said, though I am here yet this sparke is in ffrance & will not here the King wronged, wherevppon they ye said Mr Mayhew & ye said Capt Martiau grew into such anger as this deponent did thinke they would haue fallen out: And this is all yt this deponent can say

1 George Thomson, or Thompson, was one of four brothers, who, at various times, lived in Virginia; Maurice, George, William and Paul. It is probable that a fifth brother, Robert Thompson, was also in the colony. George Thompson, who was born in 1603, returned to England and became a Colonel in the Parliamentary Army during the Civil Wars. See this Magazine I, 188-192.

Captain Nicholas Martiau, or Martian, afterwards of York County, was a Huguenot and had seen the persecution of his co-religionists by the French Government, but evidently his love for France was still strong. He was afterwards a member of the House of Burgesses, a leader in the movement to depose Governor Harvey in 1635 and was an ancestor of Washington.

At this Court the sayd Capt Martiau tooke the oath of Supremacy vppon ye holy Euangelists.

At this Court there was a controuersie brought in betweene Capt William Peirce & Capt Robt Gire.

And the Question propounded to ye Court was as followeth viz. Whither by a paire of Indentures bearing date the 25th day of July last past made betweene Capt Peirce[2] & Capt Gire, the said Capt Peirce bee bound to deliuer vpp vnto ye said Capt Gire an Inuentorie of his ye Capt Peirce his whole estate & to take his oath vppon ye holy Euangelists that ye said Inuentorie is peremptorily a full entire & perfect Inuentorie of all his whole Estate & goods whatsoeuer, wth out any mention that it is full & perfect as far as his knowledge and conscience. And ye maio^r part of ye Councell viz Capt West, Mr Docto^r Pott, Capt Mathewes, Capt Tucker, & M^r ffarrar, were of opinion that Capt Peirce should as aboue said peremptorily deliuer ye said Inuentory vppon his oath, And on ye other side the Gouerno^r, Capt Smyth, Mr Persey, & Mr Secretary did iudge it sufficient if Capt Peirce deliuer the said Inuentory vppon his oath to be true & perfect to ye vtmost of his knowledge: And ye said Capt Peirce offered to doe ye same, & then his wife & seruants should likewise take their oath.

After ye abouesaid iudgm^t & opinion of ye Court deliuered the said Capt Peirce & Capt Gire did agree in ye presence of ye Court as followeth, Viz, That Capt Mathewes in ye behalfe of Capt Gire & Mr Persey in ye behalfe of Capt William Peirce shall arbitrate & conclude the controuersy now in question betweene them, & Capt William Tucker to be Vmpire in the same: And ye said Capt Peirce & Capt Gire doe bind themselues in this Court to stand to ye arbitrament that shall be made by ye said Arbitrators & Vmpire, in the full sume of six thowsande pounds of lawfull mony of England to be paid by him wch shall refuse to stand to ye arbitram^t vnto ye other of them.

---

[2] Captain William Peirce and Joane his wife were living at Jamestown 1623-4. He was member of the Council 1631-44 and had at least one child, Jane, who was the third wife of John Rolfe.

John Vpton sworne & examined sayth that about this time tweluemonthe Mr Menefy receiueing certaine siluer spoones from Caleb Page this deponents partner left fowre ounces of siluer & 5^{s} 6^{d} in ye hands of ye said Caleb Page, And ye said Mr Menefy did often require the said Page to worke it out, but this deponent sayth y^{t} by reason of his sicknes hee did not, & sayth farther y^{t} Mr Menefy is yet vnsatisfyed for it. And this deponent further sayth that in ye time of their Partnershipp they receiued goods of Menefey betweene them of the wch the said Page is to pay ye one halfe wch is 13^{l} of Tobacco.

It is ordered that Leften^{t} Allington Administrato^{r} to ye said Caleb Page shall pay to ye said Mr Menefy the said fowre ounces of siluer & 5^{s}—6^{d} of mony, & the said 13^{l} of Tobacco.

The 14th day of Nouember 1627: being the day after ye buriall of Sr George Yeardley Kn^{t} late Gouerno^{r}, the rest of the Councell met viz.

Capt ffrancis West,
Docto^{r} Pott,
Capt Smyth,
Capt Mathewes,
Mr Persey,
Mr Claybourne,
Capt Tucker,
M^{r} ffarrar.

At this time by ye opinions & voices of ye Councell Capt: ffrancis West[3], according to the Com'ission of his Most excellent Mai^{tie} directed vnto vs for ye same purpose was elected & chosen to be the present Gouernor & Captaine Gennerall of this his Maties Colony & Plantation of Virginia in as full & ample manner as by ye said Com'ission and their election may be deriued vppon him.

---

[3] Francis West, brother of Lord Delaware, who was also Governor of Virginia, was Governor of the Colony Nov. 14, 1627—March 5, 1628. John West, a third brother was also Governor. Capt. Francis West returned to England, where he lived at Winchester and died 1634. For his will see this Magazine XI, 359-360.

[Written in a different hand in the lower left hand corner of this page is the following:] Begin in this Page to finish this Book

---

A Court at James Citty the 16th of Nouember 1627 [Present]

Capt: ffrancis West Esqr Gouernor &c.
Doctor Pott
Capt Smyth
Capt Mathewes
Mr Persey
Mr Secretary
Capt Tucker
Mr ffarrar

At this Court the Lady Temperance Yeardley[4] came & did fully & absolutely confirme as much as in her lay the sale & conueyance made by her late husband Sr George Yeardley Knt, late Gouernor deceased, vnto Mr Abraham Persey Esqr for the lands of fflower [Dew] Hundred being one thousand acres, & of Weiano[ke] on ye opposite side of ye water being 2200 hun[dred] acres, And ye said Lady Temperance Yeardley did then alltogether absolutely disclaime . . . vnto ye said Abraham Persey all the [right] interest & claime in all & euery . . . of ye said lands to herselfe any . . . & appertaineing either by way Dow[er or] Thirds.

A Court at James Citty the 19th of Nouemb. 1627. present

Capt ffrancis West Esqr Gouernor &c
Doctor Pott.
Capt Smyth.
Mr Secretary.

John Southerne gent sworne & examined sayth that the eightenth day of October last past one Beniamin Browne of

[4] Temperence, wife of Sir George Yeardley, Governor of Virginia, was daughter of Anthony Flowerdew, Esq., of Hethersett, Norfolk, England. She married, secondly, Capt. Francis West, and died soon afterwards. See this Magazine XXV, 207-210, and *Tyler's Quarterly Historical and Genealogical Magazine*, II, 115-129.

Lyme in ye County of Dorset Marriner being sickly of Body yet in perfect sense & memory, & telling this deponent that he wanted meanes to releiue him self, did make a bargaine & Couenant wth Valentine Oldis, Marchant, in manner & forme following, viz that for & in consideration of ye sum'e of twenty pounds of lawfull mony of England to be paid by ye said Valentine Oldis vnto him w^th^in fowretene dayes next after ye Arriual of ye good shipp called y^e^ . . . at ye Port of London, whereof his Captaine Arthur Guy [?] for ye voiadge, he did bargine & sell & make over vnto ye said Mr. Oldis all & singuler such profitts gaines & benefitt whatsoeuer as shall any wayes belonge vnto him ye said Browne for his part & share, for his seruice in ye said voiadge: And did further couenant & agree that if it should please god to take him the said Browne out of this life before [the ar]rivall of ye said shipp at ye Port of London, . . . was y^t^ the said Valentine Oldis in . . . & frendshipp he had receaued at [his hands shou]ld alsoe receaue the said 20 pounds . . .

[The next three paragraphs are either out of place, or some portion of the original is missing.]

Vnto Mrs Pott, (being speaking of a bote) and [if] it please God, as soone as I am well I will goe to worke for you: And Mistress Pott sayd againe I will helpe you to what timber I can & you shall haue your diet here. And this deponent further sayth that hee heard Mrs. Pott say that it should be such a boate as Mr. Sharples his boate was.

It is ordered that the aboue sayd Will'm Bennet shall build & make such a boate, as Edward Sharples his boate is for Docto^r^ Pott, & to go aboute the building thereof very speedily, And to be prouided of all timber & such other things as are necessary therevnto.

Richard Cocke, Purser of the shipp the Thomas & John sayth that in the beginning of their voiadge their shipp riding in Catt Water, there did fowre of Mr Sharples his men runne away, then this deponent goeing on shoare told Mr Moore of it, & sayd if you will not supply & prouide fowre men againe, I will: then Mr. Moore sayd that he would doe, and afterwards Mr. Moore shipped fiue men aboard, And did neuer speak vnto this deponent, whither they should be vppon his owne, or on Mr. Sharples his Acco.

Capt John Hudlestone Sworne & examined sayth that he knew noe other, but that those fiue men were shipped vppon Mr Sharples his Account & not vppon Mr Moores, And that he would not haue receaued them into ye shipp for any other.

John Woolrich gent sworne & examined sayth that Mr Moore told him that he was but to shipp ten men aboard the shipp.

At this Court Will'm Perry gent deliuered in vppon his oath the Inuentory of ffrancis Weekes his estate.

James Citty the 14th January 1627, being present,

Capt francis West Esqr Gouerno^r^ &c.
Docto^r^ Pott.
Capt Smyth.
Mr Secretary.

Thomas Sawyer[5] arrested at ye suite of Edward Sharples Marchant for 210^l^ of Tobacco wth allowance of 10^l^% [100?] ll. And further at ye suite of Mr Gill for 479 l. Tobacco.

Jonas Reily & Andrew Reily arrested at Mr Gills suite for 330 l. Tobacco.

Robert Wright arrested at ye suite of Robert Marshall for 1200 l. Tobacco.

Robert Marshall arrested at ye suite of Gabriell Holland for 900 l. Tobacco.

---

[5] Thomas Sawyer, aged 23, was in 1624-5, a servant of Peter Langman, at James City. Jonas Rayley lived at Shirley Hundred, Feb. 16, 1623. Robert Wright, aged 45, who came in the *Swan*, 1608, Joane Wright, and two children born in Virginia, were in Anthony Bonall's "Muster" at Elizabeth City, 1624-5: Robert Marshall and his wife, Ann, both of whom came in the *George*, lived on James City Island, 1624-5. Edward Wigg, aged 22, who came in the *Abigail*, 1621, lived at Basse's Choice, 1624-5. George Unwin lived at Hog Island, 1623. Steven Barker lived at Martin's Hundred in 1624-5. George Fryer, who came in the *William & Thomas*, and Ursula his wife, who came in the *London Merchant*, lived at Pashbehayes on the Main, near Jamestown 1624.

Edward Wigg arrested at ye suite of Edward Sharples for 100 l. of Tobacco.

George Vnwin arrested at y^e suite of Edward Wigg for 230 l. Tobacco.

Steven Barker & Wassell Webling arrested at y^e suite of Edward Sharples for 440 l. Tobacco.

George ffryor arrested at y^e suite of George Saunders for 120 l. Tobacco, to appeare on Monday next, & M^r $Docto^r$ his suerty.

$Will^m$ Baker arrested at y^e suite of y^e Lady Yeardley for 300 l. Tobacco.

$Will'^m$ Harman[6], John Vpton, Robert ffitt & Amy Hall had their bonds of their good behauior canceled.

At this Court Mr Thomas Harwood[7] shewed that hee was much scanted for want of ground to plant at y^e Necke of land, And the Ouerseers & Guardians refused to let him any more, Where vppon the Court gaue leaue vnto him to remoue from thence & to plant elsewhere.

It is ordered that Capt ffellgate[8] shall forfeit forty waight of Tobacco for that he did not this day appeare at y^e Court, being warned by y^e Prouost Marshall.

A Court at James Citty the 21th of January 1627. p^rsent

Capt ffrancis West Esqr $Gouerno^r$ &c.

Capt Smyth

Mr Secretary.

---

6 Capt. John Upton, afterwards a prominent man in Isle of Wight County. Robert Fitt, who came in the *George*, and his wife Ann, who came in the *Abigail*, lived on James City Island, 1624-5.

7 At the census of 1624-5, Thomas Harwood, who came in the *Margaret & John*, 1622, his wife, Grace, who came in the *George*, and one man-servant, were living at Mulberry Island. This was probably Capt. Thomas Harwood afterwards a large landholder in Warwick County and member of the Council. The Thomas Harwood ,of Neck of Land, near Jamestown, seems to have been a different man. See this Magazine II, 183-185.

8 Probably Capt. Robert Felgate, afterwards of York County. See this Magazine II, 181-182.

Richard Alford[9] Com'itted prisoner at ye suite of Mr Gill for 500 l. [weight of] Tobacco.

Whereas it is credibly reported that Capt John Wilcoxes[10] is lately passed away in goeing ouer the Bay & his estate left vnsetled by that means & being diuersly ingaged vnto Edward Waters gent & others, the Court hath herevppon ordered that a Com'ission of Administration shalbe graunted vnto ye said Edward Waters vppon ye said Capt Wilcoxes his estate.

Obediens Robins[11], of Accawmacke, Chirurgion, sworne & examined sayth that about October last past he heard Capt Wilcoxes agree wth Walter Scot that he ye said Walter should haue 3 shares in ye Croppe, And this deponent further sayth that at ye same time Capt Wilcoxes profered the said Walter Scot 600 l. of Tobacco for his ouerseeing of ye men in ye Croppe besides ye shares, but ye said Walter refused the same.

At this Court Richard Richards[12] & Rich: Dolphenby came & did freely & fully surrender & giue vpp all their right tittle & interest in one hundred acres of land belonging & graunted by Patent vnto ffrancis Chapman, planter & scituate nere vnto Paces-Paines, vnto Izabella the wife of Will'm Perry of the same place gent & to hir heires & assignes for euer

John Cooke[13] Com'itted to p^rison at ye suite of Lewis Baily, for [space left here in the original]

---

[9] Richard Alford, aged 26, was in Capt. Roger Smith's Muster, "Over the Water", in 1624-5.

[10] Capt. John Wilcox, of Accomac, Va., was formerly of Plymouth, England. His will has been printed in Waters' *Gleanings* and in this Magazine II, 77-78.

[11] Obedience Robins was born at Brackley, Northamptonshire, England, April 16, 1600, and was the son of Thomas and Mary (Bulkley) Robins, of that place. He settled in Northampton County, was a Burgess at the sessions of March 1629-30, Jan. 1639, April 1642, Oct. 1644, April 1652, and November 1652, was appointed to the Council 1655, and died in 1662. A genealogy of his descendants was published in the *Richmond Standard*, Sept. 4, 1880 &c.

[12] On Sept. 20, 1628, Mrs. Isabella Perry obtained a new grant for the land here conveyed. For a note on her husband, William Perry, see this Magazine I, 451-452.

[13] John Cooke, aged 27, was in 1624-5, a servant of Mr. John Burrows, of James City.

Will'm Mills[14] aged 21 yeares or thereabouts borne at Purton in Wiltshire examined sayth that at dieurs times before Christmas last past he this examinate stolne from his Master Edward Grindon at dieurs times some Tobacco out of one his tobacco houses & from ye piles of Tobacco as much as himselfe could carry away vnder his arme, & further hee sayth that about St Johns or St Steuens day a little before Sun rising he this examinate pulled downe three boards being on the side of one of ye Tobacco houses & nailed at one end, & haueing slipped them downe went in & stole a way his capp full of currants, & carried them vnto John Tios his house, & gaue them vnto him, his wife being by: And this examinate further sayth that on Newe Yeeres day in ye morning this examinate as before went into ye store againe & stole from thence more currants & brought them away in his cloath wch the sayd John Tios & Jane his wife & Thomas Hall (who all were priuy to ye stealing of the currants) gaue vnto him this examinate to bringe them in, And this examinate at the same time alsoe stole 6 p^re of shoes & one shirte: And this examinate further syath on Sunday in the Morning being ye 14th day of this present Month, he this examinate went into the store againe and tooke from thence some Currants in a bagg wch Thomas Hall gaue him some suger in a shirte sleaue wch the said Jane ye wife John Tios had giuen him. And this examinate further sayth that John Tios did bid him this examinate take heed that he was not seene & specially take heed that one Rich: Littlefere should not see him for he was a very Knaue

---

[14] Edward Grindon, who lived opposite Jamestown, on the south side of the river, was a Burgess in 1623-24. John Tios, or Tyos, lived on the Treasurer's Plantation, as did Thomas Hall. Both had come in the *Bona Nova*, 1620. It would seem, from the purchase of the stolen currants [raisins] and sugar, that Tios and his wife were collecting materials for a Christmas plum pudding.

(To be continued)

VIRGINIA QUIT RENT ROLLS, 1704

(Continued)

Prince George County.

[Prince George at this time included, in addition to the present county, the territory now comprised in the counties of Dinwiddie, Amelia, Prince Edward and Nottoway. It is singular that this roll does not appear to include Brandon. The 4600 acres, belonging to "the merchants in London", could not have included all of Coggins Point and Martins Brandon. Nathaniel Harrison bought them from the English owners and when he made his will in 1726, it was stated that the former contained 1973 acres and the latter about 7000.]

A Rent Roll of all the Lands held in the County of Prince George for the year 1704:

A

	ACRES
Tho. Anderson	450
Wm Aldridge	160
Mr. Charles Anderson	505
Richd Adkinson	200
Tho. Adams	250
Matt. Anderson	349
Henry Ally	390
Wm. Anderson	235
Jno. Anderson	228
Henry Anderson	250
Robt. Abnernathy	100
Jno. Avery	100
	3217

B

Richd Bland	1000
Robt Burchett	375
Arthur Biggins	200
James Benford	461
Jno. Barloe	050
Charles Bartholomew	600
Philip Burlowe	350
Nich^o Brewer	100
Jno. Bishop Senr	100
Jno Bishop Junr	100
Isaac Baites [Bates]	360
Tho Busby Capt.	300
Tho Busby	200
Wm Batt	750
Coll Byrd Esqr	100
Edwd Birchett	886
Col. [Robert] Bolling	3402
Edm^d Browder	100
Matus Brittler	510
Jno Butler	1385
Andrew Beck	300
Henry Batt	790
Wm Butler	283
Tho Blitchodin	284
	12986

C

Tho Curiton	150
Hen. Chammins	300
Capt. Clements	1920
Wm Claunton	100
Robt Catte	100
Bartho Crowder	75
Tho Clay	70
Jno Coleman	200
Geo. Crook	489

Francis Coleman	150
Jno Clay	350
Wm Coleman Junr	100
Geo. Crooker	30
James Cocke	750
Robt Carlill	100
Jno Clerk	83
Richd Claunton	100
Stephen Cock for Jones' Orph.	2405
	7622

D

Tho Daniell	150
Roger Drayton	270
Joseph Daniell	50
Jo^{n} Doby	500
Geo Dowing	100
Wm Davis	100
Jno Duglas	300
Richd Durding	500
Christ^{o} Davis	50
Tho Dunkin	136
	2156

E

Robt Ellis	50
Jno Epes Senr	530
Wm Epes Senr	750
Jno Epes	300
Wm Epes	633½
Edwd Epes	500
Littlebury Epes	833½
Benj^{a} Evans	700
Tho Edw^{ds}	250
Dan Epes	200
Jno. Evans	800
Jno Ellis Junr	400

Jn° Ellis Senr	400
Mary Evans	400
Peter Evans	270
Capt. Fra Epes	226
	7243

F

Jn° Freeman	300
Wm Frost	50
Jn° Fountaine	350
Robt Fellows	418
Eliz^b Flood	100
Benj Foster	923
Jn° ffield	100
	2241

G

Jno Green	125
Richd Gord	100
David Goodgame	479
James Greithian	363
Mag^r Goodrick	900
Tho Goodwin	150
Hubert Gibeon	250
Richd Griffith	335
James Griffin	100
Charles Gee	484
Charles Gillam	200
Hugh Goelightly	500
Lewis Green	149
Wm Grigg	200
John Gillam	1000
John Goelightly	100
	5435

H

Coll. [Edward] Hill	1000
Dan^ll Hickdon	280

Robt Harthorn	243
Jno Hamlin	1484½
Coll Harrison Esqr	150
Ralph Hill	175
Wm Harrison	1930
Wm Heath	320
Edwd Holloway	100
Robt Hobbs	100
Jno Hobbs Senr	250
Edwd Holloway Senr	620
Jno Hobbs	100
James Harrison	200
Gilbert Haye	200
Richd Hudson	75
Gabriell Harrison	150
Robt Hix	1000
Joseph Holycross	84
Charles Howell	125
Sam Harwell	125
Isaac Hall	450
Jno Howell	183
Tho Howell	25
Mrs. Herbert	3925
Jno Hixs	216
Richd Hamlin	240
Tho Harrison	1077
Eliz^{b} Hamlin	250
Wm Hulme	100
Jeffry Hawkes	125
Adam Heath	300
Jno Hill	160
Jno Hardiman	872
Instance Hall	614
	17366

J

Wm Jones Junr	230
Wm Jones Senr	600
Henry Jones	200
Robert Jones	241
Edmd Irby	800
Nich. Jarrett	700
James Jackson	80
Adam Ivie	200
Tho Jackson	60
James Jones Senr	1100
Henry Ivye	450
Peter Jones	621
Richd Jones	600
Ralph Jackson	110
Joshua Irby	200
John Jones	350
	6542

K

Richd Kirkland	300
John King	50
Henry King	650
Arthur Kavanah	60
Eusobius King	100
	1160

L

John Livesley	300
Samll Lewey	100
Jno Lumbrey	400
Jno Leeneir [Lanier]	700
Mrs. Low	70
Sam Lewey for Nether'ld's [Netherland's] Orph	498
Tho Lewis Senr.	200
Hugh Liegh	762

ffrancis Leadbeatter	100
Jn° Leadbeatter	400
Wm Low	1584
	5114

M

Wm Maddox	190
Robt Munford	339
James Minge, Senr	500
Matt Marks	1500
Samll Moody	328
Francis Mallory	200
Danll Mallone	100
Jn° Mayes	365
Richd More	472
Henry Mitchell, Senr	100
Jn° Mitchell	170
Wm Mayes	763
Edwd Murrell	100
Tho Mitchell Junr	100
Peter Mitchell	305
Henry Mitchell Junr	200
ffrancis Maberry	347
James Matthews	100
Jn° Martin	200
	6839

N

Richd Newman	120
Walter Nunnaley	299
	419

O

Nich° Overburry	809
Jn° Owen	25
	834

P

Geo. Pasmore	330
Francis Poythres Senr	1283
Joseph Pattison	200
Geo. Pace	246
Nathan^{ll} Phillips	150
Jno Price	50
Wm Peoples	150
Eliz^{b} Peoples	235
Joseph Perry	275
Richd Pigeon	524
bs/Thomas Potts	200
Joseph Pritchett	50
Jno Patterson	373
Geo. Pace	1000
Ephram Pakham	300
Tho Poythres	616
David Peoples	60
Grace Perry	100
Jno Poythres Junr	916
Jno Petterson	428
Mr Micajah Perry	600
	9203

R

Jno Roberts	316
Nath. Robinson	100
Roger Reace Junr	100
Henry Read	75
Roger Reace Senr	100
Wm Reanes	250
Frances Raye	300
Jno Reeks	50
Wm Rachell	100
Timothy Reading Senr	460
Jno Riners	200

Edwd Richardson	300
Coll. [William] Randolph	226
	2677

S

Matthew Smart	100
Wm Standback	150
Tho Symmons	566
James Salmon	477
Wm Savage	150
Wm Sandborne	——
Jno Scott	300
Martin Shieffield	150
James Smith	67
John Stroud	60
Richd Scoking	100
Wm Sexton	50
James Seveaker	710
Chichester Sturdivant	214
Daniell Sturdivant	850
Richd Smith	550
Jno Spaine	118
Matthew Sturdivant	150
Capt. Stith	470½
	8272½

T

Maj^r Henry Tooker for ye Merch^ts in London	4600
Geo. Tilliman	446
Jno Tilliman	530
Wm Tomlinson	400
Adam Tapley	377
Capt. John Taylor	1700
Mich. Taburd	150
Maj^r Tooker	181
Robt Tooker	400

Robt Tester	170
Joseph Tooker	200
Wm Temple	100
Jno Thornhill	350
Jno Taylor	100
Nath: Tatham jun^{r} [Tatum]	200
Sam^{ll} Tatham Senr	100
Sam^{ll} Tatham jun^{r}	195
Henry Talley	639
Richd Turberfield	140
Francis Tucker	100
Nathl Tatham Senr.	501
Jno Thrower	250
James Taylor	306
Tho Thrower	150
Sanders Tapley	300
Tho Tapley	300
James Thweat Senr	715
James Thweat Junr	100
Eliz^{b} Tucker	212
Tho Taylor	400
Edwd Thrower	150
	14462

V

Jno Vaughan	169
Sam^{ll} Vaughan	169
Nath Urvein	150
Dan^{ll} Vaughan	169
James Vaughan	169
Richd Vaughan	309
Wm Vaughan	309
Tho: Vinson	550
Nich^{o} Vaughan	169
	2163

W

Jno Woodlife Senr	644
Wm Wallis	200
Jno Witchett	250
Capt. Jos. Wynn	860
Jno Woodlife Junr	750
Jno Winningham Jun	200
Richd Wallpooll	625
Jno Womack	550
Capt. Tho Wynn	400
Jno Wall	233
Tho Winingham	100
Eliz^{b} Woodlife	844
Richd Worthern	1600
Richd Winkles	450
Capt. Nich^{o} Wyatt	700
Antho. Wyatt	250
Valentine Williamson	250
Hurldy Wick	600
Wm Wilkins	900
Francis Wilkins	150
Robt. Winkfield [Wingfield]	107
Jarvis Winkfield	100
Henry Wall	275
Jno Wilkins	150
James Williams	1436
Geo. Williams	210
Jno White	150
Edwd Winingham	100
Sam^{ll} Woodward	600
	13684

Y

Dorrell Young	383
John Young	200
	583

A	3217
B	12986
C	7622
D	2156
E	7243
F	2241
G	5435
H	17366½
J	6542
K	1160
L	5114
M	6839
N	419
O	834
P	9203
R	2677
S	8272
T	14462
V	2163
W	13684
Y	583
Totall	127218½

Orphans Lands which is refused paying Quit Rents for viz[t]

	Acres
Mr. Jn[o] Banister orphans p Steph: Cock	1970
Capt. Henry Bates [Batte's] orph p their Mother Mrs. Mary Bates	1200
Capt. Hen: Randolph orph[s] p Capt. Giles Webb	129
Morris ffalliham orph[s] p Robt. Rivers	200
Crockson Land formerly who it belongs to now I cannot find	750
	4249

Deduct the new discovered Land 10000

accounted for 117218½ acres at 24[ls] tob[o] p 100 is 28132[ls] tobacco at 5[s] p C[t] is

	£	s	d
	£70	6	6
Sallary 10 p C[t] 2813	7	0	10½
	63	5	7½

p W[m] Epes Sherriff

VIRGINIA GLEANINGS IN ENGLAND

Contributed by Reginald M. Glencross, 176 Worple Road, Wimbledon, London, S. D. 19, England.

(Continued)

JOHN LANIER

Will dat. 27 Jan 1649 My wife Ellinor Lanier to be ex'trix in whatsoever is due to me either in the Exchequer or the Great Wardrobe or the Treasury Chamber. She to have disposing of my children. Witnesses: Edw. Maylard, John Roberts. Prob. 28 Aug. 1650 by Eleanor L. relict & extrix.

Pembroke, 135.

ELINOR LANIERE relict or widow of John L., of London, late dec.

Will dat. 23 Apr 1652. To be bur'd in St Giles' churchyard where my late husband was. To my son John L. ring etc., his father's picture & all his books. To my dau'r. Frances, silver porringer etc., moneys at my present chambers. To my dau'r. Elizabeth, Spanish silver dish etc. Whereas there is due to me from Mr. Thomas Harris for so much goods of mine as he hath now in his hands, £70, same to my dau'r. Frances for maintenance of my younger dau'r. Elizabeth. To my mother my deathshead ring. Whereas there is an estate fallen to me by death of my kinsman Mr. John Woodburne, which is yet in dispute, what is due to go between my three children John, Frances & Elizabeth, And whereas my late husband Jo. L, left me his executrix & bequeathed me his whole estate & several sums still due, same to sd. three children equally, John & Elizabeth being under 18 & unmarried. My son in law

Thomas Hubbard to be ex'or & Mr. Ambrose Jennings, of London, merchant, to be overseer. Witnesses: Will. Lullingden, Richard Seaman Prob. 22 July 1652 by Thomas Hubbard, the ex'or. *Bowyer*, 150.

[In this Magazine XXV, 407 &c, XXVI, 321 &c, a kinship was traced between Thomas Jefferson and John Lilburne, the ardent defender of popular rights in England in the Seventeenth century. It would be as interesting a study in heredity if the descent of Sydney Lanier could be traced from the family of the name who, as composers, musicians and artists, were in the service of the English court from the time of Henry VIII through the reign of Charles II.

The emigrant ancestor of the Virginia family (Sydney Lanier's ancestor) was John Lanier, who lived in what is now Prince George County in 1676. He died in 1717 leaving four sons, Nicholas, Sampson, John and Robert. It will be seen that Nicholas was a favorite name among the English Laniers. There is a short account of the Virginia family in the *William & Mary Quarterly* XV, 77-79.

The Laniers in England are stated in the *Dictionary of National Biography*, to have been of French origin. John Lanier, who died in 1572 is referred to, in 1577, as having been a musician and a native of Rouen, France. He owned property in Crutched Friars, parish of St. Olave, Hart Street, London. He was probably father of "John Lanyer, musician to her Matie". This John Lanyer or Lanier, married, Oct. 12, 1585, at the Church of the Holy Minories, London, Frances, daughter of Marc Anthony Galliardo, who had served as musician to Henry VIII and his three successors.

The most distinguished of the family, Nicholas, son of John Lanier just referred to, was baptized at the Holy Minories, London, Sept. 10, 1588. He became a musician in the royal household and in 1604 was "musician of the flutes". He held, subsequently, a high position among the royal musicians, both as a composer and performer. Among other music he composed that for Ben Jonson's masques; "Lovers Made Men" (1617), and "The Vision of Delights", as well as painting the scenery for the latter. At the accession of James I he was made Master of the Music, with a pension of £200 a year. He was also a painter and skilled amateur of works of art. In 1625 he was sent abroad by Charles I, to purchase pictures and statues, and is considered to have been the first, with the exception of Thomas, Earl of Arundel, to appreciate the worth of drawings and sketches by the great masters. With the outbreak of the Civil War the fortunes of the family declined, and Nicholas Lanier followed the Stuarts into exile. At the Restoration he was restored to his office and died Feb. 1665-6.

Another Nicholas Lanier, probably uncle to the preceding, was musician to Queen Elizabeth in 1581 &c. He owned considerable property in East Greenwich, Blackheath and the neighborhood. He had four daughters and six sons, John (died 1650), Alphonso (d. 1613), Innocent (d. 1615), Jerome (d. 1657), Clement (d. 1661) and Andrea (d. 1659). All of these were musicians in the service of the crown and some of their children succeeded to their posts.

The will of Nicholas Lanyer, gent., gave his lands &c. to his wife Lucrece, and 12 d. apiece to his sons named. Mrs. Lucretia Lanier was buried at Greenwich, May 31, 1634.

Another Nicholas Lanier, probably a cousin of the musician and painter, was born in 1568 and published two volumes of etchings. He was probably the person of the name buried at St. Martins-in-the-Fields, Nov. 4, 1646.

It is possible that the John Lanier, named in the wills above, was the emigrant to Virginia.]

DEBORA FLEETE, of Westminster, widow.

Will dat. 27 Mar. 1651. All goods to my cousins Sir Robert Filmer & Sir Edward Filmer, both of East Sutton, Kent, knights, & they to be ex'ors, towards payment of such sums as sd. Sir R. Filmer lent me & my son Henry Fleete towards the recovering of my sd. son of a great sickness & for furnishing him with provisions & necessaries for his last voyage to Virginia. Witnesses: Henry Frenoham, Thomas Davy. Prob. 23 Jan. 1651[-2] by Sir Robert Filmer, knight, one of the ex'ors. Power reserved for Sir Edward Filmer, knight etc other ex'or. *Bowyer*, 5.

DOROTHIE SCOTT of London, spinster.

Will dat. 5 Mar. 1632(-3) 8 Car. I. To my brother Thomas S. esq. a silver spoon. To my friend Mrs Elizabeth Grovenor, widow, with whom I now sojourn, £5. To her dau'r. Elizabeth G. £3. Rest of goods to my sister Deborah Fleete (and she to be) ex'trix. My friend Sir Robert Phillmer, knight, to be overseer. Witnes: Thomas Dutton, Scrivener.
Prob. 29 June 1650 by Deborah Fleete, the ex'trix.

Pembroke, 100.

[Debora Fleete and Dorothie Scott were daughters of Charles Scott, of Egerton, Kent, (and his wife Jane, daughter of Sir Thomas Wyatt, of Allington Castle) and granddaughters of Sir Reginald Scott, of Scotts Hall, Kent. Debora married William Fleet, gent., of Chartham, Kent, a member of the Virginia Company, and had (with several other sons and daughters, some of whom emigrated to Maryland) a son Henry, born 1595-1600, died about 1661, who emigrated to Virginia and became a very prominent man in that colony and in Maryland. For notices of him and his descendants, see this Magazine II, 70-76, and V, 253-254.

The people to whom the Fleets were related form another of those groups of Kentish kinsfolk so closely associated with the colony of Virginia. Charles Scott, of Egerton, had a sister, Mary, who married Richard Argall, of East Sutton, Kent, and was the mother of Captain (afterwards Sir) Samuel Argall, Governor of Virginia, and of Elizabeth Argall, who married Sir Edward Filmer, of East Sutton. Lady Filmer was, in turn, the mother of Henry Filmer, who emigrated to Virginia, and of Sir Robert and Sir Edward Filmer, named in Debora Fleet's will. Jane Wyatt, wife of Charles Scott, was aunt of Sir Francis Wyatt, Governor of Virginia, and of Rev. Hawte Wyatt, minister at Jamestown. George Wyatt, brother of Jane (Wyatt) Scott married Jane Finch, who was aunt of Henry Finch, who emigrated to Virginia, and was member of the Council, 1630 &c. The paternal grandmother of Henry Fleet, the emigrant, Katherine (Honeywood) Fleet, was aunt of Col. (afterwards Sir) Philip Honeywood, one of the Royalist officers, who took refuge in Virginia in 1649.]

SIR EUSEBY ISHAM. "A note of such debts as I require my wife to pay". To my brother Tipping £5. To my cosin William Downall 42s. To Robert Lade of Cransby £10. To my son John Isham my sorrel mare. To Mr. (sic) Barbon so much money as she will say I ought to pay her. To Saxby the man that dwelled in my grounds £10. 4s. 0d. To my son Euseby Isham "as you can" £66. 13s. 4d. To my sons William and Thomas I refer them to yourself. To the servants with you a year's wages. To Richard Berry 60s. To Steynes for a horse £4. 10s. 0d. To my man Barber if he go away 40s. To poor of Picheley £5. Small debts which I cannot call to mind I pray you see paid. Witnesses: Feargod Barbon, Ha. Kinnesman. Memorandum that I Harold Kymesman of Picheley gent wished by Sir Euseby Isham, knight, on 7th June last to write the particulars specified as he spoke it which I did in his presence. He desired that his wife should see legacies paid . . . his sickness being such and he so short taken he could not do more neither was he desirous to the articles on Feargod Barbon subscribed as a witness, And to this I will depose Sir Euseby said he could not live long and his wife should have all. Anne should have all. 27 July 1626 emat com' to Lady Ann Isham. relict of Sir Euseby Isham, Militis. 1st

January 1627 em't com' to Thomas Isham fil. nat. et ltmo. etc. *Hele*, 100.

Dame Anne Isham, late wife of Sir Euseby Isham of Pitchley county Northampton, Knight. Will 3 December 1627; proved 1st January 1627. Body to chancel at Pitchley. To my son Euseby Isham £150. To my son William Isham £200. To Euseby Isham son of said William £100. To said son Euseby Isham my Cabbinett. To Susan his wife my gilt cups. My border of Goldsmiths work to Mary wife of my son William. To my daughter Mary wife of Sir Fleetwood Dormer knight, two geldings. To my daughter Susan wife of Thomas Threlfall pearl chain and 20 marks. £100 which I owe to Euseby Glover my grandchild to be paid to him. To Susan Isham my gentlewoman £10. To each of my servants 4 marks. To poor of Pitchley £5. Residue of my goods to my youngest son Thomas Isham sole executor. I not meddling with goods left by my late husband Sir Euseby Isham to my eldest son John Isham deceased. Witnesses: Ri: Houselepp, Saml Garthwaite. *Barrington*, 4.

John Isham of Braunston, county Northampton, Esquier. Will 29 September 1624; proved 4 May 1627. Sir Eusebie Isham my father and Thomas Isham my brother executors. To Thomas Isham said brother lease of the parsonage in Braunston and tithes belonging. To Ann Lane my daughter £10. To Blaise Adams for his pains £10 and all my wearing apparel. To William Eare my servant £20. To Robert Tymes £10. To John Allen my servant £6. 13s. 4d. To poor of Braunston £10. To poor of Vichley [Pitchley?] £5. Residue of my goods to my executors. Witnesses: Wm. Southam, Thos. Makepease, Richd Cooke, John Clarke, Blaise Adams. Codicil 8 December 1626. As the said Sir Eusebie my late father is deceased I now appoint my said brother Thomas sole executor to whom all benefit of my goods. I have given into the hands of Thomas Makepeace, William Southam, Robert Foster and Henry Bree four ancient copyholders of my Manor of Braunston £20 to be lent from year to year to three of the poorest copyholders of my said Manor at 8% said profit and increase to be distributed amongst six poor widows of the town of Braunston. My executor shall provide one treble bell tunable to the four bells already in the Church. To my cosen Gregory Isham 4 milk beasts. To my brother in law Thomas Threlfall 30 hoggerells, my stone horse and 7 cows. To Hanna my maid a cow. To Robert Tymes my sorrell mare and apparel. To my servant John Allen my grey Nagg and apparel. To Isaac Moule 20s. To Zephania Southam 2 ewes and my horse Geers. To Martha Burrowes one ewe for watching with me. Witnesses: Gregory Isham, This Threlfall, John Allen, Robt Tymmes. *Skynner,* 52.

[The wills given above are those of Sir Euseby Isham, of Pytchley, (b. Feb. 26, 1552, d. June 11, 1626), grandfather of Henry Isham, the emigrant to Virginia; of Anne, daughter of John Borlase, of Marlowe, Co. Bucks., wife of Sir Euseby, and of their son John, an uncle of the emigrant. It will be noted that the famous Praisegod Barbon or Barebones, was a witness to Sir Euseby's will. For other Isham wills and notes on the family, see this Magazine IV, 123-124 and XVIII, 85-87.]

(To be continued)

PRESTON PAPERS

(From the originals in the Virginia State Library)

(Continued)

COL. WILLIAM PRESTON TO THE FIELD OFFICERS,
AUG. 24, 1782.

Sir

The act of Assembly for recruiting this States Quota of Men just came to hand In consequence of which I have appointed all the late Officers Lt Captain or the commanding Officers of Companies to meet at the Court House of this County on Monday the 15th day of September that the said act may be put immediately into Execution. You are hereby required to attend with a fair and just list of your whole Company from sixteen years of age to fifty, making a Distinction of such as are under eighteen years.

You are to give your company notice that they are to be laid of in Classes or Districts of fifteen men each, that such as have any Infirmities of Body and are not exempted may attend a Court Martial who will meet at that time & for that, as well as other purposes.

You are also to make return of what Beeves & cloaths your company hath furnished under a late act of assembly, which must by no means be omitted; as has been hitherto the case altho often required. You are likewise Required to bring with you a list of all the men your Company has furnished for the Army either by Draught or Enlistment Since the Spring of the Year 1777. If you do not of your own Knowledge know the number of men or their names you will take the best information you can get in the Company, not omitting such as deserted.

You will please to observe that there is a fine of £20 on each Officer who fails to appear as above directed, to be recovered by Information to the Court in a Summary Way But I hope a sense of our 'Duty to the Country will induce every Officer to attend with cheerfulness, and give all the Assistance we can to carry this necessary act into Execution.

I am Sir your humble Servt

Wm Preston

Copy of a Letter to the field Officers Augt 24th 1782

[Endorsement]

CIRCULAR.

War Office Nov. 8th 82

Sir

His Excellency the Governor in Council has directed me to apply to the Several county Lieutenants & recruiting Officers for an immediate Return of what money they have received & what men have been recruited.

I must therefore beg the favor of you to furnish me with this return as soon as possible.

I am, Sir, very respectfully

Your most obed. Servant

William Davies

Montgomery

[Addressed] County Lieutenant—Montgomery

[Endorsement] Answered & a return made 19th Dec. 1782

WALTER CROCKETT TO WILLIAM PRESTON.

Fort Chiswell[1] Novr 9th 1782.

Sir

The Officers and Men that were ordered out on the Tour to

---

1 Fort Chiswell, between the present Wytheville and New River, was built by Col. William Byrd (3rd) and named for Col. John Chiswell. The latter was the chief owner of the lead mines nearby, which furnished large supplies to Virginia during the Revolution and the Confederacy.

Clinch have all returned Home again, and say that there were but ten or twelve that met at the place appointed & many of them without Arms, all the others that were ordered never moved from Home. The principal reasons that they render for their not proceeding is that there was no Salt & that they would not go there to live three weeks on fresh Provision. I would thank you for your advice in the matter, as I am at a loss to know how to proceed therein.

This Bearer Henry Kiesler will be the only speedy hand to bring anything you write on the subject—

I am Sir your Mo. Obedient
& very Hble Servant

Walter Crockett

P. S. Kiesler will also carry a bushell of Salt if there be any for the use of the Men—
[Address] To Colo. William Preston
Walter Crockett—Public Service
[Endorsement] Walter Crockett to Col. Preston 9 Nov. 1782

Col. William Preston to a Collector, Nov. 12, 1782.

Montgomery S. C. T.

Whereas by a Return made this Day by John Charlton, Collector of 45th Division of Militia of this County, it appears that several have failed to pay their proportion of a Tax imposed by a late act of assembly for the purpose of recruiting this States Quota of Troops to serve in the Continental Army. You are hereby authorized and required to collect by Distress & Sale of their Property, as in the case of Parish and County Leevies the following Sum annexed to each Persons name that is to say from Lottin Romaine 1/3, Benjamin Donathan 1/3 William Lawson 2/6 & John Wylie 1/6; & return the same to me on or before the 20th of November this Instant & this shall be your Warrant for so doing.

Given under my hand this 12th day of Novr 1782
Wm Preston

To the Collector to Execute
& make Return
[Endorsement] Charltons return of his Collection
p'^{d}

GEORGE PEARY TO COL. WILLIAM PRESTON, DEC. 17, 1782.

Sir

I have sent by the bearer Wm Kavanaugh the District money for Aplegate & Langley & as for Arain Dooley, Charles Cidwell, John G. Runion & Thomas Stanton They are not in this County nor hant bin sence Last Spring & I understand all but Runian had thire famleys in Bedford County & was Trying to Shift Duty when they were hear So I can do no more & I shall humbly thank you for a Clearance for this Part of Duty

I am Sir your Humble Ser^{t}
Geo. Peary

De$^{c'er}$ the 17th 1782
To Col Wm Preston
[Endorsement] Geo. Pearys'
ab^{t} Collection
1782

COL. WILLIAM PRESTON TO COL. DAVIES.

Montgomery Decr 19th 1782

Sir

Yours of the 8th of November came to hand the 25th of that month while I was on a Journey to Botetourt where I was necessarily detained two weeks, and not finding any conveyance from there, nor since I returned till this day by Mr Granville Smith I therefore could not make the return you requested.

Enclosed you have Lieut. Rhea's[2] receipt for £95—18—4. Since the date thereof I have rec'd which I have by me. I cannot say what success Mr. Rhea has had in recruiting since the 6th of November last when we parted. Before that I know he was very industrious in the business but without success.—A few days ago I enlisted one man and sent him to Mr. Rhea in Washington. I paid him forty Dollars & he lodged thirty of them. With me untill he would be on his march. down by way of security that he would not desert.

Several of the Collectors have been deficient in making their returns and I have given them Notice that I shall move the Court for a Judgment against them; but as will probably be no Court before march I dont think it will be in my power to close this very troublesome business before then,—In the meantime I shall urge them to a settlement all I can.

I am, with great esteem, Sir your most Obt
& very hble Servt
Wm Preston

Colo Davies

Col. William Preston to the Governor.

Montgomery Dec 20th 1782

Sir

The Court of this County have directed me to lay the enclosed recomendation before your Excellency that the several Persons mentioned therein may be added to the Commission of the Peace for this County.

If your Excellency will be pleased to order the Commissions to be made out the bearer Mr. Granville Smith will forward

---

2 This was Matthew Rhea, Lieutenant and Quartermaster. He was regimental quartermaster 7th Va. Regiment, June 15, 1777, 2d Lieutenant, Sept. 9, 1778, transferred to 5th Va., Sept. 14, 1778, 1st Lt. July 4, 1779, transferred to 7th Va. Feb. 12, 1781, and served to the end of the war.

John Rhea, was ensign 7th Va., Jan. 16, 1777, discharged Nov. 1777 and died May 27, 1832. Jesse Rhea, Joseph Rhea, Robert Rhea, David Rhea, and Philips Rhea also served in the Revolution from Virginia.

it to me by a safe conveyance. This will really oblige the County as one or two Justices have removed since the recommendation was made, exclusive of those mentioned therein.

I am your Excellenceys most obed[t]
h[ble] Serv[t]

The Governor— W[m] Preston

LIST OF THE FINES RECEIVED FOR THE BOUNTY OF SOLDIERS.

List of the Fines rec'd for the Bounty of Soldiers before the 20th of Dec[r] 1782 with the names of the Collectors & No. of each Division.

No.		£		
1	John Adams	4	13	3½
2	Joseph White	5	10	2½
3	John Miller	3	7	10
4	James Newell	3	9	6½
5	Saml Ewing Sen[r]	1	14	0
6	George Duff	2	0	6
7	Philip Cannady			
8	Robert Love	2	16	3½
9	James White	4	12	1½
10	John Bustard	2	17	3
11	Flower Swift			
12	Benjamin Hartgrove			
13	Nathan Ward			
14	John Bedsolt			
15	Jacob Eliott			
16	James M[c]Donald		14	3
17	William Harraldson		6	
18	George Reives			
19	Jacob Stamper			
20	Charles Morgan	2	9	6
21	James Wade			
22	Joseph Glover		7	9
23	Moses Johnson			

24	Daniel Keith J^{r}	2	15	9
25	Enoch Osburn		10	9
26	Edmund Wood	1	15	7
27	Robert Buchanan	4	16	1
28	Robert Davis	6	3	4
29	William Campbell	4	7	1
30	Henry Patton	5	3	11
31	$Alex^{r}$ Mares	5	11	10
32	Daniel How	4	16	10
33	Andrew Crockett	4	6	9
36	John Thompson Sayers	6	5	11
37	Frederick Edwards	5	15	3
38	William Hays	2	5	10
39	George McCown	7	13	7½
40	David Doak			
41	Philip Barrier	7	12	5
42	John Ward			
43	William Love	2	14	
44	Spencer Rice	1	5	8
45	William Davis	4	9	10
46	Ezekiel Young	1	17	3
47	Richard Wynatt	2	2	10
48	Thomas Peery	3	5	9
49	Thomas Burk	3	8	2
50	John Hayes	1	16	8
51	Edmund Vancill	2	9	7
52	Israel Lorton	3	6	5
53	Joseph Polley	2	4	5
54	Daniel Witcher	1	12	1½
56	Hercules Ogill	1	15	10
57	Benjamin Baily		19	3½
58	William Doak	3	1	8
59	Isaac Petterson	2	4	1½
60	Jeremiah Pate	2	6	8
61	Isaac Stephens	3	3	7
62	James Byrns	4	4	5
63	James Maxwell	2	13	6
64	Robert Davis	2	2	11

65	Alex[r] Neily			
66	William Bobbit	7	18	
67	Saml Tinley	1	16	7
68	Aron Collier	1	10	1
69	Christian Saidon	2	9	1
70	Joseph Mares	3	9	6
71	William Kavenaugh	3	6	9
72	Samuel Ewing	2	15	3
73	Adam Wall	4	8	
74	James Moore			
75	Charles Carter			
76	George Pearis	2	17	8
77	Joshua Richardson	1	17	8
78	Stephen Sanders & Alex[r] Neeley	8	0	10½
79	William Davidson			
80	John Chapman	1	11	7
81	William M[c]farland	1	10	1

List of sums pd. by Collectors

[Endorsement]

Letters to the Governour & Col[o] Davis Dec 19th 1782 about the Collection & a memo Commissions—

(To be continued)

VIRGINIA IN 1683

(Abstracts by W. N. Sainsbury and Copies in the McDonald and DeJarnette Papers (Virginia State Library), from the British Public Record Office.

(Continued)

Order for Mrs. Bland to Give Security.

At the Court at White Hall the 26th of April 1683
present
The Kings most Exct Maty in Council
Whereas upon the Petition and Appeal of Sarah Bland Widdow and one of the Executors of John Bland[1] late of London Merchant from divers sentences given against her in the Courts of Virga His Maty in Council the third day of August last was pleased to order the Governor and Council there to take care that as well as the said Sarah Bland as the other parties in the Peticon mentioned should give good and sufficient security to make their appearances and to answer the determination of this Board a. by ye said Order more at large

1 John Bland was the 4th child of John Bland, also an eminent London merchant. John Bland, the younger, is mentioned in Pepys Diary, under date, June 12, 1680, when he states that Mr. Bland was buried in the Chancel of St. Olaves, Hart Street, London.

John Bland (Jr.) was actively engaged in business in and with the Colony of Virginia. He prepared an able remonstrance "in behalf of the Inhabitants and Planters in Virginia and Mariland" against the Navigation Act, which was printed in our Magazine I, 141-155. He is stated to have expended £10,000 sterling in Virginia. An act in Hening (1752) VI, 303, shows that John Bland owned 8000 acres in Charles City County, called Kymages.

Theoderick Bland (ancestor of the Virginia family), brother of John Bland, came to Virginia as his agent. The suit against Mrs. Sarah Bland was brought by St. Leger Codd and his wife, the widow of Theoderick Bland. John Bland was the father of Giles Bland, executed in Virginia for taking part in Bacon's Rebellion.

appeareth And the said Appellant having this day further Petitioned His Ma^{ty} in Council setting forth that having endeavoured all that within her lyeth to comply with the said Order Shee finds that by reason of the prevalency of the other parties residing there Shee cannot during her absence without great difficulty and delay procure such security as is thereby required And praying that Shee may be admitted to give security here to answer the determination of this Board in her said Appeal; His Ma^{ty} in Council was pleased to Order and It is hereby ordered that the Clerk of the Council in wayting do take good and sufficient security of the said Sarah Bland that she shall answer such determination in her said Appeal as His Ma^{ty} in Council shall think most just And it is further Ordered that Shee be excused from giving any further security in Virginia, the said order above mentioned or any other order or Instruction to the Governor or Council of Virginia touching the method of proceeding in Appeals to the Contrary notwithstanding

Francis Gwyn

Secretary Spencer to the Committee of Trade and Plantations.

May it please your Lo^{ps}

Since my last to your Lo^{ps} noe matter of moment hath occurred in this His Maties Government therefore should not now have presumed to have troubled your Lo^{ps} but in obedience to your Lo^{ps} commands in transmitting Copies of Orders of Council and political matters registered in my Office which are herewith humbly presented to your Lo^{ps} being as am commanded a Duplicat.

By His Ex^{cy} my Lord Culpeper I presume your Lo^{ps} have received the satisfaction of the intire well settlement of His Maties affaire in this Government which continues in the like good State, and have noe apprehension of their otherwise being—In which the faithful service of him shall not be wanting who beggs leave to subscribe himselfe your Lo^{ps} most humble and Obedient Servant.

Nich^{o} Spencer

Virginia July 16th 1683

LORDS OF TRADE AND PLANTATIONS TO LORD CULPEPER.

Council Chamber
24th August 1683

My Lord

The Right Hono^{ble} the Lords of the Committee for Trade and Foreign Plantations having this day read your Lo^{ps} Instructions bearing date 27th Jan^{ry} 1681-2 have commanded mee to signify their desires that your Lo^{p} give them as soon as may bee a particular and distinct Account in Writing how your Lo^{p} has observed and complyed with each of the said Instructions, with the proceedings that have been had thereupon

---

LORD CULPEPER TO THE LORDS OF TRADE AND PLANTATIONS
2 SEPTEMBER 1683.

In pursuance of your Lord^{ppes} Commands by Mr. Blathwaite Dated 24th August last, when I was extremely ill, though I should more willingly have presented it in person, you will now receive A Particular Account of Each Instruction written on the other side of it, wch being voluminous, hath taken up more time than I expected, And my sicknesse hath been a very great Hindrance alsoe, for there was nothing I desired more, and had notice come sooner, as I earnestly expected, you had been sooner obeyed by

You Lord^{ppes}
Most Humble Servant

Tho. Culpeper

S. P. O. Va. vol. 65.

INSTRUCTIONS FOR MY LORD CULPEPER WITH AN ACC'T OF HIS LOP'S COMPLIANCE THEREWITH[2].

Charles R

Instructions for Our Right Trusty and Well beloved Thomas Lord Culpeper Our Lieutenant and Governor General of Our Colony and Dominion of Virginia in America and, in his absence, to ye Commander in Cheif of Our said Colony Given at Our Court at Whitehall the 27th day of Jan^ry^ 1681-2 in ye 33th year of Our Reigne.

Whereas by Our Letters Patents under Our Great Seal of England bearing date the eight day of July in the 27th Year of Our Reigne. Wee granted unto you Thomas Lord Culpeper the Office of Our Lieut. and Govr General of Our Colony and Dominion of Virginia to hold, execute and enjoy the said Office during your natural life next @ immediately after ye death, surrender forfeiture or other determination of the Interest of Sir Wm Berkley Kn^t^.

And whereas you are from ye death or other avoydance of ye sd. Sir Wm Berkley, by vertue of Our said L'res Patents, become possessed of the said Office of Our Lieuten^t^ and Governor General of Our said Colony and Dominion; You shall therefore fit yourselfe with all convenient speed and repair to Virginia.

I was actually ready in every respect on the 15th of September last 1682 But either by the fault of the Captain, or of the victuallers (for a fault there was) The Newmayde: Fregat sailed not out of the Downes till the 2^d^ October, and stopped at Plymouth to take in Provisions till the 6th and after a tedious Danjerous Winter passage (all alone) arrived not in Virginia till the 16th December, whereas severall other Virginia ships that came into the Downes after us, sailed thence before us viz. on the 25th of September aforesaid, and takeing advantage of the Faire Easterly Wind had (all) Quick passages, particularly Capt. Arnold, and Capt. George Purvis, the latter

---

[2] Culpeper's account of how he carried out his instructions affords valuable information in regard to Virginia at that time.

whereof came to an anchour within the Capes on the last day of October.

And, being arrived there, you are forthwith to call a meeting of y[e] Members of Our Council for that Our Colony and Dominion, by name,

Sr. *Hen. Chicheley Lt. Gov*[r].

Nathaniel Bacon	Esqrs.	William Cole	Esqrs.
Nicholas Spencer		*John Custis*	
Robert Smith		Richard Lee	
Philip Ludwell		Ralph Wormly	

John Page Esq[r]

I had a full Councell on the 18th December But in regard *Col. William Byrd* was an Eminent member of the Assembly then sitting, I did not sweare him till the first councell day after the Dissolution thereof, viz. 10th January following. *Col. Matthew Kempe* died two or three dayes before my Arrival.

Joseph Bridger Esq. Mathew Kemp Esq. William Byrd Esq.

At which meeting, after having published in usual manner Our said Letters Patents constituting you Our Lieut. and Gov[r] General of Our said Colony @ Dominion, you shall take yourself and also administer the Oaths of Allegiance @ Supremacy @ all such other Oaths usualy taken @ administered as by Our Commission or y[e] powers given you under Our great Seal is directed.

(To be continued)

VA. STATE TROOPS IN THE REVOLUTION

(Continued)

Ditto paid Ditto for Arms Purchased for the Public Service	10	10	
Ditto paid John Coffer for Pay of Cap^{n} Masons Company of Minute Men in Prince William District	77	9	7
Ditto paid David Clark for Provisions furnished Cap^{n} Greens Company	1		
Ditto paid Ditto for Provisions to Cap^{n} Dabneys Company.	1	4	6
Ditto paid Harry Dudley for Ferriage to Sundry Troops..	2	4	8
Ditto paid Christopher Harwood for Provisions to Cap^{n} Smiths Company	19	13	6
Ditto paid Ditto for Cart & Horse hire to the public by S. Field	2	5	
Ditto paid Thomas Slate for making a Suit of Colours....	1		
Ditto paid Manor Dixon for a Gun sold to the Public.....	3		
To cash paid Captain James Barron for Rowe Cowper for wood to the Troops at Hampton	21	12	
To Ditto paid Ditto for Forage allowed his as a Militia Officer	17	11	
Ditto paid Ditto for Horse Hire for the Guard at Mill Point..	5	10	
Ditto paid James Ball for Waggonage & Provisions to a company of Regulars	46	12	3
Ditto paid John Hulingson for a Gun furnished the Army..	1		
Ditto paid James Shields for Corn & Fodder furnished Ditto	172	10	

	Ditto paid John Taylor balance of his Account as Quarter Master	11	2	6
	Ditto paid Martin Hawkins for Wood Etc. to the Troops at Hampton	43	12	7½
	Ditto paid George Stubberfield Balance of his Recruiting Account ..	41		
7	Ditto paid Samuel Parks for a Rifle furnished public service	5	10	
	Ditto paid Ditto for Lewis Willis for Wood Etc to Prince William Battalion	5	5	
	Ditto paid Ditto for John Picket for Provisions to the Culpepper Battalion	1	8	

(To be continued)

ORANGE COUNTY MARRIAGES

(Concluded.)

Reuben Boston—Mary Anderson, Geo. Bingham.
Jeremias Rogers—Elizabeth Ferguson, Geo. Bingham.

1810

Wm. Parrott—Judith Wayland, Jacob Watts.
Fred'k Harman—Mary Jimerson, Robt. Jones.
Hamlet Sanford—Phebe Biggers, Robt. Jones.
Rich'd White—Auney Wayt, Jacob Watts.
Reuben Stowers—Margaret Jackson, Jacob Watts.
Joel Marr—Betsey Miller, Jacob Watts.
Henry Marshall—Elizabeth Walton, Geo. Bingham.
Wm. Cane—Mary Snow, Geo. Bingham.
Abraham Estes—Sally Cox, Jacob Watts.
Joseph Kirtley—Elizabeth Sims, Jacob Watts.
Willis Loyd—Felicia Agheart, Geo. Bingham.
John Beadler—Lucinda Haynes, Geo. Bingham.
Saron Simpson—Mary Millican, Jere Chandler.
Charles Yates—Betsey Loyd, Jere Chandler.
Joseph H. Schooler—Dolly Quisenberry, Jere Chandler.
Washington Hoard—Elizabeth Adams, Jere Chandler.
Thomas Rogers—Penelope Chanceller, Jere Chandler.
John Hensley—Elizabeth Oliver, A. Brockman.
Ambrose Henderson—Lucy Acre, A. Brockman.

NOTES AND QUERIES

CORRECTIONS.

During the months in which the April and July numbers, 1920, were in course of publication, copy was exchanged several times between the various printers employed, and, by accident, the concluding portion of Orange County Marriages, was published in the April number, while the sections which should have immediately preceded, were published in the July number and in this one. Mr. Scott's valuable contribution has now been completed.

P. 141, line 1, for "Oprie" read "Opie".

P. 169, line 9 from top, for "charity" read "charily".

P. 253, line 6 from top, for "Stauard" read "Stanard".

P. 254, line 1, for "Math'l Ferry" read "Nath'l Terry", and on line 5, for "Ferry" read "Terry".

In "Proceedings of Annual Meeting" p. ix, for "S. A. Longe" read "S. H. Yonge".

WAR NOTES.

On Dec. 11, 1920, the navy decorated an officer of the army with its Distinguished Service Medal when Major Gen. David C. Shanks received the honor in formal ceremonies at the Boston Navy Yard.

The award was made in recognition of the services of General Shanks in co-operating with the navy while he was in command of the port of embarkation at Hoboken, N. J., in the transport of troops during the war.

Major General Shanks, who is a native of Salem, Va., commanded the Port of Debarkation at Hoboken, N. J., Aug. 1, 1917–Sept. 9, 1918, and Dec. 9, 1918- —. He is now in command, 1st Army Corps, headquarters at Boston.

A SOUTHERN WOMAN IN WAR TIME.

There recently came to light a private memorandum book formerly belonging to Mrs. Mary Mann (Page) Williamson, of Orange County. She had written in it various things which she did not know any eye but her own would ever see. An expression of her thoughts at the beginning of 1865 gives a good example of the hopefulness and undaunted courage of Southern women, even at this dark hour of the Confederacy. Mrs. Williamson's only son, then a mere youth, the late Joseph A. Williamson, of Frederick, Md., was serving in the Richmond Howitzers, C. S. A., and her son-in-law, Major and Surgeon (afterwards Bishop) John B. Newton, had actively served in the Confederate Army from the beginning.

"1st Jan. 1865.

Exit 1864 buried in the tomb of ages. Enter 1865 new born of time, and swaddled in a robe of snow. One more turning of a new leaf in the book of time. There is casting up of accounts and a squaring of records in Heaven and upon earth between man and his Maker—between man and man. The record of this year in the experience of *this people* has been written with a pen of iron, dipped in ink mixed with blood and tears, and the story is the repetition of the bloody annals of the three preceding years. But girding our loins at this retrospective point of affairs and buckling on the armour of a just cause, let the people resolve *D. V.* to make 1865 the birth year of our national independence."

Medical Prescriptions of 1812.

We are indebted to Mr. W. W. Scott, State Law Librarian, for two notes from Dr. Robert H. Rose, to Mrs. Scott of Orange County, containing prescriptions. Dr. Rose was a descendant of Rev. Robert Rose and married Frances Taylor Madison, a sister of President Madison.

(1)

Sunday, March 15th 1812.

Madam,

I have sent by Betty a paper of [word missing at edge of page] she shou'd take fifteen grains three times a day in a Table spoonful of Sassafras Tea. She ought to begin with them in the morning. I have given her a dose of Calomel. When she has taken all the Powders I shall be glad to see her again. My opinion is that complaint is a Tetter which I fear will be very difficult to cure. She ought to take Burdock concoction every [day?] at least a pint. I give the receipt to make it below,

I am respectfully your obt Servt,

Robert H. Rose.

Mrs. Sarah Scott.

Take two ounces of Burdock root and three ounces of iner bark of sassafras and put them into three pints of water & boil to two. Dose from a Pint to a Quart a day.

(2)

Mrs. Scott will give Diana a Tablespoonful of mixture every two hours unless her fever shou'd get highr, when it must be given once every hour. She must have glisters frequently given her during the course of the day to aid the operation of the mixture and if it should not have the effect desired she must give her a dose of Salts. At night she must take a Tea spoonful of Paregoric and also in the day after pains should be severe. She must put the sugar of lead in a quart of water and have two Tablespoonfuls injected three times a day and milk & water as often as convenient,

Robert H. Rose.

Mrs. S. Scott.

SIR RICHARD LANE.

Henry Randolph and his nephew William Randolph, of "Turkey Island", the emigrants to Virginia, not only had associations with literature through Thomas Randolph, the poet, but with law, through Sir Richard Lane.

William Randolph married, first, Elizabeth Smith, and had issue, Thomas Randolph, the poet; and second, Dorothy, daughter of Richard Lane, of Curteenhall, gent., (and his wife Elizabeth, daughter of Clement Vincent, of Harpole), and sister of Sir Richard Lane.

This Richard Lane, brother of Mrs. Randolph, was baptized at Harpole, Northamptonshire, Nov. 12, 1584. He was called to the bar from the Middle Temple, was elected reader of his Inn in 1630, and in September 1634 appointed Attorney General to the Prince of Wales. When Strafford was impeached by the House of Commons in 1641, Lane conducted his defense with so much ability, especially in his legal arguments, that the Commons desisted from the trial and accepted a bill of attainder.

Lane followed the King to Oxford and was knighted there Jan. 4, 1643–4, and was made Lord Chief Baron on Jan. 25 following; acted as one of the commissioners for the King at the treaty of Uxbridge, Jan. 1645, and was appointed Lord Keeper, Aug. 30, 1645.

Oxford surrendered on June 24, 1646, and Lane was the principal agent in drawing the articles on the King's note. On Feb. 8, 1649, he had a grant of arms from Charles II. He continued nominally Lord Keeper during the remainder of the King's life and his patent was renewed by Charles II. He followed the latter into exile and died at Jersey, April 1650. (Dictionary of National Biography).

Thos. Randolph seems to have been on intimate terms with his step-mother's family. Among his poems is an amusing and ingenious "Apologie for his false Prediction that his Aunt Lane would be Delivered of a Sonne."

William and Dorothy (Lane) Randolph were the parents of Henry Randolph, who came to Virginia, and of Richard, the father of William Randolph of "Turkey Island".

A Religious Feud in the Valley.

Rev. William Williams was a very early Presbyterian minister in the valley of Virginia. At Orange Court (then including Frederick, Augusta, &c.), Mr. Williams was fined £4 "for joyning in the holy bonds of matrimony several persons, he being no orthodox minister". This meant that he was not of the Church of England.

Some years earlier he was in difficulties with the people of his section, and sued a number of them for libel. The nature of the charges made against him are not known, but the list of defendants is of interest as giving the names of very early settlers in the lower Valley. On April 27, 1738, William Williams had a deed for 225 acre in "Opeqon." This was probably his residence.

We are indebted to Mrs. Fothergill for the following notes:

Orange Co. O. B. 1734–39, P. 331, 22 June 1738.

In the suit by complaint brought by Wm Williams Gent. against John Smith, John Petite, Danl Chancey, James Brown, Jonathan Curtis, Jonas Hedges, Cornelius Newkirk, Barent Newkirk, Enogle Urelawt, Peter Hyat, Francis Hood, Jeremiah Poor, James Sargeant, John Harris, Jno. Hays, Thos. Wilbourn, Wm. Smith, John Smith Jr., Tines Newcock, Henry Newcock, Saml Wilson, John Largant, Zebulon Centerel, Philip Jobson, William Homes, John Crabtree, John Powell, Wm. Wilburn, Lovis Dumas Sen., Lovis Dumas Junr, John Dumas, Thos. Low, Walter Homes, Wm. Hays, John Woodson, David Logan, Jonah Seaman, Paul Williams, Jno. Hiatt, Jno. Risk, Darby McCover, Jeremiah Williams, Paul Williams Jun., Jno. Grayham, Jos. King, Wm. Saterfield, Jos. Cantrell, Jno. Tradan, Jno. Pitts, Rice Smith, Andrew Clemens, Saml Hayward, Josiah Hayward, Thos. Mcleduff, Geo. Hyett, Geo. Nixon, Thos. Hart, Henry Robinson, Wm. Rush, John Sheppard, Abraham Yeates, Andrew Hampton, Wm. Beerley, Thos. Potts, Nicholas Knight, Jno. Stuard, Francis Ross, Robert Colvert, Saml Hews, Wm. Fullten, James Delehay, Saml Breeton for signing scandalous papers reflecting on ye complaintant. They were summoned by the sheriff. Some plead ignorance of the nature of the papers, others begged to be excused as they knew no harm of Mr. Williams. Others begged for the case to be continued until next court.

Wm. Williams vs Noah Hampton. Plf. awarded £9.

Jury: Goodrich Lightfoot Junr., Wm. Payton, William Xethwait, Thos. Pattey Jun., Jno. Ingraim, Jno. Burk, Luke Thornton, Alex. Waugh, George Nettles, William Jackson, John Connor, Richard Durrit.

THE COCKE FAMILY.

A bound copy of Vol. IV of your Magazine, page 442, says "Stephen Cocke[5] son of Abraham . . . and his son Jno. H. Cocke succeeded him", which interested me very much as my grandmother was Amy Elizabeth Cocke of Somerville, Tennessee, m. Dr. Josiah Higgason, born 1801 in Hanover Co., Va., and a son of Chas. R. Higgason. Before her death in 1890 she gave me some Cocke genealogical data taken from old family Bibles the which may show a slight error in the above quoted statement concerning Stephen Cocke. I am taking the liberty of sending it to you for perpetuation in your valuable journal.

This is the record:

Stephen Cocke Sr was born March 31, 1740.

Amy Jones his wife was born Jan'y 26, 1747.

The children of Stephen and Amy Jones Cocke were:

1 Richard, born 1766, d. Feb. 17, 1823.
2 Mary, born 1768.
3 Elizabeth, born 1770, ——— 1804.
4 Martha Lacy, born 1772, d. ——— 1824.
5 Sarah Stratton, born 1774.
6 Rebecca, born 1776.
7 Amy Jones, Jr., born 1778, d. June 1, 1824.
8 Thos. Jones, born 1780, d. Aug. 21, 1845.
9 Stephen, born 1784, d. April 5, 1822.

Stephen Cocke Sr died 1792 & Amy Jones Cocke died Sept 15, 1788.

Thomas Jones Cocke married Lucy Watkins Nicholson on Jany 20, 1802, (Lucy W. Nicholson was b. Feby 4, 1783, d. Nov. 2, 1836.) Their children were as follows:

1 A son born Feby 10, 1803.
2 James Nicholson b. Jany 3, 1805, d. Dec. 29, 1850.
3 Stephen William b. Feby 10, 1807, d. ———.
4 Thomas Oct. 27, 1808, d. Oct. 29, 1808.
5 Martha Ann Mch 20, 1810.
6 Amy Elizabeth b. Oct. 17, 1812, d. ——— 1899.
7 Thos. Richard b. Oct. 13, 1814, d. ——— 1883.
8 Edwin b. Aug. 27, 1817, d. July 21, 1830.
9 Jack Lacey b. May 11, 1821, d. Oct. 26, 1822.

My grandmother said her parents moved from Virginia and settled in Kentucky, afterwards in about 1825 coming to Fayette Co., Tennessee. Her father, Thos. Jones Cocke was wealthy, owned many slaves and much land, was for years a member of the County Court.

Lucy Watkins Nicholson, wife of Thos. Jones Cocke, was the daughter of James Nicholson, b. Nov. 1, 1748, and his wife Sally Harris b. May 11, 1767.

Martha Ann Cocke m. Maj. Edmund Winston of La Grange, Tennessee, on Feb. 11, 1828.

The record also gives this information:

Richard Cocke, oldest son of Stephen & Amy Jones Cocke, married Mary Watkins Dec. 6, 1797 (Mary dying Feb. 20, 1823). Their children:

1 John Watkins Cocke b. Jany 21, 1808.
2 Rich'd Cocke b. July 12, 1815.
3 Mary Ann Cocke b. Dec. 13, 1816.
4 Martha Frances Cocke b. ——.

Stephen Cocke Jr son of Stephen Sr & Amy, married Mch 10, 1806, Harriet A. Nance & their children are as follows:

1 Susan Francis Cocke, b. Dec. 29, 1806.
2 Stephen Frederick Cocke b. Dec. 29, 1809.
3 Thomas Robert Cocke b. April 23, 1815.

Thinking this data might be interesting to some of the numerous Cocke heirs in Virginia and elsewhere, and considering its reliability as I have explained, I am in hopes that you will be able to print it.

Very Respty

J. H. Dortch,
1510 Park Road, N. W.,
Washington, D. C.

Oct. 9, 1920.

John Oldmixon, 1673–1742.

The article on Oldmixon, in the *Dictionary of National Biography*, is not as explicit as it might be. Oldmixon's *British Empire in America* (1708 and 1741) must have been a rather powerful book in America for at least seventy years from its first edition. For instance in the Introduction (ed. 1741, p. xxvii), the question is put—"if it were asked why our Colonies have not their Representatives who could presently give a satisfactory answer?" And so a good deal throughout. Oldmixon has been reckoned a mere party man. He was much more than a canting Whig in his youth when he wrote on America. He disliked many things in the government at home, and mentions them often, directly or indirectly, in writing of America, mentions them never without making his opinion sufficiently clear. And what if Oldmixon inspired Burke?

The *Dictionary of National Biography* does not enough emphasize Oldmixon's stout Whig principles as applicable in the affairs of British America at that time; and not enough stress is given the fact that John Oldmixon was nephew to Sir John Bowden (or Bawden), London merchant. Oldmixon's account of Barbados, St. Kitts, Antigua, (note what he says of the precipitate Colonel Parke), Jamaica, etc., his second volume, all on the West India British islands, shows evidence of first hand information and mature judgment. As regards Barbados, Oldmixon says (Preface, p. xiii) "The inhabitants of that fruitful and pleasant island . . . . will see that he speaks things of his own knowledge; and as to the memoirs of events that happened before his time, he had recourse to the papers of an eminent merchant, Sir John Bowden, his uncle." And Sir John Bowden we learn (vol. II, ,p. 43) and Mr. John Gardner "had then (1687) the largest commissions from Barbados of any merchants in England, and perhaps the largest that ever were lodged in one house in the West India trade." Sugar is perennially interesting. For the history of sugar, at least, you cannot overlook Oldmixon and his uncle Sir John Bowden.

A. J. MORRISON.

NOTES FROM THE RECORDS OF RICHMOND COUNTY.

(1) Will of Robert Tomlin Jr., dated March 1st, 1794, proved Dec. 1, 1794, legatees: wife Sarah, sister Winifred Tomlin, niece Eloisa Tomlin McCarty, my brothers and sisters, provision in case a child is born, to wife one third of the money left her by her grandmother Browne, and one third of all the moneys she is entitled to under her father's will. Father Robert Tomlin nd brother-in-law Bartholomew McCarty executors.

(2) Will of Thomas Brockenbrough, dated June 27, 1794, proved Jan. 5, 1795, all estate to brothers John and Newman Brockenbrough

(3) Will of Robert Tomlin, dated Dec. 18, 1794, proved Jan. 5, 1795, wife Susannah, plantation he lived on, called Rainesse [?] for her life and afterwards to his son Moore Fauntleroy Tomlin, and if he died, to his (testator's) daughter Elizabeth McCarty's children, certain property to be equally divided among daughters and son, except daughter Elizabeth. Daughters Nellie, Apphia and Susannah Tomlin.

(4) Will of Samuel Peachey, dated April 1, 1795, proved April 27, 1795, brother William Peachey, cousin Mrs. Winifred Armistead, sisters Jane and Catherine.

(5) Will of John Smith Jr., dated March 23, 1787, proved June 6, 1797, wife Lucy, children John and Meriwether Smith, Elizabeth Burwell, Mary, Lucy, Ann, Sarah and Francis Smith.

(6) Will of Robert Wormeley Carter, of Sabine Hall, dated Dec. 16, 1794, proved June 5, 1797. To wife, Winifred Travers, the plantation where I live consisting of several tracts contiguous to each other, also the Fork Plantation, 30 working slaves, half males, stocks, utensils &c, &c, on said plantations, and household and kitchen furniture (except book-case and library and other things excepted), also such household servants as she shall choose, my stable and chariot servants, cooks, washing laundry servants and those who wait in the house—all these bequests to go after her death to son Landon Carter. To wife, carriage and four horses. Son George Carter all my lands in York and James City commonly called Rippon Hall, my lots in Williamsburg, and stocks, slaves &c., there, also to him my lands in Stafford called The Park or Acquia tract supposed to contain [copy torn] with all the slaves, stocks &c., on said tract, also two other negroes. To son Landon several negroes. To daughter Ann Beale [Carter] [torn], a negro. To daughter Elizabeth Carter, a negro. Whereas I have before given my daughter Elizabeth during her first marriage £1000, which although it was nearly equal to her husband's with specie, and was applied by him to the payment of his specie debts, yet as it was paid in paper money when depreciated, I give to daughter Elizabeth £500 specie in five annual installments of £100. To daughter Ann Beale Carter £1000 specie, also to her the rents and profits of my Hickory Thickett estate in Richmond County until she marries or receives her portion. Having paid my daughter Fanny Lee's portion, shall make no further provision for her. To godson Robert Hamilton, son of Mr. Gilbert Hamilton, late of Richmond County, a lot of land on Ocupason, supposed to be in Frederick County, for his life. To son Landon all rest of real estate on Ocupason. To dear and most intimate friend, Mr. Richard Parker and Elizabeth his wife, the tenements they occupy, for their lives, with reversion to my son Landon Carter. Son-in-law Landon Carter, of Cleve, Thomas L. Lee of Loudoun and my son Landon Carter, executors.

(7) Will of George Lee Turberville, of Epping, Richmond County, dated March 17, 1798, proved April 2, 1798. To be buried by the side of his mother and his lately deceased wife in the old family burying ground at Hickory Hill, Westmoreland County. Gives son John Turberville, as requested by John's mother, certain negroes given to her by her grandfather, the late Richard Corbin, deceased. Daughters Elizabeth Tayloe and Martha Felicia. Whereas by a settlement made by my father on me on my marriage, my son will possess, should I die before my father, a very considerable estate, and my daughters £1000 each, to be paid them by their uncles, I hope my father will have the money invested as this will requests. My brother, Richard Henry Corbin, Mr. Walter Jones the younger (attorney at law) and Mr. John Fawcett, executors. Brother R. H.

Corbin, General Henry Lee and Mr. John Tayloe of Mt. Airy, guardians to my daughters, and Mr. Jones and Mr. Fawcett to my son John.

(8) Will of Thomas Beale, dated June 7, 1799, proved Dec. 3, 1799. Wife Sarah the land I li-e on called Chestnut Hill, and after her death to son Thomas Beale. Children: Mildred, Jesse Ball, Eliza, Maria, Winifred Travers, Charles, George and Robert Taverner. Son Thomas Smith Beale. Sons James and Reuben. Daughter Fanny Foushee (gift to her confirmed). Children: Daughter Ann H. Belfield, William Currie, Thomas Smith, Mildred, James, Reuben, Fanny, Jesse Ball, Eliza, Maria, Winifred Travers, Charles, George and Robert Taverner. Brothers William and Reuben Beale and wife, executors.

(9) Will of Ann Hamilton, dated June 17, 1778, proved Aug. 2, 1784. Refers to will of deceased husband, Gilbert Hamilton, dated the last of August 1765, which devises his whole estate to her. Son John Tayloe Hamilton the land I live on. Son Robert Hamilton the land in Orange County my husband, Gilbert Hamilton bought of Mr. Taverner Beale, also two negroes. Daughter Judith Carter two negroes. Daughter Elizabeth Hamilton two negroes. Daughter Euphan, two negroes &c. Mr. Thomas Lawson and Mr. Robert W. Carter, executors.

(10) Will of William Peachey, dated July 30, 1798, proved Sept. 6, 1802: daughter Armistead, daughter Nicholson, son William Travers grandchildren beginning with Elizabeth B. Armistead and so on down to the youngest; daughters Winifred and Susanna. Refers to a negro given to his sister Eustace by his father's will (she was the wife of John Eustace); grandson John Nicholson, Jr. Testator owned lands in Kentucky. Son William Travers Peachey, son-in-law John Nicholson and friend Rudolph Colste[?] [Raleigh Colston?] executors. Codicil dated Dec. 18, 1798, bequest to daughter Winifred Armistead.

(11) Will of James Monroe, proved Feb. 2, 1807, "at present of the County of Richmond"; wife all estate, refers to his children and his brothers, but does not name them. Brother William executor.

(12) Will of Charles B. Carter, dated Dec. 1, 1800, proved April 4, 1808. £1000 due from Landon Carter, executor of Robert W. Carter, to my wife, which was left her by her father. All lands in Richmond and Westmoreland to be sold. Land in Lancaster called Nantipoison Neck, 800 acres, and the necessary slaves, to be left for the support of my wife, Ann Beale Carter and my sons John Hill Carter and Charles B. Carter. Daughter Winifred Beale Carter (under 21). Refers to his father as still living. Friends Edward Carter, of Prince William, Landon Carter and John Tayloe of Richmond and Thomas L. Lee, of Loudoun, executors.

GENEALOGY.

THE CORBIN FAMILY.

(Continued)

We are indebted to Earl Beauchamp, the representative of the senior branch of the Corbin family, for abstracts and copies of deeds, letters, wills, etc., relating to the Corbins, which are among his family papers and for permission to use them. We also desire to thank Mr. C. L. Kingsford, 15 Argyll Road, Kensington, London, for kind aid in the same connection. Mr. Kingsford writes: "Hall End house is still standing. The property belonged originally to the Marmions of Tamworth. In the 15th century it was acquired by one, William Sturmy, whose granddaughter married Nicholas Corbyn, of Kingswinford. The original home of the Corbyns was Corbyns Hall at Kingswinford near Dudley, about 25 miles from Hall End. The Hall End estate was, I believe, sold by the last Earl Beauchamp about 40 years ago. Some of the Corbyns were buried at Polesworth and others at Kingswinford."

GENEALOGICAL DATA FOR THE CORBIN FAMILY FROM THE DEEDS OF EARL BEAUCHAMP.

C. 1220. William son of Corbinus de Chorbeus makes a grant to the Nuns of Polesworth.

1358. William Corbin held land at Dudley.

1400. Henry Corbyn occurs as a witness to a deed relating to land at Dudley and Seggesley (Sedgeley).

1401. August 10, Charter of Henry Corbyn granting land at Kingswinford.

1407. June 29. Grant to Henry Corbyn of land at Sedgeley (near Dudley).

1414. Sept. 25. William Sturmy occurs in connection with Holt Hall at Polesworth.

1421. June 24. Quitclaim by Margery sometime wife of Henry Corbyn, of land at Sedgeley.

1427. March 2. Grant of "le Hall End" and the lands in Polesworth which were once William Gregory's, by Thomas Lonett to John Chetewynd, who on 25 June conveyed it to Henry Ludford and John Scot.

1428. April 15. William Sturmy and Eleanor his wife.

1428. Sept. 20. Settlement of lands in Kingswinford, Dudley and Sedgeley on John Corbyn and Elizabeth Everdon and the heirs of their bodies.

1430. Oct. 3. William Everdon and John Lorde grant to William Corbyn lands in Kingswinford which they had by feoffment from John Corbyn: to hold for life with remainders to John Corbyn and the heirs of his body and in default to Thomas Corbyn, brother of John Corbyn.

1431. Sept. 14. Grant by Nicholas Russell and John Lorde to John Corbyn son of William Corbyn of lands in Kingswinford, which they had by feoffment of William and Margery Corbyn. Thomas Corbyn a witness.

1432. March 20. Grant by Thomas Page to William Sturmy of Polesworth and Eleanor his wife, of Hall End and lands in Polesworth which he acquired from John Scotte and Henry Lutteford.

1438. Aug. 1. Settlement of Hall End with remainder to John, son of William and Eleanor Sturmy, with remainders to brother Edward and sisters Elizabeth and Joan.

1452. March 25. Demise by Thomas Corbyn of Kingswinford of land at Tybinton.

1452. June 26. Settlement on marriage of John Sturmy and Joan daughter of William Clerke of Dudley.

1452. July 14. Charter of Eleanor late wife of William Sturmy, to her son John.

1453. Feb. 2. Deed of Thomas Corbyn.

1459. Apr. 16. Joan late wife of John Sturmy.

1459. June 8. Demise of Hall End on trust by Eleanor Sturmy.

1467. January 19. Charter of Thomas Corbyn to John Corbyn, vicar of Womburne.

1468. Apr. 29. Wardship of Agnes and Joan daughters of John Sturmy.

1474. Dec. 12. Demise by Joan Corbyn, late wife of Thomas Corbyn, and Nicholas Corbyn, her son, of land in Tybinton, on trust.

1489. Feb. 1. Demise by Nicholas Corbyn of land in Sedgeley.

1506. Lawsuit between Nicholas Corbyn, Joan his wife, and Robert Carlile. Joan Corbyn was daughter of John Sturmy. Robert Carlile was son of Joan daughter of William Sturmy. It related to the lands in Polesworth and was decided in Corbyn's favour.

1512. Feb. 1. Demise by Nicholas Corbyn.

1513. Rental of Nicholas Corbyn. Mentions Corbyns Hall in Kingswinford. His lands worth £109 the year.

1528. May 30. Demise by Jane Corbin, late wife of Nicholas Corbin to Anne Corbin her daughter. Richard Corbin son and heir of Nicholas Corben assents.

1530. Apr. 14. Lease by Richard Corbyn of Kingswinford.

1553. Jan. 1. Deed of Thomas Corbyn of Hall End.

1563. Aug. 13. Deed of Thomas Corbyn of Hall End and Anne his wife.

1564. May 30. Grant by Thomas Corbyn of Hall End to Francis Corbyn, John Corbyn and others on trust for George Corbyn, son and heir of Thomas. Francis and John were probably brothers of Thomas.

1574. March 24. George Corbyn witness to a deed between Thomas Corbyn and Thomas Warings. Thomas Corbyn uses a seal displaying his shield "in chief three ravens"; the earliest instance.

1581. May 27. Deed of George Corbyn of Hall End.

1620. Aug. 25. Deed of George Corbyn of Hall End, for settlement of estates. Witnesses include Gawen Grosvenor, Anne Corbin, and Jane Corbin.

1621. May 26. Bond to Thomas Corbyn of Hall End.

1622. Sept. 5. Sale of lands at Polesworth to Thomas Corbyn

C.1625. George Corbyn in giving evidence in a lawsuit describes himself as about 80 years of age and bred and born at Hall End.

1635. Nov. 2. Deed of Thomas Corbyn mentioning Winifred his wife and George Corbyn his father.

1636. Mar. 29. George Corbyn alive.

1637. Nov. 14. Grant of Wardship of Thomas Corbyn to Winifred Corbyn widow, and others.

1638. June 1. Probate of Will of Thomas Corbyn of Hall End. His sons: Thomas, Henry, George, Gawyne and Charles: daughter Lettice. Brothers-in-law John Dawkins and James Prescott. Winifred Corbyn remarried (2) Cecil Warburton who died before 1646. (3) Richard Howell. Lettice Corbyn married Thomas Okeover.

1645-6. Feb. 15. Marriage Settlement of Thomas Corbyn of Corbins Hall and Margaret daughter of Edmund Goodere.

1650. Feb. 22. Receipt by George Corbyn of London, salter, for a legacy under his father's Will.

1653-4. Jan. 7. Do. by Henry Corbyn of London, draper. [The emigrant to Virginia]

1653-4. Jan. 18. Do. by Thomas Okeover on behalf of his wife.

1657. Dec. 7. Do. by Gawen Corbyn. Charles Corbyn was dead.

1656-7. Jan. 3. Bond of Henry Corbyn of Rappahanock, Virginia, merchant, to Sir Henry Chicheley, Colonel Samuel Mathewes and Thomas Corbyn, on the occasion of his intended marriage to Alice, widow of Rowland Burnham of Rappahannock, in order to secure her property to Alice.

Thomas Corbyn (eldest son of Thomas, of Hall End), had a numerous family, but all died young except one daughter Margaret who in July 1688 married William Lygon of Madresfield. Thomas Corbyn died in Dec. 1688. William Lygon had issues William, Corbyn, Thomas and Margaret. William and Thomas died before their father. Corbyn Lygon succeeded and died in 1728, having by his wife Jane Tullie a son William and two daughters Jane and Margaret; William died soon after and was succeeded at Madresfield and Hall End by his Aunt Margaret, then widow of Reginald Pyndar of Kempley, Gloucestershire. Her son Reginald took the name of Lygon and was father of William Lygon, first Earl Beauchamp.

The following short pedigree of the English family was prepared by Mr. Kingsford from the original documents. This gives an unbroken and fully proven descent from about 1400. As this outline pedigree was prepared entirely from the Corbin papers referred to, the absence of the names of wives, &c., given in the pedigree printed in the last instalment does not necessarily mean that the statements in the former pedigree are incorrect.

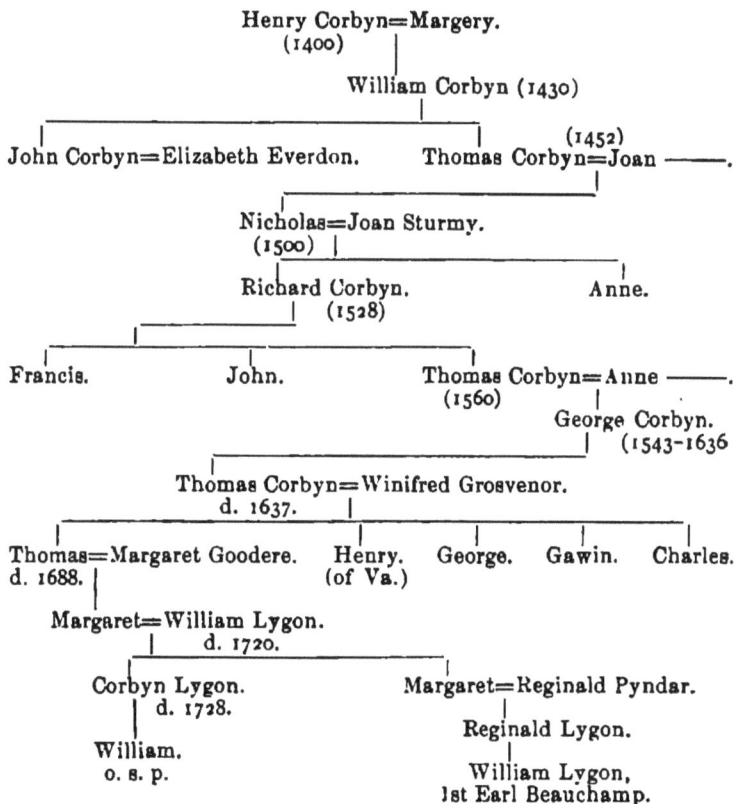

Henry Corbyn=Margery.
(1400)

William Corbyn (1430)

John Corbyn=Elizabeth Everdon. Thomas Corbyn=Joan ——. (1452)

Nicholas=Joan Sturmy.
(1500)

Richard Corbyn. (1528) Anne.

Francis. John. Thomas Corbyn=Anne ——.
(1560)

George Corbyn.
(1543-1636

Thomas Corbyn=Winifred Grosvenor.
d. 1637.

Thomas=Margaret Goodere. Henry. George. Gawin. Charles.
d. 1688. (of Va.)

Margaret=William Lygon.
d. 1720.

Corbyn Lygon. Margaret=Reginald Pyndar.
d. 1728.

William.
o. s. p.

Reginald Lygon.

William Lygon,
1st Earl Beauchamp.

(To be continued)

GRYMES OF BRANDON, &c.

(Concluded)

52. William Fitzhugh[5] Grymes, of "Eagles Nest", King George County, was born ——— and died 1830. He was a member of the House of Delegates from King George 1810-11. He married Jane Champe, daughter of Thomas Pratt, of Caroline County, and had issue:

71. Robert Carter Nicholas[6], M. D., died unmarried; 72. Richard Montgomery[6], died unmarried; 73. William Fitzhugh[6], died unmarried; 74. William Henry Fitzhugh[6], died unmarried; 75. Benjamin Franklin[6], died unmarried; 76. Mary Meade, died unmarried; 77. Virginia, married Nov. 31, 1829, Henry T. Washington of King George County; 78. Thomas Jefferson Independence[6], born July 4, 1825, died Oct. 1866, married Fanny Irving, of Alexandria, Va., and left three sons and three daughters who lived at "Eagles Nest".

53. Benjamin[5] Grymes, of "Somerset", King George County, born ———, died 1828 or 1829. He married Margaret Vivian, daughter of Thomas Pratt, of Caroline County, and had issue:

79. William Fitzhugh[6], who was in the U. S. Navy and died young and unmarried; 80. Louisa, married Edgar Snowden, of Alexandria; 81. George Washington Parke Custis[6], born ———, died 1870, married 1st, Martha, daughter of George N. Grymes (and had two daughters), married 2nd, Miss Stuart (and had a son and a daughter); 82. Quisenberry Pratt[6], died young; 83. Jane Brockenbrough, married Richard Kidder Meade, of White Post, Clarke County; 84. Eleanor A. S., married March 28, 1848, Hugh Mercer Tennant, of King George County; 85. Martha.

54. George Nicholas[5] Grymes, of "Mt. Chene" and "Mt. Stuart", King George County, born 1784, died Nov. 1853. He married Ann Eilbeck Mason, grand-daughter of George Mason of "Gunston" (she died Nov. 1864, aged 74 years) and had issue:

86. Ann N., married ——— Atkinson; 87. Elizabeth Mason; 88. Lucy Fitzhugh, married Dr. A. B. Hooe, of King George County; 89. Martha Lucretia; 90. Sarah; 91. Rosalie; 92. George Graham[6], died young; 93. Edmund Fitzhugh[6], died young; 94. Richard Barnes Mason[6], died young; 95. George Edmund[6], of King George County, married Elizabeth Hansford, and had four sons and five daughters; 96. Benjamin Richards[6], of Mathias Point, King George County, married and had three sons and three daughters.

62. PEYTON[7] GRYMES, married Catherine Catlett and had issue:

97. Robert[8]; 98. Peyton Minor[8]; 99. Mary Lewis; 100. Fanny; 101. Betty; 102. Nanny.

63. DR. ROBERT PAGE[7] GRYMES, was born at "Selma", Orange County, May 30, 1824, removed to Chesterfield County in 1846 and died May 23, 1889. He married, Mary, daughter of Dr. Joseph E. Cox, of Petersburg (she died in Richmond, Nov. 22, 1920 in the 86th year of her age) and had issue:

103. E. Buford, married Fanny Thaw; 104. Peyton[8]; 105. James[8]; 106. Robert[8]; 107. Susan, married C. T. Henley; 108. Sarah, married H. T. Wright.

64. BENJAMIN ANDREW[7] GRYMES, married Harriet Beale and had issue:

109. Kate; 110. Benjamin[8]; 111. Edwin[8]; 112. William[8]; 113. Alice, married Bolton Harrison; 114. Sarah, married Peter V. Moncure; 115. John Randolph[8]; 116. Eugenia.

65. DR. WILLIAM SHEPHERD[7] GRYMES, of Gordonsville, Va., born April 3, 1825, died March 20, 1891. He served as surgeon C. S. A. He married, June 1, 1870, at "Backwood", Orange County, Va., Mary Ann, daughter of David Meade Bernard, of Petersburg, Va., and had at least one daughter, Mrs. E. D. Gilmore, of Sewickley, Pa.

66. JOHN RANDOLPH[7] GRYMES, married in Texas and had several children.

THE LOVELACE FAMILY AND ITS CONNECTIONS

By J. Hall Pleasants, Baltimore, Md.

(Continued)

AUCHER OF OTTERDEN AND BISHOPSBOURNE, KENT, WITH NOTES ON CORNWALLIS, WROTH AND RICH.

Sir Anthony Aucher[7]: continued from page 295—The *inquisition* shows that Sir Anthony Aucher died January 9th [1558]. As this was two days after the surrender of Calais, he doubtless died of wounds received a few days previously during the siege.

Sir Anthony Aucher[7] married, apparently in 1525, Affra daughter of William Cornwallis of Brome, Suffolk, the then head of the distinguished family of this name, by his wife Eliza Stamford. At the time of this marriage William Cornwallis was dead; he had died in 1519. The identity of Affra Cornwallis is correctly given in the contemporary pedigree of Cornwallis in *Harvey's Visitation of Suffolk 1561*, (*Metcalf's Visitations of Suffolk; Exeter, 1882*, pp. 21, 22). This is confirmed by the *inquisition* upon the estate of Sir Anthony Aucher given below in which it is recited that he conveyed [in trust] the manor of Otterden, 20 July 17 Henry VIII [1525] to Sir Robert [or Edward] Guildford [Guldford] and Sir John Cornwalleys, knights, George Guildford and Thomas Hardres, esquires, Thomas Cornwalleys, clerk, and Edward Cornwalleys, gent, for purpose of a settlement on the said Affra [followed by illegible words] Cornwallys whom he proposed to marry. It is known that Sir John Cornwallis, Thomas Cornwallis and Edward Cornwallis were sons of William Cornwallis [d. 1519] of Brome. The evidence as to the identity of Affra Cornwallis is gone into in detail, because the *Visitation of Kent, 1619, Burke* and *Berry*, although giving her father's name correctly, state that he was of Norfolk. A sketch of the Cornwallis family of Brome will follow (pp. 381-2).

Sir Anthony Aucher[7] apparently left no will and his estate was administered upon in the Prerogative Court of Canterbury: "12 May, 1560, administration upon the estate of Anthony Aucher, kt. Cant. was granted to his son Edward Aucher, with consent of Walter Bradbourne", and a subsequent administration doubtless an *adm. de bonis non:* "admon. Anos. gt. Jan. 1571" (*Genealogist; Administrations; Prerogative Court of Canterbury;* 1; p. 7). The statement of *Hasted* that he left Bishopsbourne to his son Edward *by will* is certainly incorrect as the *inquisition* shows that it was settled by entail in 1552, or five years before Sir Anthony's death, upon his eldest son John, and in default of male heirs of John, successively upon his sons Edward, Thomas and William. The statement that he left a will is also incorrect.

In addition to the manors of Otterden, Bishopsbourne and Hautsbourne (or Shelvingbourne), Sir Anthony Aucher died posesssed of the manors of Kyngeston, Baddlesmere and Pasting, and of the manor and park of Lyminge (Lyming). He also held the advowson of the churches of Kyngston, Lyming, Perlesforth and Stamforth, as well as lands in various other parishes in Kent named in the *inquisition*, in which it is stated that some of these "premises descend in gavelkind", i. e. were to be divided equally among his male heirs, not passing entirely to the eldest son by entail. Certain of the above lands including the manor of Otterden were subject to the life interest of his wife Affra, but all those entailed were eventually to pass to his eldest son and heir John Aucher, who was living when the *inquisition* was taken 15 May, 1558, with contingent remainders, except in the case of Otterden, successively to his other sons Edward, Thomas and William should John die without male issue. As this John Aucher[8] died, leaving as his only heir, a daughter, the entailed lands, including the manors of Bishopsbourne, Hautsbourne, Kingston and Lyminge, finally passed to his brother Edward Aucher[8], the second son of Sir Anthony[7] in whose possession they were 15 May, 1568, when the *inquisition* upon Edward Aucher's[8] estate was taken (q. v. p. 279), except the manor of Otterden which under the terms of the settlement descended to the heirs of John's daughter Anne, who married Sir Humphrey Gilbert, the great navigator.

The following is the *inquisition post mortem*, unfortunately illegible in some important parts, upon the estate of Sir Anthony Aucher, Knight, taken 15 May, 1558 (*Chancery Inquisitions Post Mortem; Series II, Vol. 112, No. 91*):

> *Inquisition* taken at Deptford 15 May, 4 & 5 Philip and Mary [1558]. Sir Anthony Aucher died seised of the manor of Shelvingbourne *alias* Hawtysbourne, and of the manor of Bishopsbourne, which he acquired by indenture of 1st June 2 Edw VI [1548] from Thomas Culpeper of Bedgebury, esq., who had married Anne, daughter & heir of Sir William Hawte, Kt.; and from Sir James Hales, Kt., and Margaret his wife, formerly wife of the said Sir William Hawte. He was also seised of the manor and advowson of the church of Kyngeston [Kingston], co. Kent, and the manor and park of Lymenge alias Gymynge, and the advowsons of the churches of Lymnge, Perlesforthe and Stanforthe, and lands in Kingeston, Barham, Wotton, Lyminge, Eltham, Patricksbourne and Brydge, etc. On 1 Feb 6 Edw. VI [1552] he therewith enfeoffed Thomas Hardres and Thomas Cox, esquires, Alvered Randolfe and John Ramsey, gentlemen; on the 20th of the same month, they by their deed granted the premises to Sir Anthony and Dame Affra, then his wife, for their lives, with remainder to John Aucher, esq., son and heir apparent of the said Anthony, in tail male, and contingent remainders in tail male successively to his other sons Edward, Thomas and William. The manor of Otterinden he conveyed 20 July 17 Hen VIII [1525] to Sir Robert (or Edward?) Guildford, kt. & Sir John Cornwalleys, kt., George Guildford and Thomas Hardres, esquires, Thomas Cornwalleys, clerk, and Edward Cornewalleys, gent., for purposes of a settlement on the said Affra * * * * Cornewallays, whom the said Anthony intended to take to wife. He was seised of the manor of Postling, out of which he granted an annuity of 100 marks to Thomas Spylman of Canterbury, gent. (now esq.), 2 April 1 Edw. VI [1547]. Other annuities he had granted to Roger Manwood & Henry Oxenden. He acquired [? the manor of Baddlesmere] & lands from Anne, Countess of Oxford [the particulars illegible]. He

died 9 Jan * * * * The said John Aucher is his son & heir; some of the premises descend in gavel kind. The said Dame Affra & his other sons all survive.

The issue of Sir Anthony Aucher[7] and his wife Affra Cornwallis as given here are taken from his *inquisition*, the *Visitation of Kent, 1619*, and *Berry's Genealogies; Kent.* Issue: (1) John Aucher[8] of Otterden, who married Anne daughter of Sir William Kelloway, knight; he died prior to 1568; his only child and heir, a daughter Anne, inherited the manor of Otterden, and married about 1570, Sir Humphrey Gilbert the celebrated navigator; issue five sons and one daughter; many biographical sketches of Sir Humphrey Gilbert incorrectly state that his wife was a *daughter* of Sir Anthony Aucher[7]; (2) Edward Aucher[8] of Bishopsbourne—See VIII; (3) Thomas Aucher[8] d.s.p.; (4) William Aucher[8] of Nonington, married Alice Monins and d.s.p.; he was a clergyman and in 1566 was granted the "next presentation of the advowson of Lyminge" by his brother Edward Aucher; (5) Susannah Aucher[8].

VIII. Edward Aucher[8] (Nicholas[1], Henry[2], Henry[3], Henry[4], John[5], James[6], Anthony[7]). Of Bishopsbourne, Kent. Born shortly before 1540. The *inquisition post mortem* given below shows that he married 10 June, 1560, Mabel the daughter of Sir Thomas Wroth. This definitely confirms the statements to this effect in the Aucher pedigrees given in the *Visitation of Kent, 1619* (*Harl. Soc. xlii;* pp. 180-1), in *Berry* (*Genealogies; Kent;* pp. 222-3) and in *Burke* (*Extinct and Dormant Baronetages;* 2nd. ed.; pp. 27-29); while it shows the incorrectness of the statement in the Wroth pedigrees among the "*Additional Pedigrees*" in this same *Visitation of Kent, 1619* (p. 214) which states that his wife was the daughter of Sir *Robert* Wroth and a *granddaughter* of the above Sir Thomas Wroth. Sir Thomas Wroth, knight, of Durants in Enfield, Middlesex, was a prominent politician during the reign of Henry VIII and of Edward VI, and married Mary the daughter of Richard, first lord Rich, the celebrated lord chancellor. Sketches of both the Wroth and Rich families will follow. The *inquisition* upon Sir Anthony Aucher's[7] estate, 1558, shows that the manor of Bishopsbourne and other property had been settled by him by deed dated 20 Feb. 1552, upon his eldest son and heir John, with reversion to his other sons successively. The *inquisition* upon the estate of Edward Aucher[8], 15 May, 1568, shows that at his death, 14 Feb. 1567-8, he was seized of the manor of Bishopsbourne and other property. It would, therefore, appear that Edward Aucher had inherited Bishopsbourne by the death of his brother John without male heirs. Edward Aucher was probably about thirty at the time of his death. None of the published pedigrees refer in any way to a remarriage by his widow Mabel. Nor does the Aucher mural tablet in Bishopsbourne church which states that she died in 1597, refer to a remarriage. That she had remarried, however, sometime prior to 5 Oct. 1573, Richard Hardres* of Hardres, Kent, and that her son Anthony Aucher was then the ward of her father Sir Thomas Wroth, is shown by the latter's will. The will of Sir Thomas Wroth, dated 5 October, 1573 and proved 16 April, 1575, a full abstract of which will be given later, refers to "my daughter Mabell Hardres, wife of Richard Hardres, esq.", and in a later paragraph provides that "if my ward Anthony Awcher [i. e. Anthony[9]] before his age of 21 pay my executor so much money for his marriage and wardship as I or they have dispersed, then my executors shall not take any further benefit but the said Anthony to remain unmarried or marry himself at his pleasure." The *inquisition* upon the estate of Edward Aucher shows that he and his wife Mabel left two children, a son Anthony born in 1562, and a daughter Elizabeth. Although the *inquisition* refers to a will of Edward Aucher, dated 3 Feb. 10 Elizabeth [1567-8], no such will can now be found in the Prerogative Court of Canterbury, London, nor in the local courts of Kent at Canterbury or Rochester.

The following *inquisition post mortem* was taken upon the estate of Edward Aucher 15 May, 1568 (*Court of Wards and Liveries: Inquisitions post mortem.* Vol. II, fol. 26), and in the absence of a will is of especial interest:

> Inquisition taken at Deptford Strand, co. Kent, 15 May 10 Elizabeth [1568], after the death of Edward Aucher, esq. He was seised of the manor of Bishopsbourne, manor & advowson of Lyminge &c. 22 August 1566 he had granted the next presentation to Lyminge to his brother William Aucher. 27 Sept. 8 Eliz. [1566] Edward Aucher and Mabel his wife granted to their kinsman James Aucher of Cherington the keepership of Cherington Park. In Mich. term 8 & 9 Eliz. a recovery was had by Sir Thomas Wroth, father of the said Mabel, and Robert Eyre, esq., to uses of an indenture made between the said Edward & his wife, 30 Sept. 8 Eliz. [1566], referring to the settlement made on their marriage 10 June 2 Elizabeth [1560], under which Lyminge was entailed on said Edward Aucher & his brother William, in tail male successively, remainder to Edward's right heirs. On 20 February 6 Edward VI [1552], Bishopsborne

* The Hardres were a prominent family in the parish of Hardres, Kent, and in the next century a baronetcy was conferred upon a descendant of Richard Hardres. The Hardres pedigrees in the *Visitation of Essex, 1612 (Harl. Soc.* xiii; p. 211), *Visitation of Kent, 1663-1668 (Harl. Soc.* liv; p. 73) and *Burke's Extinct and Dormant Baronetages* (2nd. ed. pp.242-3) erroneously state that this Richard Hardres married *Mary*, daughter of Sir Thomas Wroth. This is disproved by Sir Thomas Wroth's will, cited above, which shows that it was his daughter *Mabel* who married Richard Hardres.

& other property was settled in tail as above, with remainder over to the right heirs of Sir Anthony Aucher, dec[d]., father of the said Edward. The recovery of Mich. 8 & 9 Eliz. [1566] and deed therewith connected are made to enable the jointure of the said Mabel to be more conveniently placed as regards a dwelling house, to raise money to pay the debts of Edward Aucher, and to provide for the bringing up and advancement of his children. The deed puts a condition on the succession by William & his heirs male, viz. that they shall not do anything contrary to this deed; and in such event, or for failure of such issue, the remainder to be to Elizabeth Aucher, daughter of the said Edward. The said Edward, as Edward Aucher of Bishopsborne, esq., son of Sir Anthony Aucher, Kt., dec[d]., made his will 3 February 10 Eliz. [1567-8], providing for his daughter Elizabeth and son Anthony. He bequeaths £5 to Mary Wroth. He died at Bishopsborne on the 14th Feb. 10 Eliz. [1567-8]. Anthony Aucher, son & heir of the said Edward is aged five and a half years.

Issue of Edward Aucher[8] and his wife Mabel Wroth:

(1) Sir Anthony Aucher[9], knight; of Bishopsbourne. He was born 1562, and died 13 Jan. 1609-10. He was knighted 4 July, 1604 at Chatham. He is said to have married twice. By his 1st wife, a daughter of Robert Barham, he had no issue. By his 2nd wife Margaret, daughter of Edwin Sandys, Archbishop of York (q. v.) he had issue (1) Sir Anthony Aucher[10] (died 1637); (2) Edwin Aucher[10] of Willesborough; (3) Elizabeth[10] married Sir William Hamour, (4) Margaret[10] married Sir Roger James. There is thus a double connection between the Aucher and Sandys families, as his nephew Sir William Lovelace, the younger (1584-1627), son of his sister Elizabeth (Aucher[9]) Lovelace, married Anne Barne, the niece of his wife Margaret Sandys. This Anne Barne was the daughter of Sir William Barne and Anne Sandys, another daughter of Archbishop Sandys. The above mentioned Sir Anthony Aucher[10], knight (died July, 1637), had a son Sir Anthony Aucher[11], knight (1613-1694) who was created a baronet July 4, 1666. The title is now extinct. See *Burke's Extinct and Dormant Baronetages, 2nd. ed.* p. 28, and *Berry's Genealogies; Kent*, p. 223, for later lines.

IX. (2) Elizabeth Aucher[9]. Born between 1561 and 1565. She is referred to in her father's *inquisition* as having been provided for under his will. She married about 1580 or 1581, Sir William Lovelace, the elder, knight, of Bethersden, Kent (1551-

1629). She was buried 3 December, 1627, in Canterbury Cathedral. Sir William Lovelace and his wife Elizabeth Aucher[6] had issue (1) Richard Lovelace (1582-1602); (2) Sir William Lovelace, the younger (1584-1627), leaving issue q. v. ante pp. 87-90; (3) Mabel Lovelace (1584-1627) mar. Sir John Collimore, knight. See the *Virginia Magazine*, xxvii-xxviii, for the Lovelace pedigree.

CORNWALLIS OF BROME, SUFFOLK.

The pedigree of Cornwallys [Cornwallis] of Brome, Suffolk, which appears in the *Visitation of Suffolk* made by Harvey, Clarencieux king-of-arms, in 1561, carries the family back to the middle of the fourteenth century and is very complete (*Metcalfe's Visitation of Suffolk; Exeter, 1882;* pp. 21, 22). An examination of the pedigree will show that Affra Cornwallis, wife of Sir Anthony Aucher[7], was a sister of Sir John Cornwallis of Brome, Steward of the Household of Prince Edward [Edward VI] and an aunt of Sir Thomas Cornwallis, Member of Queen Mary's Privy Council and Comptroller of Her Majesty's Household. Of this same family is the celebrated Lord Cornwallis of the American Revolution. The following is from the contemporary pedigree in the *Visitation of Suffolk, 1561:*

The arms of Cornwallis as given in the *Visitation:* Arms Sable, guttée d'eau, on a fess dancetté Argent three Cornish choughs [proper]. Crest: On a mount Vert a stag lodged regardant Argent attired Or gored with a chaplet of laurel Vert, and vulned on the shoulder Gules.

I. Thomas Cornwallis[1]. Of London, merchant. Married Jane da. of William Hansard. He was Shrive [Shrieve or Sheriff] of London temp. Richard II [1378] and was born in Ireland whence this surname cometh. He died in 1384 and was buried at St. Margaret's in the Vintry. Son and heir:

II. John Cornwallis[2]. Married Phillippe de. and one of the heirs of Robert Buckton [Bucton] of Brome, Suff., esq. Issue son and heir:

III. Thomas Cornwallis[3] of Brome. Married Phillippe da. and one of the heirs of Edward Tyrrell of Dowham, Essex, esq. Issue (1) John[4], son and heir d.s.p. [1506]; (2) Edward[4], d.s.p. [1510]; (3) Robert[4], d.s.p.; (4) William[4]—see IV; (5) Katherine[4] married Francis Frewsmere.

IV. William Cornwallis[4] of Brome. Married Eliza da. and one of the heirs of John Stamford, esq. [Burke refers to him as *Sir* William Cornwallis which is doubtless an error as regards the title, and states that he died in 1519. This date is confirmed by the probate in the Prerogative Court of Canterbury, 1519, of the will of William Cornewalys, esquire, of Ocley (i. e. Oakley adjoining Brome) Suffolk;

London; Bedfordshire; Norfolk]. Issue (1) Sir John Cornwallis[5] of Brome, married Mary da. of Edward Sulyard of Otes, Essex, esq. knighted at the taking of Morley [Morlaix—1523]. He was Steward of the Household of Prince Edward [afterwards Edward VI] for six years until his death [died 1544]. Buried in Barkshamsted in Bucks [Herts]. He had issue by his wife Mary Sulyard, among other children, Sir Thomas Cornwallis[6], knight, Member of Queen Mary's Privy Council, Treasurer of Calles [Calais] and Comtroller of Her Majesty's Household; (2) Thomas Cornwallis[5], Archdeacon of Norfolk; (3) Edward Cornwallis[5]; (4) William Cornwallis[5]; (5) Francis Cornwallis[5]; (6) Elizabeth Cornwallis[5] married ——— Singleton; (7) V. Affra Cornwallis[5] married Sir Anthony Aucher of Otterdon [Otterden], Kent, kt, [and is the ancestress of the Lovelaces of Bethersden]; (8) Dorothy Cornwallis[5] married John Head of Kent; (9) Katharine Carnwallis[5], a nonne [nun] of Elstow [a Benedictine nunnery near Bedford]; (10) Prudence Cornwallis[5] married Royden Eden; (11) Edith Cornwallis[5] married ——— Barwyke.

For the Cornwallis pedigree from this point down, see *Burke's Extinct Peerages* (ed. 1866; pp. 137-8), *Collins's Peerage of England* (ed. 1812; ii; pp. 537-559), and *The Dictionary of National Biography* (xii; pp. 242-7). Sir Thomas Cornwallis[6] (1519-1604) son of Sir John Cornwallis[5], and nephew of Affra (Cornwallis[5]) Aucher, was prominent in the reign of Mary, but held no offices under Elizabeth on account of his catholicism. He rebuilt Brome Hall. His grandson Frederick Cornwallis[8] was created a baronet in 1627, and elevated to the peerage as Baron Cornwallis of Eyre in 1611; and the fifth baron, Charles Cornwallis[12], was in 1753 made Viscount Brome and Earl Cornwallis. The latter's son, Charles Cornwallis[13] (1738-1805), second Earl and first Marquis Cornwallis, was the celebrated Lord Cornwallis, the British commander in the American Revolution.

Collins (p. 541) gives very full quotations from the will of William Cornwallis[4] of Brome, dated 8 November, 1519, and probated 29 November, 1519. He makes a bequest to the parish church of Brome and requests to be buried in the church of St. Nicholas, in the adjoining parish of Oakley. He names his wife Elizabeth and his eldest son John and refers to, but apparently does not name, his other sons. He names his daughters Prudence, Edith, Affra, Catherine and Dorothy, apparently all unmarried at the time of his death. *Collins* also refers to a will of his widow Elizabeth Cornwallis of Thrandeston, dated 30 May, 1537, but does not quote from it. *Collins* states incorrectly that it was his daughter *Frances* who married Sir Anthony Aucher[7].

WROTH OF ENFIELD, MIDDLESEX.

The Wroth and Aucher families are connected through the marriage in 1560 of Edward Aucher (1539?-1568) of Bishopsbourne, Kent (see ante pp. 378-381) and Mabel, the daughter of Sir Thomas Wroth (1516-1573), knight, of Enfield, Middlesex. This Sir Thoms Wroth, who was very prominent in public affairs in the reigns of Henry VIII, Edward VI and Elizabeth, married Mary daughter of Richard, first lord Rich of Leez, lord chancellor under Edward VI (see note on Rich post, p. 390).

The father of Sir Thomas Wroth (1516-1573) was Robert Wroth (-1536) of Durrants in Enfield. This Robert Wroth was attorney of the Duchy of Lancaster, and one of the commissioners appointed in 1529 to enquire into the possessions of Cardinal Wolsey; and sat for Middlesex in the reformation parliament (1529-1535). He married Jane, the widow of Thomas Goodere and the daughter of Sir Thomas Hawte of Haute Court, Kent, and died in 1536. A full pedigree of the Hawte or Haute family carried back to the reign of Henry III will be found in the *Visitation of Kent, 1619*, (*Harl. Soc. Publ.* xlii; 214). The Wroths claim descent from William de Wrotham, constable of Dover Castle in the reign of King John, whose descendant John Wroth in the reign of Edward III was shrive or sheriff of London in 1331, lord mayor in 1361, and representative of Middlesex in several parliaments. Either through his marriage or the marriage of his son Thomas, for the old pedigrees vary as to this point, with Maud the daughter and heir of Thomas Durant (d. 1348), who built Durrants in Enfield, this became the seat of the Wroth family in Middlesex.*

The following sketch of Sir Thomas Wroth, whose daughter Mabel married Edward Aucher, is taken largely from the *Dictionary of National Biography* (lxiii, 163-5). While this sketch and the other published pedigrees make brief reference to his seven sons, neither the names nor any information whatever is given in regard

* The pedigrees of Wroth, none of which appear to have been compiled before the seventeenth century, are so conflicting as to the early lines that it seems inadvisable to select arbitrarily any one and reproduce it in detail here. The interested reader is referred to the following visitation pedigrees of this family: *Visitation of Essex, 1612 (Harl. Soc. Publ.* xiii; 33), *Middlesex Pedigrees (Harl. Soc. Publ.* lxv; 17) and *Visitation of London, 1633, 1634, 1635 (Harl. Soc. Publ.* xvii; 374). The pedigrees which appear in various county and local histories are equally conflicting and unreliable. There is still another pedigree tracing the family from a Geoffrey de Wrotham who flourished in the reign of King Stephen (1135-1154). This chart pedigree which appears in full in the *Archaeologia Cantiana* (xii; 310-16) was filed as evidence in a chancery suit commenced in 1788 by William Henry, Earl of Rochford and John Lane, esq., plaintiffs, against Sir John Dashwood, King, baronet, the Baroness Le Despencer and others, defendants, to dispossess them of certain old Wroth estates in Enfield, Middlesex. The suit was won by the plaintiffs. The whole question should be restudied by modern methods of genealogical research.

to the seven daughters whose existence we learn of through his will. The writer has fortunately been able to secure from the probate records an abstract of this will which has not been previously published, and which adds much to our knowledge of him and his descendants.

Thomas Wroth, the eldest son of Robert Wroth, of Durrants in Enfield, and his wife Jane Hawte, was born in 1516, and upon the death of his father in 1536, inherited Durrants. He was a ward of the king. He was educated at St. Johns College, Cambridge and in 1536 became a student of law at Gray's Inn. October 4, 1536, his wardship and marriage was granted by Henry VIII to Thomas Cromwell. In 1539 Sir Richard Rich, later Lord Rich and Chancellor of England, paid Cromwell three hundred marks for the right of disposing of Wroth in marriage, and provided for his third daughter Mary by betrothing her to him. Wroth, 24 April, 1540, granted livery of his lands, and in that and the following year Rich secured for Wroth the manor of Highbury, forfeited by Cromwell, and the manors of Beymondhall, Herts, and lands in Chestnut, Wormley and Enfield, belonging to various dissolved monasteries.

Wroth went to parliament, 18 December, 1544, as one of the knights of the shire for Middlesex, and appears to have again represented Middlesex from 1547 to 1552. Through the influence of his father in law he was appointed in 1545 one of the gentlemen of the bed chamber of Prince Edward and retained this position during all of Edward's reign, and was knighted, 22 February, 1546-7. He was sent by the king with a letter of congratulation to the Protector upon the victory of Pinkie, September, 1547, and July, 1548, was a witness against Bishop Gardiner for his sermon preached at St. Paul's. Upon the Protector's fall Wroth was appointed one of the four principal gentlemen of the privy chamber, his ordinary salary of £50 being doubled to help ensure his fidelity to Warwick. On the day of the Protector's execution he was sent to Sion House to report on the number and ages of Somerset's children and servants, and 7 June, Wroth was given a twenty-one year's lease of Sion House, which however he surrendered later for charitable purposes. He was granted, 24 July, 1550, the manors of Barfield, Chigwell and West Ham in Essex. He was appointed, 14 April, 1551, joint lord lieutenant of Middlesex with Paget, and in the last year of Edward's reign was one of the commissioners for the lord-lieutenancy of Middlesex, and knight of the shire in Edward's last parliament. Although he never actually became a member of the Privy Council, he was one of those whom Edward proposed in March, 1551-2 to "call in commission." He was a great favorite of King Edward, who is said to have died in his arms. Wroth was in 1552 on a commission for the recovery of the king's debts, and this same year was one of the "adventurers" in a voyage to Morocco.

Wroth signed the king's letters patent limiting the crown to Lady Jane Grey, but took no other part in Northumberland's insurrection. He was committed to the Tower, 27 July, 1553, but was released. Although urged by Lord John Grey, Jan. 27, 1553-4, to join Suffolk's rising, Wroth escaped to the continent, probably by royal license obtained through the influence of his father-in-law Lord Rich from Queen Mary. He remained at Frankford and Strassburg during the remainder of Mary's reign, but on Elizabeth's accession he returned to England. He again represented Middlesex, 29 December, 1558, as knight of the shire, and was appointed in 1562 special commissioner on the government of Ireland, being in Dub in in 1563 and 1564. In 1569 he was commissioner for the musters in Middlesex and for the lord-lieutenancy of London. Wroth's will shows that he held numerous manors in addition to those already referred to, which he had doubtlessly acquired by purchase. The date of his death, 9 October, 1573, as given in the *Dictionary of National Biography*, is probably incorrect, as this is the date of the codicil of his will, which was not probated until 16 April, 1575. He therefore probably died early in 1575.

The will of Sir Thomas Wroth, dated 5 October, 1573, with a codicil as just stated, dated 9 October, 1573, was proved in the Prerogative Court of Canterbury, 16 April, 1575 (*Pyckering, 16*). Although the will is a very lengthy one, it seems advisable to give a full abstract of its contents, both on account of the additional light it throws upon Wroth and his descendants, and as a picture of the times which it presents. His directions for a simple funeral throw an interesting sidelight upon his character ,and his desire that the "gilt boll pinked with a cover that King Edward gave me" should descend with Durrants, the principal family seat, shows the great value which this evidence of his sovereign's favor possessed in his eyes.

> Will of Thomas Wrothe of Enfeld, co. Middlesex, knight, 5 October, 1573. I desire to be buried where I die "without all sumptuousness either of herroldrie other than my armes upon my herse or of blackes but onlie my frendes children and servauntes in their usuall aparrell bringing my bodie to the place of buriall." I bequeath to my eldest son, Robert, my manors and lordships of Bardfeld Magna, Chigwell & Westhatche, co. Essex, with all the lands thereunto belonging, being a full third part of all my manors & lands. Whereas by Indenture dated 1 December, 10 Eliz. made between me, Sir Thomas Wrothe, of one part & Sir Robert Riche, Knt., Lord Riche, Peter Osborne esq^r. & William Wrothe, gent. of the other, it was covenanted that within one year from that date I should convey by fine, feoffment or recovery to the said parties the manor and

park of North Petherton, co. Somerset & all lands, fishings, rights, &c. thereunto belonging, all which I have since conveyed to the said parties & I devise the same to the persons to whom the uses thereof are limited by the said Indentures. I bequeath to Marie, my beloved wife, the Manors of Durantes and Gortons with appurtenances in Enfeld, co. Middlesex, the manor of Twying co. Herts, the Manor of Newton Pleycis als Newton Wrothe, co. Somerset & all my messuages and lands called Cranes or Cranes Farme in Enfeld & the lands called Breknox in Chestnut, co. Herts, & all other my messuages, lands, &c. in Enfeld, Edmonton als Eddmeton, co. Middx., in Twyng, co. Herts, & in Newton Pleycis als Newton Wrothe & Netherperton, co. Somerset, other than the premises already conveyed, as aforesaid, to have & to hold to my said wife, for term of her life & on her decease the same to my executors for 21 years to pay my debts & perform my legacies, & after that the same to my son, Robert, in tail male, in default to my son Richard, in tail male, in default to my son Thomas, in tail male, to my son Edward in tail male, to my male issue, in default to the male issue of Robert Wrothe Esqr. my late father, in default to my right heirs. I bequeath to my executors the manor & parsonage of Hampstead, co. Middx., & the manors of Narthall and Downebarnes, co. Middx., the manor of Bishop's Lydiard co. Somerset, the manor of Theydon Bois, co. Essex, & all lands, &c. to the said manors belonging, for 21 years, to pay my debts and legacies, & after this term, the same to be divided amongst my children, then living at their ages of 21. I bequeath tc my daughters, Elizabeth, Anne, Marie & Frances Wrothe, to such as shall not be married before my death, £400 each, & £40 each in ready money "towards everie of their charges of their wedding apparrell and dynner." To my younger sons, Richard, Thomas, Edward, John, Gerson & Peter Wrothe £500 each, at their ages of 22; if any die ,his portion to be divided among the survivors. To my daughter, Mabell Hardres, wife of Richard Hardres, esquire, £20. To my daughter, Judith Burgoine, wife of Robert Burgoyne, esquire, £20. To my daughter, Wynefred Goddard, wife of Thomas Goddard, esquire, £20. To William Wrothe, son of my brother John Wrothe, deceased, £20, at his age of 24. To my brother Oliver Wrothe's daughters, Margerie and Suzan Wrothe, £20 each at their days of marriage or age of 21. To my sister, Dorothey Lewkenor, widow, £20. To my sister, Dame Anne Penruddock, now wife of Sir George Penrudock, Knt., £10. I will that my wife Marie, shall have for term of her life the custody & occupation of all my household goods at Enfeld, excepting my plate, corn, cattle & hay, & after her death the same to such person as the manor of Durantes shall appertain; to my said wife £100 & so much plate as is worth £100. To each of my servants one whole year's wages. I desire my wife to have the bringing up of my unmarried daughters, she to have £10 a year for each of them. I desire my executors shall have the bringing up of my younger sons & until the death of Sir Morrice Barkley, Knt., who has the custody of the park of North Petherton co. Somerset, shall have not more than £20 a year for each such son until his lawful age, for the which & the payment of my legacies my executors shall take the rents & profits of all lands being demesne lands of Hiburie, co. Middxs. as I now have by lease of the Queen, except the three last years of the said lease which I give to my younger sons. I bequeath to my executors my manor of Bassets fee in co. Sussex, my wood & woodground called Strodewick Woods belonging to the same, my wood & other ground called Charterhouse Wood in Tottenham, co. Middxs, my reversion of the ground, wood & pasture, called Roughe Cattall in the parish of Chestnut, co. Herts, which latter ground I have in reversion after the death of my said sister Dame Anne Penruddock, to sell the same to pay my debts & legacies, but if my son Robert, his male issue, or in default, my next male heir, pay my executors £250, then my said bequest of the ground call Roughe Cattall shall be void & the same shall remain to such person as pays the same; & if my said heir pays £300 the bequest of Charterhouse wood shall be void & he shall have the same. To my son Robert, my lease of the parsonage of Enfeld which I hold of Trinity College, Cambridge, for 60 years to begin immediately after the expiration of John Buttes lease, he to pay my executors £50, towards the finding of my younger children; I also bequeath to him my lease of a house in Warwick Lane, London, which I hold of the Dean & Chapter of St. Paul's, London, he to pay my executors £400. I bequeath to my wife Marie, for life, & after her decease to the heir male of my body, in tail male, my meadow in Enfeld, called Little Lothersey, which I bought of my nephew Cock, & my pasture at Milmarshe Gate that Stockell now holds, which I bought of one Wright, of Edmonton & all other my lands in Enfeld, not before bequeathed. Whereas my younger son, Edmond, is bound prentice & to get his living by merchandise, I bequeath to him £300, part of his legacy of £500, one year after his years of apprenticeship shall expire, £100 being already delivered to his master, Francis Wotton, by William Smith, late of London, mercer, when he bound apprentice. To bequeath to such person as the manor of Durants shall come, all my leases of lands in Enfeld, as are parcel of the Duchy of Lancaster & also "the bason and ewer of sylver which my father gave me and one gilt boll pinked with a Cover that Kyng Edward gave me and myne owne harneys for my bodie and also all myne other armor and weapon for warre and all my bookes and also my sealing ringe." All the residue of my plate, goods & chattels to be sold for the performance of my will. I will that there be a strong chest bought with locks which shall stand in my loving friend's house Mr. Peter Osborne, "eche of my executours havinge a sondine keye so as none shall open the Chest but by the consent of the whole into which chest all suche somes of money as shall growe to myne executours for the performaunce of my will shalbe Laied to be kept untill suche tyme as they have occasion according to this my will to defraie and laie out the same." I make my friends, Mr. Peter Osborne, esquire, my cousin James Morrice, esquire, my brother William Wroth, gent, & my friend William Clerk gent. my executors & give to each £20. If my ward, Anthony Aucher, before his age of 21 years pay my executors so much money for his marriage & wardship as I or they have disbursed, then my executors shall not take any further benefit, but the said Anthony to remain unmarried, or marry himself at his pleasure.

Signed: Thomas Wrothes. Witnesses:—Robert Hayes, Toulke Heath, George Tenacre.

Codicil dated 9 October, 1573. I bequeath to my executors the lands I late purchased to me & my heirs for ever of the heirs of Henry Iden esquire, deceased, in Islington, co. Middxs, in trust for my nephew, William Wrothe, son & heir of my late brother John Wrothe, & the heirs of the said William for ever, he to pay for the cost of purchasing the same. To my daughters, Elizabeth, Anne & Marye, "for their naturall paines taken ever aboute me and chieflie in this my last sickness" £60 each, & £60 to my daughter Frances because she is youngest & least able to provide for herself. I forgive Richard Childs, my servant & bailiff, all the money he owes me upon his accounts. I will that my wife shall not take the bequest of £100 in money & £100 in plate unless she permit my executors to take the whole benefit of the bequest made to her by Lord Rich, as to one of his daughters.

Witnesses: Henry Knolls, Hector Nunes, Robert Burgoine, George Tenacre, Robert Blowen, John Ansley. Proved:—16 April, 1575, by Master Christopher Robinson, public notary, proctor to the executors named in the will.

Sir Thomas Wroth, who had married in 1539 or 1540, Mary daughter of Richard, Lord Rich of Leez, is shown by the will to have left by her seven sons and seven daughters. The statement made in several of the old visitation pedigrees that all the sons except Robert and Thomas died without issue is open to doubt. Issue:

Sons:

1. Robert Wroth of Durrants in Enfield, Middlesex. Born about 1540; died 1606. He married Susan, daughter of Francis Stonard (or Stoner) of Loughton, Essex, by whom he left issue, which carried down the Durrants line.
2. Richard Wroth. Living 1573. Not traced.
3. Thomas Wroth. Died 1610. He was of the Inner Temple, London; he acquired a considerable fortune and was later of Blundenhall, Kent. He married Joane daughter and coheir of Thomas(or John) Bullman(or Bulmer) of London.
4. Edward(or Edmond) Wroth. Living 1573. Not traced.
5. John Wroth. Living 1573. Not traced.
6. Gerson Wroth. Living 1573. Not traced.
7. Peter Wroth. Living 1573. Not traced.

Daughters*:

8. Mabel Wroth. Probably the eldest daughter and born about 1542. She died in 1597. She married 1st, 10 June 1560, Edward Aucher of Bishopsbourne, Kent, by whom she had issue (1) Sir Anthony Aucher and (2) Elizabeth Aucher mar. Sir William Lovelace (1561-1629), the elder, of Bethersden. Mabel Wroth married 2nd, about 1571-1572, Richard Hardres of Hardres, Kent. For full details of her and her Aucher descendants see ante pages 378-381. No attempt has been made to trace her Hardres descendants.
9. Judith Wroth. Married prior to 1573 Robert Burgoyne. Not traced.
10. Wynefred Wroth. Married prior to 1573 Thomas Goddard. Not traced.
11. Elizabeth Wroth. Unmarried in 1573. Not traced.
12. Anne Wroth. Unmarried in 1573. Not traced.

---

* *The Visitation of Essex, 1612 (Harl. Soc. Publ.* xiii, 33), which alone of the old pedigrees refers to any daughters, gives only one daughter, *Margaret*, who is stated to have married 1st ———— Izacke and 2nd Thomas Wyatt of Barkyn, Essex. This is probably an error as it is entirely unsupported by the will, which makes no mention of a daughter Margaret.

13. Marie Wroth. Unmarried in 1573. Not traced.
14. Frances Wroth. Unmarried in 1573. Not traced.

RICH OF LEEZ, ESSEX.

Mary, the daughter of Richard Rich, first baron Rich of Leez (or Leighs), Essex, and lord chancellor in the reign of Edward VI, married in 1539, Sir Thomas Wroth of Enfield. While the life of Lord Rich may be found in full in such general works as the *Encyclopedia Brittanica*, the *Dictionary of National Biography* and *Campbell's Lives of the Lord Chancellors*, a few brief notes here on the career of this talented but not over scrupulous nobleman will be of interest to his very numerous American descendants.

Richard Rich, first baron Rich and lord chancellor, the son of Richard Rich of London and his wife Joan Dingley, was born about 1496 in the parish of St. Lawrence, Jewry. His first appearance in public life was on the commission of the peace in Hertfordshire in 1528, and in the year following he was a reader of law in the Middle Temple. He was knighted in 1533 and became solicitor general, acting as a "lesser hammer" under Thomas Cromwell in the suppression of the monasteries. He took a discreditable part in the trials of Bishop Fisher and Sir Thomas More. Although an acquaintance of the latter's in the Temple in former days, he misrepresented a friendly conversation to secure his conviction and was charged by More with being light of tongue, a perjurer, a great dicer and gamster and of not commendable fame. Rich was in 1536 made first chancellor of the recently created Court of Augmentations and acquired from Henry VIII as his share of the spoils nearly a hundred manors in Essex. Anne Askew testified that Rich personally screwed the rack at her torture. Rich was under the will of Henry VIII appointed one of the executors to administer the kingdom during Edward's minority. He was created Baron Rich of Leez (or Leighs) February, 1547-8, and in the following month became lord chancellor.

At first a supporter of Protector Somerset, Rich in October, 1549, deserted to the Earl of Warwick (later Duke of Northumberland), whose son Sir Henry Dudley had married Rich's daughter Winifred, and he afterwards presided over the trial of Somerset. He resigned as chancellor in 1551, on the ground of ill health, and with the exception of an occasional appearance in the Privy Council in the reign of Mary, and when summoned by Elizabeth for consultation about her proposed marriage, he rarely in his latter days appeared at Court.

His principal residence was Leez, or Leighs Priory, in Essex. He died at Rockford, Essex, 12 June, 1567, and is buried in Felsted church, where there is an elaborate monument to his memory.

Rich was a Roman catholic at heart, for although he aided Henry VIII in despoiling the monasteries, and assisted in dispossessing bishops Bonner and Gardiner in the reign of Edward VI, when Mary was on the throne he founded a chaplaincy providing for the singing of masses in Felsted church. He appears however to have been equally detested by catholic and protestant alike. In 1564 he established Felsted school.

Rich had by his wife Elizabeth Jenks (or Gynkes), daughter of William Jenks of London, a wealthy grocer, fourteen, or according to other accounts, fifteen children. It has also been stated that he had four illegitimate children. His grandson Robert, third Lord Rich, was created Earl of Warwick in 1618. The latter's son of the same name and title was a prominent puritan and took an active part in the affairs of the Virginia Company and of the New England Companies. In the *Visitation of Essex, 1552* and *1612* (*Harl. Soc.* xiii; 13, 276) and in *Sargeaunt's History of Felsted School, 1889*, will be found rather full details of Chancellor Rich's children and their descendants.

The descent of Chancellor Rich as given in *Burke's Extinct Baronetage* (2nd ed. 1861; p. 441) and in the *Dictionary of National Biography* (xlviii; pp. 123-6), traces his origin to (I) Richard Rich, sheriff of London in 1441, whose second son was (II) Thomas Rich of London, whose son (III) Richard Rich married Joan Dingley and had a son (IV) Richard Rich, first baron Rich of Leez and lord chancellor. The early Rich pedigree as given in the *Visitation of Essex, 1612*, is obviously absurd as it makes the Lord Chancellor, who was born in 1496, the son of a John Rich who died in 1458.

The Rich arms are: Gules, a chevron between three cross crosslets or [Rich]. Azure, two bars argent, each charged with a martlet between two crosslets sable, on a chief or a rose between two fleur de lis gules [Jenks].

Children of Richard, first baron Rich of Leez, and his wife Elizabeth Jenks:

Sons:

(1) Robert Rich, second baron Rich; born about 1537; died 1581; married Elizabeth daughter and heir of George Baldrey, alderman, of London. His son Robert, the third baron, was in 1618 created Earl of Warwick. Richard Rich, soldier, adventurer and author of *Newes from Virginia*, published in 1610, is supposed to have been the illegitimate son of Robert Rich, the second baron.

(2) Thomas Rich. Married ——— Fisher and died before his father.

(3) Sir Hugh Rich, Knight of the Bath. Married Ann, daughter of John Wentworth of Codham.

Daughters:

(4) Margery Rich. Married Henry Pigot of Abington, Cambridgeshire.

(5) **Mary Rich.** Married in 1539 Thomas Wroth, knight, of Durrants in Enfield, Essex. She was living in 1573. Her marriage to Wroth is referred to in his will and in all contemporary pedigrees. Their daughter Mabel Wroth through her marriage with Edward Aucher was the ancestress of the Lovelaces of Bethersden. See Aucher and Wroth ante pages 378, 379, 384.

(6) Anne Rich. Married Thomas Pigot (Picot) esq. of Straton, Bedfordshire.

(7) Dorothy Rich. Married Francis Barley of Kinton, Herts.

(8) Ethelred Rich. Married Henry Drury, esq. of Hawsted [Halstead], Suffolk.

(9) Audrey Rich. Married Robert son and heir of Sir William Drewry, knight, of Halstead, Suffolk.

(10) Elizabeth Rich. Married Robert Peyton, esq., of Iselham [Isleham?], Cambridgeshire.

(11) Winifred Rich. Married 1st Henry Dudley, son of the Duke of Northumberland; 2nd Roger, Lord North; a descendant of this marriage was the celebrated Lord North, prime minister of George III during the American Revolution.

(12) Frances Rich. Married John, Lord Darcy of Chiche.

(13) Agnes Rich. Married Edmund Mordaunt of Thunderly, Essex.

(14) Barbara Rich.

(To be continued)

Pages 393-396 - Title page and Contents.

GENERAL INDEX

Titles of Separate Articles are Indicated in Small Capitals.

www.ingramcontent.com/pod-product-compliance
Lightning Source LLC
Chambersburg PA
CBHW031817270326
41932CB00008B/451
* 9 7 8 3 3 3 7 3 8 8 6 1 4 *